HISTORIC STRUCTURES

Historic Structures

The Prague School Project, 1928–1946

By F. W. Galan

CROOM HELM
London & Sydney

Croom Helm Ltd, Provident House, Burrell Row,
Beckenham, Kent BR3 1AT

Croom Helm Australia Pty Ltd, First Floor,
139 King Street, Sydney, NSW 2001, Australia
First published in this edition 1985 by Croom Helm

British Library Cataloguing in Publication Data
Galan, F.W.
  Historic structures : the Prague School
  project, 1928–1946.
  1. Czech literature—History and criticism
  2. Structuralism (Literary analysis)
  I. Title
  891.8'609   PG5003.2.S7/
  ISBN 0-7099-3816-0

Grateful acknowledgment is made for permission to quote from the following:
"The Truest Poetry Is the Most Feigning," *W. H. Auden: Collected Poems*, ed. Edward Mendelson. Copyright 1979 by Edward Mendelson. Reprinted by permission of Random House, Inc.
"At the Fishhouses," *The Complete Poems 1927–1979*, by Elizabeth Bishop. Copyright 1947 by Elizabeth Bishop, copyright renewed 1974 by Elizabeth Bishop. Reprinted by permission of Farrar, Straus and Giroux, Inc.
"Little Gidding," *Four Quartets*, by T. S. Eliot. Copyright 1943 by T. S. Eliot, copyright renewed 1951 by Esme Valerie Eliot. Reprinted by permission of Harcourt Brace Jovanovich, Inc.
"An Ordinary Evening in New Haven," *The Collected Poems of Wallace Stevens*. Copyright 1954 by Wallace Stevens. Reprinted by permission of Alfred A. Knopf, Inc.
"The Circus Animals' Desertion," *The Collected Poems*, by W. B. Yeats. Copyright 1940 by Georgie Yeats, copyright renewed 1968 by Bertha Georgie Yeats, Michael Butler Yeats, and Anne Yeats. Reprinted by permission of Macmillan Publishing Co.

IN MEMORIAM

Dr. Ladislav Galan (1912–1971)
and Dr. Štefan Haas (1910–1977)

Contents

Preface   **ix**

A Note on Translation   **xiv**

Abbreviations   **xv**

1. A Brief Introduction   **1**
2. Language Diachrony and Literary Evolution   **6**
3. An Attempt at a Historical Ordering of Poetic Structure   **45**
4. The Semiotic Reformulation   **82**
5. Readers' Reception History and the Individual Poetic Talent   **141**
6. A Summary Conclusion   **202**

   Appendix 1. A List of Lectures on Poetics, Aesthetics and Semiotics Given in the Prague Linguistic Circle, 1926–1948   **207**

   Appendix 2. A List of Secondary and Related Sources   **215**

   Index   **243**

I have seen it over and over, the same sea, the same,
slightly, indifferently swinging above the stones,
icily free above the stones,
above the stones and then the world.
If you should dip your hand in,
your wrist would ache immediately,
your bones would begin to ache and your hand would burn
as if the water were a transmutation of fire
that feeds on stones and burns with a dark gray flame.
If you tasted it, it would first taste bitter,
then briny, then surely burn your tongue.
It is like what we imagine knowledge to be:
dark, salt, clear, moving, utterly free,
drawn from the cold hard mouth
of the world, derived from the rocky breasts
forever, flowing and drawn, and since
our knowledge is historical, flowing, and flown.

ELIZABETH BISHOP, "At the Fishhouses"

Preface

The work of the Prague School offers a theory of literary history which, among many other things, vindicates structuralism against the frequent charge that its approach, whether in linguistics, literary study or related fields, is inherently unhistorical. Born of the insight that a language system is complete at every moment of its existence, the structural approach is well equipped to deal with synchronic language states but unfit—or so the critics claim—to do justice to diachronic change. After a brief introduction to the problematics of literary history in chapter 1, I try to demonstrate that the methodological rift between synchrony and diachrony, between structural and historical linguistics, is by no means a necessary and logically unavoidable consequence of Ferdinand de Saussure's trenchant thesis which inaugurated the structural study of language phenomena at the start of this century. Indeed, overcoming this methodological impasse, resolving the apparent incompatibility between traditional and modern linguistic inquiries, has been the principal challenge faced by the scholars of the Prague Linguistic Circle, Roman Jakobson (1896–1982) in particular, as I endeavor to show in chapter 2.

Once they had reconciled structural linguistics with linguistic change, the Prague structuralists, principally Roman Jakobson and Jan Mukařovský (1891–1976), sought to extend the structural and historical approach to the investigation of literary evolution. Chapter 3 focuses on Mukařovský's exemplary attempt at an "analysis and historical ordering of poetic structure" and on the subsequent debate about the merits as well as defects of his historicizing method. Even though Mukařovský and Jakobson did not draw on the inchoate doctrine of semiotics when working on the problems of the history of Czech versification, they both soon found it an indispensable tool for the proper location of literature and art within the larger social context. The ramifications of the semiotic break from the formalist confines of immanence are the subject of chapter 4. The last chapter, devoted in part to the problems of so-called *Rezeptionsgeschichte*, suggests that the semiotic conception, elaborated by Mukařovský's pupil, Felix Vodička (1909–1974), defined a new and fertile area in the study of literary history. Finally, the semiotic model of communication showed the way toward integrating the creative poetic personality into structuralist theory, thereby enabling the Prague scholars to heal the other Saussurean rift between the *langue*—or the system—and the *parole*—or the individual utterance—and so to round off a comprehensive theory of literary art in its historical evolution.

Although this book examines and describes a theory of (linguistic and literary) history, it is not a history of the Prague Circle's own development. The constitution and organization of scientific institutions such as the Prague Linguistic Circle is doubtless a worthwhile subject. But the Circle's archival material being unavailable, and the writing of the evolution of theoretical thought being notoriously difficult, I keep to the minimum references to the social conditions and historical circumstances *entre deux guerres*, the period during which the Prague savants laid the groundwork for structural and semiotic poetics. For similar reasons, I do not hazard conjectures either about the operation of the Circle during the traumatic years of World War II or about the Circle's dissolution in 1948, shortly after the Communist government, newly in power, officially endorsed Marxism to the exclusion of any other critical approach. Nevertheless, I do strive to present an account of the Prague School's theory of literary history which pays considerable attention to the temporal, evolutionary dimension of the Circle's own theoretical development. This is not an examination of select topics in the structural theory of literary criticism; nor is it, as I have said, a presentation of the Prague School's entire history, which spanned the years 1926 to 1948, although appendix 1 should give the reader some idea of the scope and variety of the Circle's literary and semiotic activities (just as appendix 2 should indicate the many possible points of contact, overlap or convergence between Prague structuralism and other schools of critical thought). Rather, my work is an effort at delineating, in all its convolutions and complexities, the gradual evolvement of the structuralists' ever-refined and ever more penetrating comprehension of the vicissitudes of literary history during two crucial stages, 1928–1935 and 1940–1946. Of the Prague researchers' many other concerns, I touch only on those which have an important bearing on their—and our—understanding of that most recalcitrant issue in the study of literature: literature's changes in time and its place in the overall structure of art and society.

Perhaps the most appropriate way to read this study is as an exercise in cultural translation. Much of the material, to be sure, will appear linguistically strange, not to say exotic, to the Anglo-American reader, as will the numerous references to the history of Czech poetry. But since structuralism is to a great extent a linguistically based theory of literary art, the "parochialism" of the Prague scholars should be readily understandable. At least I try to make up for the difficulties of the second and third chapters with an excursion into film, which, despite the invention of the talkies (and of television), remains the "language" closest to our ideal Esperanto. Besides, the structuralists' discussion of cinema indicates how deeply rooted they were in their own time, how avidly and presciently they responded to the most adventurous developments of the new medium, which combined the best of avant-garde and mass art. But the more serious problem is really cultural—of differences in scale, the hierarchy of values, and associated cross-cultural expectations.

It is surely symptomatic of deep-seated cultural differences that the New Critics, for instance, remained for the longest time almost completely unaware of the parallel, yet frequently far more advanced, theoretical notions articulated by the Russian formalists and Czech structuralists; that the first English translations, *Russian Formalist Criticism: Four Essays* (1965) and *A Prague School Reader on Esthetics, Literary Structure, and Style* (1964), appeared years after the New Criticism's own demise; that these two anthologies offered slim, even skimpy selections, showing a curious preference for the two Slavic movements' immature or insubstantial statements; that both of these readers continue to be used despite the existence of superior collections, namely, *Readings in Russian Poetics: Formalist and Structuralist Views* (1971) and *Semiotics of Art: Prague School Contributions* (1976); that, consequently, English and American critics acquainted with Slavic literary theory still take as the key texts Viktor Šklovskij's "Art as Device" (1917) and Jan Mukařovský's "Standard Language and Poetic Language" (1932), when available studies such as Jurij Tynjanov's "On Literary Evolution" (1927) or Mukařovský's "On Poetic Language" (1940; reprinted in his book *The Word and Verbal Art* [1977]) provide incomparably more representative accounts of the respective movements' assumptions and achievements; and that, finally, while Russian formalism may have received due hearing in Anglo-American criticism after it had become something of a critical rage in France, Czech structuralism, studiously ignored by the French, is to this day a rather faint and unassimilated voice in the general theoretical discussion. Cultural misapprehensions obviously die hard. In this respect, literary criticism has proved to be particularly susceptible, for, in contrast to American linguistics and anthropology, it has put off for decades the challenge of facing up to the methodological implications of structuralism (as well as of semiotics): seeking repeatedly to go "beyond" formalism, Anglo-American critical theory has kept on returning to the nineteenth-century master disciplines, Hegelian metaphysics and Marxian political philosophy, although historically the proper successor of formalism is indeed nothing other than structuralism.

The difficulty of bridging the gap between diverse traditions is further compounded if the necessary effort calls for unexpected, and possibly unsettling, cultural adjustments. This is how a recent observer succinctly put it in a review of Mukařovský's book *Structure, Sign, and Function:*

> The disadvantage of writing in a minority language and exemplifying theories with the analysis of works from a "provincial" culture (as most scholars, with a twinge to the sense of their own inadequacy, regard Czech language and literature) may turn out ultimately to be to Mukařovský's advantage. For the sheer power of his theories, the scope of their application, the range of reference and the grasp of aesthetic universals make Mukařovský seem a true Renaissance Man, like his great contemporary Thomas Masaryk; it is his critics and imitators from the "metropolitan" cultures of Western Europe and the United States who are made to look narrow and provincial.[1]

Many may find this statement exaggerated, but it does highlight the fact that artistic and intellectual breakthroughs are more often apt to occur along the little-noticed periphery than in the putative centers of international culture. As Roman Jakobson himself learned,

> the cultural history of a small country demands exceptional discipline and strict self-denial. *L'art pour l'art* of endless debates, the motley polyphony of simultaneous tasks, a profusion of byways—all this is luxury. In contrast to the cultures of larger countries, what leaps to the eye here is a more rigorous line of development, a more clearly unveiled dialectic of history. . . . Czechoslovakia lies at the crossroads of various cultures and its distinctive cultural character throughout history . . . has consisted in the creative merging of streams whose sources are at some distance from one another. The great charm of Czech art and social ideology during the most productive periods of its history stems from the masterful crossing of diverse, at times even contradictory, currents.[2]

Thus, while in the politics of superpowers small countries stand no chance against big countries, in the study of art, which, like art itself, is supposed to be a realm of freedom and desire, David can—we must continue to hope—on occasion show the way to Goliath. In the present (and rather modest) case, that way points toward an interdisciplinary study of art, culture and society—a viable methodological synthesis of linguistics, poetics, aesthetics and semiotics, disciplines which, in the Anglo-American scholarly world, are usually kept apart, much to their mutual detriment.

It remains for me to pay tribute to those Czech scholars—notably, Miroslav Červenka, Květoslav Chvatík, Mojmír Grygar, Milan Jankovič, the late Oleg Sus and others—who in the 1960s produced the first critical analyses of the Prague School and thus paved the way for the present commentary. As it turned out, they helped revive structuralism at considerable personal risk: in the seventies, they were all faced with either silence or exile. I am also in debt to the work of Lubomir Doležel, Ladislav Matejka, Peter Steiner, Jurij Striedter (a recent arrival from Germany), Jiří Veltruský, Thomas G. Winner and, not least, René Wellek, who in the last decade or so have joined forces in promoting the Prague School literary theory in the English-speaking countries (see appendix 2). In a personal way, I owe most to the patience and tolerance of Lubomir Doležel: in both his historical and theoretical essays he best exemplifies the unbroken continuity between the original and present-day structural thought. Among friends, Jonathan Arac, Eugene Hill and Brian Stock helped me in the very beginning, while Wallace Martin came to my aid toward the end. My thanks go also to two of my colleagues: to Michael Holquist for his continuous interest and to Sidney Monas for having read the whole manuscript with good cheer.

I should like to acknowledge with thanks the support of several institutions which generously provided funds that permitted me to carry out research and to carry on writing, most especially the Canada Council Doctoral Award, the Massey College Junior Fellowship, the Ontario-Quebec Post-Doctoral Exchange Fellowship and the University of Texas Research Institute Grant. Earlier versions of parts of this book appeared in the following publications: a précis of the whole study, drawing mainly on the contents of chapter 2, in *PMLA* (March 1979), another section of this chapter in *Essays in Poetics* (April 1980), a slightly revised chapter 3 in *Zeitschrift für Ostforschung* (March 1980), the film segment of chapter 4 in a longer essay on cinema in *Semiotica* (no. 1/2, 1983), portions of chapter 5 in *Sound, Sign, and Meaning: Quinquagenary of the Prague Linguistic Circle* (1976) and in *The Structure of the Literary Process: Studies Dedicated to the Memory of Felix Vodička* (1982) and, finally, a draft of the entire chapter 5 in the series Toronto Semiotic Circle Monographs, Working Papers and Prepublications (no. 1, 1981). I am grateful to the editors for their permission to reuse these materials.

I owe my appreciation most of all to Stephanie Merrim, wife and colleague, for the friendship as well as fortitude and forbearance which she has amply proved over the years, themselves a small chapter in history, that it has taken me to come to terms with my subject. Yet I dedicate this work to the memory of my father and my uncle. Sadly, this book does little to compensate for their absence, but I know full well that they would have been greatly pleased by its presence.

F.W.G.
Austin, Texas

NOTES

1. L. M. O'Toole, *British Journal of Aesthetics* 19 (1979): 378.
2. "O předpokladech pražské linguistické školy" (On the Premises of the Prague Linguistic School), *Index* 6 (1934): 6, 8.

A Note on Translation

Since the following work is essentially one of commentary on and interpretation of a body of theoretical thought, translation emerges, in this context, only as a special, limiting case of the same critical operation. The goal of all these interrelated activities is, of course, truth of statement and accuracy of comment, but, as in all interpretation, a certain "attitude" or "turn" is unavoidable. Throughout my study I have sought to make that interpretive point of view consistent and coherent, be it in narrative commentary or direct citation. For this reason I offer my own translations, except for one or two instances where the available versions seemed unimpeachable, in the quoted passages, regardless of whether the originals are in Czech, Russian, German or French. Even though I have tried to provide translations which are as exact and literal as possible, I have struggled not to lose sight of the demands of English idiomatic usage, and, in the battle between the two imperatives, I have usually opted for the latter. In short, unless otherwise indicated, all translations—and all responsibility—are mine.

Abbreviations

The following abbreviations of the most frequently cited works and scholarly groups are used in the text, notes and appendices.

TITLES

Charisteria   *Charisteria Gvilelmo Mathesio Qvinqvagenario a Discipvlis et Circvli Lingvistici Pragensis sodalibvs oblata*. Praha: Pražský linguistický kroužek, 1932.

CJP   *Čtení o jazyce a poezii* (Readings in Language and Poetry). Ed. Bohuslav Havránek and Jan Mukařovský. Praha: Družstevní práce, 1942.

CPE   *Cestami poetiky a estetiky* (On the Paths of Poetics and Aesthetics), by Jan Mukařovský. Praha: Československý spisovatel, 1971.

KCP 1–3   *Kapitoly z české poetiky* (Chapters in Czech Poetics), by Jan Mukařovský. 3 vols. Praha: Svoboda, 1948.

PS   *The Prague School: Selected Writings, 1929–1946*. Ed. Peter Steiner. Austin: University of Texas Press, 1982.

RF   *Russian Formalism: History-Doctrine*, by Victor Erlich. 3rd ed. New Haven: Yale University Press, 1981.

RJ   *Roman Jakobson: Echoes of His Scholarship*. Ed. Daniel Armstrong and C. H. Schooneveld. Lisse: de Ridder, 1977.

RRP   *Readings in Russian Poetics: Formalist and Structuralist Views*. Ed. Krystyna Pomorska and Ladislav Matejka. Cambridge, Mass.: MIT Press, 1971.

SA   *Semiotics of Art: Prague School Contributions*. Ed. I. R. Titunik and Ladislav Matejka. Cambridge, Mass.: MIT Press, 1976.

SE   *Studie z estetiky* (Studies in Aesthetics), by Jan Mukařovský. Praha: Odeon, 1966.

SLP   *The Structure of the Literary Process: Studies Dedicated to the Memory of Felix Vodička*. Ed. Peter Steiner, Miroslav Červenka and Ronald Vroon. Amsterdam: John Benjamins, 1982.

Sl. sl. 1–9   *Slovo a slovesnost* (The Word and Verbal Art) 1–9. Praha, 1935–1943.

SSF   Structure, Sign, and Function, by Jan Mukařovský. Trans. and ed. John Burbank and Peter Steiner. New Haven: Yale University Press, 1978.

SSM   Sound, Sign, and Meaning: Quinquagenary of the Prague Linguistic Circle. Ed. Ladislav Matejka. Michigan Slavic Contributions no. 6. Ann Arbor: Department of Slavic Languages, University of Michigan, 1976.

SV   Struktura vývoje (The Structure of Development), by Felix Vodička. Praha: Odeon, 1969.

SVA   Studies in Verbal Art: Texts in Czech and Slovak, by Roman Jakobson. Michigan Slavic Contributions no. 4. Ann Arbor: Department of Slavic Languages, University of Michigan, 1971.

SW 1–5   *Selected Writings*, by Roman Jakobson. Vol. 1, *Phonological Studies*; vol. 2, *Word and Language*; vol. 3, *Poetry of Grammar and Grammar of Poetry*; vol. 4, *Slavic Epic Studies*; vol. 5, *On Verse, Its Masters and Explorers*. The Hague: Mouton, 1962–1981.

Travaux 1–8   *Travaux du Cercle Linguistique de Prague*, 1929–1939.

WVA   The Word and Verbal Art, by Jan Mukařovský. Trans. and ed. John Burbank and Peter Steiner. New Haven: Yale University Press, 1977.

SCHOLARLY GROUPS

Opojaz   Petersburg Society for the Study of Poetic Language, 1916–1930.

PLC   Prague Linguistic Circle, 1926–1948.

HISTORIC STRUCTURES

1 ‖ A Brief Introduction

No metaphor, remember, can express
A real historical unhappiness;
Your tears have value if they make us gay;
O Happy Grief! is all sad verse can say.

W. H. AUDEN

In twentieth-century intellectual history, the sixties and early seventies will most likely be known as the period of structuralism. In France, at least, structuralist methodology, which originated in linguistics, radically affected a wide spectrum of disciplines in the humanities, including, of course, literary theory, during this period. To this day, structuralism (and its methodological *envoi*, poststructuralism) continues to be a vital and developing enterprise; yet its culmination has been located midway through the first decade—more precisely, in 1966–1967.[1] At that time, coincidentally, the Johns Hopkins symposium "The Languages of Criticism and the Sciences of Man," with its impressive *pléiade* of principal structuralists, helped introduce the structuralist conception of poetics or critical theory in North America.[2]

Perhaps because of the gathering momentum of French structuralism on both sides of the Atlantic, hardly anyone in the West took notice of another important event in the history of the movement taking place in Eastern (Central) Europe. On the occasion of the 75th birthday of one of the founders of modern structural poetics, Jan Mukařovský, there appeared in Prague an extensive selection of his literary and aesthetic essays, *Studies in Aesthetics*. This fourth volume in Mukařovský's collected works had unfortunately been delayed for nearly twenty years during which structuralist thought was taboo in Czechoslovakia.[3] Concurrently, Mukařovský's disciples published in his honor a *Festschrift* entitled *Structure and Sense of a Literary Work of Art*, thereby firmly reestablishing a continuity with the prewar school often known as the Prague Linguistic Circle.[4] Thus, Czech structural linguistics and poetics, previously exposed to devastating ideological attacks, became once more an admissible, and soon widespread, approach to the study of language, literature and art in the very country in which it had been engendered.

Unfortunately, mainstream Anglo-American scholarship—whether in

Slavic studies or literary theory—has until recently lagged behind Continental work on the latest structuralist developments.[5] The first two book-length American discussions of formalism and structuralism are typical in their exclusive focus on the historical poles of Russian formalism in the twenties and French structuralism in the late fifties and sixties, and in their glaring neglect of the crucial contribution of Czech structuralism of the thirties and forties.[6] But if structuralism is to exercise, as Geoffrey Hartman once demanded,[7] a genuine historical consciousness vis-à-vis itself, the long hiatus caused by the omission of Czech structuralism must be filled. The following study will endeavor to show that such a task is imperative not merely for historical completeness but also for recognizing the still-unmatched achievements of the Czech structuralists in literary (and semiotic) theory.

‖●‖●‖●‖●‖●‖

What most sharply distinguishes Czech structuralism from the other twentieth-century literary theories is its commitment to literary history. For Russian formalism and French structuralism, the problem of literary history is rather peripheral, if not irrelevant; for the Czechs, it is crucial. In order to understand why the Czech structuralists arrived at this position, it is necessary at the outset to retrace their evolution within the wider framework of literary history in this century.

Everyone will agree that an ideal theory of literary evolution should be able to deal at once with the literary and historical aspects of its subject. In other words, it ought to trace the mutations, in time, of literature's aesthetic or poetic features while firmly anchoring them in a wide, ever-changing social context. What is needed is a way to correlate, with sufficient precision, the principles of literary history with the laws governing social processes and practices. A full-fledged theory of literary development, then, would have to steer the difficult course between two extremes: a theory which provides a history, but not mainly of art, and one which, by studying art itself, excludes the full dimension of history.

Thus, on one side we find the "Lives," histories dating from Plutarch until the end of the eighteenth century, which were composed of individual portraits chronologically strung together according to the artists' birthdates. This group includes, too, much of the nineteenth-century positivistic preoccupation with source and influence studies, as well as its successor, Wilhelm Dilthey's *Geistesgeschichte*, which favored broadly philosophical rather than aesthetic pursuits. In all such histories, limited attention, if any, is paid to the aesthetic element in the examined works, since art served, in most cases, as a foil for the study of the "lives and times," of religious, moral and psychological environments. On the other side, we encounter nearly all major twentieth-century critical approaches, which, like the *Geistesgeschichte*, revolted against prevailing positivism in literary study: the Cambridge School of "Practical Criticism," New Criticism, the Geneva School's "critique de conscience," Russian formalism and the like. These schools share the ability to analyze the complexities of a text, but all fail—in different degrees—to treat it historically. They either totally extract the work from a temporal continuum or, when handling it as a changeable phenomenon, tend to isolate it from the neighboring realms of culture and society.

Indeed, one could compose a "negative" history of modern literary criticism by assembling its failures to develop a coherent, all-encompassing literary history. The tenacity of these failures is truly remarkable, considering the vehemence with which they have been exposed time and again. No doubt a great majority of present-day critics of a historical orientation could accurately be depicted, to use the words of Walter Benjamin, as antiquarians possessing "no theoretical armature," whose method, like that of collectors, is merely additive.[8] Consider Benjamin's impassioned critique of Emil Ermantiger's representative anthology *Philosophie der Literaturgeschichte*, branding historians as custodians of dead wood who have lost touch with the needs of their own time.[9] Or consider Roland Barthes' polemic concerning Racine, some thirty years later, in which he argues against the kind of literary history that at best draws up lists of works.[10] The resulting picture confirms that the literary history of the academies, the stronghold of historical scholarship, is and has been in a shambles. Incidentally, official Marxist literary history in the Soviet Union and elsewhere has fared no better, owing to the dogmatic interpretations imposed by Party orthodoxy.

Neither modern textual exegetes who prefer to dispense with the recalcitrant issues of literary theory nor the historically inclined academicians who perceive no theoretical problem worth attacking have responded to the call for a new synthesis in the theory of literary evolution. Such synthesis would seek, according to György Lukács' astute study "Zur Theorie der Literaturgeschichte," to join two disciplines, each of which elucidates different facets of literary phenomena: aesthetics, on the one hand, grappling with the "permanent," and sociology, on the other, investigating the "variable."[11] The creation emerging from a fusion of these seemingly antagonistic disciplines would be literary history proper.

Nevertheless, interest in literary history subsided, especially after the demise of the *Geistesgeschichte* some thirty years ago, only lately to be revived.[12] Members of the so-called Konstanz School, headed by Hans Robert Jauss, have elaborated a theory of *Rezeptionsgeschichte* which shifts the burden of investigation from the text and its producer to the reader's "horizon of expectation."[13] The study of literature, of its continually changing reception, is thus wedded, at least partially, to the study of society. Parts of this theory, however, have an undisputed source in the writings of a school "furthest from the dogma of the irreconcilability of structural and historical analysis,"[14] that is to say, in Prague structuralism. And this juncture brings us to our own topic. We can now turn to the beginning of Czech structuralist investigations into literary history during the period 1928 to 1934. Since in structuralism literary theory is intimately linked with linguistics, we shall first examine the notion of the immanent evolution of language. Next we shall discuss the extent of Czech structuralism's indebtedness to the ideas of Russian formalism. In the final section of the following chapter we shall trace the growth of structuralist theory and of its conception of literary evolution.

NOTES

1. Cf. Fredric Jameson, *The Prison-House of Language: A Critical Account of Structuralism and Russian Formalism*, p. ix.

2. Cf. *The Structuralist Controversy: The Languages of Criticism and the Sciences of Man*, ed. Richard Macksey and Eugenio Donato. See also the special issue of *Yale French Studies*, nos. 36–37 (1966).

3. *Studie z estetiky (SE)*. The first three volumes were brought out under the title *Kapitoly z české poetiky (KCP)*.

4. *Struktura a smysl literárního díla* (The Structure and the Sense of Literary Work), ed. Milan Jankovič et al.

5. See Hans Günther's introductory *Struktur als Prozeß* and Jurij Striedter's substantial "Einleitung" to Felix Vodička, *Die Struktur der literarischen Entwicklung*, ed. Frank Boldt, pp. vii–ciii. The most informative essay on the Prague School's literary theory is Miroslav Červenka, "Die Grundkategorien des Prager literaturwissenschaftlichen Strukturalismus," in *Zur Kritik literaturwissenschaftlicher Methodologie*, ed. Viktor Žmegač and Zdenko Škreb, pp. 137–68, and the most comprehensive study to date is Květoslav Chvatík, *Tschechoslowakischer Strukturalismus: Theorie und Geschichte*, trans. Vlado Müller. Still, the testimonial volumes, *Sound, Sign, and Meaning: Quinquagenary of the Prague Linguistic Circle (SSM)* and *The Structure of the Literary Process: Studies Dedicated to the Memory of Felix Vodička (SLP)*, along with the numerous articles listed in appendix 2, show that more research in this area is currently going on in American than in German literary studies, at least among emigré scholars.

6. Cf. Jameson's *Prison-House* and Robert Scholes' *Structuralism in Literature: An Introduction*. See also Jonathan Culler, *Structuralist Poetics: Structuralism, Linguistics, and the Study of Literature*, which, although fully aware of Jakobson's contribution to modern poetics, largely ignores his ties to Prague structuralism.

7. "Structuralism: The Anglo-American Adventure," *Yale French Studies*: pp. 137–58, rpt. in Hartman, *Beyond Formalism: Literary Essays 1958–1970*, pp. 3–23. This synoptic essay, however, signally fails both as a critique of structuralism and as an explanation of its origins. By overlooking Lévi-Strauss' express indebtedness to the principles of (structural) phonology as formulated by L'Ecole

de Prague (another name for the Circle), Hartman confuses the structural and the anthropological features of Lévi-Strauss' work. In consequence, his Anglo-American expedition is a mythic trip, not an analysis of structuralism. As usual, the legend has taken deep roots; it lives happily on, for example, in Edith Kurzweil, *The Age of Structuralism: Lévi-Strauss to Foucault.*

8. Cf. Benjamin, "Theses on the Philosophy of History," in his *Illuminations*, ed. Hannah Arendt, trans. Harry Zohn, p. 262. This powerful meditation on history was written in 1940 and first published in 1950. The degree of naiveté with which such critics make their appeals to the "facts of history" has been sharply exposed in recent works by the historian Hayden White. See especially his "Interpretation in History," *New Literary History* 4 (1973): 281–314, rpt. in his *Metahistory: The Historical Imagination in Nineteenth-Century Europe.* Also consult White's collection of essays *Tropics of Discourse: Essays on Cultural Criticism.* White turns the tables, as it were, on literary critics, and seeks their assistance in the interpretation of historical narrative in which "facts" are inevitably embedded.

9. This text remains untranslated. Cf. "Literaturgeschichte und Literaturwissenschaft," in Benjamin's *Angelus Novus*, pp. 450–56. It first appeared in the journal *Literarische Welt* in 1931.

10. Barthes, "History or Literature," in his *On Racine*, trans. Richard Howard, pp. 153–72. (The original appeared as *Sur Racine* in the Editions du Seuil in 1963.)

11. *Text + Kritik* nos. 39–40 (1973): 24–51. The original paper, "Megjegyzesék az irodalomtörténet elméléhez," appeared in 1910.

12. For an obituary of this critical theory, see Karl Vietor, "Deutsche Literaturgeschichte als Geistesgeschichte: Ein Rückblick," *PMLA* 60 (1945): 899–916.

13. See most of all the first two essays, "Literary History as a Challenge to Literary Theory," and "History of Art and Pragmatic History," in Jauss' collection *Toward an Aesthetics of Reception*, trans. Timothy Bahti, pp. 3–45, 26–75; cf. Paul de Man's introduction, esp. pp. xvii–xviii.

14. Jauss, *Toward an Aesthetics of Reception*, p. 72.

2 | Language Diachrony and Literary Evolution

It almost scares
A man the way things come in pairs.

ROBERT FROST

If Northrop Frye's masterwork *Anatomy of Criticism* can be seen as an annotation of T. S. Eliot's observation on the simultaneous order of all existing works of art,[1] the entire development of the theory of literary history, as conceived by Jan Mukařovský and his Prague School colleagues, may be taken as an extended commentary on Roman Jakobson and Jurij Tynjanov's manifesto "Problems in the Study of Literature and Language." Published in 1928 in the avant-garde futurist journal *Novyj Lef*, the manifesto's eight terse theses, which focus almost exclusively on the theory of literary (and, of course, linguistic) history, represent a profound revision of classical Opojaz formalism.[2] Even though Russian formalism itself, already moribund, never followed up the ramifications of these theses, their role in structuralism is, as we shall see, paramount.

This manifesto principally demonstrates the close and highly instructive parallel between the study of literature and that of language. Jakobson and Tynjanov appropriate for literary analysis the basic categories of Ferdinand de Saussure's *Cours de linguistique générale*,[3] as modified by later linguistic theory: the dichotomy of *langue* and *parole*; the opposition of synchrony and diachrony; and, finally, the functional point of view. The first Saussurean bifurcation, *langue-parole*, inaugurated a new linguistic school. According to Saussure's theory, the true object of linguistic study is not the individual utterance but "a language [*langue*], i.e., a system of distinct signs . . ." (p. 10, cf. p. 15). *Parole*, the speaker's individual execution, affords material that is too heterogeneous and many-faceted, in Saussure's view, for the linguist's firm theoretical grasp. Hence a methodological priority must be given to the investigation of the system of language. The Saussurean concept of *langue*, moreover, stresses the social character of language communication. No language can be complete in any one person, but only within a collectivity of speakers. Put differently, a set of linguistic norms or conventions is prerequisite for a fully communicable individual utterance. Thus *langue* necessarily presupposes, and precedes, *parole*.

The notion of *langue* enables us to see that language retains its systemic character at each separate moment of its existence, because any language always forms a complete system. To understand the particular *langue*, one no longer has to resort to cumbersome and speculative reconstructions of linguistic data of the past; instead, thorough analysis of the contemporary language system yields the required answers. According to Saussure, we can therefore study language in two distinct ways: synchronically (or statically), by examining the reciprocal relationships of individual linguistic phenomena which exist simultaneously, and diachronically (dynamically), by tracing, ultimately reconstructing, a given linguistic datum in its evolutionary stages from, say, its Indo-European prototype to its present form. The synchronic approach is fully adequate for the study of *langue*; only by examining individual language changes or *parole* need we arrive at a diachronic study of language phenomena.

Since synchronic linguistics has as its object a self-contained system, the chief method of historical linguistics, usually known as geneticocausal, can be replaced by a teleological mode of explanation, or, as Jakobson preferred to say, by the means-ends model of language.[4] It is no longer necessary to inquire under what circumstances and from what sources a certain linguistic fact came into existence. What one now has to determine is the *function* of that particular fact with respect to the language system as a whole. Consequently, the new Prague School linguistics views language as a formal unity in which every part can be understood only in a relation to every other part and to the hierarchically ordered whole, and not as a mere mechanical sum of scattered linguistic occurrences.

Obviously the second bifurcation, that of synchrony and diachrony, is central for the understanding of literary evolution. Here Tynjanov and Jakobson, while acknowledging the fruitfulness of the separation of synchrony from diachrony as a working hypothesis, are compelled to go beyond Saussure: "The history of a system is in turn a system. Pure synchronism now proves to be an illusion: every synchronic system has its past and its future as inseparable structural elements of the system" (p. 79). Saussure, in an overreaction to the genetically minded neogrammarian philology of his predecessors, insisted not simply on the primacy of synchronic study but also on its strict methodological separation from diachrony. He warned that the linguist studying a language state must ignore diachrony altogether, for "the intervention of history can only falsify his judgment" (*Course*, p. 81). In point of fact, this cardinal insight of structuralism, the ever-present completeness of the language system, was for a considerable time to be its major pitfall. To this day most French structuralist ventures are trapped within the confines of synchronic analysis. In Jakobson and Tynjanov's proclamation we witness the first integration of the two dimensions viewed as dynamic complements.

When seen through the prism of linguistic categories, literature, like language, is comprehended as a system governed by specific structural laws. Hence, the main task of literary history is the elucidation of the principles which determine literary system and its changes. Such a synchronic literary system should be distinguished, according to Jakobson and Tynjanov, from the traditional concept of a literary period. As in Saussure's *langue*, all that matters is the public's current linguistic or literary consciousness, not the historical age and provenance of individual words or works. Literary synchrony can thereby embrace "not only works of art which are close to each other in time but also works which are drawn into the orbit of the system from foreign literatures or previous epochs" (*RRP*, p. 80), thus providing a basic theoretical framework for a comparative literary study.

All the works contained in a synchronic consciousness build the background for a complex of literary norms. It is this normative background which permits, in any period, the creation of certain works but not of others. It follows that no literary work can be interpreted in isolation, since the previous works have established a norm to which every new work must react, whether by conforming to the norm (archaists or epigones) or by rejecting it (innovators). Parallel to Saussure's *langue-parole* opposition, Jakobson and Tynjanov pose a heuristic division between an individual work of art and a set of artistic norms. Accordingly, the analysis of literary evolution moves from the consideration of disjointed instances to the study of the interconnected complex of norms, so that, in the end, a "limited series of actually existing types of structural evolution" (p. 80) could be postulated (although admittedly, the last proposal advanced little beyond this initial blueprint).

If literature is viewed as a relatively autonomous system, most historical changes must occur within the system in accord with the internal or immanent laws of literary history. As Jakobson and Tynjanov assert, "every system necessarily exists as an evolution, whereas, on the other hand, evolution is inescapably of a systemic nature" (p. 80). Indeed, most changes can be explained as obeying the laws of immanent evolution—or intertextuality, if you will—but this is by no means true of all changes. After all, literature does not develop in a vacuum, independent of other historical events and conditions. Although the immanent laws cast light on the character or the function of each change, they do not, as our theorists were quick to notice, "allow us to explain the tempo of evolution or the chosen path of evolution when several, theoretically possible, evolutionary paths are given" (p. 80). In order to understand fully the principles of literary change, literary series must be integrated with other historical series. Only by means of a *"system of systems"* (emphasis mine) which would correlate the two series coexisting in manifold relations of tension, indirection, opposition or complementarity can we gain an all-encompassing perspective on literary evolution.[5]

The significance of Jakobson and Tynjanov's propositions for the theory of literary history can hardly be overestimated. The two scholars addressed themselves directly and forcefully to the cardinal fallacy that had plagued Saussurean linguistics and, to a degree, also Opojaz formalism. From now on, both fields of endeavor, linguistics as well as literary theory, could systematically treat their respective objects of investigation not as statically synchronic but as dynamically diachronic. Modern linguistics and linguistically grounded literary theory have thus come full circle from the separation of the two investigative methods to their new, equally seminal, synthesis.

Innovative as it is, "Problems in the Study of Literature and Language" in fact stems from two works of 1927: Tynjanov's "The Problem of Literary Evolution" and Jakobson's "The Concept of the Sound Law and the Teleological Criterion."[6] These antecedents point to a concrete bridge between the Petersburg and Prague schools, which is still more explicitly documented by the following historical circumstances. Roman Jakobson, who had been a Prague resident since 1920, became one of the founding members of the Prague Linguistic Circle in 1926 and its first vice-president. "The Concept of the Sound Law" was presented at the Circle's fourth meeting on 13 January 1927. Unfortunately, a brief summary, published in 1928, is all that is extant. Jurij Tynjanov, visiting from Leningrad, also attended one of the Circle's sessions on 16 December 1928, when he delivered a lecture, "Le problème de l'évolution littéraire." Not even a précis of that lecture has seen print; Tynjanov may have presented another version of his Russian paper from the previous year.[7] In the light of these events, Victor Erlich's assessment of the theses as "the attempt to revise Russian Formalism in quasi-structuralist terms" becomes particularly revealing.[8] Indeed, Jakobson and Tynjanov's joint statement of principles symbolizes the transition from Opojaz formalism to PLC (Prague Linguistic Circle) structuralism.

To be sure, in Tynjanov's essay on literary evolution we encounter all the key concepts: system, its functions, norms and mutations, as well as the interaction of the literary system with contiguous systems in literary history. The 1928 manifesto merely defines Tynjanov's perception of the nature of literary process in the precise terminology of structural linguistics as designed by Prague structuralists. Yet it appears that Jakobson, above all a linguist, faced a greater challenge than the literary critic Tynjanov. For one thing, Tynjanov's contribution is in many ways the outgrowth of numerous incisive remarks made in earlier formalist writings; here Tynjanov concentrated his skills toward a succinct theoretical statement, while other studies tackled specific problems of Russian literary history. In addition, there is no inherent theoretical obstacle to pursuing literary history, no grounds for severing historical research from the study of individual texts, though there is always considerable practical complexity.

In contrast with those engaged in literary study, linguists—having been revolutionized by synchronic theory—saw no pressing need for diachronic research or for the modification of Saussure's tenets. Jakobson's chief objective, then, was to revise the Geneva School's adamant espousal of the categorical fissure between synchronic and diachronic studies. To quote from his 1927 lecture:

F. de Saussure and his school broke a new trail in static linguistics, but as to the field of language history they remained in the neo-grammarian rut. . . . This antinomy between synchronic and diachronic linguistic studies should be overcome by a transformation of historical phonetics into the history of the phonetic system. . . . phonetic changes must be analyzed in relation to the phonetic system which undergoes these mutations. (*SW* 1, pp. 1–2)

The neogrammarian theory propounds a lawlike regularity of sound changes—namely, if a phoneme is altered in one word, a similar alteration must affect every other word which contains such a phoneme—but it does not provide an adequate theoretical explanation of their occurrence. The sound changes are thought of as unmotivated, fortuitous and blind and presumably happen only because of destructive outside interference. Since Saussure subscribed fully to the notion of linguistic permutations as arbitrary and nonsystematic (as opposed to the perfect intelligibility and order of static systems), the following methodological principle—an unmistakable echo of the above-quoted statement—adopted at the First International Congress of Linguists constitutes a major breakthrough in the modern science of language: "The history of language [*la langue*] . . . should not confine itself to a study of isolated changes but should seek to consider them as functions of the system they help sustain."[9] This proposition presents a meeting ground for the two most influential linguistic movements of the time, the Geneva and Prague schools, for it was produced jointly, along with four other propositions, by Charles Bally and Albert Sechehaye on one side and Roman Jakobson, Vilém Mathesius and N. S. Trubeckoj on the other. However, the principal creator of this crucial premise was Jakobson, as is clearly documented by his response to "Quelles sont les méthodes les mieux appropriées à un exposé complet et pratique de la phonologie d'une langue quelconque?"—one of the topics of the Congress.[10]

The gist of Jakobson's polemic with Saussure and his disciples can perhaps be conveyed most tellingly by following up the consequences of

Saussure's famous chess analogy. Chess, according to Saussure, offers the best model for the workings of language. First of all, in chess, as in language, one can dispense with the knowledge of "Realia," the external facts about, say, the place of the game's origin or the material of which various chess pieces are made; all one needs to know is the nature of the system, that is to say, its basic rules. This set of rules is of course unchangeable, given once and for all. And it is only within the system, depending on the position on the board, that individual pieces (in language, phonological elements) and their moves (changes) acquire meaning and value. Moreover, in Saussure's view, the configurations of the system are always momentary, since the pieces shift from one instant to the next. As in chess, the changes in language occur only in certain spots. Notwithstanding the local character of one change, its repercussions are extensive, so much so that the magnitude of the ensuing effect on the whole system is often inestimable. Most importantly, the temporal dimension seems to have no bearing on the game, since each particular move is absolutely distinct from the preceding and subsequent situation. In other words, one could grasp the present position of each player without knowing anything about the previous course of the game.[11] Likewise, no knowledge of etymology is requisite for a correct understanding of a word's current meaning.

For Saussure, there is in fact a single difference, albeit of enormous significance, between action in chess and evolution in language: in chess, every player "*intends* to bring about a shift and thereby to exert an action on the system"; language, on the other hand, "premeditates nothing" (*Course*, p. 89). Otherwise, since Saussure asserts that language changes take place spontaneously and randomly, there would have to be "un joueur inconscient ou inintelligent" (an unconscious or unintelligent player) (*Cours*, p. 127). Thus language shares with chess its systemic character in a state of synchrony, but when inspected diachronically, individual changes seem to play havoc with the entire system. In this way, Saussure sought to prove the irreconcilability between the systemic nature of language states and the arbitrariness of language change and, consequently, "the absolute necessity of making a distinction between the two classes of phenomena in linguistics" (*Course*, p. 89).

In a monograph, *Remarques sur l'évolution phonologique du russe comparée à celle des autres langues slaves*, written in 1927–1928 and published a year later, Jakobson proposed to think Saussure's analogy through to the end.[12] In doing so, he also offered on a more practical level an abundance of recondite examples culled from Proto-Slavic and Proto-Russian as well as several modern Slavic languages. To start with, he refuted Saussure's contention that language is a system which somehow ceases to act as such the moment it undergoes a change. Instead of accepting the idea of blind outside destruction, of a "cambriolage phonétique," an unforeseeable phonetic "burglary," Jakobson strove to resolve the contradiction of a system's nonsystemic change by arguing that many changes to which a language is exposed have a clearly therapeutic character. In other words, whenever there is a disturbance of the system's synchronic equilibrium, there is also an opposing tendency to restore the lost balance.

Just as in a game of chess the loss of one piece often calls forth a whole series of moves on the part of the menaced player wishing to reestablish the balance, so in a given language, in the same way, there is a need of a whole series of phonetic innovations striving toward a reestablishment of stability of the phonological system. And it may happen to the members of the language community, just as it happens to a chess player, that means are used which, though they reestablish the balance in one point of the system, risk the rise of disastrous consequences in another of its points.[13]

Not only is language, in Jakobson's conception, unceasingly dynamic, but its changes *do* exhibit a great deal of purposive, self-maintaining regularity. It is no longer taken for a passive vehicle which is under constant threat from outside; on the contrary, like any self-regulating system, language is capable of adjusting itself to any "blind" jeopardy.

Similarly, Jakobson contests the validity of Saussure's claim concerning the unpremeditated character of language; or, rather more to the point, he substitutes for the unintelligent and unconscious language master a "collectivité des sujets parlants" (a collectivity of speaking subjects)—a notion perfectly congruent with the Saussurean tenet of language as a social instrument. This apparently simple correction nonetheless points to the main shortcoming of the *Cours*, namely, the lack of a theory of *parole*. As far as the system of *langue* is concerned, the individual hovers somewhere on the margins, his or her influence on the system being minimal. But for *parole* the individual is indispensable, since "speaking" is the prime cause for language evolution. Consequently, without a theory of *parole* there can be no concept of systemic linguistic change—or diachrony.

‖●‖●‖●‖●‖●‖

Language does not decay or deteriorate in the course of time,[14] for the active participation of the language community helps to restore equilibrium whenever a particular linguistic change threatens to upset it. To perceive the process of language evolution in all its complexity, we must not analyze an individual change in isolation as a local disturbance but must examine the circumfluent system as a whole. Only from the viewpoint of the holistic system, according to Jakobson, will the general principles of language change emerge.

The constant reciprocity of change and counterchange entails, on the level of sound, three kinds of phonological changes: dephonologization,

phonologization and rephonologization. Jakobson set out to outline these categories in another definitive study, "Prinzipien der historischen Phonologie," presented at the First Phonological Congress held in Prague in 1930.[15] Each of the three categories consists of several subgroups, but it should suffice here to describe the basic principles. In dephonologization, the binary relationship between phonemes after mutation has lost the phonological opposition which existed before. In phonologization, this process is reversed: phonemes which were not opposed phonologically are in a state of opposition after mutation. In rephonologization, both the original and resultant pairs remain phonologically opposed, yet the structure of the binary opposition changes in the process of mutation. Moreover, mutations transform not only individual phonemes but groups of phonemes. Finally, several mutations can take place at the same time; in that case, the so-called bundle of mutations (*Mutationsbündel*) must be analyzed in its entirety.

As can be seen, a vast multiplicity of linguistic changes may occur, whether individually or in a bundle. But the underlying purpose behind all of them remains the same: the preservation of language equilibrium. The evolution of language, however, is not comprised solely of a chesslike assortment of combinatory variants that, on the whole, balance each other in a series of destructions and novel creations of phonological differences. Language is more complex than that. Jakobson and other structuralists proposed that there is not one (for example, English) language; rather, there are several *functional dialects* or styles—be they standard, practical, theoretical or poetic—within it. In order to exhibit greater flexibility, and not stagnate on one level, language must operate on several stylistic planes. In addition to the repertory of phonological combinations, there is also a process which the members of the Prague School called the "permutation of functions" (*Umschaltung der Funktionen*). Here a phoneme alters its function by shifting into another functional dialect—we could think of a three-dimensional chess game. While the state of equilibrium is always preserved in one language dialect—that is, any dephonologization is compensated for by a phonologization—a phoneme's migration to another dialect, on the contrary, tends to cause a rupture in the system.

It is the permutation of functions, this extra flexibility and open-endedness, which accounts for language's continual efficacy. Like any system, organic or mechanical, language wears out its parts, whether phonemes, individual words or idioms. A permutation of functions, in turn, permits the renewal and refurbishment of those aspects that are felt to be stylistically stale and ineffective. When, for instance, some parts of emotive language lose their expressiveness, they may fulfill another function in strictly referential language. In other words, the dynamic vitality of language rests in its ability to find new replacements for abandoned means of expression or to rejuvenate ossified forms. Ultimately, Jakobson established this reciprocal balancing of loss and gain and of ever-shifting permutations as one of the permanent linguistic principles: "The spirit of equilibrium and the simultaneous tendency toward its rupture constitute the indispensable properties of that whole that is language" (*Reader*, p. 137).

Regardless of whether various mutations contribute to the maintenance or disturbance of the equilibrium, they cannot be understood apart from the system they create. By the same token, the system itself cannot be abstracted from the changes which it generates and to which it is subject. Consequently, since numerous changes are registered in the synchronic consciousness of the language community, diachrony and synchrony intersect:

The most characteristic form of the projection of diachrony into synchrony is the attribution of a different function to the terms of a change; thus two phonological stages are judged as the attributes of two different functional dialects, as two styles. Conversely, the characteristic form of the projection of synchrony into diachrony is the generalization of a style—two styles become two stages. (*SW* 1, p. 19).

The two prevalent diachronic components found in the consciousness of a language community are archaisms and neologisms. Both antiquated and innovative linguistic forms not only exist simultaneously in the usage of a community, according to the age of its members, but often coexist in the language of a single speaker as well. Eventually, some obsolete forms are dropped, while other forms, if productive, engender still newer forms. From the synchronic standpoint, then, language appears as a many-layered hierarchy of several contending "styles," which, when viewed diachronically, mark individual stages in evolution.

A comparative typology of phonological systems further illuminates the systemic nature of linguistic evolution. In every phonological system there are two sets of oppositions, namely, the binary opposition between phonemes of the same type—the correlative phonemes—and phonemes which do not constitute a system of parallel oppositions—the disjunct phonemes. A series of phonological oppositions of the first type establishes a phonological correlation, and a set of such correlations, in turn, provides the basis for typological classification of individual languages. There are, to be sure, phonological correlations which coexist in one language but not in another. Thus the correlations voiced-voiceless consonants and long-short vowels characterize the phonological system of Czech. But in Russian we see the following correlations: voiced-voiceless consonants, soft-hard consonants and dynamically stressed-atonic vowels. Furthermore, strict phonological rules regulate the relationships between certain correlations within one language. These are the so-called laws of implication. One can conceive of three alternative arrangements of these laws: both correlations are present; one correlation is present, the other absent; and both correlations are absent. For example, one law of the second category, discovered by Jakobson in 1922, states that free dynamic stress and independent opposition of long and short vowels cannot both be present in one system. Since these "connections between the correlations of the phonological system" have, according to Jakobson, "infailliblement valeur de loi" (without fail the value of a law) (*SW* 1, p. 23), they help us reduce that immense array of phonological mutations to a few fundamental principles. Consequently, our "predictive power" in historical reconstruction increases considerably, and the previously vexing and insoluble problem of language evolution gives way to a systemic explanation.

Another bone of contention between Saussure and Jakobson, this time concerning linguistic borrowings, brings us closer to the concerns of literary theory and history. Briefly put, the problem of linguistic borrowings gives rise to a principle which is applicable not only to small units like phonemes, morphemes or words but, with modifications, also to larger verbal structures. In literary theory this problem is studied as literary influence, whether the influence is of one poetic generation on another or of one foreign literature on another. Saussure, desirous of protecting the purity of the system, argued that, considered synchronically, borrowings do not really count as such since they are fully integrated into the system and thus are no different from any other "signe autochtone" (linguistic sign) to which they now stand in opposition. In diachrony, however, the assimilation of an "emprunt de phonème" (loan-phoneme) seems to exhibit little, if any, systemic connection with "les aires de contagion" (affected zones). The regularity of change that a phoneme exhibits in the evolution of one language is destroyed when it migrates into another language, because now the loaned phoneme is affected by time as well as space. There are instances, in Saussure's view, where imitation of a neighboring dialect takes place irrespective of the traditional prototype, that is to say, capriciously and at random. In that case, we should distinguish between a phonetic change, which exhibits regularity, and the borrowing of phonemes, which does not. The obvious contradiction of this process did not escape Saussure's attention but rather reinforced his belief in the necessary rift between the diachronic and synchronic methods.

To rectify Saussure's unsatisfactory procedure, Jakobson reasoned that, on the contrary, the laws of diachrony and synchrony are intimately bound together if seen as a relation between the means employed and the results attained. The direction inherent in a language change demands the use of certain means in order to fulfill its goal—Jakobson prefers to speak of obtained results since in language the goal is not always reached. When the available means happen to come from the system of language "B"—in which they performed a distinct function—the other system of language "A" appropriates such means for its own purpose. With respect to language borrowings, we can see, then, that any new linguistic borrowing introduced into the system must correspond in great measure to a need already present in the system:

> . . . when the system of idiom "A" "imitates" the system of idiom "B," the selection and revision of the functional values of the adopted elements always takes place from the point of view of the system "A," in correspondence with the evolutionary possibilities and inclinations of the latter. (p. 107)

Thus by analyzing the state of language before the change which was brought about by a borrowing, and then examining its reverberations on the whole system, Jakobson once again provided a viable solution to what had seemed to be a fortuitous and unmotivated linguistic phenomenon. The issue of literary influence, by extension, should be approached primarily from the standpoint of the affected literature viewed as a cohesive system. Far from defying a systematic explanation, the functional conception of linguistic borrowings lent additional support to the notion of language as a system, whether in synchrony or in diachrony.[16]

In this way, the theory of immanent evolution explains the kinds of language changes which take place, namely, either to ensure equilibrium or to increase stylistic flexibility. Moreover, it offers a principle of their classification. Yet several important points remain unaccounted for. These are, as Jakobson and Tynjanov pointed out in the 1928 manifesto, the tempo of evolution and the direction of change when several other options seem equally conceivable. Similarly, the theory of immanence, system-bound as it is, leaves little room for the action of the individual—and we shall see later that this was a stumbling block that hampered the elaboration of a full-fledged literary history for many years. As in modern biology—in which phylogeny, the evolutionary development of the species, is a precondition of ontogeny, the development of the individual—so, too, in linguistics, Jakobson argued, the individual's role amounts at best to the "speeding up" of the phylogeny. For structural linguistics, in other words, the importance of the individual speaker is by and large negligible. Instead of inquiring into the genesis of a linguistic innovation, its source in the individual person, the structuralists consistently sought to investigate the function of such a change, that is, the way it fulfilled the demand created by the impersonal or suprapersonal system.

In sum, structuralism subscribed to a strictly teleological (or means-ends) mode of explanation of language phenomena. Language no longer appeared as an aggregate of unrelated facts or, diachronically, as a haphazard collection of fortuitous changes; the concept of *Gestalteinheit*, the formally unified whole, successfully superseded the concept of *Und-*

Verbindung, the mechanical whole. Jakobson's crowning accomplishment lay in his thoroughgoing application of the teleological point of view to the problems of language history. Once the functional approach disclosed the purpose behind any phonological mutation or any innovation occasioned by language-borrowings, language could clearly be seen to function as a regulated system not merely on the vertical axis of synchrony but also on the horizontal axis of diachrony. Thus Jakobson achieved a final dialectical synthesis of the principles of comparative philology and those of Saussure's *Cours*. For the former explained language as having a history but lacking a systemic character, and the latter understood it as a unified system which, however, could not be grasped historically. By achieving this synthesis the Prague Circle linguists succeeded for the first time in defining the laws of language evolution.

‖●‖●‖●‖●‖●‖

The next step in the development of a theory of language evolution would logically be to move beyond the conception of immanence and to integrate the language series with other orders of social phenomena. Even though Jakobson did not elaborate on the nature of this interrelationship, he should be credited with the acute perception of the problem. This problem is exceedingly complex, since there are definite limits to how far we can go in positing some universal correlation between the evolution of language and society unless we advocate a wholly deterministic view. Instead of constructing a grandiose, all-encompassing theory, then, we are compelled to confront head-on the specifics of each case examined. Clearly, not even an exhaustive analysis of linguistic as well as extralinguistic data can lead to a general theory of systemic evolution. Still, a theoretical knowledge of immanent principles guiding the development of every (semi-) autonomous order of events can help in solving particular problems that affect the life of language and, indirectly at least, of society at large.

The most convincing testimony of the Prague School's unflagging interest in a wide variety of issues concerning nearly every aspect of the study of language is the Circle's collective contribution to the First Congress of Slavicists, held in Prague in 1929.[17] These "Theses" not only adumbrate the School's pet projects of synchronic and diachronic phonology; they pay as much attention to topics such as linguistic geography, Slavic lexicography, the study of Old Church Slavonic and the importance of functional linguistics for language pedagogy. Especially with regard to the last item, the state of the Czech language, the Circle repeatedly demonstrated an active, even aggressive, interest. In fact, a few years later the Circle's members got embroiled in a heated controversy with the linguistic establishment, the so-called purists, about concrete usage and rules of contemporary Czech. In contrast to the Copenhagen School, another branch of structural linguistics, the Prague School did not occupy itself merely with the refining of language theory; it concerned itself in equal measure with the relation between language and language users, that is to say, society.

One of the salient ways in which we often use language is in literature. This may seem a rather trivial thing to say, yet modern linguists in general (as opposed to many nineteenth-century philologians) have studiously refused to apply their tools to the language of poetry, and the Prague School is a striking exception in this respect—the only other significant exception being the school of Vosslerian stylistics.[18] The third section of the "Theses" discusses the key problem of language's basic functional systems, or, better, subsystems: first of so-called standard (literary) language (*jazyk spisovný*) and then of poetic language (*jazyk básnický*), which, as we shall see, far from being substandard, is seen rather to conform to standards of its own. These pages, which present a far-reaching definition of the nature of poetry, have been justifiably singled out as "among the most valuable in the Prague School repertory."[19]

Before we can approach the problem of poetic language, we must differentiate standard language from the common language of the populace (*jazyk lidový*), with which it may be in danger of being confused. In contrast to the popular language, standard language is characterized by a far heavier functional load, that is, by a greater variety of tasks it is called upon to carry out. Above all, standard language gives expression to the life of a nation's culture and civilization, to its science, philosophy, religion, law and the like. The system of standard language, consequently, is distinguished from the other contiguous linguistic systems by a number of distinctive functional traits, all of which can be subsumed under the rubric of intentional normativeness. This is why we can speak of language "politics" (as in the attempts at puristic reforms and purges and other forms of linguistic censorship) as well as language "aesthetics" (as in the sense of language decorum and verbal etiquette with its social norms for suitable usage of speech). Because standard language establishes the general norm, it only follows that such language gravitates toward stability, which, however, is at the same time coupled with flexibility and versatility in the continuous selection of requisite means of expression. This selection, in every national language, is motivated by a desire for specificity, a demand that the chosen means correspond to the characteristic needs of the language in question. But standard language is set apart from the colloquial language most of all by its pronounced tendency toward intellectual abstraction, particularly evident in various professional discourses. Unlike common language, standard language must foster verbal exchange about matters with little if any bearing on life's everyday concerns or about newly discovered and invented things or, when communicating about familiar affairs, must enable language users to describe things with exactitude and in all their complexity. While on the whole conservative with respect to grammar and phonology, standard language is more creative lexically, since one of its main goals is an ever more precise linguistic articulation of logical categories (as, for example, in the formation of "word-concepts"). Syntactically, too, standard language has to meet a number of intellectually challenging demands, such as adequately expressing the intricately interconnected nature of mental processes (for instance, through complex arrangements of subordinate clauses). Not surprisingly, the most effective instrument of standard language is written discourse, whereas spoken standard language stands closer to the vernacular forms of common language. From the social viewpoint, during the course of its development, standard language is torn between two contradictory impulses: on the one hand, its tendency to become the common coin or, as the "Theses" have it, to function as "*koinē*"; and, on the other hand, the tendency to become the privileged property of the ruling class, an insignia of social status. A reflection of societal pressures, standard language is clearly subject to the contending claims of "aristocracy" and "democracy."

But what of poetic language? As the "Theses" argue, when viewed in terms of synchronic linguistics, poetic speech appears as the *parole*, or "as an individual creative act which is evaluated against the background of the immediate poetic tradition (poetic language—*langue*) on the one hand, and against the background of the contemporary language of communication on the other." Put another way, as in linguistics, in the study of poetry we must first investigate the normative backdrop (or implicit "context") both of the standard language of communication and of poetic language, since an individual literary work cannot ultimately exist—nor can it be adequately understood—independently of this complex of norms and conventions. Thus poetic language is intimately bound up with the standard language but must always be distinguished from it. Not only might a breach of rules in standard language be permissible poetic usage, but much more importantly, the two subsystems have distinct social functions with respect to extralinguistic reality: standard language has a communicative function, whereas poetic language has an aesthetic one. Accordingly, we may say that the dominant tendency of the first linguistic domain is toward the normalization of the range of expression; and of the second, toward the realization of new possibilities. This functional antinomy between the operations of "practical" and "poetic" means of language, first proposed by Opojaz linguist Lev Jakubinskij some dozen years earlier,[20] in the Prague School vocabulary is labeled that of "automatization" (*automatizace*) and "actualization" (*aktualizace*). In the language of communication, understanding is facilitated when all language elements are automatized, or we may also say nonactualized: language seems to refer, unobstructed, to the objects under discussion. Poetry, in comparison, is bound to strike us as oblique and indirect. In the formulation of the "Theses," "poetic language is directed toward [*zamíření; Einstellung*] the act of expression itself," and thus "all strata of the linguistic system, which in the language of communication have only a subservient role, acquire more or less autonomous value in poetic language."[21] In other words, if standard language tends to provide a schematic, conventional account of events, poetic actualization amounts to the breaking of the customary scheme.

The analysis of a poem centers on demonstrating the degree of actualization of its component parts. Again, analogous to the global linguistic system, "a poetic work is a *functional structure* and the individual elements can only be comprehended in their relation to the whole" (emphasis mine). The function of each actualized and nonactualized element differs from poem to poem, even when such elements are, objectively, identical. Whether, and to what degree, a given linguistic element has been actualized becomes evident by comparison either with the contemporary state of standard language or with the prevalent aesthetic canon. Indeed, it is the merit of structural phonology, the authors of the "Theses" maintain, that it alone can disclose the governing principles of poetic structures, in particular, the sound structures of poetry. All the traditional approaches to versification are bound to miscarry, failing as they do to recognize the basic phonological law of verse technique—namely, that two seemingly identical rhythmic structures from different languages are likely to have distinct values attached to them, since they consist of phonological elements with different roles within their respective sound systems. Poetic phonology, then, must always examine the degree to which poetry, or the individual poet, exploits—actualizes—the phonological inventory of the pertinent standard language. In every verse language, it is rhythm which tops the hierarchy of structural values. As the organizing principle of verse structure, it binds to itself such phonological facets as verse melodics and "euphony" as well as canonic devices like rhyme and alliteration. Besides rhythm, one of the prime devices of poetic actualization is the parallelism of sound structures vividly embodied in rhyme patterns: "the confrontation of consonant phonic structures," according to the "Theses," "throws into relief the coincidences as well as noncoincidences among syntactic, morphological and semantic structures." Rhythmic-syntactic figures further underscore the autonomy of verse structure: with their special intonation which through repetition creates the so-called melodic impulse they deform still more palpably the automatized sound organization of standard language. Yet poetic actualization is not confined only to the sound stratum. It affects the poet's lexicon, too, especially through poetic neologisms, archaisms or barbarisms. Such unconventional locutions set off poetic language from standard language both phonologically (by calling attention to the words' acoustic makeup, to which speakers are usually indifferent) and morphologically (by actualizing the words' constituent morphemes). And syntax in its turn, thanks to the dense interaction with verse rhythm, melody and semantics, generates additional stimuli for poetic actualization by charging especially those syntactic features which remain underutilized in the language's grammatical system.

Just as the same structural element is apt to have different functions in various contemporary language systems (as well as, of course, within assorted coexisting poems), its function in the given poetic system will change in time as well:

An artistic phenomenon of the past may . . . last or may be revived as an effective factor in another environment and become an element in the new system of artistic values, but of course its function changes in the process and the phenomenon itself is subject to corresponding changes.

The "Theses" therefore warn against any sort of investigative "egocentrism" which might lead us to negate the pastness and, in many cases, the historical remoteness of individual poetic manifestations. Instead, they call for an immanent or internal typological categorization of poetic genres as they functioned at the particular time. This typology must recognize that a poem, like any work of art, is a *sign* with a specific function, namely, to be directed toward the very act of verbal expression, and not toward what may thereby be signified in nonartistic terms. In literary evolution, we must reconstruct the original function of the phenomenon under investigation within the original system (the linguistic and poetic canon) and then follow its successive temporal modifications. The final article of the "Theses" defines in no uncertain terms the proper subject of historical study:

The immanent characterization of the evolution of poetic language is frequently replaced in literary history by a cultural-historical, sociological or psychological deviation, that is, by a reference to heterogeneous phenomena. Instead of mystifying causal relationships among heterogeneous systems, we have to investigate the poetic language in itself.

Roman Jakobson and Jan Mukařovský, who were in reality the principal authors of this section of the "Theses," do not venture any further.[22] They are so concerned with the autonomous or intertextual functioning of literature as literature that, at this point, they see no good reason for an inquiry into the social, or "heterogeneous," aspect of literary evolution. All they manage to hint is that while the "distinctive feature of poetic language is its highlighting of the aspects of struggle and re-formation [*přeformování* (of standard language)], the character, direction and scale of this re-formation vary greatly"—without indicating any of the decisive factors which help determine the ongoing change. Briefly put, this part of the "Theses" basically remains within the tenets of advanced formalism; it is not yet a full-fledged statement of the principles of a structuralist literary criticism. Jakobson and Mukařovský write a valuable complementary sequel to the earlier manifesto of Jakobson and Tynjanov but methodologically they do not dramatically advance beyond it. For the future development of a structuralist literary theory, the main contribution of the "Theses" lies in the introduction of these key concepts: the poem as a functional structure; poetic language as a language marked by actualization of expressive means; and the notion of the sign as the dominant feature of the artistic system of literature.[23]

‖●‖●‖●‖●‖●‖

The conception of immanent literary evolution, too, had largely been articulated in the writings of the Russian formalists. Such was the message another leading formalist, Boris Tomaševskij, carried to Prague in his speech ("La nouvelle école d'histoire littéraire en Russie") to the Circle on 7 February 1928.[24] Tomaševskij sketched a brief history of formalism, separating its development into two stages. During the first period the formalists tried to illuminate the technical facets of poetic composition—art as the sum of poetic devices was the slogan of the day—but in the second period the focus shifted toward the study of literary history. The traditional conception, sarcastically labeled the "literary history of the generals," conceived of literary "progress" as a succession of masters and their respective influences. In its place the formalists offered a version of literary history which was not a peaceful legacy but, rather like the Marxist idea of class struggle, one long battle for artistic supremacy—if not a permanent revolution, at least a permanent reform.[25] Not only is there a positive influence of one author's attraction to his or her master, argued the formalists, there is also, and often more decisively, a negative influence of rebellion and repulsion, "the tendency to react against the dominant literary forms of the period" (p. 235), to engage in a kind of guerrilla activity against literary conventions. Thus, again as a kind of reaction, the formalists were keen on studying those realms which had escaped from the desiccating embrace of academic history, those less dignified or "barbaric" genres like melodrama, crime fiction, diaries, travelogues and so on. For they now claimed that the emergence of a new literary school is often but a "canonization of the effort of those writers who were neglected during the preceding epoch" (p. 236). This novel view of literary history necessitated the study of other issues and areas previously untouched by literary historians (but now investigated under the aegis of comparative literature), such as the grounds for the reception and assimilation of models from foreign literatures; literature in translation as an integral part of a given national literature; and, above all, the study of contemporary literature as a desirable complement and corrective to the historicist perspective.

The formalists gradually moved from the analysis of individual poetic devices to the study of their role within the work taken as a whole, and even to the study of entire literary systems. Tomaševskij attributed this change in formalist research to the discovery of poetic function and its historical relativity.[26] Previously, most formalist studies had been comparatively static and descriptive, whereas their approach now was dynamic and evolutionary. The functional approach resulted in a totally new perspective on the process of literary evolution:

it did not present itself as a series of forms substituting for one another, but as a continual variation of the aesthetic function of literary devices. Every work found itself oriented in relation to the literary milieu and every element in relation to the entire work. That element whose value is determined by one era completely changes its function in another. . . . The true life of a literary work's elements manifests itself in the continual change of function. (p. 239)

The process of the poetic function's temporal mutations, however, remained a thesis without any detailed explanation, unsupported by concrete examples. Together with the Jakobson-Tynjanov propositions, Tomaševskij's assessment of the formalists' accomplishments, although still forward-looking, remained a blueprint which the formalists themselves—owing mainly to unfavorable political circumstances—were unable to develop.

Fortunately, the Prague Linguistic Circle proved to be a most fertile ground where formalist ideas were easily transplanted and where they continued to grow vigorously. For the Czechs were far from unprepared for the importation of formalist theory. The local formalist tradition dated all the way back to the reception of aesthetic ideas worked out by Johann Friedrich Herbart (1776–1841), a contemporary of Hegel, who, rather than examining the philosophical import of art, concentrated on art's formal relationships.[27] Jan Mukařovský, the Circle's foremost specialist in aesthetics, is a direct descendant of that tradition. Nonetheless, the formative years 1928 to 1930 can be called, without hesitation, the Circle's formalist period, at least in matters of literary theory.

Indeed, Mukařovský's major work of that time, the study of a celebrated narrative poem by Karel Hynek Mácha, *Máj* (1836), recapitulates, so to speak, the whole development of formalist ideas. *Mácha's "May": A Study in Aesthetics* consists of three chapters, each reenacting a successive stage of formalism: the first two are descriptive and synchronic, while the third is interpretive and diachronic.[28] Even within the first two chapters, formalism's chronology is repeated. The first employs a complicated linguistic apparatus in a manner reminiscent of Jakubinskij's and Osip Brik's early forays into metrics and sound repetitions to explain what critics traditionally referred to as the musicality of Mácha's verse. The second, emulating Tynjanov's studies of poetic meaning from the mid-twenties, unravels the causes of *May*'s semantic vagueness. Whether discussing the patterns of sound organization in terms of parallelism, inversion and sequence or the poem's semantic aspect in terms of the syntagmatic relationship between the semantic core and accessory meanings of nouns and adjectives, Mukařovský displays the formidable intricacy of synchronic analysis. Their scintillating analytic performance notwithstanding, these phonological and semantic investigations might appear at first glance to exhibit linguistic excess. W. H. Bruford, an early commentator on Czech structuralism, observed that Mukařovský "would seem to have been guilty of a misplaced abstraction,"[29] an impression created by a strictly static description in which the poem is extracted both from the poetic series—that is, poems that may have anticipated it—and from other series of social phenomena.

The third chapter, however, which Mukařovský devotes to a comparative study of the poem's theme, goes a long way toward correcting the impression of misplaced abstraction. The thematic and comparative approach would suggest a rather more traditional orientation than the earlier sections, but the very method which Mukařovský calls a genetic analysis of forms dispels any doubts that he may have renounced the formalist position. Not at all. Instead of the poem's genesis or a source study, the author analyzes the changing inheritance that Mácha bequeathed to the poets of the following two generations. This inheritance consisted largely of a thematic problem, namely, how to render the epic, by definition an objective narrative, in a subjective mode. But before one proceeds to discuss the theme (or "content"), one must break it down to its basic components, that is, motifs, just as the sound stratum has to be segmented to phonemes or syntax to words. A motif, in Mukařovský's definition, is a "semantic unit that is immediately higher than a word and a syntagma" (p. 110). Mácha's *May* and Hálek's *Alfred* (1858) as well as Vrchlický's *Satanela* (1874) share a complex of motifs: love, sentencing, execution of one of the lovers, and amorous quarrel as the source of the tragic denouement. Mukařovský sets forth the manner in which each poet combined this set of motifs to tackle the problem of making an epic narrative more subjective.

This intermixing of the genres which traditionally—before Byron, that is—had stood in stark opposition demands two things: that the subjective elements embodied in the narrator's presence be emphasized and, conversely, that the objective, impersonal narrative be toned down. Each of the three poets, needless to say, handles this problem differently. In Mácha's *May* the subjective element enters the poem with the introduction of the first person narrative: the lyrical "I" both participates in the poem's action and reflects and comments upon it. The objective aspect of the story, on the other hand, is undermined by a suppression of the causal links between the various elements that comprise it and by an almost total lack of narrative suspense. In the next poem, Vítězslav Hálek's *Alfred*, we witness a partial distancing of the narrator from the scene. While Mácha's lyrical "I" identified fully with the protagonists' thoughts and emotions, even to the point of assuming responsibility for their deeds, Hálek's narrator, at a distance, passes a moral judgment on the heroes' acts. The objective side is also colored by the narrator's aloofness: he must make sense of actions with which he is far from familiar and, consequently, interposes his own point of view between the story and the reader. The poem's storyline thus loses its immediacy and concreteness. The third poem, Jaroslav Vrchlický's *Satanela*, follows its immediate precursor, *Alfred*, in the use of personal address to the poetic personages and to the reader yet differs from it in one important respect. The narrator no longer takes the whole story seriously. He tells an old tale whose actors interest him only intermittently, if at all. And, conversely, Vrchlický observes the action with great detachment, so that it is presented as concrete and objective. In a complete turnabout, the epic narrative is finally divested of its subjective stance, and Mácha's original experiment is set on its head. In fact, since Vrchlický inserts a motif of laughter into a story considered somber and tragic by both Mácha and Hálek, *Satanela* ends up as a muted parody of the two preceding poems.

In this conception, Mukařovský does not put stress on the generational conflict as the driving force of literary evolution as much as on the limited number of possible poetic answers to a given problem. It is the circumscribed potential of any poetic idiom, genre or even aesthetic canon which, in Mukařovský's view, accounts for the never-ending process of poetic innovation. Once an artistic norm has been officially established, the next generation cannot, as a rule, adopt their predecessors' poetic idiom wholesale, or else it meets the fate of all epigones: instant oblivion. The new schools of poets assimilate certain parts of the existing canon and put them to a novel use; for the rest, the poets employ their imaginative power to create new thematic variations or, eventually, seek their inspiration from lower, uncanonized genres. According to the notion of immanent evolution, then, a poet is not free to choose any random configuration or structure of elements—any form—but must confront the canon inherited from his or her precursors. It is not by delving into the poet's private or social life that the critic can uncover the reasons why and the way in which the particular poem came about. Rather, it is necessary that the critic come to grips with the state of aesthetic norms of the time, to which the poet must have reacted. But aesthetic norms are historically relative, since the complex of norms valid for one generation is modified, and in some instances rejected, by the next. It is precisely this historical permutation of aesthetic canons, their continuous supersession, that explains literature's evolutionary dynamism.

In a lecture surveying formalist literary theory, "On Current Poetics," delivered in April 1929,[30] Mukařovský reiterated and enlarged upon the dynamism and relativity of artistic norms and forms: "A literary work of art appears to us, even when we approach it from the point of view of form, as *a member in an evolutionary series*, conditioned by what preceded it and conditioning what will follow it" (p. 111; emphasis mine). The same principle, claimed Mukařovský, applies *ipso facto* to the category of genre. The genre should not be defined thematically, he argued, since the same theme is apt to find expression in various genres, for instance, in a legend as well as a ballad, a short story or a drama; on the contrary, we should define it formally. In this way, genre appears as a "fixed set of formal devices" (p. 113), where the defining devices may be, in Mukařovský's view, the metrical form (in the *chansons de geste*, for example, the characteristic features are the *laisses*, the *tirades monorimes* and the decasyllabic verse), or certain sound qualities (in the Russian eighteenth-century ode the dominant component was the intonation), a lexical choice (as in the heroic epic) or a technique of composition (the difference between the novel and the short story). Moreover, a genre is constituted not only by individual formal devices but by their combinations. In time, understandably, the particular combination of such devices can change: some elements remain unaltered, maintaining the genre's continuity, while the influx of new elements assures its expressive freshness and elasticity. But in extreme cases even those elements with which the genre is generally identified may disappear, whereas the secondary elements are preserved. In the romantic epic, as was the case with Mácha, the typical feature of the genre—the epic action—faded away, yet the division of the poem into "books" was retained. Subject to vast changes, the same genre may, over a long period of time, produce two almost unrecognizable "evolutionary members." As examples, Mukařovský cited the picaresque novel and the contemporary novel or the Spanish and modern romance. He concluded, accordingly, that we "can safely define the genre only for a given period, and not as a universally valid category." "Even for the principal poetic categories such as the lyric and the epic," he went on to say, "we would be hard put to find a simple and unambiguous definition that would be valid for all time and all literature" (p. 114).

Like Jakobson in linguistics, Mukařovský in literary theory had moved, by the end of the twenties, an impressive distance from the initially exclusive synchronic approach. Still, despite the fact that he examined Mácha's complex of motifs as dynamically evolving in time and in another study, "Variants and Stylistics," analyzed the development of a single text's stylistic revisions,[31] Mukařovský's work from this period falls distinctly short of being historical. It also falls short of being structural. As long as the theory of literary history remained confined within the bounds of immanence—and refused to consider the import for literary evolution of the reciprocal relationships among literature and the other arts and, further afield, among literature and other social phenomena—this theory was a straightforward outgrowth of formalism. In actuality, the very terms of structuralism, first utilized in the "Theses"—functional structure, the nature of the sign, literature as the system of signs—had not yet been clarified. In *Mácha's "May"* Mukařovský took the word *struktura* to mean approximately the same as a host of architectural terms like *konstrukce* (construction), *stavba* (formation or building) and *osnova* (lay out); he thought of the term *znak* (sign) as merely a linguistic unit. It should come as no surprise, then, that, on republication of this work in 1948, Mukařovský voiced reservations about his early methodology, downgrading it as his phase of "Herbartism," as just one leg, if an important one, of a long and involved journey.

‖●‖●‖●‖●‖●‖

Structuralism itself begins to germinate only after 1930. In many ways, its development can be equated with the development of a theory of literary history. However, before structuralism reached the point when it produced a theory advancing beyond the immanent conception, the basic structuralist terms had to be clearly defined. Hence we can divide the process of structuralism's germination into two stages: 1930–1932, the period of terminological formulation, and 1932–1934, the time of intense work on literary history.

The first definition of structure occurs, with almost emblematic appropriateness, in Mukařovský's response to Chaplin's *City Lights*, "An Attempt at a Structural Analysis of Acting."[32] Although this coincidence may well be a historical whim, it seems to confirm richly Saussure's belief in the fruitfulness of the science of semiotics: the sign had to be freed from language so that its nature could be clearly comprehended. In Mukařovský's formulation, structure is "a set of elements which are aesthetically actualized and grouped in a complex hierarchy which is united by a domination of one of the elements over the rest . . ." (p. 254). A structural analysis sets out to locate the "dominant" (*dominanta*) and the assembly of relationships between the dominant and all other elements of the structure. Mukařovský's study, a model of structural approach, is so tightly knit that no summary can possibly do it justice. But the following lines should give some sense of his method. In Chaplin's film, the dominant consists of expressive gestures. Consequently, both auditory elements (the pitch, intensity and color of voice or the tempo of articulation) and bodily movements expressive of the actor's relation to the stage space are subordinated. Chaplin's voice is in fact either replaced by music or completely suppressed, and his bodily movements, insofar as they are distinguishable from gestures, have much the same (expressive) function as gestures. In other words, *City Lights* had to remain a silent film for the gestures to become the dominant structural component.

Generally speaking, there are two kinds of gestures, sign-gestures and expression-gestures. The designation for the first category emphasizes the social character of signs: sign-gestures in Mukařovský's terminology are those whose expressiveness, like that of most words, has been curtailed by common use, that is to say, by convention. From such ritual gestures it is impossible to gauge the person's sincerity and the intensity with which he or she expresses emotions. A gesture must thus depart in some way from the prevailing convention if its individual expressiveness is to be perceived. When a gesture convincingly conveys the emotion of which it is a sign, and so becomes an expression-gesture, it usually appears as an accentuation of the conventional manner: the smile is broader or the bow deeper. A gesture, however, may just as well camouflage the genuine intention behind it and become a pretense. Here we see what Mukařovský calls the interference of an individual expressive gesture in social sign-gestures. Such interference may occur successively, so that a coordination of a series of gestures which unfold in time is disrupted—a sudden, unwitting expressive gesture obtrudes on the sign-gestures; or it may happen simultaneously, as is the case when the sign-gesture communicated by, say, facial mimicry is at the same time belied by an individually expressive gesture conveyed by the movement of the hand. Throughout the film, according to Mukařovský, there is a dynamic interplay between the two sets of gestures, which are in continual catachreses: in Chaplin's mask—a worn-out evening coat but a cane and a bowler—or in the very theme of a beggar who entertains grand social aspirations. Further, the catachrestic interplay explains the role of the two supporting actors, the blind flower girl and the drunk millionaire. Each character is designed to perceive a single set of interfering gestures: the girl's blindness leads her to acknowledge only social sign-gestures, whereas the millionaire's intoxication makes him register the individual expression-gestures. In this way, the unerring identification of the dominant has revealed step by step the principle underlying the whole structure.

Literature, like acting and mime and social gesticulation, is composed of signs. A sign serves for supraindividual communication and is therefore a social fact *sui generis*. What cannot be communicated socially is not a sign; nor is it the business of criticism to investigate such phenomena. Structuralism, in literary theory, opposes the kind of study that purports to treat those matters which are not expressed in and communicated by the text. Mukařovský's *bête noire*, as his devastating review "The Artist's Personality in the Work's Mirror" abundantly illustrated, was psychological criticism.[33] By failing to come to grips with the semiotic character of art, psychological criticism seemed to incorporate every fallacy that had come under attack during the formalists' polemic against biographical, philosophical and social criticism. In short, psychological criticism did not, and still frequently does not, recognize that art is a mediation, not a causal result of a certain set of conditions. A sign stands for another object; it cannot *be* that object. "The theorist of art must," according to Mukařovský, "seek justification for the work's every quality in the structure of the work he analyzes, in the work of art itself." Conversely, "the correspondence between the work and its author's psychological state is neither necessary nor unexceptional but merely arbitrary" (p. 146). Unlike structuralism, psychological criticism ultimately misses the most fundamental point, namely, that a poetic work is a "sign that has been created in order to be understood as a work of art" (p. 145).

A structural analysis of a work of verbal art, then, tries to identify the characteristic properties of poetic language. But poetic language, as we have seen already in our discussion of the "Theses," is nothing more than a particular use of standard language in which certain elements become actualized. Just as an individual expressive gesture could be appreciated only in juxtaposition with social sign-gestures, so poetic language comes to be aesthetically effective when it is measured against standard language. As Mukařovský put it in another essay from 1932, "Standard Language and Poetic Language," "The interference in the norm of standard language, and a systematic interference at that, makes possible the poetic use of language; without this possibility there would be no poetry at all" (p. 117).[34] The defining characteristic of poetic language is not so much any discernible property but a process, the process of actualization. Poetry aims at maximum actualization "in order to push into prominence the very *act* of expression, or speaking itself" (p. 114; emphasis mine). Actualization should not, however, be conceived in quantitative terms. Actualization, it must be reemphasized, can function only in conjunction with automatization, that tendency which defines standard language. If all elements were poetically actualized, put in the foreground, as it were, there would be no background against which to observe them. In other words, "actualization of any element . . . is necessarily accompanied by automatization of one or several other elements" (p. 119).

Thus we once again approach the problem of the dominant. In verbal art, the dominant is that element of the work's structure which sets into motion all other elements, thus organizing into a complex hierarchy a set of relationships that is only potentially present in standard language. Everyday language is comprised of elements which stand in relationships of equivalence to one another. The dominant upsets the system's equilibrium, the norm of standard language, and points in a direction in which actualization takes place. Consequently, depending on the dominant, in one instance, intonation may start to govern meaning or, in another, may in turn be governed by it; a word's actualization, similarly, may develop in relation to the lexical inventory or to the sentence or even to the text's sound stratum. The dominant thus establishes a hierarchy in which one set of elements converges toward the dominant, while another set, composed of nonactualized elements, tends in the opposition direction. Still, elements which diverge from the dominant are not merely the ones that remain nonactualized with respect to standard language. As the "Theses" explicitly stated, poetic language functions against the background of twin norms of standard language and the aesthetic canon. For this reason, even though a certain element in a work may appear as actualized with respect to the former, it can in fact be nonactualized if the poet's diction conforms fully with the norms of the latter. The degree of actualization of that impulse toward continual linguistic change and poetic innovation, however, varies according to whether it occurs against one set of norms or the other. Intensive actualization takes place vis-à-vis the normativeness of standard language, whereas moderate actualization which subsequently ensues operates in contrast with the prevailing aesthetic canon. And the poetic dominant changes accordingly.

When we take all these factors into consideration, we arrive, with Mukařovský, at the definition of the organizing principle of verbal art:

The reciprocal relationships of all the poetic work's elements, actualized as well as nonactualized, create its *structure*. This structure is dynamic, containing both the tendencies of convergence and divergence, and is an artistic phenomenon which cannot be taken apart since each of its elements gains value only in a relationship to the whole. (p. 122)

It should be noticed that the definition is dynamic itself, for it embraces at once the *langue-parole* antinomy and, as we shall discuss in detail in the following pages, that between synchrony and diachrony. An individual poetic expression cannot be understood, as we know, apart from the linguistic norms and aesthetic canon which underlie it. At the same time, every single poetic act has a unity of its own given by the dominant. A poem is, in Coleridge's phrase, a unity in multeity, which is to say that every poem, as well as every writer's distinct *oeuvre*, combines a multitude of elements into a new unity, creating a new dominant in a new structure. Consequently, the particular principle controlling any one poem can be comprehended only from within the work's or author's unique structure. While the norms of language and literature guarantee that we read and describe a poem as poetry, they do not help us to interpret it. If we know the poetic *langue*, we know what a given poem or poems share with all other poems and with language in general. But if we are to grasp the singularity of the poet's production as *parole*, we can do this solely by pinpointing the structure's dominant.

Let me now briefly illustrate the historical operation of this structural principle with examples from Mukařovský's study "On the Problems of Czech Symbolism: The Poetry of Karel Hlaváček."[35] The symbolists, who took the lead in the Czech poetry of the 1890s, reacted in several ways to the poetic structure established by the previous generation, above all, by Jaroslav Vrchlický. The dominant position in Vrchlický's poetic works was taken over by a strong and continuous line of intonation. Indeed, for Vrchlický's contemporaries, the clear-cut, ostentatiously sonorous intonation was the highest gain, or, as Mukařovský put it, a true structural conquest (*výboj*), of his poetic output. Yet this structural victory of the intonational contour occurred at the expense of verse rhythm, which had become wholly automatized in order not to disturb the smooth flow of intonation, and of verse semantics, since all of the potentially disruptive verbal material had to be consigned to a subordinate position. Thus Vrchlický's word order takes second place to rhythm and intonation—so much so that the usual hierarchy of verbal expression, in which intonation follows upon meaning, is turned upside down. Here both individual meaning and theme, the highest unit, serve as base support for Vrchlický's high-flown intonation. The great challenge for the generation of the symbolists, consequently, was to repair this gross imbalance, to direct its rebellion (*odboj*) against Vrchlický's dominant: to subjugate intonation and to elevate the semantic aspect to a role of structural prominence. (Incidentally, note how Mukařovský's new vocabulary of evolutionary struggle and revolt reflects the impact of the formalist doctrine.)

Different symbolist poets, of course, took different evolutionary paths. As we know from the Jakobson-Tynjanov declaration as well as from the Circle's "Theses," the choice of the dominant path of poetic development and the scale of the ensuing structural transformation are in principle quite indeterminate. While some Czech symbolists chose to actualize the semantic or syntactic components of the sentence, Karel Hlaváček (1874–1898) recast the relation between the whole semantic construction of his texts and their theme. To begin with, Hlaváček drastically reduced his poetic lexicon. The frequent recurrence of the same, or phonically similar, words resulted in deliberate (intonational) monotony. In its extreme repetition of entire lexical groups, the pull of Hlaváček's poetry was toward a (partial) homonymy: by yoking words together phonically he conjured up their semantic resemblance or near-identity, where in reality there was none. Yet in the reader's mind such verbal similitude could well be "unwittingly assumed owing to the illusion rooted in the linguistic unconsciousness that a sound is necessarily bound to a meaning and even to the very reality to which the meaning points" (p. 123). Relying heavily on devices like alliteration, paranomastic equation of unrelated word roots and neologism, Hlaváček sought to create the impression that all of his poetic lexicon descended from a single, if indefinite, Word. Like Mallarmé, Hlaváček ultimately desired to compose a poem consisting of only one vocable, which would be repeated ad infinitum with the slightest if any shades of meaning, until the world became contained within the word. No wonder the *oeuvres* of Mallarmé, Hlaváček and a number of other symbolists were so slim. The symbolists' preferred dominant, the all-embracing word, ran against the grain of theme's constitution: while the repetitive word froze the lexical meaning into a static construct, the theme, any theme, of necessity had to unfold successively. The symbolists' poetic context (or, better, contexture) thus strove to blot out its own built-in temporal dynamism. The symbolist dominant, the orientation toward semantic immobility, posited a goal which could not be reached. There was but a thin bar separating the lone word from total silence.

The dominant, as we have just observed, is a conclusive and dynamic principle that not only molds into a distinctive unity a number of disparate elements but also differs in every accomplished poet and poetic generation: there is no single poetic dominant, but several possible ones. This view considerably alters some of the traditional concepts of literary theory. Most strikingly, it assails the privileged position accorded to the thematic aspect of literature in previous aesthetics. The theme is no more than another element of structure, which may or, as with the symbolists, may not be in the dominant position. In this context, structuralism takes one step further the formalist polemic against the content-bound approach of other critical schools. As Mukařovský asserts in "Standard Language and Poetic Language," there is just one method of dealing with "content" in art—the semantics of theme. In his definition, "the theme of a poetic work is its highest unit of meaning" (p. 123). It is that structural element which is not directly tied to the linguistic sign; in terms of the familiar New Critical heresy, the theme is what we can paraphrase. Moreover, the theme can be transposed into another semiotic series—for example, novels into film—without any significant modification of meaning. In other words, the theme is precisely what is not lost in translation. This divergent property which characterizes the theme does not, however, entitle it to any special consideration. It remains a part of a larger structure. In fact, as Mukařovský claims,

the principle that the theme is not equivalent to "reality" which the work is supposed to express as effectively or as truthfully as possible but that it is rather a part of the structure whose laws it obeys and has value according to its relationship to the structure applies also to those works in which the theme is dominant. (p. 123)

What has been asserted here is once more the predominantly centripetal movement in literature, the convergence toward the work's dominant. Before evaluating the efficacy of each element, thematic or not, on the scale of values external to the work, we must first determine the element's role within the structure. The question of evaluation, according to Mukařovský, is as follows: "in what way and to what extent does the element fulfill the function which is assigned to it within the structural whole" (p. 130). Even though, judged by external criteria, an element may be evaluated negatively when it breaks with the pertinent aesthetic or linguistic norm, its value with respect to the whole structure can be positive—precisely because of its deviation. As the structuralist maxim has it, "the criterion of evaluation is provided by the context of a particular structure and is therefore invalid for any other context" (p. 130).

Value judgments indeed pose an often intractable problem. It was the last block on the Prague School's road toward the theory of literary history. But Mukařovský's research in "A Literary Work of Art as a Complex of Values" paved the way.[36] Of course, aesthetic valuation typifies the sole attitude commensurate with the aesthetic nature of art. Every work of verbal art, however, contains a number of values other than the aesthetic one, be they intellectual, ethical or social. Especially in genres such as biography or the historical novel, the inclusion of "extra-aesthetic" values is undeniable, and the question of veracity and historical verisimilitude and of the corresponding judgment is no doubt legitimate. Historically (depending on the period) and socially (depending on the type of readership), there is therefore a constant oscillation between the aesthetic and nonaesthetic appreciation of any work. Yet what Mukařovský calls the "epistemological postulate" (*noetický požadavek*), namely, the view that a work of art must be judged above all aesthetically, remains unaffected by the presence of extra-aesthetic values. These values matter only insofar as they form a part of the work's aesthetic structure. In an epic, for instance, it is of no relevance for the aesthetic evaluation whether the given hero existed or not, although such a fact carries, under some circumstances, an extra-aesthetic value. But what does matter aesthetically is the purpose a moral or social value may fulfill in the work's composition: this value defines the relationships among the epic heroes and the degree of their importance, as in the opposition between the positive and negative hero. Even the absence of some extra-aesthetic value, such as the suppression of moral judgment in naturalistic novels, can act as a structural component if the reader's attention is drawn to it.

The presence or absence of extra-aesthetic values, their function as the work's compositional elements, is at times so much taken for granted that they escape the reader's notice. Only when there is a shift in valuation, and the reader's set of values no longer coincides with the extra-aesthetic values built into the work, does the role of the latter start to be appreciated on aesthetic grounds. In a revival of an older novel, for instance, the social differentiation manifested in the work can be at odds with the contemporary social arrangement, and thus the values can distinctly function as compositional elements, because they are now freed from the social pressures clouding their original reception. A conflict between the values of a work and those held by the reading public can be deliberately used, as in early romanticism, to intimate a sphere of values higher than those of ordinary life or, contrariwise, as in the poetic decadence and satanism of late romanticism, to celebrate values that are much below the socially acceptable norm.

This complexity and historical dynamism of value judgments led Mukařovský to recognize another mode of literary investigation, the sociology of literature. The existence of extra-aesthetic values establishes close links with the work's social function. Just as the aesthetic evaluation is the sole adequate approach to an artwork, so the aesthetic function is its principal goal. Similarly, as there are extra-aesthetic values, so a work can have several other extra-aesthetic functions, such as ethical, religious or social. In some cases, according to Mukařovský, "society may assign the work another function than that which was ascribed to it by the poet" (p. 278). It is the task of sociology of literature to investigate the reasons for the work's social appeal. While the aesthetic reception of any art is, in Mukařovský's view, always limited to a very small group of people who are endowed with special propensities or have had appropriate training, the public reception, based as it often is on art's extra-aesthetic functions, fluctuates greatly. It is important, for this reason, to "distinguish between the changes of extra-aesthetic values in poetry and their evolution in the society's consciousness and in the social praxis" (p. 280). Consequently, structural poetics concentrates on the work's artistic structure, whereas the sociology of literature inquires into the relationship between literary evolution and the evolution of general values underlying social practice. Still, this division of labor requires one qualification: to the same extent that structural analysis should account for extra-aesthetic values, literary sociology should consider "the possible deformation of extra-aesthetic values by the aesthetic value" (p. 279). In other words, poetics cannot treat its object as if it existed in a vacuum, cut off from social reality, and literary sociology, by the same token, cannot lose sight of art's aesthetic principles.

From the recognition of the sociology of literature as the appropriate discipline for the study of extra-aesthetic values and functions, there is but a small step toward a comprehensive literary history. An interview with Mukařovský which appeared in a Prague weekly in 1932 shows that the topic of literary history soon received top priority on his critical agenda.[37] This interview is remarkable in several respects. The term *structuralism* appears here for the first time as a designation for a new school of literary criticism to be distinguished from formalism.[38] *Structure* is explicitly defined in terms of a part-whole relationship as a "whole whose nature is determined by its parts and their reciprocal relationships, and which in turn determines the nature and relationships of the parts." Furthermore, the dynamic nature of structure is emphatically reiterated: "the relationship of its parts is felt to be not static, as if given beforehand, but unique and unrepeatable; . . . structure is not a stable but a fragile equilibrium." But it is with regard to what we identified as the *langue-parole* dichotomy that Mukařovský's definition takes a surprising turn:

It is clear that the value of respective parts does not depend on *a priori* norms but is given by their relationship to the whole. The value of the entire work, then, is determined by the degree to which it is able to fulfill the structural principle that underlies it. Structure, in other words, is a phenomenological and not an empirical reality; it is not the work itself, but a set of functional relationships which are located in the consciousness of a collective (generation, milieu, etc.). Several distinct structures with distinct dominants and distinct hierarchies among their parts can gradually be realized, in different times or, as the case may be, milieux, on the basis of the same work of art. Thus, the nature of structure is not univocally given by the work. The structure becomes explicit, however, once we perceive the work against the background of a vital tradition from which this work diverges and which it reflects. If the background of the tradition shifts, the structure changes too—the dominant is altered, etc. Owing to such a change the work assumes a completely new appearance.

It is the very reality of a work's structure, and not just the presence of extra-aesthetic values and functions, that makes literary history the uppermost concern of literary study. Not only must a work be understood in the context of the linguistic and aesthetic norms that surround it, but the norms themselves must be viewed as a part of a larger setting, that is, "the consciousness of a collective." The structural dynamism and historical relativity thus increase still further. We have seen that each work is defined by a special dominant governing a special structure. Now it is the structure of the work itself that undergoes numerous changes, whether in time ("generation") or space ("milieu").

Mukařovský's theory conceives of art as a process of continual permutations of functions, norms and values. Yet it would be a mistake to conclude that this theory is so relativistic that it is incapable of verification and judgment. Quite the opposite. The wide-ranging analysis of norms and of "collective consciousness" must ultimately clarify a particular work. The argument is that no work can be adequately comprehended apart from the context in which it is unavoidably anchored. Conversely, our research in the "vital tradition" can provide the much-needed correctives for the work's interpretation. In sharp contrast with traditional literary theory, structuralism insists on locating the dynamic principles of evolution within the literary series, not outside it. Since structure appears as a fragile whole, it is subject to continuous regroupings of elements and permutations of functions. This evolutionary dynamic is given, in Mukařovský's words, "by the evolving series itself." He offers the following explanation, couched in the vocabulary of intentionality: "Every structure, namely, contains, as well as an affirmation, also the possibility of its negation. The affirmation consists of those properties which are intended and designed, and the negation of the properties which were an indirect if necessary consequence of that intention and design." The term *structure* does not refer here so much to one work as to literature in general and is thus synonymous with the term *series*. (Such an occasional substitution of terms is the result of the isomorphic character of structures, of *langue* and *parole*.) As we have seen, if one poetic school selects intonation as the structural dominant, the semantic independence of words in a sentence thereby becomes weakened, and the next poetic generation then reacts negatively to such a weakening of ties among words and makes precisely the complex semantic interrelations the new dominant. The chief task of literary history is, in Mukařovský's view, to uncover the law of these modifications and replacements of dominants and the corresponding reorganizations of structural elements into new hierarchies, for such changes "do not take place randomly, but evidently have their own strict order."

||●||●||●||●||●||

By 1934 all parts of Mukařovský's (as well as Jakobson's) multifaceted theory finally fall into place. With four of his major studies published that year, structuralist theory reaches full maturity. During this prolific period Mukařovský definitely parts ways with formalism, develops a sophisticated concept of the semiotic principles of art and, last but not least, offers two separate treatises on the history of Czech verse. Unfortunately, it is necessary to omit one of the treatises, Mukařovský's lengthy work "The General Principles and Evolution of Modern Czech Verse," as well as Jakobson's companion study, "Old Czech Verse," because of both their insuperable linguistic difficulties and the specifically Czech nature of the issues treated.[39] But the discussion of Mukařovský's study "Polák's *Sublimity of Nature*" in the next chapter should adequately convey the tenor of structuralist theory of literary history.

Mukařovský's new historical and dialectical orientation comes out clearly in his review of Šklovskij's *Theory of Prose*, which appeared in a Czech translation.[40] In his opinion, the main significance of Šklovskij's theories was their polemical extremism, the uncompromising rejection of all extrinsic approaches to art. As Mukařovský writes, "against the unqualified emphasis on the 'content' one had to propose a radical antithesis emphasizing the 'form,' so that we could arrive at the synthesis of the two, that is, structuralism" (p. 346). In a truly dialectical fashion, Mukařovský discerns even in the works of this most militant of the formalists the seeds of formalism's negation. Formalism, he declares, dealt with much more than "form," that meretricious husk enveloping the precious kernel (or so said the traditional aesthetics). When talking about composition, for instance, Šklovskij did not stop at the description of what might be called the work's architecture (that is, the proportion and succession of narrative parts) but also discussed the problem of signification. Mukařovský singles out a place in Šklovskij's analysis of *Don Quixote* where Šklovskij treated Cervantes' change of attitude to his hero. Whereas in part 1 of the novel, in Šklovskij's view, Don Quixote's behavior alternates between wisdom and folly, in part 2 he always appears deceived and befuddled. Šklovskij attributed this shift to Cervantes' new comprehension of the old material: his hero is no longer a mere butt of all the jokes and stories—he now lives them. Cervantes' humanity thus acquired the function of a compositional element. Admittedly, this was a very minor issue in Šklovskij's essay, but Mukařovský's point is well taken: even in Šklovskij one could detect the presence of extra-aesthetic values. The incipient dissolution of the conventional form-content dichotomy, the realization that a work of art is a semantic whole in which every part—"content" as well as "form"—expresses meaning, was, according to Mukařovský, the starting point for the structuralist overcoming of formalist limitations.

Mukařovský's restatement of Šklovskij's well-known industrial metaphor best illustrates the gap separating structuralism from its immediate precursor. According to Šklovskij, a formalist critic should be concerned with the internal laws of literature; he or she should not be "interested in the condition of the world market or in the policies of the trusts," as his ("textual" and "textile") metaphor had it, "but solely in the count of yarn and weaving techniques."[41] Mukařovský argues in response that it is impossible to separate the problem of weaving techniques from the situation on the world market, since it is the market mechanism of supply and demand which conditions the development of the weaving techniques. In structuralism, in other words, while the internal laws are still the center of investigation, the external factors which influence the course of literary evolution are also considered. Besides, as Mukařovský points out, the external factors affecting literature do not act chaotically but "obey a strict order and have their lawlike development" (p. 349). Thus we arrive at a new, distinctively structuralist conception of literary evolution:

we are able to take into account at one and the same time the continuous evolution of poetic structure, which consists in a constant reshuffling of elements, and those outside interferences which, although they do not themselves sustain continuity, explicitly determine each of its phases. From this viewpoint, every literary fact appears to be the result of two forces: the inner dynamism of structure and the outside intervention. (p. 348)

Structuralist literary history, following the design of Hegel's philosophy, is thus based on the principles of dialectics. Formalism is as much an integral prerequisite for structuralism as the immanent conception of literary evolution is for the structuralist conception. Without the theory of immanence, the later development could not possibly have happened. At the same time, the structuralist theory of literary history rejects several aspects of formalist immanence and partially returns to the earlier extrinsic approaches.[42]

As a result of this synthesis of intrinsic (formalist) and extrinsic (sociological) approaches, the structuralists had to fight critical battles on two fronts. They had to ward off a facile identification with the formalists and, simultaneously, stress the merely secondary role played in literary evolution by external social factors. They were formalists only to the extent of holding that the primary causes for literary changes have to be sought within the literary series, and social scientists to the extent of recognizing that literature properly belongs to the wider realm of culture and society. No longer could the structuralists be content with the study of literature alone. Inevitably, they had to accept the challenge posed by that most intransigent of problems, the interaction of literature and other orders of social reality such as science, politics, economics, religion and others. How they faced up to that challenge, where they succeeded and where they failed, is the subject of the next chapter.

NOTES

1. See "Polemical Introduction," in *Anatomy of Criticism: Four Essays*, p. 18.

2. "Problemy izučenija literatury i jazyka," *Novyj Lef* 2, no. 6 (1928). The English translation by Herbert Eagle is included in *Readings in Russian Poetics: Formalist and Structuralist Views (RRP)*, pp. 79–81.

3. The first edition of the *Cours* by Charles Bally and Albert Sechehaye dates to 1916, the second revised edition to 1922. All French quotations are taken from the critical edition by Tulio de Mauro (Paris: Payot, 1972). English quotations are from Wade Baskin's translation, *Course in General Linguistics*.

4. See "Efforts toward a Means-Ends Model of Language in Interwar Continental Linguistics," *Selected Writings (SW)* 2, 522–26. This is the key formulation: "the elemental demand to analyze all the instrumentalities of language from the tasks they perform emerged [in the 1920s] as a daring innovation" (p. 523). The third section of this volume, "Toward a Nomothetic Science of Language" (pp. 369–604), provides the amplest context to date for the understanding of the rise and progress of modern structural (or law-seeking) linguistics.

5. An incisive observation by a recent commentator supplies plenty of grist for our mill: "Tynjanov and Jakobson do *not* take [the] step of assuming that the

methods in the study of language can be directly transferred to the other areas of social and cultural activity. Indeed, in suggesting that the correlation between systems 'has its own structural laws, which must be submitted to investigation,' they explicitly go *beyond* structuralism [that is, of course, the French brand—FWG], which has so far proved notoriously incapable of proposing a theoretical framework within which such questions might be posed" (Tony Bennett, *Formalism and Marxism*, p. 36). It is most paradoxical that the founding structuralists, nearly all of them highly distinguished linguists, were never tempted to commit the kind of linguistic fallacy that misled their French successors, most of whom lacked extensive training in linguistics. Perhaps the most flagrant instance of this methodological cul-de-sac in the study of the arts was reached in works by Christian Metz, such as *Film Language: A Semiotics of the Cinema* (1968), trans. Michael Taylor (New York: Oxford University Press, 1974). For detailed discussions of the formalists' theories of literature as system, consult Erlich's chapter "Literary Dynamics," in *Russian Formalism*, pp. 251–71, and Jurij Striedter's "Vorwort" to his edition of *Texte der russischen Formalisten*, vol. 1 (München: Fink, 1969), pp. ix–lxxxiii, both parts of which exist in English: "The Russian Formalist Theory of Prose" and "The Russian Formalist Theory of Literary Evolution," trans. Michael Nicholson, *PTL: A Journal for Descriptive Poetics and Theory of Literature* 3 (1977): 429–70 and 3 (1978): 1–24.

6. Cf. the English translation of "O literaturnoj evoljucii," in *RRP*, pp. 66–78, and *Časopis pro moderní filologii* 14 (1928): 183–84; the English translation is in Jakobson's *SW* 1, pp. 1–2.

7. A full account of these events can be found in the excellent editorial notes to the volume of Tynjanov's studies *Poetika/Istorija literatury/Kino*, ed. E. A. Toddes et al. (Moskva: Nauka, 1977), esp. pp. 518–36; see also Jakobson's reminiscences in "Jurij Tynjanov v Prage," in *SW* 5, pp. 560–68.

8. Erlich, *Russian Formalism*, p. 135.

9. *Actes du Premier Congrès International de Linguistes à La Haye du 10–15 Avril 1928* (Leiden: A. W. Sijthoff), p. 86.

10. *Actes*, pp. 33–36. Two other eminent Russian linguists, Sergej Karcevskij (1887–1955) and Prince Nikolaj Trubeckoj (1890–1939), were cosignatories of this statement. Vilém Mathesius (1882–1945), the Circle's first president, collaborated on the formulation of the final theoretical propositions to the Congress. For contemporary accounts of the emerging theory of the Prague School, see Mathesius' articles "New Currents and Tendencies in Linguistic Research," *Mnema* (Praha: Jednota českých filologů, 1927), pp. 188–203; "Ziele und Aufgaben der vergleichenden Phonologie," *Xenia Pragensia* (Praha: Jednota československých matematiků a fysiků, 1929), pp. 432–45; and "La place de la linguistique fonctionelle et structurale dans le développement géneral des études linguistique," *Časopis pro moderní filologii* 18 (1931): 1–7. The pupil of Mathesius, Josef Vachek, also produced articles for foreign audiences: "What Is Phonology?" *English Studies* 15 (1933): 81–92, and "Several Thoughts on Several Statements of Phoneme Theory," *American Speech* 10 (1935): 243–55.

But perhaps the single most telling formulation of the Prague School's position is Trubeckoj's "La phonologie actuelle," *Journal de psychologie* 30 (1933): 227–46, just as his *Grundzüge der Phonologie* (= *Travaux* 7 [1939]), translated by

Christiane A. M. Baltaxe as *Principles of Phonology* (Berkeley: University of California Press, 1969), is one of the most comprehensive expositions of the School's linguistic functionalism and structuralism (the volume includes Trubeckoj's bibliography). The latest, and probably the last, statement of this position is the magnum opus *The Sound Shape of Language*, coauthored by Jakobson and Linda R. Waugh (Bloomington: Indiana University Press, 1979), a volume which includes a fifty-page list of references.

11. The analogy, like the rigid synchrony/diachrony division, breaks down at this point. To cite only one example in which the time element plays a crucial role: when the same position on the board is repeated for the third time, the game necessarily ends in a draw. Similarly, within a synchronic cut we always find elements of language that seem to be either anachronisms or neologisms.

12. Vol. 2 of *Trauvaux du Cercle Linguistique de Prague* (1929). All subsequent quotations are from *SW* 1, pp. 7–112.

13. This excerpt has been translated by Josef Vachek in his *The Linguistic School of Prague: An Introduction to Its Theory and Practice*, p. 14. All other quotations are from *SW* 1.

14. Saussure's pessimism is strikingly revealed in a passage concerning, incidentally, the Czech language, in which the zero sign occurs in the genitive plural of *žena* (i.e., *žen*). After observing that language seems content with the opposition between something and nothing, Saussure comments: "La langue est un mécanisme qui continue a fonctionner malgré les détériorations qu'on lui fait subir" (Language is a mechanism which continues to function despite the deteriorations to which it is subjected) (*Cours*, p. 124).

15. *Travaux du Cercle Linguistique de Prague: Réunion Phonologique Internationale tenue à Prague (18–21/XII/1930)* 4 (1931): 247–66. This essay exists in English: "Principles of Historical Phonology," in *A Reader in Historical and Comparative Linguistics*, ed. and trans. Allan R. Keiler (New York: Holt, 1972), pp. 121–38. The Prague Congress produced a valuable document entitled "Projet de terminologie phonologique standardisée," which attempted to define the basic categories of phonetics and phonology. According to the "Projet," the phoneme is "a phonological unit not dissociable into smaller and simpler units" (*Travaux* 4: 311). However, a considerably more refined definition, worked out by Jakobson in 1932, states that by the term *phoneme* "we designate a set of those concurrent sound properties which are used in a given language to distinguish words of unlike meaning" (*Ottův slovník naučný nové doby, Dodatky* [Otto's Encyclopaedia of Modern Times, Supplements], II/I [1932], p. 608). The English translation is in Jakobson's *SW* 1, p. 231, and also in the useful volume *Approaches to English Historical Linguistics: An Anthology*, ed. Roger Lass, pp. 6–7. Another handy anthology is *Classics in Linguistics*, ed. Donald E. Hayden et al. The translation of the "Projet" definition is provided by Vachek, *The Linguistic School of Prague*, p. 45. For a succinct general account of Jakobson's theory, consult Linda R. Waugh, *Roman Jakobson's Science of Language*.

16. For further illustrations of this argument, especially regarding the notion of "nomogenesis," see Jakobson's later study of a related topic: "Sur la théorie des affinités phonologique" (1938), *SW* 1, pp. 234–46; English version in *A Reader in Historical and Comparative Linguistics*, pp. 241–52.

17. *Travaux du Cercle Linguistique de Prague: Mélanges linguistiques dédiés au Premièr Congrès des Philologues slaves* 1 (1929): 7–29. The "Theses" are best known in the French version, but there are certain discrepancies between that rendition and the Czech original which was included in the same volume—unfortunately without pagination. I have found it desirable to offer my own translation from the Czech. Complete English translations of the "Theses" published under the title "Manifesto Presented to the First Congress of Slavic Philologists in Prague" can be found in *Recycling the Prague Linguistic Circle*, ed. and trans. Marta K. Johnson, pp. 1–31, and, in John Burbank's version, in *The Prague School: Selected Writings, 1929–1946 (PS)*, ed. Peter Steiner, pp. 3–31.

18. For example, see "Linguistics and Literary History" by Leo Spitzer, the best-known representative of this school in America, in his *Linguistics and Literary History: Essays in Stylistics*, pp. 3–39.

19. Karl D. Uitti, *Linguistics and Literary Theory*, p. 143. Interestingly, the "Theses" do not, however, bring the discussion of the two "functional dialects" (in Jakobson's older terminology)—or as we may say, between common colloquy and uncommon poetry—into any sort of alliance. To that extent, the individual parts of the "Theses" bear the signatures, as it were, of their respective authors. To simplify matters, the following commentary also draws on the subsequent restatements by Bohuslav Havránek (1893–1978), "Úkoly spisovného jazyka a jeho kultúra," and Jan Mukařovský, "Jazyk spisovný a jazyk básnický," from the Circle's volume *Spisovná čestina a jazyková kultura* (Standard Czech and Language Culture), ed. Bohuslav Havránek and Miloš Weingart (Praha: Melantrich, 1932), pp. 32–84 and 123–56; sections from these two articles appeared in English: "The Functional Differentiation of the Standard Language" and "Standard Language and Poetics Language," in *A Prague School Reader on Esthetics, Literary Structure, and Style*, ed. and trans. Paul L. Garvin, pp. 3–16, 17–30 (the reader includes a handy critical bibliography). Havránek's investigations in this field have been brought out under the title *Studie o spisovném jazyce* (Studies in Standard Language) (Praha: Nakladatelství Československé akademie věd, 1963). The complete bibliography of his publications from the Prague Circle's period is in *Studie a práce linguistické: K šedesátým narozeninám akademika Bohuslava Havránka* (Linguistic Studies and Works: On Bohuslav Havránek's Sixtieth Birthday) (Praha: Nakladatelství Československé akademie věd, 1954), pp. 529–51.

20. See especially Jakubinskij's paper "O zvukach stichotvornogo jazyka" (On the Sounds of Verse Language), *Poetika: Sborniki po teorii poetičeskogo jazyka* no. 1 (1919): 37–49. To be sure, there were considerable differences between Jakubinskij's (or Opojaz') "psychophonetics" and Jakobson's (and eventually the Prague School's) phonological interpretation of poetic language. Consult Ladislav Matejka's discussion "The Roots of Russian Semiotics of Art," *The Sign: Semiotics around the World*, ed. R. W. Bailey et al., pp. 146–72, esp. pp. 155–59.

21. Here is a subsequent, more sophisticated definition: "While the structure of the pertinent standard language provides the basis for the shifting structure of [poetic language], it furnishes the basis only for the signifying side (*signifiant*) of the linguistic sign; [poetic language's] signified side (*signifié*) is constituted by other distinct structural relations" (Bohuslav Havránek, "K funkčnímu rozvrstvení spisovného jazyka," *Časopis pro moderní filologii* 28 [1942]: 412). This formulation

seems to look forward to the Moscow-Tartu School's conception of primary and secondary communication-modeling systems: see B. A. Uspenskij, V. V. Ivanov, V. N. Toporov, A. M. Piatigorskij, Ju. M. Lotman, "Theses on the Semiotic Study of Cultures (as Applied to Slavic Texts)," *Structure of Texts and Semiotics of Culture*, ed. Jan Van der Eng and Mojmír Grygar, pp. 1–28. The other major texts of this latest development of Slavic literary theory are collected in *Semiotics and Structuralism: Readings from the Soviet Union*, ed. Henryk Baran, and *Soviet Semiotics: An Anthology*, ed. and trans. Daniel P. Lucid.

22. "Deux Lettres de Roman Jakobson," *Change* no. 3 (1969): 51, and "Lettre sur le Cercle de Prague à J. P. Faye et L. Robel," *Change* no. 4 (1969): 224–26. The "Theses" were presented as a collective statement of the Circle without individual attributions.

23. Many readers may be familiar with the principles of structural linguistic analysis from the later works of Roman Jakobson, notably "Linguistics and Poetics" (1960), "Poetry of Grammar and Grammar of Poetry" (1962) or the numerous exegeses of specific poems now collected in *SW* 3. In this sense, Jakobson may be said to have returned during the last phase of his career to the methodological stance of formalism/structuralism from the late 1920s and early 1930s.

24. This lecture was translated by Jan Mukařovský and published as "Nová ruská škola v bádání literárně-historickém," *Časopis pro moderní filologii* 15 (1928): 12–15. All quotations are from the expanded version, "La nouvelle école d'histoire littéraire en Russie," *Revue des études slaves* 8 (1928): 226–40.

25. For a similar historical account of the growth of the formalist doctrine, see Boris Eichenbaum, "The Theory of the Formal Method" (1926), in *RRP*, pp. 3–37.

26. Perhaps the most illuminating excursus on the historical instability of major categories of literary history is Roman Jakobson's denunciation of what may be called "realistic fallacy," the literary historian's indiscriminate use of the term *realism* as if it were a "bottomless sack" into which at least nine separate meanings could be stuffed. Realism is not an ideal or transcendental concept but an eminently historical one; its character changes depending on how the goal of maximum verisimilitude is conceived by the writer and then perceived by the reader— whether the writer, for instance, seeks to deform or conform to the reigning tradition in the name of a closer approximation to reality or whether it is the reader who rebels against the prevailing artistic code or, on the contrary, views the code's subversion as a distortion of reality. Instead of misusing the term as an honorific catchword of every new *Sturm und Drang* movement, we may do well, Jakobson implies, to restrict the meaning of *realism* to that trend in nineteenth-century prose whose principal technique was the "condensation of the narrative by means of figures based on contiguity," as when Tolstoj focuses metonymically or synecdochically on Anna Karenina's handbag while describing her suicide. But even in this instance we should bear in mind that the "requirement of consistent motivation and realization of poetic devices" cannot possibly be established once and for all ("O realismu v umění," *Červen* 4 [1921]: 300–304; cf. "On Realism in Art," trans. Karol Magassy, *RRP*, pp. 38–46). Although written in Russian (the original version is in *SW* 3, pp. 723–31), this article was published in Czech translation shortly after Jakobson's arrival in Czechoslovakia.

27. See, in this connection, the informative survey article "Semiotics in Bohemia in the 19th and Early 20th Centuries: Major Trends and Figures" by Peter Steiner and Bronislava Volek, in *Sign: Semiotics around the World*, ed. R. W. Bailey et al., pp. 207–26, Steiner's·"'Formalism' and 'Structuralism': An Exercise in Metahistory," *Russian Literature* 12 (1982): 290–330, or the numerous studies by Oleg Sus (consult appendix 2). The extent of the Prague School's debt to the ideas of the Russian formalists is examined in Ladislav Matejka, "Postscript: Prague School Semiotics," in *SA*, pp. 265–90, and in Jurij Striedter, "Einleitung," in Felix Vodička, *Die Struktur der literarischen Entwicklung*, ed. Frank Boldt, pp. vii–ciii.

28. Jan Mukařovský, *Máchův Máj. Estetická studie* (Praha: Universita Karlova, 1928). For the French résumé, see pp. 155–63. It should be noted that this study was recommended for publication by Mukařovský's teacher, Otakar Zich (1879–1934), a well-known aesthetician in the tradition of Herbart. Zich's precursors in aesthetics were Otakar Hostinský (1847–1910) and Josef Durdík (1837–1902).

29. W. H. Bruford, *Literary Interpretation in Germany*, p. 12. For an opposing view, which effectively refutes claims such as that of Bruford, see Lubomir Doležel, "The Conceptual System of Prague School Poetics: Mukařovský and Vodička," in *The Structure of the Literary Process: Studies Dedicated to the Memory of Felix Vodička* (*SLP*), ed. Peter Steiner et al., pp. 109–126, esp. pp. 111–14.

30. "O současné poetice," *Plán* 1 (1929): 387–97. Quoted from *CPE*, pp. 99–115, the final volume of Mukařovský's collected papers.

31. "Varianty a stylistika," *Studie a spomínky prof. dr Arne Novákovi k 50. narozeninám* (Vyškov: Obzina, 1930), pp. 52–53; reprinted in *KCP* 1, pp. 206–10.

32. "Pokus o strukturní rozbor hereckého zjevu: Chaplin ve *Světlech velkoměsta*," *Literární noviny* 5, no. 10 (1931): 2–3. Quoted from *SE* (2nd ed., 1971), pp. 254–59.

33. "Umělcova osobnost v zrcadle díla (Několik kritických poznámek k uměnovědné teorii i praxi)," *Akord* (1931): 253–63; *CPE*, pp. 145–55.

34. "Jazyk spisovný a jazyk básnický," *Spisovná čeština a jazyková kultura*, ed. Bohuslav Havránek and Miloš Weingardt (Praha: Melantrich, 1932), pp. 123–56. Quoted from *CPE*, pp. 116–44. This essay was part of the debate with the "purists" (see discussion above).

35. "K problémům českého symbolismu (Poesie Karla Hlaváčka)," *Charisteria*, pp. 118–25; revised version in *KCP* 2, pp. 209–14; see also "Předmluva k vydání Hlaváčkových *Žalmů*" (Foreword to the Edition of Hlaváček's *Psalms*) (1934), rpt. in *KCP* 2, pp. 219–34.

36. "Básnické dílo jako soubor hodnot," *Jarní almanach Kmene (Jízdní řád literatury a poesie)*, ed. Adolf Hoffmeister (Praha: Kmen, 1932), pp. 118–25. Quoted from the revised version, in *KCP* 1, pp. 275–80.

37. "Rozhovor s Janem Mukařovským," interview conducted by Bohumil Novák, *Rozpravy Aventina* 7, no. 28 (1932): 226. All quotations are from the same page.

38. For the sake of historical accuracy, I must mention what is probably the earliest appearance of this term, although made in the context of linguistics rather than poetics: "Were we to comprise the leading idea of present-day science in its

most various manifestations," Roman Jakobson wrote in a magazine report on the First Congress of Slavists, "we could hardly find a more appropriate designation than *structuralism*. Any set of phenomena examined by contemporary science is treated not as a mechanical agglomeration but as a structural whole, and the basic task is to reveal the inner, whether static or developmental, laws of this system. What appears to be the focus of scientific investigation is no longer the outer stimulus, but the internal premises of the development; now the mechanical conception of processes yields to the question of their functions" ("Romantické všeslovanství—nová slavistika" [Romantic Panslavism—New Slavic Studies], *Čin*, 31 October 1929; quoted from *SW* 2, p. 712).

39. The two studies, Mukařovský's "Obecné zásady a vývoj novočeského verše" and Jakobson's "Verš staročeský," appeared in the third volume, *Jazyk* (Language), of the grand encyclopedia *Československá vlastivěda*, ed. Oldřich Hujer (Praha: Sfinx, 1934), pp. 376–429 and 429–59.

40. "K českému překladu Šklovského *Teorie prózy*," *Čin* 6 (1934): 123–30. Quoted from *KCP* 1, pp. 344–50.

41. This is Victor Erlich's translation in *RF*, p. 119. The original, *O teorii prozy*, appeared in 1925.

42. Mukařovský reiterates this point in a highly instructive lecture, "Vztah mezi sovětskou a československou literární vědou" (The Relationship between Soviet and Czechoslovak Literary Scholarship), *Země Sovětuå* 4 (1935–1936): 10–15, given to the Society for Cultural and Economic Relations with the USSR in Bratislava, February 1935. Ever so tactfully, Mukařovský here eulogizes the demise of the formal method and bemoans the rise of the officially sanctioned sociological method whose conception of literary evolution is "more primitive and less dialectical than in the understanding of Marx, Engels and Lenin" (p. 13).

3 | An Attempt at a Historical Ordering of Poetic Structure

> Last season's fruit is eaten
> And the fullfed beast shall kick the empty pail.
> For last year's words belong to last year's language
> And next year's words await another voice.
>
> T. S. ELIOT

Mukařovský's major treatise of 1934, "Polák's *Sublimity of Nature*," shows at great length how the new structuralist precepts are to be applied in practical criticism.[1] Like many formalist studies,[2] this experiment in historical and structural categorization of poetic structure amounts to a substantial revision, if not quite a reevaluation, of the historical record. Mukařovský's purpose is very well served, as we shall see, by a descriptive poem in the manner of Thomson's *Seasons* composed by a decidedly minor Czech poet, Milota Zdirad Polák (1788–1856). *The Sublimity of Nature*, unlike Mácha's *May*, is seldom, if ever, read today and can scarcely be considered a "touchstone" of Czech literature. Yet this obscure poem, strewn with archaic and arcane expressions, awkward neologisms and impenetrable compound formations, is, as Mukařovský claims, of considerable importance for Czech literary history.

On what grounds do we judge a work of art historically important? There are two extremes to be avoided in approaching works of the past from the point of view of the literary historian. One is the "investigative egocentrism" that the Circle's "Theses" warned against, the eagerness to judge all by the criterion of relevance to the present. The other is the methodologically naive attempt to re-create the place of the work in its pristine form and its authentic, unretouched environment. Both approaches equally fail to come to grips with the ineluctable changeability of each work's structure. Thus the standpoint of the present blinds the historian to oftentimes vast changes in the standard language which separate the language of the given work from the current linguistic usage: structural elements which may have appeared as intensely actualized in the past can strike us now as glaringly clichéd and automatized. A similar kind of progressive differentiation occurs in the sphere of extra-aesthetic values, not to speak of the inevitable evolution of the aesthetic canon itself.

The other attitude to the artistic products of the past, which we may call archival, is just as likely to come to grief. If pushed to its limits, this stance leads to the untenable view that in order to identify oneself with, say, the fourteenth century one must expunge the knowledge of the intervening centuries. Among the more formidable hurdles, facing a medievalist especially, is the likelihood that for its original audience the work's aesthetic function may have been overtaken or swallowed by other functions, whether religious or political. But for literary history it is axiomatic that the criterion of evaluation must take account, first and foremost, of the aesthetic function. Yet even where the work's aesthetic functioning seems beyond doubt, our judgment may still be insufficiently historical. As Mukařovský insists, in any aesthetic appraisal we "necessarily look at the structure realized in the work to be evaluated as a stable and clearly delimited entity." This freezing of the aesthetic object runs contrary to the requirements of historical investigation, in which we "must view the poetic structure in a constant movement as an incessant regrouping of elements and a permutation of their relations" (p. 110).

What then, we must ask, is the proper historical criterion to bring to bear on this evolutionary flow? Mukařovský's answer is, the contribution to change: "The sole decisive value for the literary historian stems from the work's relation to the dynamism of evolution: the work which in some way regrouped the structure of the preceding period appears as a positive value, while the work which accepted that structure without changes appears as a negative value" (p. 101). In this way structural history hopes to arrive at an aesthetically value-neutral account of literary development. This does not mean that Mukařovský's structuralism sidesteps the issue of value judgments: it simply strives to avoid the fixity that any aesthetic preference injects into the continuum of literary change. Admittedly, the very selection of items for inclusion involves some judgment of value, as does all causal explanation of the work's effect on the structure of the literary period. But in order to avoid the misprision of modernizing and antiquarian tendencies, both of which unwittingly follow what Northrop Frye has called the high priori road, the structuralists propose to distinguish the evolutionary or historical from the aesthetic value. The assessment of the latter as a rule reflects more the judge than the object of judgment. While the sense of the aesthetic value is, in Frye's description, "individual, unpredictable, variable, incommunicable, indemonstrable, and mainly intuitive,"[3] the historical value can be objectively ascertained. Faced with the tides of the historical process, Mukařovský is, at this stage at any rate, captivated more by its variety and variability than by universality and invariance.

With Mukařovský's exegesis of *The Sublimity of Nature* we are plunged midstream into the period of Czech literature perhaps richest in linguistic and literary transformation, the Czech renascence. At this time the school of poets headed by Antonín Jaroslav Puchmajer (1769–1820) broke the hegemony of syllabic versification which had taken root in Czech poetry from its earliest days. The Puchmajerian reform, however, swung to the opposite extreme: against the protean changeability of syllabic verse it pitted the rigid syllabic-accentual system with complete realization of the metrical scheme. Shaken by this upheaval, Czech prosody subsequently became a scene of battle among not just two but three contending metrical schools, the syllabic, the syllabic-accentual and the quantitative (časomíra), each backed up by well-argued scholarly disquisitions. The student of English literature finds a comparable state of affairs in the sixteenth century.[4] Here, too, several metrical systems, including the syllabic and syllabic-accentual, vied for prominence but were thought by some to lack the dignity of Greek measures. Such poets as Roger Ascham or Sir John Cheke tried to imitate the classical iambic line, and a metrician such as Gabriel Harvey championed the heroic hexameter. And Renaissance England also witnessed a protracted theoretical dispute concerning metrics. Finally, here, too, the Greek imports met with limited success; in the end it was the syllabic-accentual line as practiced by Shakespeare and Marlowe that won the day. But to sense more fully the enormous distance the present-day reader feels from *The Sublimity of Nature* and other poetic production of that time, the Anglo-American reader has to go as far back as the fourteenth and fifteenth centuries, to the transition to Modern English. Only by entering the strange, uncertain metrical and linguistic world of someone like Lydgate can we glimpse the momentous transition that Czech language and literature were subjected to only some hundred and fifty years ago.

The historical mission of *The Sublimity of Nature* comes into focus against the backdrop of such poetic and prosodic fermentation. Despite the turbulence of literary change, Mukařovský argues that no drastic breach occurred in Czech versification. After all, the emerging system was not purely qualitative or accentual but syllabic-accentual. Not only did the old syllabic and the new syllabic-accentual metrical structures coexist for some time but, what is more important, they shared several features. These were the isosyllabism of verse-line, its interior division into regular units of two syllables and the utilization of word boundaries as a device of rhythmic organization. Even in this instance of extensive prosodic change, besides a group of conflicting elements which propels the prosodic system forward, Mukařovský detects a group of the selfsame elements which guarantees its identity throughout. "The point is not," as he asserts, "to place one side in a polemical antithesis against the other, but, on the contrary, to find the common denominator of opposite tendencies, the direction of evolution" (p. 120).

As a demonstration of Mukařovský's descriptive and interpretive strategy, let us now look at the opening six lines of the poem *The Sublimity of Nature:*

V šedivině | věků když pu‖stota v jícnu | strašných nocí
Korala i | smrt a temnost ‖ s živlů vztekem | litým mocí
Válčili na|jednou skrze ‖ hrůzy dálné | rozlitiny
Rozkaz vyšel | slavně skrze ‖ veškerosti | zmateniny;
Světe bud'! | I dělily se ‖ látek vlno|bitné toky,
Temnost mračen | vysvětlela, ‖ hloubné suši|li se moky.

(At the dawn of the ages, when the wilderness murked in the abyss of the dreadful night, and death and darkness battled with furious elements brimming with power, suddenly across the terrifying immensity of waters, a glorious command rose out of the cosmic chaos: Let there be the world! And the matter of the surging flow sundered, the darkness of the clouds brightened, the mire of the deep dried out.)

The poem's metrical form is rather unwieldy, each line consisting of sixteen syllables. The French alexandrine, in comparison, has only twelve syllables. The rhythmic tendency of the poem is clearly trochaic, but to analyze its metrical design in greater detail, Mukařovský computes, throughout the first song of the poem, the main word stresses as they variously fall on each syllable and obtains the following percentile frequency:

I.	II.	III.	IV.	V.	VI.	VII.	VIII.
99	3	60	8	76	3	61	0.5
IX.	X.	XI.	XII.	XIII.	XIV.	XV.	XVI.
96	3	65	3	77	1	65	—

The above correlation of the number of stresses per syllable translates into this diagram:

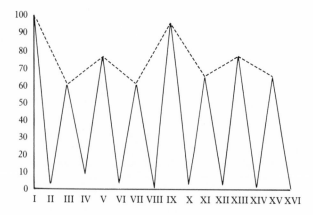

The two geometrical curves, the full line signifying the rising and falling percentages of stress and the broken one connecting the rhythmic downbeats on odd syllables, lay bare the poet's manipulation of the rhythmic impulse. The schematic picture confirms that, since the percentages are high in odd and low in even syllables, the verse is indeed trochaic. In addition, it shows the great regularity of the median caesura after the eighth syllable. The lower peaks on the fifth and thirteenth syllables indicate a further halving of each hemistich into two dipodies. Moreover, the diagram displays the nearly perfect symmetry of the two hemistiches; the eight-foot metrical scheme is in effect a doubling of the four-foot trochees employed by the preceding generation. The poem's metrical blueprint is thus as follows:

$$-\cup-\cup \mid -\cup-\cup \parallel -\cup-\cup \mid \cup-\cup$$

Above all, Mukařovský's use of the statistical and diagrammatical method reveals where the rhythmic pattern of *The Sublimity of Nature* diverges from the prevailing metrical norms. The Puchmajer generation sought to make the rhythm identical to the metre, and so in its verse the dipodic mark nearly always coincided with the word boundary. The main innovation of *The Sublimity of Nature* was the disruption of this rhythmic monotony by frequent shifts, as in the first hemistich of the third line, of the dipodic marks inside the words, 20.9%, to be exact. On rare occasion, as in the first line of the poem, even the caesura falls inside the word. Such departures from the steady metrical beat create a strong impression of rhythmic syncopation. And the effect is also reinforced by varying the clusters of syllables within the individual dipodies. Since the trochee contains two syllables, the standard arrangement of two trochees into a dipody would appear to be 2–2. In *The Sublimity of Nature*, however, 34% of the syllabic groupings are asymmetrical, 3–1, 1–3 or 1–2–1, which once again highlights the poem's general tendency toward rhythmic diversity. Distinct euphonic and syntactic configurations, finally, add further nuance to the dominant prosodic feature of the poem: the releasing of rhythmic energy from the constraints of a rigid metric scheme.

This complicated verse pattern, however, exacted a high price. To fill up the long dipodies the poet frequently had to resort to four-syllable words, as in the very first dipody, for instance. The polysyllabic formations serve yet another purpose: they either straddle the boundaries between adjacent dipodies—see the term *vlnobitné* in the penultimate line—or help conceal the regular divisions inside individual dipodies. But like most languages, Czech does not abound with lexical units of such length, and it is precisely this factor which explains the presence of many topheavy neologisms, for example: *rozlitina* or *zmatenina*. The demand for rhythmic variation thus conditions the choice of lexical material. Of course, rhythmic considerations do not determine the entire verbal selection. Nevertheless, the common occurrence of neologisms does have broad implications for the poem's semantic makeup. Most of the newfangled expressions in the poem do not so much name new objects as provide poetic synonyms for already existing words. Thus *zmatenina*, coined *ad hoc* by adding the suffix *-ina*, duplicates the word *zmatek*, meaning chaos, confusion—but with a difference. While the poet's coinage has the same reference as the standard term, the manner of its referring seems less definite and immediate.

In *The Sublimity of Nature*, these peculiarly redundant constructs, together with a host of other poetic locutions, tend, according to Mukařovský, to assume the form of periphrasis. Periphrastic tropes, instead of seeking to point directly to a given object, indicate one of its properties or describe the object's creation and working or, as in the example cited, move to another, more general and abstract, semantic plane. In this conception, which clearly goes beyond the traditional definition, periphrasis covers the whole domain of indirect signification, subsuming not only metonymy and synecdoche but also certain trite metaphors (such as "stars" for "eyes") which, though common enough, are not thought of as "proper" names. Every use of periphrasis results in the displacement of customary designations, which in turn deepens the sense of distance between words and things. Periphrastic figures always accentuate the function of verbal mediation: they refer to their corresponding objects obliquely or circuitously via the verbal representations ordinarily associated with those objects. If in everyday communication it seems as if words or signs coincide, or dovetail, with the things they represent, indirect periphrastic designations throw emphasis on the autonomy of verbal signs, their nonidentity vis-à-vis extralinguistic facts. Put differently, whereas in communicative language verbal signs stand for nonverbal phenomena, in poetic periphrasis words stand above all for other words, as signs of signs.

To be sure, the direct or proper designation is not readily apprehensible behind every periphrastic expression. In that case, when the appropriate synonym does not offer itself, the direct designation exists potentially, "given as it is by the semantic connections within the total context of a sentence . . ." (p. 155). It follows that periphrasis, especially where its possibilities are systematically exploited for structural purposes, brings about a twofold semantic disaccord: referential, between the sign and its designatum, on the one hand; and syntactic, between the word and other component parts of the verbal concatenation forming a particular sentence, on the other. Catachresis, zeugma and the like are the classical categories defining those instances in which there is an explicit clash between a periphrastic (or other) figure and its neighboring terms in the sequence. In *The Sublimity of Nature*, Mukařovský argues, the trend toward periphrasis, the purposeful separating of the poetic vocable from what it is supposed to denote, permeates the poem's diction and gives it the character of a jigsaw puzzle. As Mukařovský describes it, "the riddle is put forth by the periphrasis and its solution by the direct designation which, once discovered, reveals the 'thing' itself . . ." (p. 157). What at first appeared to be a purely rhythmic requirement for multisyllabic word forms now turns out to have significant consequences indeed for the semantic construction of the whole poem.

Before going on to trace further repercussions of the interdependence of metrics, semantics and other structural aspects of the poem, it should be noted that Mukařovský's investigation of poetic meaning signals a substantial advance over the earlier formalist researches. The slogan *Slovo kak takovoe!*—the sense of which the German phrase *das Wort an sich* (roughly, the word as such) conveys rather nicely—embodied the formalist claim of the self-sufficiency of the poetic word. In poetry, the formalists maintained, the utterance loses the transparency necessary for informational language and, consequently, blocks access to exterior reality: the word in poetry is opaque, self-referential, intransitive, valuable in its own right. Sharing the futurist fascination with the materiality—the *Dinglichkeit*—of poetic expression, its concrete sound shape, Opojaz theorists (except for Jurij Tynjanov) paid little attention to literary semantics. The Russians would have wholly subscribed to the New Critical maxim that the poem must not mean but be. This kind of poetic isolationism, typical of extreme formalism, would no longer do for the Prague structuralists. For them, the poet's stock of words, no matter how eccentric and fanciful, unavoidably bears some relation to the world of things, even if its mode of referring is as circumlocutory and equivocal as in the poem at hand. And the task of poetics, or, better still, poetic semantics, is not to stamp out the reference but rather to shed light on the rules of poetic signification. Mukařovský's inquiry into contextual semantics takes the first steps in that direction.

Tackling the problem of structural motivation, Mukařovský amplifies and restates another original formalist idea. Opojaz critics held that every literary work is a self-contained, and self-reflexive, entity and that the presence of various devices in it must be justified by its particular artistic constitution, not by external verisimilitude, psychological plausibility or the writer's social engagement. But the weakness of the formalists' own position stands revealed, for instance, in their unwarranted deflation of the concept of character, as when Šklovskij contends that the figure of Don Quixote is nothing more than a compositional device to knit together otherwise incongruous plot elements. Though ingeniously inverting traditional critical attitudes which disregard the protagonist's textual existence, this formulation, too, fails to satisfy. It was such a simplistic reduction of complex realities to a single proposition that prompted Hegel to call the procedure—in a different but not altogether irrelevant context—a "mono-chrome formalism."[5] Mukařovský, by contrast, following Hegel's lead, argues for a two-sided, dialectical motivation of every literary phenome-non. Thus, in analyzing *The Sublimity of Nature*, it would be equally erro-neous to attribute the motivation of its lexical material either to the need for rhythmic differentiation or to the periphrastic drift of the poet's ex-pression. In Mukařovský's explanation, the poem's focal points are to be located, on the contrary, exactly at the intersections of the two motivating series, the rhythmic and the semantic, which ultimately circumscribe the poetic vocabulary.

The principle of two-way motivation extends, of course, to the core of the poem's semantic organization, its theme. *The Sublimity of Nature* is an apotheosis of nature, registering its ever-changing cycles. The connection between the theme and the periphrastic vocabulary is self-evident, since the periphrastic stress on the qualities of an object yields its description, and description plays a key role in the composition of Polák's poem. Were we to stop here and propose that the descriptive theme is really the upshot of the poem's lexical selection, we would be caught up in the old formalist fallacy. We must therefore raise the question as to what else—dialecti-cally—motivates the theme of this poetic composition. So far we have es-tablished a set of structural linkages embedded in the poem and the poetic series to which it belongs. Let us recapitulate: the stasis of Czech versifica-tion calls for a subtler rhythmic gradation; the poet responds by employing four-syllable terms, thereby systematically syncopating the dipodic verse unit; this decision affects the poem's lexicon and is only partially suc-cessful as the poet finds himself repeatedly compelled to fall back on nonce words; these novel linguistic creations in turn underscore the periphrastic orientation, and the periphrastic disposition ties in with the descriptive theme. Now, if the structural chain of double, reciprocal motivations is not to exclude the theme, it becomes clear that we must at this point break open the bounds of immanence. In other words, we have to address the problem of where the poem fits not only in terms of literary development but also in terms of the sociocultural situation of the times.

In the case of *The Sublimity of Nature*, what we should call the exter-nal motivation turns out to be exceptionally strong—so much so that, in Mukařovský's view, it furnished the poet not merely with the theme but with the whole ready-made genre. As Mukařovský observes, early in the nineteenth century, descriptive poems, divided in imitation of the epic into songs or books, were regarded as an elevated genre with a special appeal to the higher social classes. At this time, Czech society still bore traits of feudal stratification in which the higher classes espoused cultural values without much relation to the concerns of the population at large. A crucial difference was one of language. Members of the upper class hardly spoke

Czech at all. The national renascence was, before everything, a struggle against foreign, particularly German, cultural and political domination. In this light, the social aim of *The Sublimity of Nature* becomes easily discernible. Borrowing from abroad what was considered a sophisticated and exclusive genre, the poet intended to win over the upper classes to the cause of resurgent Czech culture. To put the matter in a nutshell, the external motivation of *The Sublimity of Nature* was the desire for the expansion of Czech national awareness among the social strata most susceptible to foreign literary and cultural fashion.

Mukařovský's recognition that any historical interpretation restricting itself to the immanent literary order necessarily falls short of providing a full and positive answer represents a watershed in the elaboration of structuralist theory. As his exegesis and historical appraisal of *The Sublimity of Nature* amply proves, the structuralist account of literary evolution forsakes none of the gains of the formal method, while making no concessions to traditional thematic criticism. Even though structuralism restores the literary theme, and through it the social actuation, to a place of great structural significance, by no stretch of the imagination does it come close to seeing literature as a product or a reflection of the *moment, race* and *milieu*—or any other set of nonliterary circumstances. The endogenous course of literary development retains complete methodological primacy. In Mukařovský's new argumentation, literary evolution obeys (as the motto to his study taken from Hegel's *Vorlesungen über die Philosophie der Geschichte* makes explicit) first of all the principle of *Selbstbewegung*, of self-motion. It is a dialectical process which, to quote Mukařovský, "is carried by the dynamics of the evolutionary series itself and ruled by its own immanent order" (p. 91). As an autonomous system, literature exhibits an inherent propensity for transformation, generating from within its internal tensions and contradictions the incentive for future change. Accordingly, all change is by definition systemic, and hence the unfolding of the evolutionary pattern is to a high degree coherent and continuous. As Mukařovský avers, the dynamically evolving structure alone can secure the methodologically indispensable line of literary continuity.

At the same time, the dialectical principle is as germane to the rapport of literature with other social phenomena as it is to intertextual literary connections or the structural correlations within a single work. The thoroughgoing and consistent application of dialectics enables Mukařovský to postulate that literary evolution is ultimately "the synthesis of the inner dynamics of poetic structure and outside interventions" (p. 165). Nonetheless, Mukařovský cautions, we must bear in mind that, however potent or persuasive the specific case may be, the external intervention at best motivates the direction of change but cannot by itself initiate the modification of the literary system. For this reason it would be inappropriate to grant special consideration to the literary theme, coming as it usually does from outside the literary sphere. Focus on the theme would, unavoidably, present us with a picture of literary evolution as "a discontinuous collection of accidental events" (p. 166), when what we need is an intelligible historical scheme.

Only by adhering to the dialectic of structures does Mukařovský justify the claim that the prime job of literary history is "the discovery of a continuing line of evolution which stems from poetry's specific function" and, simultaneously, reiterate that structuralism in no way diminishes the importance of extraliterary orders. His argument is well worth quoting at length:

It would be a mistake to place literature, due to its specific function, in a total vacuum. We are aware that the evolutionary series generated by the dynamism of individual structures which change in time (political, economic, ideological and literary structures, for example) do not run parallel without any contact, but are *parts of a higher structure*, and that this structure has its hierarchy and its dominant (the predominant series). Since, of course, it is a vital structure, not a fixed system, this highest construction, fraught as it is with internal antinomies, is also constantly moving and reorganizing: individual elements alternately assume the dominant position, none remaining permanently in the forefront. In other words, it is impossible to reduce the history of one series to the status of a commentary on the history of another series under the pretense that one of them is subordinate while the other is superior. Literary history is neither the history of national idea (ideology) nor the history of national economy—to take the two extreme standpoints which, though seemingly antithetical, are nevertheless related by their shared basic epistemological fallacy—but is precisely *literary* history. Parts of a single higher structure, individual series constantly affect each other. Still, one series' intervention in another always occurs only if it is mediated by the immanent evolution of the affected series (p. 166; emphasis mine).

Even when cast in the sweeping perspective of general human affairs, literature loses little of its homogeneity, coherence and order. Mukařovský's thesis echoes to some extent Jakobson's position regarding phonemic borrowings, a problem, we remember, that frustrated Saussure. There the incursion from another vernacular could be adequately understood only after a diagnosis of what Jakobson called "the evolutionary possibilities and inclinations" of the affected series. Here Mukařovský reminds us that, despite the fact that outside infringements may issue from various directions and may affect any of the work's structural elements, what matters in the final analysis is the intrinsic functioning of the literary system itself, the unity of its evolution. And the unity of evolution, he insists, "is maintained by external interventions' having neither the same provenance nor the same direction, but by the very laws that govern the internal movement of literature" (p. 167). Mukařovský's two fundamental assumptions, it may bear repeating, are that literature follows the dialectical give-and-take of automatization and actualization and that its primary function is to throw into relief the act of verbal expression. But while Jakobson grappled with what we may call intramural connections between one language and another, Mukařovský pushes the principle of structural ordering to embrace the totality of literature's relations to other series of social reality.

At this point we arrive at the crossroads of historical poetics and literary sociology. In *The Sublimity of Nature* the motivation of the theme remained vague and one-sided until one identified the social forces in terms of which the poem functioned. Besides the aesthetic function, *The Sublimity of Nature* manifested a conspicuous social function, and here the knowledge of social conditions proved essential. Mukařovský touched on the radically polyfunctional character of literary works earlier; now he adopts the theorem of ethnographer Petr Bogatyrev (1893–1971) that the functions themselves also constitute a structure which has a dominant and around which all the work's other functions rally. Whether investigating folk songs, costumes or magic rites, Bogatyrev came across the same phenomenon, namely, that folkloric objects perform several functions at once and that the hierarchy of such functions changes with time, environments and social classes. The Christmas tree, to cite one of his examples, had a purely aesthetic function for the educated classes in Eastern Slovakia, but when the local peasants took over the custom, the dominant function became magical and religious, with the aesthetic function receding into the background.[6] Literary artifacts, too, often serve ideological, philosophical, religious and numerous other functions in addition to the aesthetic. To account for the changing structure of functions in a wider social framework is, as we know, the very aim of literary sociology.

While literary history deals primarily with the work's production, the internal and external motivations of its constituent elements, literary sociology surveys the work's effect with respect to larger social concerns. A full-scale structural history, then, scrutinizes the literary work of art from a dual and mutually reinforcing perspective: that of the (functional) structure of literature *per se* and that of the structure of literature's functions. The structuralist critic in the end confronts the "structure of structures" (or the "system of systems" in Jakobson and Tynjanov's terminology), the manifold complex of interactions between literary and social history. Although Mukařovský, understandably enough, does not offer any definitive answers here, he at least proposes a formula that carries some weight:

. . . the set of [literature's] functions and their reciprocal relations comprise a structure which is also constantly reshuffled, evolving, on the basis of its own order. During this evolution, the influences within the changing artistic makeup of literature itself and/or the changes in the internal evolution of the other series with regard to which literature functions (i.e., which it affects) operate as external interventions. The problem of the dominant is very complicated here, since on the one hand it follows from the very notion of structure that various functions may play the dominant part, yet on the other there is clearly the *permanent*, exceptional position of the aesthetic function which makes the work of poetry poetic. Therefore the poetic function is always *de jure* dominant, although *de facto* it is frequently displaced from this position by another function. The tension resulting from this conflict among functions creates the immanent dynamism of that structure of which they are the parts. (pp. 167–68)

‖●‖●‖●‖●‖●‖

With the historical account of *The Sublimity of Nature*, Prague structuralism made a noticeable dent in literary scholarship, for it challenged the academic establishment on its own ground. Indeed, soon after appearing in the prestigious review *Sborník filologický* (Philological Miscellany), Mukařovský's study became the subject of heated critical controversy. No other work of Mukařovský's, before or after, seems to have elicited such an intense and wide-ranging response. It is advisable, therefore, to dwell on this debate, and particularly so, as it prefigures many of the methodological skirmishes in the last two decades surrounding the newer versions of structuralism. As early as 1934, structuralist ideas came under attack from every major critical position: the academicians, the Marxists, the formalists and the phenomenologists.[7]

The first thing that strikes the observer of the controversy regarding Mukařovský's attempt at a structural literary history is the peculiar lack of balance in nearly all the comments. One group, mainly of academic historians, considered solely the practical side of Mukařovský's analysis, steering clear of methodological issues. Generally, everyone agreed with his characterization of the poet Polák's historical role as a transition figure who correctly perceived the rhythmic monotony and inefficacy of the Puchmajerians' verse but himself produced a type of metre which was at best a mixed blessing. It was left up to Mácha and the next generation to make the decisive break, designing the Czech iambic and dactylotrochaic feet. In the reader's report, Miroslav Hýsek (1885–1957) summed up the academics' view succinctly: "Mukařovský's study . . . indeed sheds new light on the beginnings of Czech poetry; even if his conclusions will not always meet with complete approval, the principal solution is highly suggestive and praiseworthy" (p. 45).[8] In short, according to the academicians, Mukařovský had done a solid piece of historical research—irrespective of his structuralist experiments in literary historiography.

Hýsek's colleague at Charles University, Miloš Weingart (1890–1939), sounded a very harsh critical note, however.[9] Weingart's objections, motivated by a growing personal disagreement with the Linguistic Circle (to which he had earlier belonged), would not be worth mentioning, had he not—amidst a barrage of cavils—hit upon some troublesome spots in Mukařovský's presentation. Weingart was the only one to question the authority of the statistical and diagrammatic method, if not the concrete results of Mukařovský's inquiries, which remained uncontested. By refusing to take the quantifying method at face value, he raised pertinent questions as to the size, the choice and the methodological *a prioris* which might guarantee the sample's aptness for the given interpretation. At the base of Weingart's invective, it is true, was a willful misconception of Mukařovský's claim that structural literary history is capable of examining all literary relationships, those within the order of literature as well as those without. Construing this to be the mechanical sum-total of existing factors, Weingart proceeded to chide Mukařovský for not comparing the two versions of the poem (there may have been a grain of truth to that) and, more irrelevantly, for neglecting other parts of the poet's *oeuvre*, mainly prose. Despite this pointless enumeration, Weingart quite correctly spotted Mukařovský's failure to relate *The Sublimity of Nature* to other poems in the genre of descriptive poetry and to foreign literary models. In a similar vein, René Wellek has recently complained about the missing middle zone in Mukařovský's critical project.[10] Mukařovský constantly moves, in Wellek's view, between the extremes of minute analysis and general theory. Perhaps what is lacking is not so much Mukařovský's *Einfühlung*, which is what Wellek suggests, as an awareness of a wider, historically fuller context of general or comparative literature, the kind of knowledge informing the works of the great Romance philologists like Erich Auerbach, Leo Spitzer or E. R. Curtius or an encyclopedic critic like Northrop Frye. Mukařovský's own interests, it should quickly be added, branch out instead toward general aesthetics and, with the exception of music, musical theatre and dance, toward the study of all the individual arts.

The divide running through Mukařovský's essays in criticism may account for the lopsidedness of the reactions to the Polák study. For the other group, composed mostly of the Circle's members, pushed aside any consideration of the analytic half of Mukařovský's treatise, concentrating entirely on the problem of structural method. As a consequence, neither group of critics paired Mukařovský's methodological assumptions with his critical practice, although several members of the Circle expressed unease, as we shall see, with Mukařovský's theoretical formulations. Thus a large unresolved contradiction underlying his critical strategy went unnoticed.

To allow for the incessant change within the literary process, Mukařovský appealed, as he had implicitly done in the 1932 interview, to the dichotomy between the "work of art" and the "aesthetic object" proposed by aesthetician Broder Christiansen.[11] In this correlation, the work of art means the material artifact, whereas the aesthetic object stands for its immaterial analogue common to the consciousness of a collectivity. Mukařovský further tried to shore up his thesis by invoking Karl Mannheim's concept of *Kultursoziologie*, a branch of social studies investigating structures lodged in the social consciousness.[12] That being the case, the work of art, Mukařovský argued, acquires its proper identity and clear-cut meaning only in relation to the norms in the given readership's consciousness. Mukařovský had no difficulty at all in demonstrating how the first readers of *The Sublimity of Nature* avidly welcomed it as a path-breaking poetic endeavor, how within a short space of time this avidity turned to indifference and how the poem experienced a brief revival toward the close of the century—all in step with the permutations of prevailing artistic norms. Here, in fact, we see the seeds of reception theory later elaborated by Mukařovský's disciple, Felix Vodička.

The trouble with this notion, however, lies in the fact that Mukařovský does not look into the relationship between the two correlates. Bent as he is on proving the ever-changing appearances that the work as aesthetic object takes on in different linguistic, aesthetic, cultural and social environments, he leaves out the work of art as such from the field of observation. The work of art comes close to resembling a Kantian *noumenon*, perceptible and knowable only through its appearances. Mukařovský seems to be saying something like that himself when he remarks that it is doubtful "whether a definite confrontation of the work's concrete diversity with the gross structural outline of the corresponding aesthetic object is at all possible" (p. 100). Hence every critical reading or, to borrow the term from phenomenologist Roman Ingarden, every "concretization" of necessity produces a partial account of the work's overall structure. Moreover, all concretizations are inescapably relative historically and socially, since they are bound to occur in conjunction with the complex of literary and nonliterary norms upheld by the reading community. This relativity, however, calls into question the status of Mukařovský's own inquiry, whose goal is scientific objectivity, statistical verifiability (or more to the point, falsifiability) and, to some degree, invariability.

Put very simply, the question is: how can the structuralist method, equipped though it is with scientific armature, escape being historically relative? Isn't Mukařovský's analysis just another concretization of *The Sublimity of Nature*? If so, the separation of the aesthetic from the historical value would be of no avail, because not merely the aesthetic value but the whole set of structural relationships must be contingent on the observer's time and place. The other alternative might be that, as the use of statistics seems to imply, the structuralist analysis treats the work on the level of its material vehicle, as a work of art. But then, does it not short-circuit the social dimension of literature, the study of which is one of its cardinal objectives? Besides, Mukařovský explicitly defines literary structure, and its motion in time, not as an empirical but as a phenomenological reality. What needs clarification here is the way in which we apply the tools of empirical analysis to a nonempirical, immaterial order, the social consciousness in which literary and other structures are embedded. Otherwise, if the results of analysis are to preserve their validity, the theoretical frame of reference would have to be restated. Mukařovský soon attempted to do just that within the framework of semiotics, but his new effort was not quite free from methodological confusion, either.

Another discrepancy between Mukařovský's tightly argued theory and the variegated reality which resists such an out-and-out formalization came into view in F. X. Šalda's article "An Example of Structural Literary History."[13] Šalda (1867–1937), *doyen* of Czech literary criticism and also a member of the Circle, was very much in sympathy with Mukařovský's methodology, commending it for successfully spanning the bridge between Herbartian formalism and Hegelian historicism (cf. p. 27 above), as well as with his practice, which Šalda felt displayed "considerable acuity and historical expertise" (p. 60). At the same time, Šalda noted that Mukařovský was on less solid ground in his sociological explanation of the provenance of the poem's subject matter. Theoretically Mukařovský was doubtless right in stating the relation of the literary and extraliterary orders in terms of structural hierarchies governed by dynamically charged dominants. But lacking a satisfactory structural sociology, how could the literary critic analyze the social interaction which would determine the priority of social forces bearing on the literature of the period? In the case of *The Sublimity of Nature*, the situation appeared straightforward enough, the craving for a national revival indeed being the overwhelming political concern of the times. Nevertheless, as Šalda pointed out, another convincing explanation could be found in the popular deistic speculations inspired by natural philosophy, which in the late eighteenth century cried for a poetic expression modeled on the admired descriptive poetry of the West. Here Mukařovský had no criterion at his disposal to adjudicate between the two contending explanations or, more exactly, between the degree of their explanatory relevance. Šalda harbored no intention to undermine Mukařovský's thesis. On the contrary, he ended his essay by expressing the hope that the Polák study would put a stop to all "blanket accusations of [the structuralists'] aestheticism and *l'art pour l'art* attitude . . ." (p. 68).

Still, for a group of the most vocal opponents of the new structural approach, Mukařovský did not go far enough in berthing literary activity in the basic social praxis. Like the structuralists—Mukařovský, Jakobson and Bogatyrev had especially close personal ties with many progressive artists—the young left-wing critics were on the whole very keen on contemporary avant-garde art with its celebration of formal experiment free from all nonartistic constraints.[14] Now, however, in their challenge to structuralism, the Marxist critics were in part spurred on by the doctrine of socialist realism and the concomitant theory of reflection proclaimed at the First Congress of Soviet Writers in 1934. To espouse faithfully the official Marxist point of view, one could scarcely make allowance for art's relative autonomy, let alone for the total autonomy advocated by extreme formalism, which, in any case, had meanwhile become anathema in the Soviet Union.[15] Kurt Konrad (the pseudonym of Kurt Beer, 1908–1941), one of the Czech leftists, was ready to concede that the Prague School's refusal to disengage literature from the larger social context meant a sizable improvement over the theoretical presuppositions of the Opojaz. He argued, nonetheless, that Mukařovský's attempt to wed structuralism with dialectical Marxism offered a false compromise, as shown in the characterization of the social conditioning of literature as a set of outside impingements. That procedure, in Konrad's view, amounted to "a mechanical rending of the dialectic into two poles which, instead of dialectically interpenetrating, appear as alien bodies colliding with one another on the surface" (p. 75).[16] As long as the structuralists insisted on the possibility of changing hierarchies within the "structure of structures," Konrad maintained, they would remain entrapped in an idealist epistemology. Their version of the connection between the cultural sphere (or superstructure in the Marxist idiom) and the socioeconomic matrix (base or substructure) must produce what Konrad, after Marx, called a "false totality" (p. 70). Echoing such established theoreticians of art writing in Russia as György Lukács and Michail Lifšic, Konrad urged the structuralists to recognize Marx's principle of determination by the economic means of production and consumption as being, in the last instance, the permanently governing social dominant.

Whether or not we can go along with such "economicism," Konrad managed to derive from it a rather trenchant insight pointing to a key deficiency in Mukařovský's conception. According to Konrad, the structuralist picture of social totality was misconstructed, principally because, looking for solutions in the ideological rather than the economic realm, it failed to disclose the very basis of all human action—the socially engaged person, that member of the collectivity on whom all the partial social series, including art, ultimately converge. Thus, "'the bad,' relativistic and ill-integrated structural totality," as Konrad put it, "results from isolating and abstracting the fruits of human activity from the activity itself and hence from its proper 'agent' . . ." (p. 73). Undeniably, Mukařovský, reacting to the psychologism which at the time was the most widely practiced extrinsic criticism, sought to minimize the role of the individual artist, and in "Polák's *Sublimity of Nature*" metonymically reduced the poet Polák to the body of his writings. It was this antipersonalistic bias, built into the structural theory, that rendered a distorted description of the interrelatedness of art and society. Similarly, Konrad also decried a reductionist tendency as damaging to Mukařovský's analytic strategy. In the book on Mácha, for example, Konrad objected to Mukařovský's unwarranted breaking up of the theme into syntagmas, particularly since the usually unmotivated relation of individual words to their referents is of a different order than that between the theme and the depicted reality—an objection Mukařovský was soon to take to heart, not because he suddenly embraced Marxism but because he realized that such an atomization runs counter to the holistic concept of structure. Konrad clinched the argument with the idea that the individual motifs can tell us no more about the theme, which is an integral whole (that is, more than the sum of its parts), than can an "isolated brick reveal the secret of a building" (p. 80).

Just as Mukařovský mistakenly detaches art from its creator and the thematic content from the context of reality, so, in Konrad's view, the explanation of the historically evolving structures disconnects literary history from its social foundation. As a consequence, the Circle's literary historiography "culminates in an utterly fetishistic worship of the 'continuous evolutionary line,' of the blind law of [autonomous] development . . ." (p. 90). Záviš Kalandra (1902–1950), another left-oriented critic who was also a leading exponent of surrealism, repeated the same charge by identifying structuralism as another expression of the *more geometrico* which "at every step of the analysis wants to be mathematically exact and, in its historical synthesis, crystal clear."[17] Fearing the real individual with "myriad appetites and apprehensions, abilities and imperfections" which would wreak havoc with the rigid formulas of immanent evolution, Mukařovský's structuralism found itself "cursed with illegitimate abstractions and condemned to seek refuge in mystic hypostases." With artistic personality eliminated from the field of observation, the Marxist literary historian, Kalandra asserted, is apt to feel a *horror vacui* and must therefore reject "the idealistic 'immanent development' and look for the laws of literary history in the depth of its roots, where the creative individuality responds to a given state of literature under the conditions determined in the last instance by the mode of commodity production and the class position of that individual." In stark contrast to the structuralist conclusions, Kalandra contended that in reality the poetic structure in its entirety was established not by the internal circumstances of literary writing but by the poet Polák's personal predilections, which accurately reflected the needs of his social class.

In spite of the heated rhetoric of their attacks, the Marxists' arguments were little marred by doctrinaire zeal. It seems that both Konrad and Kalandra leaned strongly toward the liberal stance of the Frankfurt School—Konrad made an approving reference to Karl August Wittfogel, a member of the Institut für Sozialforschung—which tried to prevent the literary analysis from becoming a crude exercise in deciphering social references. The two theorists, after all, were most appreciative of those facets of Mukařovský's critical project dealing with the specific characteristics of literature, which they hoped to incorporate into a future Marxist art theory. This new theory would at last transcend the limitations of the mechanistic model of social equivalence associated with early Marxist thinkers such as Franz Mehring and G. V. Plechanov and eventually resurrected by A. A. Ždanov, Stalin's commissar for culture. Unfortunately, about a decade and a half later it was the sterile orthodoxy of socialist realism, reducing all cultural phenomena to a direct ideological reflex of class interests, which received official endorsement in Czechoslovakia. (Neither Konrad nor Kalandra, however, were to see this: Konrad perished in a German concentration camp; Kalandra was sentenced to death in a Stalinist purge for alleged Trotskyite deviations and, despite international protests from Albert Einstein, Bertrand Russell, André Breton and others, executed in 1950.) This measure spelled structuralism's banishment, which lasted all through the fifties, with an inestimable loss to Czech literary scholarship. At present, regrettably, we witness much the same situation, in which structuralism is once again treated as a *theoria non grata*.

In 1934, luckily, a wide-open methodological discussion was not only possible but most welcome. Kalandra, for one, invited by the Circle, expounded his critique at a meeting on 10 December 1934 dedicated to the methodological problems of Mukařovský's Polák study. Other speakers in this debate were A. L. Bém, René Wellek, Petr Bogatyrev, Sergius Hessen (a philosopher), Roman Jakobson and, of course, Jan Mukařovský. The fact that the Circle convened a special session to deliberate on the issues raised by Mukařovský's monograph indicates the degree of significance and seriousness it was accorded by other interested scholars. The proceedings, too, were exceptionally well documented, save the observations by Bogatyrev and Hessen, which, as was customarily the case, went unrecorded.

In the opening statement, Alfred Bém (1886–1945?), a Russian literary historian best known for his work on Dostoevskij, subjected Mukařovský to a criticism from the standpoint of formalism. On the whole, his critical pronouncements were like a negative image of the Marxists' censures. First, Bém thought that the combination of what was basically formalist poetics with cultural sociology ended up an unwieldy misalliance. As much as the Marxist critics accused Mukařovský of artificially segregating literary activity from other social occupations, Bém denounced him for their implausible unification. Further, neatly inverting the Marxist belief in the essential affinity of literature with what it portrays, Bém put emphasis on the irrepressibly mediating nature of artistic creation. Even though social factors do exert influence on the literary work, Bém conceded, they do so only as material, no different from the rest of the poet's experience, which the poet must mold, or deform, in conformity with what Tynjanov dubbed the principle of construction (*konstruktivnyj princip*). In Bém's words, "material, social or otherwise, does not predetermine the work's formal structure but is itself subordinate to it" (p. 333).[18] Literature, in this view, does not—in fact cannot—reflect the circumambient world; it deflects it. Bém's, clearly, was formalism pure and simple, which—albeit a healthy antidote to vulgar sociologism—merely posited the constructive principle of deformation without clarifying its general mechanism.

As a next move to protect the privileged status of literary discourse so vehemently denied by the Marxists, Bém distinguished, unsuccessfully, between the literary and the other series of social reality; he surmised, it seems, that literature alone exhibits a double articulation, material and mental, although elementary knowledge of economic value theory would quickly have set things straight. Anyway, the thrust of Bém's contention was that literature is not a property of some global social consciousness but merely of a particular segment of society, the readers. Though true, this clarification, unbeknownst to Bém, served to bring out the potential circularity of Mukařovský's hypothesis—namely, that it defines literature in every instance by the consensus of a readership and then defines the readership itself by a common perception of the literary phenomena. Yet as far as Bém was concerned, the existence of literature in the readers' consciousness proved that "the history of the literary series does not take place within the social structure as a part of it, but only in a variable relation to it as an independent evolutionary line" (p. 332). But then, Bém was also unhappy with Mukařovský's concept of the evolutionary series, which, like Konrad and Kalandra, he considered a hypostatized construct "without any correspondence to reality" (p. 331). Besides, how can there by an evolution devoid of teleology, queried Bém, taking note of just one of several paradoxes lying at the heart of Mukařovský's aesthetics, with which we shall deal later. Finally, Bém complained about the ambiguity of Mukařovský's defining structure holistically as an entity whose every element "gains value only in a relationship to the whole" (p. 332) and then assigning priority to the limitless evolutionary series—an ambiguity Mukařovský never quite resolved.

In a rejoinder, however, Roman Jakobson reminded Bém that a single "literary work," which according to Bém is the only objectively given reality, is just as much an abstraction as is "literary evolution." In Jakobson's words, "the literary work presupposes literary evolution to the same degree as evolution presupposes the work."[19] Appealing to the *langue-parole* dichotomy, the very backbone of structuralist theory (which the other discussants chose to ignore), Jakobson went on to say that precisely "the existence of the system [of actual norms] makes possible the individual expressions as well as the reactions to them." The literary work, then, is an

integral whole, but it is simultaneously a component part of a larger totality; and since the constitutive relations are, so to speak, infrastructural,
differential and immaterial in the former as in the latter, the two structures
are—we are led to assume—homologous, although Jakobson did not specify the nature of their interrelation, either. Jakobson's sole reservation concerned Mukařovský's term *collective consciousness* (which I also eschewed
to avoid confusion with the Jungian category), proposing *convention* or *collective ideology* in its stead. His objections to Bém were much more severe,
for Jakobson, a founding father of formalism, ironically saw Bém as heir to
the mechanistic attitude of the Opojaz, which the Circle's structuralism
wanted to overcome with the dialectical method. Thus Jakobson warned
against setting too much store by the idea of deformation, since, as he put
it, "the choice of material creates an indissoluble dependence on the material." It was such a dialectically balanced statement, succinctly embodying
the tenor of structuralist thought, that, while correcting Bém's error on
the one side, aimed to disarm the Marxist critics on the other.

One of Bém's—and not only Bém's—strictures, however, Jakobson
did not address, and that involved evaluation. The question was as follows. How can one draw the line of literary evolution without choosing
every link in the chain to represent a specifically literary value? Or, isn't
value judgment an indispensable prerequisite for establishing the affilia-
tion of items to literature? Mukařovský, as we have seen, acknowledged
the problem, but ventured no further. Like Northrop Frye, I have suggested, he viewed his task as primarily one of description and organization
of material, with evaluation as an ever-present by-product. Explicit judgments of value, in this view, are the chief objective and the proper domain
of the review and the personal essay rather than of scholarship. René
Wellek, in the most cogent and constructive criticism of all, rejected that
distinction. Any endeavor to winnow out the historical from the aesthetic
is doomed from the start, Wellek insisted, for the one is irrevocably implicated in the other. Literary objects are, one and all, aesthetically valorized.
Insofar as we treat literature as literature, we deal with values and, like it
or not, pass value judgments. When studying works of literature, therefore, one cannot possibly escape one's subjectivity, one's own historicity.
The attempt to do so only leads the investigator to approach the work of
art, in Wellek's description, "as a neutral carrier of value, as if the value
were somehow superimposed on it and could be arbitrarily thought away"
(p. 442).[20] What is worse, the promotion of change and novelty as the sole
historical criterion at the expense of aesthetic accomplishment puts someone like Marlowe, who initiates a particular literary period, higher on the
scale of values than, say, Shakespeare, the master who comes at its peak.
In addition, the criterion of innovation and experiment poses anew the

problem that we must have some sense of what to take as a significant change, since mere newness may easily be worthless. For Mukařovský, a historically valuable innovation is always the one which recasts the dominant metric structure of the given literary era. To this extent, one might argue, the "ordering" of *The Sublimity of Nature* is really a study in the development of versification, not of poetry. If we are to have a full-blown history of poetry or, for that matter, of any prose genre, what we badly need is a "theory of artistic values and of their experience" (p. 443). But as Wellek readily conceded, such a theory was nonexistent.

Undaunted, Wellek confronted this, the most knotty of theoretical issues, once more in his next paper, "The Theory of Literary History,"[21] profoundly convinced that in order to be tenable, Mukařovský's conception of historic structures—according to Wellek by far the most impressive attempt yet to attack the problem—must be drastically modified. Why? Because in principle "there is no structure outside norms and values" (p. 180). This assertion eloquently sums up what was to be the leitmotif of Wellek's lifelong critical enterprise. Here is the gist of his argument:

Only through *tendencies* discoverable by a scale of values can historical evolution be discovered. The relativity of the individual work to this scale of values is nothing else but a correlate of its individuality. All values are historical individualities and are always comprehensible only inside the network of historical relations. So the series of developments will be constructed by reference to values but these values emerge only by contemplating these series. (p. 189)

Wellek, of course, realized that the last sentence described a logical circle in which he sought to assess the historical process in terms of values that themselves could only be derived from history (p. 191). But, following the eminent German historiographer Ernst Troeltsch, Wellek thought this was an accurate picture of how the historian must go about delineating a historically validated scheme of things: "values grow out only from the historical process of valuation, which they help to make us understand" (p. 185). Surprisingly, though intimately familiar with current phenomenological literature, Wellek nowhere mentioned the hermeneutic circle of understanding as a conceivable way out from what threatened to be a vicious circle. Yet without some such interpretive *Zirkelschluß*, without a normative horizon of critical expectations or what today we could call general epistemic premises, Wellek's own proposal was bound to falter. This is best evident in the fact that, from within that circle of history, Wellek proved unable to postulate the desired universal value or a possible hierarchy of evaluation standards. In its original setting, his insistence on the inextricable presence of value in the literary structure appeared as a singularly penetrating insight, but an insight still in search of its theory.

Unfortunately, the other term in Wellek's initial assertion, *norm*— which he saw as suffusing the structure of the literary work—did not, on the evidence, fare much better. Like value, the concept of norm remained without the necessary underpinnings of an articulated theory. Let us quote again from Wellek's account of the mechanism of selecting historically notable literary products:

> . . . when we consider a work of art created in the past, this process of choosing has been already accomplished in a rather mysterious manner. Some works of art have merely sunk into oblivion, while others have risen to eminence and cannot be overlooked, though they were unknown or little known in their own time. It is difficult to describe this process in detail, but, of course, it is nothing but the result of an innumerable series of individual acts of judgment. (p. 183)

While descrying fully the vexing peripeties of literary events, this observation, citing as it does the "mysterious manner" of historical transmission, loses sight of the normative nature of this process. "Individual acts of judgment," no matter how idiosyncratic and self-indulgent, can only occur within the certain parameters provided by what in a sense are coercive, obligatory standards or norms of each period. Though slightly less binding, because less codified, than language rules, moral customs or legal systems, aesthetic norms must conform just as much to the period's constitutive *sensu communis*. And the historian's goal is to unearth from all available personal testimonies the underlying set of shared assumptions, beliefs and critical anticipations which go into the (positive or negative) individual appraisal of the work or works. It follows that relevant judgments, as the material of literary history, are not individual but supraindividual. Of course, historical accidents, whether in the work's production or in public reception, do happen in literature just as elsewhere. It is for this reason that the exclusively immanent treatment, as Jakobson and Tynjanov pointed out, is likely to fall short of explaining the most interesting cases. But it is equally clear that the one-sided focus on the individual will fail to divulge an intelligible pattern even in the most settled of times that have no startling masterpieces or rediscoveries.

Wellek, it seems, at the outset approached the problem of history as system with an unexpected bias. Witness this remark: "The concept of development of a series of works of art seems *prima facie* an extraordinarily difficult one" (p. 186). Could one not claim exactly the opposite? Could art possibly withstand and arrest the progress of time? Wellek himself refuted those who, accepting Schopenhauer's dictum that art has always reached its goal, view it as some transtemporal, ahistorical presence. Perhaps the best counterargument is that, *pace* Schopenhauer, the same—if true— holds for philosophy (as well as for any other humanistic pursuit). Suffice

it to place side by side the analogous convictions of Alfred North White-
head and Northrop Frye that the histories of philosophy and of literature
comprise, respectively, a series of footnotes to Plato and the Bible. The key
point is that such a stress on the basic invariant can in no way belittle the
importance of subsequent variations. Wellek's doubts, in other words,
rather than being grounded philosophically, must have stemmed from his
study of the repeatedly frustrated efforts at a literary history of English:
"all histories of English literature," he was forced to conclude, "are either
histories of civilization or collections of critical essays" (p. 175).[22] Still,
these sundry aborted projects cannot serve as a theoretical proof that it is
impossible or even extraordinarily difficult to portray the internal movement of literary series. There is plainly no inherent reason why literary
study could not reenact what we may call the Saussurean turn, namely, to
define its proper object by granting precedence to the exploration of the
system of literary conventions or norms over that of individual works. And
at first sight there is nothing within the literary system to hinder the con-
stellation of such conventions from passing through various transformations and rearrangements over the course of time.

   We can now draw nearer the root of Wellek's principal difficulty, and
that is his misconstruing of the structuralist version of evolution. Like
Bém, Wellek perceived its close resemblance to biological evolution and
likewise could not imagine a teleological development emptied of *telos*, of a
purposeful end. At the same time, he was very much aware that the term
did not apply to literature in either of the senses employed by Ferdinand
Brunetière, the foremost proponent of evolutionism (pp. 186–88). In the
history of literature there can be neither a metamorphosis like that of cater-
pillar into butterfly nor yet a gradual morphological advancement toward
an ideal generic form. Therefore, to preserve what he styled "the individuality of *historical* reality" (emphasis mine), Wellek urged that this could
only be done by "relating a teleological series to a value" (p. 188), thereby
encircling himself in the old contradictory chain of reasoning. What he
overlooked was not only that the biological metaphor—especially that
adopted from nineteenth-century biological thought—in literary criticism
is highly misleading but that one must radically differentiate between
natural and artistic (for the sake of contrast, let us say: artificial) evolution,
just as one has to make a sharp distinction between the concepts of "organic unity" and "structural whole."[23] Indeed, this difference runs so deep
as to cut across the nexus of the most fundamental ideas about both the
order of nature and the organization of society. It may deservedly be designated as a change in paradigm (in Thomas A. Kuhn's sense)—a change
from romanticism to modernism, from mimesis to abstraction, and, in a
way, also from inductive (empirical) objectivism to deductive (structural)

constructivism. Simply stated, in modern linguistics, and *mutatis mutandis* in poetics, *organism* is to be taken in a formal or methodological rather than ontological sense.

This is how Ernst Cassirer described the matter in his lecture to the Linguistic Circle of New York on 10 February 1945:

Language [and, let us add, literature—FWG] is neither a mechanism nor an organism, neither a dead nor a living thing. It is no thing at all, if by this term we understand a physical object. It is—language, a very specific human activity, not describable in terms of physics, chemistry or biology. The best and most laconic expression of this fact was given by W. von Humboldt, when he declared that language is not an *ergon* but an *energeia*. (p. 110)

And most important of all, the modern science of language sees that "Language is a 'symbolic form.' It consists of symbols, and symbols are no part of our physical world. They belong to an entirely different universe of discourse. Natural things and symbols cannot be brought to the same denominator. Linguistics is a part of semiotics, not of physics" (p. 115).[24] Now we can comprehend why literary theorists can disregard the lesson of structural linguistics only at their own peril. Language, literature and other kinds of discourse enjoy a special status, a unique mode of existence, and pertain, along with other objects endowed with meaning, to the domain of semiotics, discussed in the next chapter. What counts in the semiotic realm above all is system. The phonological theory of the Prague School, in particular, demonstrates how the sounds of a language comprise a system of diacritical relations by means of which we "distinguish words of unlike meaning." This network of phonic oppositions, as we have seen, exists in evolution, too. However, instead of progressing toward a final outcome, a metaphysical resolution of some sort, the evolution of language is inner-directed: its goal is to protect the system's dynamic stability, to propagate language's systemic equilibrium. (In fact, *evolution* seems rather a misnomer, with its undesirable connotations of natural development—but we still do not have a neutral term for the temporal existence of semiotic phenomena.) And even during times of linguistic turmoil and transition, clearly, the rules and principles of the language system must be available to every member of the *masse parlante*, for its continuous functioning depends on the agreement among the speakers of the given community. In sum, language, a semiotic system, has no existence apart from or outside of social consciousness.

Yet Wellek, even while exposing the unsuitability of the organological theories, refused to locate literature and literary development in the consciousness of a collectivity. Following Nicolai Hartmann's analysis in *Das Problem des geistigen Seins*,[25] he went so far as to deny altogether the possibility of a collective's consciousness: the collective can enter consciousness only as an object, not as a subject, of knowledge; hence, there can be no adequate awareness of the "collective spirit" in the concrete consciousness. Whatever the merits of this reasoning may be, and critics have argued that Hartmann's epistemology is riddled with contradictions, it helps underscore the fact that Mukařovský, too, could be guilty of explanation by an unknown category, leaving social consciousness undefined. Unfortunately, every language theory that posits a linguistic consciousness, or rather competence, is to this day caught on the horns of the same dilemma. Since the sole manifestation of linguistic competence is the speaker's verbal performance, there is no recourse to an independent testing procedure that could move us beyond the orbit of language. Wellek's own proposal, though, was still less satisfactory. Protesting against Mukařovský's thesis that the aesthetic object, like the meaning of the individual lexical unit, is what is common to all the states of "collective" consciousness, he countered that the aesthetic object is rather the ideal analogue of the work's artifact, not the impoverished, lowest common denominator of the public consent.

But before treating the problematic concept of the ideal aesthetic object, an obvious misunderstanding must first be clarified. The confusion appears to be occasioned by the two seemingly incompatible strands in Mukařovský's theory mentioned earlier, that is, the empirical and the phenomenological. Certainly, if his definition of the aesthetic object were empirical, it would produce utterly trivial statements, like much of the sociology of cultural consumption. To make any sense at all, this definition must be founded phenomenologically. On this theory, we perceive any given intentional object—a vase, say—only from a definite standpoint. Within the flow of consciousness, our perceptions continually change, the angles of our apprehending vary and so reveal the perceived object in ever-differing patterns of color, shape, texture and so on. The variation of perspective then yields different *Abschattungen*, or profiles of the selfsame thing, the synthesis of which are its essential features, not the crude common denominator.[26] Thus the aesthetic object may be identified as that unity created by the totality of all partial apprehensions of the concrete material vehicle. In other words, phenomenologically, the aesthetic object is apprehensible; Wellek's ideal object, by contrast, is not. As an ideal it can only be approximated in all "valid" readings, past, present and future. This naturally begs the question, because again we stand in need of a prior criterion of validity or value. Moreover, we must ask, how can we avoid drawing purely relativistic conclusions regarding the critics' realizations of the work? Wellek's answer is that one individual's experience of the work's values is richer and more rewarding than another's and that, in a supposedly dialectical reversal, the reader's most intense subjectivity gives expression to the highest objectivity (cf. 1934 lecture, appendix 1).

This proposition, however, raises more problems than it can solve. Like the Marxist reliance on social contradictions, it is prone to spin off endless equivocations. But more crucial than that is Wellek's complete obliteration of the all-important structural analogy with language, unwittingly suggesting a chimerical superspeaker that no linguist could take very seriously. Wellek, though, quickly realized the absurdity of this proposition and dropped the idea. By the time of "The Theory of Literary History," he had introduced the parallel between the system of rules and the individual speech act and the system of literary norms and the individual form. Nonetheless, like other critics of Prague structuralism, he still seemed not to have thought through the implications of the Saussurean *langue*—with unwanted consequences for his own theoretical views. To recapitulate: Wellek's insistence on the problem of the value-constituted nature of the structure of literature overshadowed its equally essential—and theoretically much more fruitful—norm-boundedness. For deprived of the normative background, the evolvement of literature presented itself as a discontinuous, piecemeal affair. And without giving literature's semiotic status its due, literary norms could not be seen as implanted in the social consciousness. The whole development of aesthetic forms thus had a rather tenuous and fragile life, always contingent on the strength or weakness of individual judgments. Rather than being a social or collective enterprise, literary history appeared as a special legacy passed, or not passed, from one historian to another in a series of individual acts. All this should explain Wellek's recent disillusionment (indeed despair) with the project of evolutionary history. As he now maintains, "there is no progress, no development, no history of art except a history of writers, institutions and techniques."[27] But it seems more likely that the germs of his misgivings, apprehensions as well as misapprehensions, go back to his earliest days.

Yet in the climate of the Circle's debate, the shortcomings in Wellek's search for critical alternatives to Mukařovský's history did not in the least detract from the cogency of his other criticisms, which, as we noted in the beginning, were most cohesive and stimulating—so much so that through his commentaries Wellek can be said to have augured the Prague School's future theoretical concerns. For example, not by coincidence did Mukařovský consecrate his next monograph to the problematic of function, norm and value and in so doing work out a scheme of literary axiology, if not quite a theory of evaluation; similarly, he was to rectify in his theoretical program every other omission so ably illuminated by Wellek. With exceptional acumen and prescience Wellek seized upon trail-blazing works by two scholars whose thought left a lasting imprint on the development of literary and aesthetic structuralism: the Polish philosopher and aesthetician Roman Ingarden (1893–1970) and the German psychologist and linguist Karl Bühler (1879–1963), both of whom were strongly influenced by

Husserl's phenomenology. Their respective books were *Das literarische Kunstwerk: Eine Untersuchung aus dem Grenzgebiet der Ontologie, Logik und Literaturwissenschaft* and *Sprachtheorie: Die Darstellungsfunktion der Sprache*.[28] Besides common origins in the phenomenological camp, the two studies also shared a common fate—which was, until recently, one of grave neglect by the scholarly world, completely out of keeping with their signal achievements. Regrettably, I can here offer no more than a bare outline of the few pivotal ideas put to such good use in Wellek's critical gloss.

Of the two, Bühler, a frequent contributor to the Circle and Trubeckoj's collaborator in Vienna, perhaps suffered the worse lot.[29] Most Anglo-American readers will probably know his name only from a brief mention in Jakobson's famous 1958 presentation of the functional model of verbal communication, for which Bühler had laid the ground some quarter-century earlier.[30] It was the Organon-model of language, reproduced below, that Wellek used to focus on what was amiss in Mukařovský's "Polák's *Sublimity of Nature*" and his other essays.

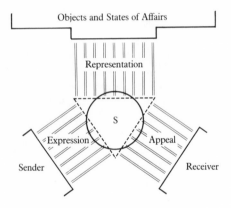

The starting point for Bühler's "first axiom" was everyday conversation, a dialogue in which one person tells another about something. In putting the accent on ordinary linguistic exchange, Bühler was merely heeding, as he said, the age-old advice of Plato's *Cratylus*; yet in modern language study this was an almost shocking thing to do, considering that nineteenth-century philology examined in the main written texts and twentieth-century linguistics analyzed separate sentences abstracted from the actual speech situation. From the standpoint of normal verbal intercourse, it immediately becomes evident that each sign (designated by the circle) contains three fundamental variables (designated by the triangle). The sign, in other words, functions not only with respect to the referred-to objects and states of affairs, as linguists hitherto took for granted, but also with respect to the speaking subject as well as the recipient of the uttered message. Depending on which of these three inalienable factors of the speech event the given sign is preeminently oriented toward, it performs, as the diagram shows, the referential, the expressive or emotive and the appellant or conative functions, respectively. In short, the sign can equally be an instrument of representation as of expression and appeal and so be classified semantically, in Bühler's nomenclature, as a symbol, a symptom or a signal.[31]

Now, in Wellek's opinion, owing to their teleological bent, structuralist investigators have gone askew in that Mukařovský and others handled literary signs as signals, neglecting the fact that they are also symptoms and symbols. Though not entirely inaccurate—we have noted that Mukařovský had, in "Polák's *Sublimity of Nature*," made inchoate gestures toward reception theory—this impression could arise simply because Bühler's triadic scheme left out the function of the self-focused or autotelic sign itself, the aesthetic function. Consequently, Mukařovský was to supplement the Bühlerian model with the (impractical) aesthetic function, which stands in a dialectical relation to the three practical functions. And Jakobson, as we know, finally expanded it to involve six functions, adding the phatic and the metalinguistic, with their focus on verbal contact and on the code. Be that as it may, Bühler's functional triad had a salutary effect on the Prague School by providing a much more viable typology of functions than that put forth in the 1929 "Theses." For by taking to heart, apparently, Saussure's understanding of linguistic facts as social in nature, the Circle's functionalism suffered at an early stage from sociological relativism. In that view, in addition to referential and poetic functions, language had the *koinē* function, the function of scientific language and any number of other "functional dialects" which could be infinitely multiplied. Bühler, in contrast, reduced the enormous variety of functional styles down to the few essential universals. But for Wellek's purposes, the semiotic triangle of Bühler lent significant support to his critique, much to the point, that the structuralists should at last stop overreacting to the dangers of psychologism, since within the very frame of semiotics one is obliged to come to terms with the producer of the message or, in literary discourse, the artistic personality. All one has to do is to distinguish the artistic (or, we might say, semiotic) subject implied in the work from the empirical person of the author. No one would doubt, Wellek argued, that the works of every poet or writer, even if anonymous, exhibit "an individual signature, a certain physiognomy or, if you will, a personality structure distinct from the features of the works of another writer" (p. 443). In the light of subsequent structural theory, Wellek's description can rightly be viewed as a preliminary sketch of the concept Mukařovský was to christen the "semantic gesture." And in the light of the most recent poetics and semiotics, we can also see that, besides aiding Wellek to chart the path of Prague School theory, Bühler, by inquiring into such parts of speech as deixis and interjection, pioneered what is now known as speech act theory and the productive field of text pragmatics.[32]

The third and, in most verbal communications, dominant moment of Bühler's Organon, that of representation, received short shrift in Muka-řovský's poetics as well. The reasons for this attitude are obvious, since representation of immediate reality is the obverse, and complementary, facet of the individual expression. The structuralist suppression or, per-haps more fairly, underestimation of those two communicative features be-trays the same fear of "premature foreclosure"—of that (for a literary critic) unseemly rush from word to world, from the realm of verbal artifice to the rival realm of the real.[33] That such a fear of "psychologistic" or "in-tentional" and, even more, "mimetic" fallacy is ill-founded, indeed that it is just a childhood disease of a fledgling poetic theory, the structuralists themselves came to realize thanks in part to the advanced formulations by Roman Ingarden.[34] Like Bühler, Ingarden sought to strip to (ontological) essentials the multitude of elements making up the structure of the literary work of art. By means of a phenomenological reduction, he dissected the work of literature into the following basic intentional strata:
1. The stratum of linguistic sound formations, of word sounds and pho-netic formations of a higher order.
2. The stratum of word meanings created by the sentences comprised in the structure of the work.
3. The stratum of represented objects, of intentional objectivities pro-jected by units of meanings.
4. The stratum of schematized aspects through which the represented ob-jects manifest themselves.
Roughly, the multilayered formation of the four strata—plus their tem-poral extension—merely establishes the work's structural skeleton, con-taining numerous gaps or "spots of indeterminacy." These spots are then filled at all levels through individual concretizations in the readers' aes-thetic experience. In other words, whereas the hierarchically stratified or-ganization of the work exists in a state of potentiality, in concretizations as an aesthetic object it attains the final "polyphonic harmony," its actual Gestalt.

The genuine breakthrough as far as Wellek was concerned lay in the fact that, within the terms of Ingarden's phenomenological investigations, not only poetic sound and sense but also such constituent parts as charac-ters, the whole furniture of the world (Ingarden's "represented objects") and, last but not least, the ideas or the *Weltanschauung* of the literary work admitted rigorous immanent analysis. For Ingarden, these highest semantic constructs, too, appeared as indigenous to the work, not exterior to it, and graspable only by means of a sociological canvasing of the literary and social milieu, which is what Mukařovský propounded. Thus, taking his cue from Ingarden, Wellek could say that it is from the "intentional reality of the artistic work that there emerges a certain attitude to and interpretation of the world, a 'deeper meaning,' a metaphysical quality," which is "just as immanent as the intentional world of realities and relationships" (p. 444). Moreover, he submitted, since the work's interpretation of the world is phenomenologically accessible without the critic's having to leave the territory of literature, the literary historian could also, ideally, trace the dialectical vicissitudes of such ideas as are expressed in works of poetry and prose fiction—provided, of course, that he or she solved the stubborn problem of translating the "poetic" ideas into the discursive language of theoretical concepts. Although amenable in the abstract or *von oben* (to use the terms of the experimental aesthetician Gustav Theodor Fechner) to Ingarden's type of philosophical scrutiny, this cluster of semantic phenomena brought home only too vividly the compelling question about the frontiers of the linguistic analysis of poetic structures.[35] As we have observed, up to this point Mukařovský had to restrict his study to individual poetic designation and motif, with the larger semantic context remaining well beyond the reach of his, and everyone else's, analytic apparatus. And, to be sure, the poetic world view continued to be the stumbling block for the structuralists for many years to come. But Mukařovský, at any rate, instead of wholly assimilating the phenomenological mode of analysis, went on to pursue the problem *von unten* along the tracks of linguistic semantics and cultural sociology or, better still, semiology. Indeed, the entire future course of the Prague School poetics is best understood as a quest for a progressive semantization of each and every element comprising the structure of the literary work.

In the reply to his critics at the conclusion of the Circle's debate, Mukařovský, understandably enough, shied away from the issues of poetic representation and ideation as being, for the moment, out of the purview of structuralism. He did, however, answer the rest of the charges leveled against his methodology in "Polák's *Sublimity of Nature*," particularly in regard to literary evolution, which, we must remember, was the central topic of the controversy. This is how he summarized the reasons for going beyond his initially formalistic premises:

If the explanation of evolutionary changes is not to be limited to the monotonously reiterated principle of the desire for novelty, it is imperative to seek an explanation in what lies outside literature, starting with the influence of other literatures and ending with the most diverse segments of human culture. However, human culture is not suspended in a vacuum either, but is rather borne by a collective, and the evolution of the collective, of that concrete social entity, indicates the direction of cultural evolution. For this reason it is necessary to account for the relation between the history of literature and the history of society. In the abstract, we could formulate this perhaps as follows: to evolve means always to become something different, but without impairment of identity. Both presuppositions are indispensable, their contradictoriness notwithstanding. This holds for literature, too, if we admit that it has a certain lawlike evolution of its own. Yet to become different implies for literature, which is a part of the vast domain called culture, to be oriented toward one of the other series—toward, for example, another literature, another of the arts, another kind of verbal expression or toward philosophy, science and the like. Not even theoretically, therefore, can we isolate literature from that domain unless we suppress the dialectical antinomy which is a prerequisite for evolution. Since culture as a whole, however, is carried by the development of society, we have to take into consideration the relation between literature and society, as well.[36]

Thus, over and against Ingarden's phenomenological vivisection of the literary object, Mukařovský spotlighted the determining interplay of aesthetic conventions and the social environment. This difference of operation was very much in tune with their dissimilar objectives. Ingarden's set purpose was to disclose the universal ontological essence of the literary work as an intentional object of a special kind. The goal of Mukařovský, on the other hand, was to discover the algorithm of literary change. Such an algorithm proved easily discoverable, but as affecting solely the internal movement of literary innovation, and so brought about results which, in Mukařovský's view, were as banal as they were false. The next challenge for the literary theorist rested in the subtle interaction among literary, artistic and social activities which, combined, at any time determined the course and pace of literature's development. The telltale signs of this intricate and dynamic interaction were practically everywhere: in the circulation of high-, middle- and lowbrow literary genres and the cultural taste of the corresponding (though loosely corresponding) social classes or, conversely, in the various aesthetic objects that distinct social or age groups realized in accordance with their perception of the state of literary structure. But, Mukařovský repeated, downplaying Wellek's emphasis on the value-guided nature of this process, all concretizations, all literary commerce, can materialize only with a view to the horizon of norms and conventions and habits, even though these must vary socially, nationally and historically. Mukařovský conceded, though, that the issue of evaluation did require further study, that his own solution had been largely a negation of traditional scholarly beliefs. "The absolute objectivity of aesthetic value, that is, its complete independence from the observer," he agreed, "is necessarily a mere postulate, but one which nonetheless must forever be posited" (p. 191). And he granted a final point to Wellek, namely, that it was indeed time to start thinking in structural terms about the place of individuality in literature. In a statement that anticipated his future conception, he announced that "one of the fundamental dialectical antinomies in literary history is . . . between the subjectivity of the individual and the objectivity of the artistic structure" (p. 192).

With the debate about *The Sublimity of Nature*, the Prague School's theory of literary history reached its apogee. Mukařovský read another paper, "An Attempt at a Scheme of the Structural History of Czech Literature," at the Second International Congress of Slavists in Warsaw, in September 1934, but, like his contribution to the First Congress, it remained unpublished.[37] After that, nearly a decade elapsed before Mukařovský returned to the problematics of evolutionary structures—though naturally the sixth, historical, sense imbued all his aesthetic criticism—expressly historical studies having in the meantime appeared from the younger structuralists, René Wellek, Felix Vodička and Josef Hrabák. There were at least two reasons, we may surmise, why Mukařovský's own research interest in the theory of literary history temporarily subsided. For one thing, Mukařovský must have felt that the driving forces of literary evolution, albeit on the level of versification alone, had in principle been sufficiently elucidated. True, his account of historical process showed it to be too linear, irreversible, precluding the vital possibility of renovation of antiquated forms, but to amend it he had first to grapple with the role of poetic personality, as his last pronouncement forecast. For another thing, as the Circle's debate amply testified, fresh vistas soon opened up in literary study under the impact from pure phenomenology, cultural sociology, Gestalt psychology and related fields.

To get a better idea of the magnitude and complexity of the additional tasks now confronting the Prague structuralists, it might be instructive to glance back at Aristotle's *Poetics*. In *Peri poiētikēs* (perhaps best conveyed in English as "On Poetic [Art]"), Aristotle, like his formalist successors some two millennia later, located the quiddity of poetic art, *poiēsis* or poeticalness, in the number and sequence of the parts of which the poem is composed.[38] Translated into Charles Morris' convenient categories, poetics is really poetic syntactics, the study of relationships among the constituent elements. Unlike the Petersburg students of poetic language or the Chicago Neo-Aristotelians, however, Aristotle himself did not rest content with the syntax of poetry, with enumerating poetry's compositional features and their combinations. Within the treatise on the poetic, even in the fragmentary shape in which it came down to us, he also took care of the other two modalities of signification, the semantic and the pragmatic: the doctrine of mimesis concerned itself with artistic representation and that of catharsis with the work's healing effect on the audience. Indeed, in this respect, no other poetic or literary or dramatic theory since has been nearly as incisive or comprehensive. And modern poetics, in a sense only recently exhumed, can be thought of as still reassembling, annotating and amplifying the principles from the extant Aristotelian fragments, occasionally filling in the lacunae.[39] But now consider the vast new dimensions the study of literature acquires when, in the twentieth-century view, poetics, along with linguistics, is seen to form just one area in the global science of signs: Peirce's and Morris' semiotic, Saussure's semiology, Bühler's sematology . . .

NOTES

1. "Polákova *Vznešenost přírody*. (Pokus o rozbor a vývojové zařadění básnické struktury)" (Polák's *Sublimity of Nature*: An Attempt at an Analysis and Historical Ordering of a Poetic Structure), *Sborník filologický* 10 (1934): 1–68; quoted from *KCP* 2, pp. 91–176. Mukařovský submitted the study for publication in July 1933 and read portions of it before the Circle on 13 February of that year.

2. See, best of all, Nikolaj S. Trubeckoj's "*Choženie za tri morja Afanasija Nikitina*, kak literaturnyj pamjatnik," *Versty* 1 (1926): 164–186; in English, "Afanasij Nikitin's *Journey beyond the Three Seas* as a Work of Literature," in *RRP*, pp. 199–219.

3. "On Value-Judgements," in *The Stubborn Structure: Essays on Criticism and Society*, p. 66.

4. What follows is an elaboration of René Wellek's suggestion; cf. his "The Literary Theory and Aesthetics of the Prague School," in *Discriminations: Further Concepts in Criticism*, p. 287.

5. "Ein einfarbiger Formalismus," in *Phänomenologie des Geistes* (Frankfurt: Ullstein, 1973), p. 20; see J. B. Baillie's translation, *The Phenomenology of Mind* (New York: Harper, 1967), p. 78 (this work first appeared in 1807).

6. "Der Weihnachtsbaum in der Ost-Slowakei: Zur Frage der strukturellen Erforschung des Funktionswandels ethnografischer Fakten," *Germanoslavica* 2 (1932–1933): 254–58; consult also several of Bogatyrev's articles translated in *SA*.

7. For instance, think of *l'affaire Picard* of the mid-1960s, the long and bitter feud between the conservative scholar Raymond Picard and the "new critic" Roland Barthes, which is examined in Serge Doubrovsky, *The New Criticism in France*, trans. Derek Coltman; see also Edward Wasiolek's informative introduction (pp. 1–38).

8. "Zpráva o studii dra Jana Mukařovského 'Polákova Vznešenost přírody. Pokus o zařadění vývojové'" (A Report), *Věstník české akademie věd a umění* 42 (1933): 44–45. We should notice that Mukařovský submitted the study in June 1933—this explains why he makes scant reference to semiotic theory, to which he turned only in the following year. See also Kvido Hodura's review in *Naše řeč* 18 (1934): 295–97 and L'udovít Novák's judicious report in *Slovenské pohl'ady* 50 (1934): 570–71; Novák likewise reported on "The History of Czech Verse," in ibid. 51 (1935): 55–60.

9. "Úvaha o zkoumání českého individuálního jazyka, zvláště básnického, a o t. zv. strukturalismu" (A Reflection on Czech Poetic Language and on the So-

called Structuralism), *Časopis pro moderní filologii* 22 (1935): 79–85. Mukařovský's rejoinder appeared in ibid. 22 (1936): 204–7, together with Weingart's further response, pp. 207–8. Finally, in a follow-up article which came out in a subsequent issue under the same title (pp. 365–70), Weingart voiced his opinions on the indebtedness of Mukařovský to the ideas of Russian formalism.

10. Wellek, "The Literary Theory and Aesthetics of the Prague School," p. 296.

11. Cf. *Philosophie der Kunst*, pp. 41, 49ff.

12. Cf. *Die Gegenwartsaufgaben der Soziologie: Ihre Lehrgestalt* (Tübingen: J. C. B. Mohr/Paul Siebeck, 1932).

13. "Příklad literárního dějepisu strukturního," *Šaldův zápisník* 7 (1934–1935): 59–68.

14. Contributions to the long debate over the politics of modern art have conveniently been gathered in three volumes of *Avantgarda známá a neznámá* (Avant-Garde Known and Unknown), ed. Štěpán Vlašín et al. For further information, one may consult the fascinating anthology *Poetismus*, ed. Květoslav Chvatík and Zdeněk Pešat, which reprints, among other things, two humorous poems entitled "Roman Jakobson" and "Dopis Mukařovskému" (A Letter to Mukařovský) (pp. 336 and 351–53, respectively), by Vítězslav Nezval, to whose work both Jakobson and Mukařovský in turn devoted several critical essays.

15. Compare, for instance, Hans Günther's collection of Russian essays, *Marxismus und Formalismus*, which also includes, quite properly, the Czech discussion by Kurt Konrad, "Der Streit um Inhalt und Form: Marxistische Bemerkungen zum neuen Formalismus," pp. 131–61 (see also note 16 below); another useful anthology is *The Futurists, the Formalists, and the Marxist Critique*, ed. Christopher Pike; consult also Růžena Grebeníčková's informative piece, "Cesty marxistické literární teorie a léte třicátá" (Marxist Literary Theory in the Thirties), *Československá rusistika* 6 (1961): 88–101.

16. "Svár obsahu a formy: Marxistické poznámky o novém formalismu" (The Strife of Content and Form: Marxist Comments on the New Formalism), *Středisko* 4 (1934): 56–65. This piece surveys Mukařovský's work up to the Polák study. Konrad, "Ještě jednou svár obsahu a formy" (Once More on the Strife of Content and Form), appeared in the next issue, *Středisko* 4 (1934): 98–99, as an appendix discussing *The Sublimity of Nature*. Both articles are reprinted in Konrad, *Ztvárněte skutečnost* (Shape Reality!) (Praha: Československý spisovatel, 1963), from which all quotations are taken.

17. "O metodu literární historie: Metodologické poznámky k. J. Mukařovského Polákově 'Vznešenosti přírody'" (The Method in Literary History: Methodological Remarks), *Tvorba*, 29 June 1934: 102–3. (This and all other quotations are from p. 102.)

18. "Methodologické poznámky ke studii Jana Mukařovského 'Polákova Vznešenost přírody,'" (Methodological Remarks), *Časopis pro moderní filologii* 21 (1935): 330–34.

19. This statement appeared in a brief report on the Circle's activity in *Sl. sl.* 1 (1935): 192.

20. "'Dějiny českého verše' a metody literární historie" (The Development

of Czech Verse and the Methods of Literary History), *Listy pro umění a kritiku 2* (1934): 437–45.

21. *Travaux* 6 (1936): 173–92. Most of the ideas first discussed in these articles became incorporated into three chapters of *Theory of Literature*: "The Analysis of the Literary Work of Art," "Evaluation" and "Literary History."

22. Wellek returned to this topic in a lecture to the Circle on 1 October 1937; it was published under the title "Vývoj anglické literární historie" (The Development of English Literary History) in *Sl. sl.* 4 (1938): 96–105, and later developed into the book *The Rise of English Literary History* (Chapel Hill: University of North Carolina Press, 1941). Professor Wellek reminisces on his Prague years and his participation in the PLC in the article "Vilém Mathesius (1882–1945), Founder of the Prague Linguistic Circle," in *SSM*, pp. 11–13.

23. Cf. Wellek's earlier article "Wordsworth's and Coleridge's Theories of Poetic Diction," in *Charisteria*, pp. 130–34, for his recognition of the similarities between nineteenth- and twentieth-century views on poetic language.

24. "Structuralism in Modern Linguistics," *Word* 1 (1945): 99–120. See also W. K. Wimsatt, "Organic Form: Some Questions about a Metaphor," in *Day of the Leopards* (New Haven: Yale University Press, 1976), pp. 205–23, for the tremendous obstacles encountered by someone not paying enough attention to the symbolic or semiotic character of art. For a detailed discussion of organismic theories, consult Morton Beckner, *The Biological Way of Thought*. The philosophical implications of the recent advances in molecular biology are discussed in Jacques Monod, *Le hasard et la nécessité: Essai sur la philosophie naturelle de la biologie moderne* (Paris: Seuil, 1970) and François Jacob, *La logique du vivant: Une histoire de l'hérédité* (Paris: Gallimard, 1970). (Both books now exist in English: see appendix 2.)

25. Subtitled *Untersuchungen zur Grundlegung der Geschichtsphilosophie und Geschichtswissenschaften* (Berlin: W. de Gruyter, 1933).

26. Cf. Edmund Husserl, *Ideen zu einer reinen Phänomenologie und phänomenologischen Philosophie* (Halle: Niemeyer, 1928), par. 41. *Ideen* appeared originally in 1913 and the English translation in 1931.

27. "The Fall of Literary History," in *The Attack on Literature and Other Essays*, p. 77. The most explicit statement about his defeat in producing an evolutionary history can be found in Wellek, "Reflections on My *History of Modern Criticism*," in ibid., pp. 135–58. See also Wellek's review of Claudio Guillén, *Literature as System*, in *Yale Review* 61 (1972): 254–59, esp. pp. 256–59. Wellek's role in the Prague Linguistic Circle and in the dissemination of the Circle's theoretical ideas abroad is critically assessed in Ladislav Matejka, "Literary History in a Semiotic Framework: Prague School Contributions," in *SLP*, pp. 341–70, esp. pp. 346–56.

28. (Halle: Niemayer, 1931); (Jena: Fischer, 1934). For a convenient introduction, one may go to Robert E. Innis, *Karl Bühler: Semiotic Foundations of Language Theory*.

29. See his "Phonetik und Phonologie," *Travaux* 4 (1931): 22–53, and "Das Strukturmodell der Sprache," *Travaux* 6 (1936): 3–12.

30. "Closing Statement: Linguistics and Poetics," in *Style in Language*, ed. Thomas A. Sebeok, pp. 350–77, esp. pp. 353–57; rpt. in *SW* 3, pp. 18–51.

31. This classification might seem confusing to those accustomed to C. S. Peirce's semiotic. (Cf., e.g., "Logic as Semiotic: The Theory of Signs," in *Philosophical Writings of Peirce*, ed. Justus Buchler, pp. 98–119; most of his semiotic writings date to the turn of the century.) Only the category of symbol (or the arbitrary and unmotivated sign of Saussure) is the same for both Bühler and Peirce. Symptoms are Peirce's indices, as signals would also have to be. On the other hand, Bühler is little concerned with "icons" since for him such an instance of verbal iconicity as onomatopoeia presents a marginal and uninteresting case. See in this regard Gérard Genette's discussion of Bühler's "Hermogenisme" in *Mimologiques: Voyage en Cratylie*, pp. 422–23. One might also consult Roland Barthes' comparative table of sign categories in *Eléments de sémiologie* (Paris: Seuil, 1964), par. II.1., although it does not include Bühler's scheme.

32. However, in England and America these new disciplines consider the work of philosopher and logician Charles W. Morris their direct forerunner. In his "Foundation of the Theory of Signs," in *International Encyclopedia of United Science*, vol. 1, published four years after the *Sprachtheorie*, Morris elaborated an analytic scheme similar to Bühler's, dividing the process of sign functioning or semiosis into semantics, pragmatics and syntactics. Here, semantics studies the referential aspect of signification, pragmatics groups together the emotive and conative functions to examine signs' effect and efficacy with respect to sign users and syntactics deals with the relations among signs. It is worth remarking that Morris acknowledged Bühler's assistance in the writing of his later book, *Signs, Language and Behavior*. Morris' semiotic parallels the Prague School's semiology in several other respects: for example, his definition of the aesthetic sign as the sign whose denotatum is value would seem agreeable to Wellek, except that Morris' theory of value is of course behavioristic (cf. "Esthetics and the Theory of Signs," *Journal of Unified Science (Erkenntnis)* 8 [1939]: 131–50). A comparison between the two semiotic schools merits further study and promises to be far more fertile than comparing structuralist literary theory with that of the New Criticism. The first steps have been taken in Maria Renata Mayenowa, "Classic Statements of the Semiotic Theory of Art: Mukařovský and Morris," in *SSM*, pp. 425–32, and in Peter Steiner, "Jan Mukařovský and Charles W. Morris: Two Pioneers of the Semiotics of Art," *Semiotica* 19 (1977): 321–34.

33. Cf. Jonathan Culler, *Structuralist Poetics*, p. 130.

34. Ingarden's two key books on literary theory exist in English translation: *The Literary Work of Art: An Investigation on the Borderlines of Ontology, Logic, and Theory of Literature*, trans. George G. Grabowicz (contains a fine introduction by the translator and a bibliography); and *The Cognition of the Literary Work of Art*, translated from the German edition by Ruth Ann Crowley and Kenneth R. Olson; the Polish original, *O poznawaniu dzieła literackiego*, appeared in 1937. For a brief report on Ingarden's work in aesthetics, see "Bericht über meine Studien zur Ästhetik," in *Contemporary Philosophy: A Survey*, vol. 4, ed. Raymond Klibansky (Florence: La Nuova Italia, 1971), pp. 106–10; for his contribution to literary studies, consult Eugene H. Falk, *The Poetics of Roman Ingarden*.

35. Even when rebuking Jakobsonian linguistic poetics at the 1958 conference, Wellek found it fitting to bring up Ingarden's concept of literary stratification; see "Closing Statement: From the Viewpoint of Literary Criticism," in *Style*

in Language, pp. 410–11. Ingarden, upon reading the German translation of *Theory of Literature*, took exception, however, to a number of points in Wellek's presentation of his ideas—see Ingarden, "Preface to the Third German Edition," in *The Literary Work of Art*, pp. lxxix–lxxxiii, as well as his rebuttal, "Werte, Normen und Strukturen nach René Wellek," *Deutsche Vierteljahrschrift für Literaturwissenschaft und Geistesgeschichte* 40 (1966): 43–55.

36. "Replika J. Mukařovského," *Sl. sl.* 1 (1935): 190–93; quotation on pp. 190–91. For a French translation of these comments, see *Change* no. 3 (1969), entitled *Le Cercle de Prague*, in particular "Formalisme russe et structuralisme tchèque," pp. 54–60.

37. Cf. Mukařovský's report on the proceedings of the Congress, *Sl. sl.* 1 (1935): 69.

38. *Aristotle's Theory of Poetry and Fine Art*, 1447a, trans. S. H. Butcher [1894], p. 7.

39. See Tzvetan Todorov's comment about the rebirth of poetics: "the close links between [Aristotle's and the Russian formalists'] approaches . . . span twenty centuries of misguided contempt of the literary text by critics who refuse to consider text and text alone" ("Quelques concepts du Formalisme russe," *Revue d'esthétique* 24 [1971]: 129–43; quoted from "Some Approaches to Russian Formalism," trans. Bruce Merry, in *Russian Formalism*, ed. Stephen Bann and John E. Bowlt, p. 6)—which, while historically true, gives an overly parochial version of poetics, again alienated from its proper semiotic environment.

4 ‖ The Semiotic Reformulation

Reality is the beginning not the end,
Naked Alpha, not the hierophant Omega

....

But that's the difference: in the end and the way
To the end. Alpha continues to begin.
Omega is refreshed at every end.

WALLACE STEVENS

The rise of semiotics (to use the now standard term), which furnished the conceptual basis for the Prague School's theory from 1934 on, betokens the final break with the ideas of formalism. If up to this time the Circle's approach could be labeled formalist in the broadest sense of the word—the notions of historical and sociological poetics being undeniably a direct continuance of Opojaz proposals—after 1934 this appellation becomes misleading, historically as well as theoretically. The Czech semiotics of art is in fact an original conception. Whatever outside impulse or inspiration there might have been originated in Saussurean linguistics and the German language philosophy of Husserl, Bühler and Cassirer, rather than the short-lived semiotic researches of Michail Bachtin and his school.[1] Consequently, many unforeseen avenues of inquiry opened up for the scholars of the Prague Circle which the members of Opojaz would scarcely know how to integrate into their rather narrow theoretical framework. In literary study such novel, and at the same time mostly traditional, topics included poetic symbolism, myth and the characteristic semantic properties of individual styles. Also, the structuralists were eager to test the tools of semiotic analysis on material from the other arts—film, theatre, the visual arts, music and even ethnographic artifacts like folk costume. Indeed, the crowning achievement of the Prague School, apart from the breakthrough in phonology, was its creation of semiotic aesthetics.

Historically, among the most vivid and telling descriptions of the realm of the semiotic must surely figure the following account by Saint Augustine. In his *Confessions*, in the chapter on "The Growth of Speech" (book 1, chapter 8), he wrote: "So little by little I inferred that the words set in their proper places in different sentences, that I heard so frequently, were signs of things. . . . Thus to those among whom I was communicated the signs of what I wished to express. I entered more deeply into the stormy society of human life . . ." Augustine also quickly learned that words are in no way the sole means of communicating, because one can express thoughts and refer to things, and often more effectively, by gestures such as "change of countenance, nods, movements of the eyes and other bodily members . . ."[2] This thumbnail sketch displays the fundamental guideposts of any semiotic theory: words are not identical with but only stand for things; verbal and nonverbal signs alike are used for communication; and communication is a social activity par excellence. Not surprisingly, the three key concepts find an echo in the work of Ferdinand de Saussure, father not only of structural linguistics but of modern semiotics.[3] Like Augustine, who realized that the *signum* is a Janus-faced entity consisting of the material *signans* and the immaterial *signatum*, Saussure maintained that the verbal sign binds together into a seamless unit not a name with a thing but the phonic *signifiant* with the conceptual *signifié*. Furthermore, Saussure, too, was very much aware that language is only one—even if the most versatile—of many signifying codes or systems; to understand better the processes of signification, Saussure urged that we study other vehicles of human communication besides language, whether those parasitic on language (like the alphabet for the deaf and flag signals) or others which are independent from it (like symbolic rituals and social customs). Last, possibly drawing support from the emerging sociology of Emile Durkheim, Saussure claimed that all signs without exception fall under the heading of social facts, that is, the special class of phenomena carrying the stamp of collective approval.[4]

Signs, then, are the province of three tightly intermeshing disciplines: semiotics, a global science of signs—verbal, visual, auditory, gestural, tactile, even olfactory—and their various implementations in everyday communicative exchange and in art; semantics, or the study of meaning, linguistic as well as logical; and sociology (or, roughly, pragmatics in Morris' sense), the discipline probing into the sociocultural dimensions of sign use and sign behavior.

Let us begin with the linguistic aspect of the problem of signification. In the study of verbal meaning, the ground of investigation shifts from phonic forms to semantic contents, from significant sounds to their corresponding concepts and objects. (In literary theory, by analogy, this change of focus characterizes the trajectory from formalism to structuralism.) The central issue in semantics, the meaning of meaning, poses what is unquestionably the most refractory problem in linguistics—and not only in linguistics, for it simultaneously lies on the borderland between philosophical logic and cognitive psychology. Although the epistemological status of signs and signification has been a hotly debated topic practically from the beginnings of philosophic speculation, it seems a peculiarly modern, twentieth-century concern. Since the appearance of Michel Bréal's *Essai de sémantique* (1897) and Gottlob Frege's "Über Sinn und Bedeutung"

(1892), linguists and logicians, of both natural and formal languages, have concentrated unprecedented energies on this tangled and controversial subject. Until recently, however, the paths of linguistic and logical inquiries have seldom crossed, and a methodological rift similarly divides general semiotics, which issues from Saussurean linguistics in Europe, while emanating from Peircean logic in America. The Prague School's contribution to linguistic semantics lags considerably behind its accomplishments in phonology. But the same is true of all other linguistic movements during the interwar period. To this day, as a matter of fact, the nature of language meaning seems largely to elude the theoretical grasp of linguistic students.[5]

Semantics aroused the interest of Prague structuralists at an early stage. Bohumil Trnka's survey, "Semasiology and Its Significance for Linguistics," acknowledged the immense importance of this field of language study.[6] According to the School's functionalist point of view, in a sense semantics takes priority over phonetics, since, if we recall the basic argument, the speech act usually proceeds from function to form, or, in other words, from a search for the appropriate meaning to a selection from the available means of expression. It was the introduction of the criterion of meaning into the study of sounds, as we know, which transformed phonetics into phonology. Yet in the sphere of the signified, Trnka candidly conceded, it is incomparably more difficult than in the sphere of the signifier to answer Saussure's call that we stand firmly on the ground of language itself, because so far even the most perspicacious of linguists had derived their principles either from psychology, the nineteenth-century master-science, or from logic or even from extralinguistic reality (the latter study, known as onomasiology, examines how certain orders of things, say, parts of the body, acquire their various denominations).

It was left to Sergej Karcevskij (1884–1955), pupil of Saussure and member of both the Prague and Geneva schools, to shed new and original light on this unyielding problematic of signs and their meaning in an essay entitled "Du dualisme asymétrique du signe linguistique."[7] The starting point of Karcevskij's observations was the familiar fact that the two faces of the linguistic sign do not stand in a one-to-one, reversible relationship. Both the sign's formal and semantic facets are prone to alteration: the signifier gravitating toward homonymy and the signified toward synonymy. Put differently, one and the same sign can have several functions or meanings (for example, *seal* [a signet ring] and *seal* [a sea mammal]) and, conversely, two distinct signs can embody approximately the same meaning (for example, *statue* and *sculpture*). Every sign, then, is potentially a synonym and a homonym at the same time, since in each case it results from a "crossing of two series of mental facts [*faits pensés*]" (p. 88). The homonymic series is constituted by psychological associations which conjure up the appurtenant thoughts or things for a given set of sounds, whereas the synonymic series is created by logical categories in which a given signification appears as a variant of the same class of concepts. Both series are of necessity open-ended. It remains forever unpredictable, on the one hand, in what "play of associations" (p. 91) the particular sign (that is, the vehicle of meaning) may participate and, on the other hand, how a different signification enters into a particular class of concepts (after all, no two words are thought to be absolutely synonymous).

If all signs are in principle so pliant and adaptable, evidently ready at any moment to assume a new function and/or find expression in another form, is language a realm of infinite possibilities? Karcevskij's vehement answer is no! Precisely the insertion of signs into one or the other series, which allots them a purely relative, differential or diacritical value, curtails any excessively idiosyncratic application.[8] We must come back to the fact that language is above all a social institution. A collective or supraindividual instrument, language is nevertheless constantly called upon to serve personal and subjective needs. To function properly, it must oscillate between the general and the individual, between the abstract and the concrete. This linguistic operation is facilitated by the circumstances that, as part of the *langue*, semiotic values exist only potentially,[9] while in individual utterance or *parole* these "virtual signs" become activated by being applied to a new aspect of concrete reality. But, of course, it is impossible for reality as such to be totally new, since it would be incomprehensible as well as unnameable: there is, in short, no perception without immediate categorization. As Karcevskij states, "the new becomes incorporated into the categories of the old and is recognized as a new genus of an old species [*un genre nouveau d'une espèce ancienne*]" (p. 89). Here is the rest of the argument:

[The new] is always a genus and not an individual. To recognize or understand a fact means to incorporate it into the ensemble of our knowledge, to establish the coordinates at the intersection of which this fact can be recovered. For what is really new is their relationship, their intersection, not the coordinates themselves. It goes without saying that an act of knowledge does not capture the individual fact. The real is infinite. In every situation we only retain certain elements of it, rejecting all the rest as irrelevant from the point of view of our interests. In this way we end up with a concept—the schematic product of an integration—intended from the first to serve as a general type. (p. 89)

Just as a "unique" fact is fated to be unintelligible, so too a "unique" word is inconceivable, for, like a fact, it is the outcome of a particular crossing of two general coordinations, this time the formal or grammatical and the semantic. It follows that a word likewise always designates a genus, not what is individual, or, in the more exact terms of modern logic, a verbal sign always presents a token of an existent type. Even a brand-new coinage is bound to behave like a sign, which means, as Karcevskij observes, that it is "capable of signifying analogous situations" (p. 92).[10] In the same breath, this neologism automatically becomes a generic term, finding itself included, as it must, in a synonymic series. But under these circumstances, we may ask, how can we tell whether a sign is well suited to represent what it is supposed to stand for? (*Aliquid stat pro aliquo*, something standing for something else, we recall, is the standard definition of the sign as framed by the Schoolmen.) Here Karcevskij postulates the double-edged notion of a *tertium comparationis*. On the synonymic side, it is the idea of conceptual class, as we have seen, which, in a concrete situation, provides a "center of radiation" (p. 91) of analogous values; with a view to the pertinent class we can determine whether the sign is "adequate" or "transposed" (figurative). And on the homonymic side, the center of radiation consists of an expanding cluster of associations gathered around the given sign's semantic value, and the *tertium comparationis* is provided by the everchanging situation in which the sign is deployed. Indeed, the exact value of the sign can be satisfactorily gauged solely within the specific context of its use. As Karcevskij writes,

every time we apply a word as a semantic value to concrete reality, we thereby recover a group of more or less new representations. Put differently, we continually transpose the semantic value of our sign. But we do not perceive this unless the deviation of the sign's value on this occasion from its "adequate" (usual) value is sufficiently great to make an impression on us. The identity of the sign is nevertheless maintained. The sign persists, in the first place, because our thought is prone to integration and refuses to take into account unexpected modifications in the complex of representations. The identity of the sign similarly appears to persist, in the second place, because, by introducing a *tertium comparationis*, we have thus motivated the new value of the old sign. (p. 91)

To be sure, the *tertium comparationis* as the referent of the particular situation is not an essential prerequisite in every context. In scientific discourse the value of a term is solidly established by its position within a system of ideas, and the possibility of deviation from the normative usage is for all intents and purposes eliminated. In ordinary speech situations, as well, a regulatory framework of ideas operates, though a much more lax one, which Karcevskij proposes we term the "ideology of everyday life" (p. 91). The ideological paradigm, if we might call it that, a sort of social contract cementing the ties within the speech community, offsets the quirks and caprices of individual interlocutors. According to Karcevskij, should we choose to call someone *Mr. Fish*, for instance, homonymically transposing the designation for vertebrate water animals (*piscis*), we thereby immediately inject this locution into a synonymic series comprised of such terms as *phlegmatic, flaccid, cold, unfeeling* and so forth. In this way, on the semantic level, signs not only transmit difference, as they do on the phonological level (for example, |p|en and |d|en), but simultaneously communicate difference and resemblance, homonymity and synonymity. To accomplish this intricate task, signs must be both mobile (to extend the range of applicability) and stable (to assure successful communicability) at the same time. Thanks to its supple semiotic mechanism, language thus manages to fight shy of two extremes: the fixity of simple naming, of leveling down to a "repertory of tags" (p. 88) valid once and for all, which is the ambition of mathematical and logical "languages"; and its opposite, outright dependency on the concrete situation, outside of which the signs cease to signify, as in the case of aphasics suffering from a similarity disorder, whose discourse deteriorates into a heap of deixes.

It is the "asymmetric dualism," the functional imbalance built into the very structure of signs, which enables language to negotiate between the contrary pulls of the social and the individual, the general and the particular, the abstract and the concrete, the already-known and the yet-unknown, the stable and the mobile—in short, to discern sameness in difference and, equally important, to discriminate between dissimilars. This structural irregularity or disproportion affects each of the four semiotic planes of language—the semantic (lexicological and syntagmatic) and the formal (morphological and phonological)—thereby enhancing its subtlety and flexibility. Take, for example, the morphological plane. In an inflectional language like Russian, one morpheme form may serve several case endings or meanings and, alternately, diverse morphemes may serve one case. Again in Russian, the form of the imperative can also be conveyed by the infinitive and can itself convey another verbal mood (or meaning), namely, the subjunctive. Yet there is a vital distinction between formal or grammatical and strictly semantic transpositions. While grammatical forms are socially shared, enforced to the point where individual manipulation is reduced to a minimum, on the semantic level there remains a "residue which resists all attempts at decomposition into 'objective' elements" (p. 91), whence, finally, the necessity of the *tertium comparationis*. Still, this ability to enlarge the register of transposed values of the same sign and to discover alternative signs to express analogous meanings or values is unmatched in nonverbal means of communication. For although a siren, say, can announce alarm as well as the end of a work shift and alarm can be sounded by other devices such as bells, the interplay of synonymity and homonymity is negligible here. This inflexibility distinguishes signs from mere signals.

The sign's lopsided structure also helps generate the historical movement of language, which Karcevskij eloquently depicts:

The *signifiant* (sound) and the *signifié* (function) continually glide along the "slope of reality." Each "overflows" the boundary assigned to it by its partner: the *signi-*

fiant seeks functions other than its proper function and the *signifié* seeks to express itself by means other than its sign. They are asymmetric; coupled together, they are in a state of unstable equilibrium. It is due to the asymmetric dualism in the structure of its signs that a linguistic system can evolve: the sign's "adequate" position being continuously displaced because of adaptations to the exigencies of the concrete situation. (p. 93)

Now the significance of semantics for general linguistics and particularly phonology emerges in full force. Language is in a process of perpetual "drifting,"[11] not only because its internal balance is constantly subverted, the system seesawing back and forth between *l'écart* and *l'équilibre* (or, in Jakobson's technical idiom, a dephonologization calling forth a stabilizing phonologization), but also because the very structure of the sign invites unending transformation. The structure of the verbal sign and the structure of the language system are homologous in that they operate on the same principle of dynamic equilibrium, or perhaps more accurately, productive disequilibrium. But while Jakobson's investigations of diachronic sound changes were confined to recording a sequence of phonological mutations without explaining the occurrence of particular changes at a particular time or the rapidity of such changes, Karcevskij shows the modifications language must undergo when confronted with the steady pressure of extralinguistic events. True, on the phonic level language functions to a great extent immanently, but this no longer applies to the semantic level, where, through acts of signification and communication, words are continually made to fit new realities. It is semantics, therefore, to which we should turn in the search for possible correlates between social action and "speaking."

Indeed, in addition to showing how semantic study builds upon and complements phonological study, Karcevskij indicated how to reintegrate *langue* and *parole*, which Saussure kept apart for heuristic reasons. Once we understand that the general scheme of things, of which language is both part and reflection, obeys such patterns as the type-token relation— the sign and the designatum alike arising at intersections of general coordinates—"speaking" will no longer be inimical to the language system and all changes will appear as systemic, not fortuitous. Unfortunately, perhaps overwhelmed by the extraordinary intricacies of his insight, Karcevskij managed to erect only the supporting pillars of his envisioned theoretical edifice, an elaboration of Saussure's *Cours*.[12] Nor did he find any followers among the younger members of the Prague Linguistic Circle.[13] He was simply ahead of his time; even so adept a student as Mukařovský took some ten years to assimilate the principles of asymmetric dualism.[14]

We might do well to backtrack at this point and, to trace more sharply the curve of Mukařovský's development, look briefly at his initial foray into the area of semantics, the second chapter of *Mácha's "May,"* which belongs to his presemiotic period. As I have pointed out earlier, Mukařovský here takes the concept of the sign to be synonymous with that of the word and is unconcerned with the asymmetry in its duplex structure. Nor does he delve into the questions of reference and of the truth of reference, but, like his formalist mentors, approaches the poem as a verbal construct *sui generis* not subject to these referential considerations.[15] Nevertheless, within the self-imposed limits of the internal analysis of textual properties, Mukařovský carries out his assignment with skill and conviction. In the main, Mukařovský's semantic explorations revolve around Mácha's handling of the poetic epithet, with the hinge-pin of the analysis being the conception of the "semantic nucleus" and "accessory meanings" (pp. 79–80).[16] It has often been observed that most words do not have a sole meaning given once and for all but that, chameleonlike, they acquire new shades of meaning under changing circumstances. Thus the word *earth* may, depending on the sentence, convey the connotations of *planet*, *globe*, *ground* or *soil*. Despite the varied overtones of accessory meanings, however, we can tell that the word *earth* possesses a central core of meaning which helps us reidentify it in diverse situations as the same word. (In homonymic usage, by contrast, we have in fact two words, albeit with identical sound shape.) One way to eliminate some less desirable semantic associations is by attaching an adjective (say, *fertile*) to the noun, whereby we single out those features which set the given phenomenon apart from the related ones. This is done by means of the so-called logical attribute. But the poetic *epitheton*, to attain its aesthetic effect, cannot simply qualify the appropriate noun but, like other figures, must seek to "give a foreign air to our language." As Aristotle argued and Mukařovský and the formalists appear to repeat almost verbatim, for diction to become "distinguished and nonprosaic" it must exploit all rhetorical devices, including the epithet, which "deviate from the ordinary modes of speech."[17]

The use of the epithet as a deviating, poetic trope is especially striking in Mácha. Witness the first two lines of *May*:

Byl pozdní večer—první máj,   (It was a late evening—the first of May,
Večerní máj—byl lásky čas   A crepuscular May—the time of love)

The phrase "a crepuscular May" differs markedly from the other expressions, for here the adjective is not subordinated to the noun it is supposed to modify but, rather, seems to go against it semantically.[18] There is a tension within the phrase created by the fact that, while the noun "May" indicates a particular series of days with mornings, noons or evenings, the epithet "crepuscular" cuts down this time span and so collides with the noun's semantic nucleus. This semantic disagreement is at its strongest in Mácha's locutions such as "ztracené světlo" (dead light), in which the adjective denies the existence of that which the noun is asserting; and it is also present, though less conspicuously, in expressions such as "daleká noc" (removed night), where a spatial signification is juxtaposed with a temporal one. In all these cases the noun's semantic nucleus, instead of establishing the "axis of signification" of the whole phrase, becomes suppressed, which brings about what Mukařovský describes as the "alternate surfacing and sinking of individual vague meanings" (p. 79) encircling the noun. In other words, where the logical attribute minimizes the number of accessory meanings, Mácha's poetic (or transferred) epithet multiplies them still further than is customary in standard informational language.

Even when Mácha's adjectives seem perfectly logical and unexceptional, they nevertheless function aesthetically because of their deliberate accumulation within the space of a few consecutive lines, which elevates these adjectives semantically above their adjacent substantives. This bunching of adjectives is then underscored by sound repetition (as in the first line: pozd*ní*—prv*ní*), by selection from the same semantic field (as when the poet amasses numerous attributes signifying colors in a short stanza) or, finally, by their prominent position at either the beginning or the end of the line or colon. This procedure, too, results in a slackening of the ties between adjectival epithets and their substantives and, with it, a releasing of a plethora of accessory meanings. The following two lines of the poem illustrate another type of weakening of the axis of signification:

Tam v modré dálce skály lom   (There in the blue distance a cliff's rift
Květoucí břeh jezera tíží   Weighs down on the blossoming shore
                                     of the lake)

Here the phrase "skály lom" (cliff's rift), a combination of a substantive with a substantive attribute in the possessive (genitive) case, strikes us as forced and peculiarly redundant. If we dropped the word "rift," the meaning of the entire phrase would scarcely be impoverished. Yet the word "cliff," which we would keep in ordinary discourse, is grammatically subordinated to the noun in the nominative case. Hence the principal semantic complex shifts from its proper place to the subordinate position of an attribute, with the noun in the nominative having the role of a mere grammatical prop. In this way, the semantic axis becomes disengaged as one semantic unit is split into two words, which once again impregnates the poetic expression with copious accessory meanings. Moreover, we note that in the two lines above the subject-predicate relation is also greatly out of kilter. Normally, the subject forms the semantic axis which the verbal predicate serves to determine or modify. But the verb "weigh down," just like Mácha's adjectives, gathers extra semantic power, representing the opposite of what we would expect, namely, that the cliff "towers above" the lake shore. Mácha's startling verb thus adds connotations of load and volume which immediately disappear when the line is transposed into informational language as "the cliff stands by the lake."

The semantic contrast between the subject and predicate is in places intensified into hyperbole, as well as personification, a species of pathetic fallacy through which Mácha, joining other romantics, credits inanimate objects with human actions. It goes without saying that all such poetic figures put a premium on the qualifying and subordinate verbal predicate at the expense of the superordinate substantive subject. The semantic inversions, caused by embracing or extensive epithets and emphatic verbs as contrasted with the neutralized nuclei of nouns in significant positions, ultimately topple the syntactic hierarchy of sentence structure. When the semantic axes of these many syntagmas (syntactic arrangements of subject and verb) become wobbly, the individual words of the phrase cease to relate as determining and determined. In syntactic isolation, lexical units lose their referential capacity and, deprived of their semantic center, give free reign to a multitude of peripheral meanings. Consequently, our attention is drawn not to the logical relations among the parts of the sentence but, on the contrary, to the "consonance and interpenetration of accessory meanings" (p. 108). This special feature of Mácha's style is most manifestly evidenced by one of the poem's leitmotifs, that of the reflection on the lake's surface which ricochets and blurs the lights and shapes of the ambient landscape. Here, tangibly and on a scale larger than the syntagma, the agitated accessory meanings without a fixed pivot are seen "rippling outward in all their variegated mutability" (p. 79). In sum, the semantics of poetic terms, tropes and motifs and of their manifold conjugations run parallel and jointly contribute to what traditional criticism impressionistically described as the dimming or obscuring of meaning in Mácha's poetry.

Although his analysis of poetic signification in *May* is as keen as it is inclusive, Mukařovský does not take up Mácha's manipulation of metaphor and metonymy. Nonetheless, he suggests elsewhere, following the example of Boris Tomaševskij, that the two master tropes, as well, lend themselves to a parsing into semantic nucleus and accessory meanings.[19] With other poetic figures, metaphor and metonymy share the principle that within each a novel and unexpected word (sometimes christened the vehicle) in a certain semantic context replaces another, more conventional term (the tenor). But the two rhetorical figures diverge in every other respect. In metaphor the two terms, the standard and the transferred, overlap to some degree in their accessory meanings and not in the basic semantic features, which, as Mukařovský insists, do not connect at all. Metaphor, hence, is neither a submerged simile nor an image that, to quote Aristotle, "puts the thing vividly before the eyes,"[20] because, in Mukařovský's view, "the basic meanings of the customary word and that which now enters the context affect the consciousness slightly, at times not at all, muffled as they are by the overshadowing accessory meanings" (p. 896). For example, in a commonplace metaphor like "stars" for "eyes," it is not the central meanings of "celestial body" and "organ of sight" that interact but the subsidiary meanings of "brightness" or "twinkling."

When the tension between the habitual term and its substitute fades away, so that the expression is no longer felt to be semantically double-edged, what we have is a "dead" metaphor—a metaphor like "the root of the word" or "the foot of the table" which has blended indiscernibly into its context of usage. If a fresh metaphor is relatively context-free, metonymy, on the other hand, is context-bound. It completely depends on the material, existential contact between the object designated by the standard literal term and another object designated by the new, figurative term. The connection may be spatial, temporal or causal. Where the connection between the two designated objects, and thus the figure's metonymic two-sidedness, is unknown—for instance, the fact that "redcoats" are English soldiers wearing red uniforms—the trope is not understood as such. In this kind of a metonymy there is no verbal interplay of any kind between the terms' principal and accessory meanings; rather, the connecting link exists solely on the level of objective, extraverbal reality. The figurative impact of a metonymic trope can also be lost by its overuse in such clichéd expressions as "reading Shakespeare" or "living by one's wits," which automatically take the place of literal expressions. To remain vital, therefore, metonymy as well as synecdoche (distinguishable from metonymy only by convention) must, just like all metaphoric tropes, preserve their crucial twofold aspect of, to coin a phrase, contextual double entendres.

In drawing so sharp a distinction between metaphor and metonymy, one motivated exclusively by the language code and the other exclusively by concrete reality, Mukařovský parts ways with Aristotle and most modern theorists of metaphor (metonymy generally being a topic of little theoretical interest). Even the proponents of the newer verbal-opposition theory who come closest to concurring with Mukařovský that metaphor "turns" on a selection from a repertoire of marginal, not central, meanings still claim that one must take into account the relevant properties of the referred-to objects.[21] According to this view, metaphor is no mere pairing and alternation of two previously unrelated terms,[22] but, at least as importantly, the fruit of a novel perception of resemblance between two things which ordinarily stand far apart. Furthermore, we may add, as metaphor should not be demoted to a search for purely verbal synonymy, so, conversely, metonymy should not be wholly cast out from the verbal sphere. For all such universalizing philosophical statements, not infrequent in poetry, as "The real is the rational" can be taken as abstract verbal and nonmaterial metonymies (or *pars pro toto* synecdoches), since "the rational," here imputed to everything, has acquired its meaning in normal usage in which it applies to less than everything. In other words, metaphor does not boil down to a dictionary choice among mutually substitutable expressions, and metonymy, by the same token, does not shrink to a case of concrete and material contiguity.

Mukařovský's problematic attempt at categorically separating the verbal from the nonverbal features of poetic figures exactly parallels his sorting out, in the Mácha study, of those forms in poetry which are intrinsically linguistic, the highest unit, as we know, being the syntagma, from the extrinsic motifs, that is, narrative units larger than the syntagma. Yet Mukařovský himself is forced to admit in several places that the borderline—say, between the so-called semantic personification occasioned by apportioning an exceptional semantic load to a verb (for example: "břeh je [jezero] *objímal* kol a kol" [the shore *embraced* the lake round and round]) and the motif personification actuated by an "external idea"—is far from clear. Unfortunately, the motif is already beyond the ken of his semantic (although not, as we have seen, of his thematic) inquiry, which is geared only to the analysis of the "verbal" facets of poetic language. In the end, all this points to the fact that Mukařovský conceives rather narrowly—formalistically—both of the fundamental modes of discourse: poetic language, on the one hand, is completely self-contained and nonreferential, while standard informational language, on the other, is completely tractable and transparent, providing as ready an access to exterior referents as if the need of a *tertium comparationis* never arose. But, to repeat, this undertaking of Mukařovský's was merely the first of a long series of gradually advancing investigations into literary semantics.

‖●‖●‖●‖●‖●‖

It was once again the study of film, which had earlier accelerated the understanding of immanent structural interrelations, that now forwarded the structuralists' comprehension of the interdependence of aesthetic signs and reality. Sensitive to the semiotic implications of the film medium, Jakobson, among others, hailed the emergence and impact of this youngest of the arts in most glowing terms:

In art it was the cinema that disclosed clearly and emphatically to countless viewers that language is merely one of the possible sign systems, just as astronomy had revealed that the earth is only one among numerous planets, thereby radically changing the view of the world. The voyage of Columbus had in essence already signaled the end of the myth of the Old World's exclusiveness, yet only the modern success of America dealt it the final blow. Similarly, film was at first regarded as no more than an exotic colony of art, and only as it developed step by step did it smash the ruling ideology [of the latter half of the nineteenth century, that period of a violent inflation of linguistic signs].[23]

The reason why cinema, rather than any of the traditional arts, helped undermine the hegemony of the verbal sign, fostered so prominently by the belief of realistic and naturalistic literature in the mimetic potency of the word, was really quite simple. Cinema reversed the fundamental principles of artistic representation. Whereas in literature, as well as other arts, the elementary materials are signs which stand for or signify people and things, in film the elementary materials are the people and things themselves, literally the furniture of the world, whether still or in motion.[24] Thus in a novel, for instance, the verbal signs constituting the narrative organize themselves so as to re-create the world of things, but in film the world is there, very recognizably, from the very beginning. The task of the filmmaker, therefore, is not so much to duplicate or create the semblance of the world, which is achieved by and large automatically, as to impose a narrative order on the randomness of the photographed reality.

How can this be done? How can there be an art whose medium is physical reality as such, and not the verbal, visual or auditory signs of literature, painting or music? An answer to this dilemma, which still leads, or misleads, some to deny the cinema's claim to art, can be found in Saint Augustine, who here, too, anticipated much of modern semiotic thought. As Augustine observed, along with the signs representing objects, there are also objects that may be deployed as signs. And so Jakobson could assert, as Tynjanov did before him, that "it is precisely things, visual and auditory, transformed into signs, which are the specific material of cinematic art" (p. 45).[25]

The familiar film terminology of closeups and medium, full and long shots directs our attention to the characteristically cinematic conversion of persons and objects into signs, which is in most cases by dint of part-for-whole synecdoches. Hence a closeup of marching feet can represent an army, driving wheels an automobile, a gun a gunman, flipping calendar pages the passing of days and so on in endless permutations. As Jakobson says, "film works with various and varied fragments of objects which differ in magnitude, and also with fragments of time and space likewise varied; it changes the proportions of these fragments and juxtaposes them in terms of contiguity, or similarity and contrast" (p. 46). Owing largely to its concrete physical nature, however, film mostly follows the course of metonymy as a means of linking separate shots, which helps explain its strong "realistic" leanings: at least as much as the nineteenth-century realistic novel, cinema condenses narrative by means of figures founded upon contiguity.[26] Filmic metaphors arise at the abrupt junctures of montage typical of the Soviet film of the 1920s, where the motivation of the metaphor tended to be ideological and didactic, or in the equally outmoded technique of lap dissolves, extended filmic similes. In exceptional instances metaphor comes about through the use of closeup, as when Eisenstein photographs a pair of eyes to signify conscience.[27] Of more recent films, Karel Reisz's *Morgan!* (1966) comes to mind as an example of a predominantly metaphoric mode, in which metaphors are produced through the hero's associating certain kinds of human physiognomy, gesture and behavior with corresponding features in the animal kingdom: if Achilles, in the classical example, is a lion, then Morgan, in the picture, is a gorilla. But the film's subtitle, *A Suitable Case for Treatment*, indicates how farfetched this type of construction is felt to be in most present-day cinema.[28]

But let us return to Jakobson's essay, written at a time when the advent of sound upset many cherished theoretical assumptions about the "inherent" possibilities of cinema. Here Jakobson and other structuralists, wholeheartedly welcoming the new technical invention, showed greater perspicacity than such astute commentators as Erwin Panofsky or Rudolf Arnheim.[29] Displaying the fine historical sense, Jakobson cautioned against comparing the sophisticated, developed art of silent movies with the incipient state of the talkies, still groping for appropriate forms of expression. In fact, Jakobson claimed, it may well have been the very perfection achieved in silent masterpieces, "this completion of a classical canon [that] contained its own demise as well as the necessity for a thorough reform" (p. 46). He further argued, in a way which prefigures current theories about the anxiety of influence, that in a country like Czechoslovakia, unburdened by a tradition of classical silent works, the transition to sound film should be much less troublesome than, for example, in Russia. Besides, filmmakers have no reason to fear the introduction of sound, since sounds function in cinema as auditory objects and, just like any other objects, are immediately transformed into signs. This being the case, sound cannot possibly be alien to motion pictures, because sonic reality is subject to the same semiotic conversion as visual reality. In sound film, silence, too, becomes an auditory object and is "valued as an actual absence of sound" (p. 47), in other words, as a sign of real silence. Perhaps the best modern example of the distinct effect of the nonpresence of sound in film is a minute of memorial silence in Michelangelo Antonioni's *The Eclipse* (*L'Eclisse*, 1962). And speech in cinema is likewise only a special kind of auditory object and as such no different in kind from street noise, machine din or nature murmur. The only means of eliminating all auditory objects—speech, silence and other natural sounds—is through music, which, thanks to its nonrepresentational quality as an "art operating with signs that do not relate to any objects" (p. 47), shields the audience from acoustic reality. This ineluctable semiotic transformation of sights as well as sounds in principle distinguishes spoken film from the theatre—the seeming resemblance between the two being a major source of worry to film purists—since in the former speech is converted into another auditory object, while in the latter it is, as Aristotle insisted, a mode of human action, real and not reproduced.

Working, at this new stage of development, with both visual and auditory signs, film's potential range of expression became enriched rather than impoverished. Not only could one now metonymically bring together disparate details of the visual world, but one could also create new cinematic configurations by combining the photographed objects with the appropriate, or inappropriate, sounds. Separate scenes, as well, could be linked by purely aural means, providing continuity even when action visually moved to another location. In fact, two avant-garde film directors, both of whom happened to be closely associated with the Circle, accepted the challenge of sound, striving, in the words of Vladislav Vančura (1891–1942), to perfect a technique of the "auditory dissolve" and the "auditory grotesque" in order to devise a "symphony of detonations"; Jindřich Honzl (1894–1953) proposed to experiment with the dialectical tension between word and picture, or what he called the "permanent conflict between auditory 'images' and the reality that the auditory 'image' stands for."[30] Finally, the most important contribution of sound, as the Circle's theoreticians and practitioners realized, was that the rhythm of the spoken word could serve as the base for the overall dramatic rhythm of alternating shots and thus significantly condition the movie's completed Gestalt.[31]

Yet despite his acuity in spotting the yet untested possibilities of filmic semiosis of sound, and despite his exceptional care not to impose arbitrary critical injunctions on the quickly evolving art of the movies, some of Jakobson's judgments about permissible means of cinematic expression were nonetheless belied by later developments. For example, arguing against the alleged subservience of the talkies to the theatre, Jakobson asserted that, as types of behavior rather than auditory objects, stage devices for conveying interior speech like the soliloquy, aside or stage whisper were profoundly foreign to the nature of cinema. But, like modern art in general, film refuses to heed its own innate inhibitions and promiscuously crosses over to other artistic domains. Ingenious contemporary comedy such as Woody Allen's *Annie Hall* (1977) adopts lock, stock and barrel the devices Jakobson censured to what now seem perfectly cinematic purposes—which, incidentally, goes to show that, as in the earliest days, comedy continues to be in the vanguard as far as the expansion of film vocabulary is concerned. Jakobson also promulgated the so-called law of chronological incompatibility, namely, that only a succeeding, not a preceding or simultaneous, action can follow a filmed event (cf. p. 48). In a manner analogous to Homeric poetics, Jakobson submitted, a past action in sound film can appear only as a narrator's or a character's reminiscence; and a simultaneous event can be presented only as if it were a consecutive one or by a simple omission of one of two parallel actions. If the sequence of two scenes is motivated not by contiguity but by similarity or contrast—that is to say, metaphorically—this law may be circumvented; but such rapid montage is likely to startle or puzzle as, in Jakobson's apt wording, "semantically overloaded" (p. 48). Again, nowadays the viewer deciphers without much difficulty a whole battery of crosscuts, flashbacks and flash-forwards, multiple exposures and split-screen actions—not only in past, "simultaneous" or future tense but as hypothetical modes of conditional or imperative.

In all fairness, though, Jakobson was not far off target in spotlighting the "linear" character of film time. Even today cinematic attempts at reshaping the flow of time give films a contrived, cerebral and, for movies, uncharacteristically highbrow quality: suffice it to recall any of Alain Resnais' films. Dramatic soliloquy, likewise, is still a rare occurrence, most likely to show up on the screen in the guise of a comic monologue or, as in Laurence Olivier's *Henry V* (1945), drastically recast in "oblique" close-ups with offscreen recitation. In one crucial respect, however, the subsequent development of cinematic narrative structure did prove Jakobson correct: it did by and large relinquish montage and the metaphoric play with pictorial images in favor of more continuous plot construction, as akin to prose as the montage was to poetry. It is as if Jakobson, with a head start of about twenty years, foreshadowed the theories of André Bazin and his school, so influential to this day.[32]

Mukařovský's contribution to the film semiotics of the thirties appears no less foresighted, for he shared Jakobson's unbiased view of the current—that is to say, passing—stage in the history of film art. For this reason, Mukařovský's two essays on film may be read as a sequel amplifying the ideas of Jakobson's article.[33] As much as Jakobson, in true formalist tradition, was bent upon identifying the specific "hero" of cinematic art, Mukařovský, expressing a more structuralist concern, set out to analyze the nature of aesthetic norms in film. Both theorists concurred, to be sure, that the function and the potential range of an artistic device, the specific hero included, cannot be grasped atomistically apart from the assembly of structural norms that underlie it. Such norms, as mentioned earlier and discussed in subsequent sections, are certainly not prescriptive or forever binding. In Mukařovský's structural aesthetics, "a norm can only be the product of the development of art itself, a petrified imprint of a historical activity" (p. 100). Instead of legislating *a priori* exactly what a particular art can or cannot do, Mukařovský wanted to uncover the "basic possibilities provided by the character of the material and the way in which the given art masters it" (p. 101). The confusion attending the birth of the art of cinema, compounded by the cinema's unprecedented dependence on technology, sprang precisely from a general ignorance of the specifically cinematic norms—the norms to measure up to or—just as effective artistically—to deviate from.

Because film is a most syncretic art—one could say it is the *Gesamtkunstwerk* of the twentieth century as was the opera of the nineteenth—from its inception it leaned toward one or the other of the arts: the theatre, the novel, painting and so on. This bewildering fluctuation took place in the early stages when, unsure of itself, film sought support from these sister arts. Had film possessed greater "certainty in handling the material," instead of being helplessly subordinated to it, such recurrent "transgressions of boundaries" would have been historically quite legitimate. For, once able to integrate into its structure of signifying devices the aesthetic impulses from the neighboring arts, the motion picture could follow its own path of development. According to Mukařovský, the arts are subject to a single legitimate limitation, namely, that "a given art does not cease to be itself even when it spills over into the territory of another art" (p. 101).

Consider, for example, the irreducible difference between space in cinema and in the theatre. No better proof is needed that no two arts ever fully merge: they either achieve "the same effect through different devices or attain different effects through the same device" (ibid.). Besides the obvious disparity between the three-dimensional stage and the two-dimensional screen—that is, between a real space and a projected illusory one—there is the fact that film tends to obliterate the distinction between animate and inanimate objects, between actors and props, which is central to the theatre. In film, people and things are open to much the same (metonymic) fragmentation or dismemberment. Whether you think of Chaplin and the Murphy bed or Keaton and the locomotive, of the two principal characters and the Manderley mansion in Alfred Hitchcock's *Rebecca* (1940) or the man and woman and windshield wiper in Claude Lelouch's *A Man and a Woman* (*Un homme et une femme*, 1966), the human protagonists and their slightly less animate antagonists, large and small, are on almost equal footing. In other words, rather than being the undisputed center as in the theatre, in film the human figure is usually a part or fragment of the total picture—which brings film space closer to pictorial space.

Film does, indeed, share the two key devices of painting, of illusory or virtual space. One such device is the reversal of perspective and depth perception, as when a gesture or movement is directed not toward the background of the picture but outward toward the viewer. The Lumière brothers put this device to good effect in the famous scene with an onrushing train (*L'Arrivée d'un train en gare de la Ciotat*, 1895); and a similar effect of reversed depth perception can be obtained in a tracking shot by mounting the camera on the forward-moving train or dolly. The other device is the use of special angles from below or above, substituting a vertical for a horizontal viewpoint, in which case, as Mukařovský notes, "the illusion [of pictorial space] is intensified by deautomatizing the position of the axis of vision" (p. 102). Still, there is one form of representing space that sets film apart from painting—space depicted by means of the film shot. Every new shot requires either refocusing the camera on another object, or part thereof, or relocating the camera in another space. And as the camera shifts and moves, so in a way does the spectator. Here painting is no match. "Only through the discovery of the shot," according to Mukařovský, "did film stop being an animated picture" (p. 102). The possibility of changing shots led to the elaboration of the closeup, that eminently filmic technique, which not only magnifies the photographed object but, in addition, makes us aware that what we see is a mere detail, a slice cropped out from the three-dimensional space that lies beyond the frontal and lateral limits of the shot. It is this heightened awareness of the space outside the picture, of signified things left out, which distinguishes photography from cinema, the former presenting us with a comparatively static detail and the latter with a dynamic closeup. The sensation of the presence of momentarily invisible space is increased in sound movies, especially in reaction shots in a dialogue, where instead of the speaker we see the addressee, all the while being intensely aware of the space, outside our purview, from which the sound issues.

If film space is similar to yet distinct from stage and pictorial space, is it perhaps more akin to space in literature? Indeed it is, affirms Mukařovský, for film space is neither real as in the theatre nor illusory as in painting, but, as in literature, it is space imbued with *meaning*. A series of separate shots which breaks a unified space into segments operates on the same principle as the sentence. It forms a significant whole. Moreover, in both instances this totality is not expressed at once but unfolds successively. A single shot, like the isolated part of the sentence, cannot convey the meaning of the whole, which, nonetheless, is potentially present in every element of the scene or the sentence. For this reason Mukařovský proposes that we term space in cinema "space-signification." "The illusory [i.e., pictorial—FWG] partial segments presented in consecutive images," Mukařovský argues, "are partial signs of this space-signification, the totality of which 'signifies' the complete space" (p. 104). Since, as a whole, this space emerges from a differentiated shot sequence, it follows that space functions as a semantic element only thanks to the change in shots. Owing to the power of film space and, as we shall see, of film time to signify, it is no idle fancy to speak, as did Boris Eichenbaum, of film sentences or film tropes.[34]

Notwithstanding the semantic kinship between literature, a structure of verbal signs, and cinema, a structure of audiovisual as well as verbal signs, there is one paramount difference between the two arts. This dissimilarity prevents a mechanical transposition of literature into cinema, for while the verbal sign knows no spatial limits, the shot, the filmic sign, is spatially bounded. As Mukařovský did not fail to notice, however, space-signification—conveyed as it is, for instance, through dynamic closeups signifying the space outside the visible frame—does approximate the boundlessness of the word.[35] Nevertheless, although there are words devoid of all spatial properties, a film shot apart from or transcending space is inconceivable. Thus, even if film can deal in abstractions, it cannot by definition picture them. Weighed down by the ubiquity of concrete reality, cinema lacks the abstracting and condensing faculty of the word.

The ability to switch at will from one semantic context to another, on the other hand, is yet another characteristic common to both literature and cinema. In the latter medium, such a change of context is executed by shifting the action to another space, a shift which, in film, is always semantically charged. Sudden transitions into another place of action, unexpected montage juxtapositions, may, as Jakobson warned, prove to be so semantically overloaded as to disorient the viewer. While a change of shots within a scene takes place in a unified, homogeneous space, a transition to another space, a change in the scene of action, disrupts the continuity between successive shots. In Mukařovský's account, there are three cinematic devices that facilitate a changeover to a new space. In current terminology, these are the jump cut, the dissolve and the match cut. Depending on the structure of a particular movie, each device can signify diverse occurrences. The jump cut, yoking together two or more noncontiguous events, may communicate a telegraphic version of the plot action. The fade out may indicate a temporal lapse between two events; and the dissolve, a superimposition of a fade in over a fade out, usually alludes to a dream, a recollection or an imagined, hypothetical action. The third bridging device, the match cut, links two distinct scenes through an exclusively metaphorical parallelism, as, to give a more recent example, in Stanley Kubrick's *2001: A Space Odyssey* (1968), setting side by side the functions of a prehistoric bone-instrument spinning in the air and a futuristic space station orbiting in space as analogous extensions of human capacities. Besides the metaphor, another purely semantic transition between two spatially unconnected incidents is by means of the filmic anacoluthon, a visual joke, where, according to one movie cliché, a shot of two people in passionate embrace is succeeded by a shot of fireworks. Finally, sound film further eases a progression from one scene to a subsequent but spatially remote one: a destination is first mentioned and then shown. As Mukařovský, Jakobson and most later commentators agreed, it is the gradual techniques of transition, rather than quick montage, that are gaining the upper hand as cinema gets a better grip on its artistic means. In sum, sound film's successive unfurling of action gravitates toward ever-greater spatial continuousness, with the effect of letting people and parts of people and objects draw attention according to their natural weight, instead of manipulating perception through cinematic tricks.

A last but most important feature shared by film and literature is that these are principally arts of telling a story, film rather more so than literature. In lyric poetry the story-line is dispensed with or kept to a minimum. A plotless film, by contrast, is at best an epiphenomenon, which is a consequence of cinema's radical inversion of the rules of artistic signification mentioned at the outset of this discussion. In other words, mimesis, that traditional goal of artistic representation, is achieved more or less automatically in motion pictures; what is not, and cannot be, arrived at through mechanical reproduction is mythos, plot or narrative, that significant collocation of people and things to be designed by the film creators. This is to say that plot, in film as much as in verbal art, is a specific form of meaning, of a meaning displayed over time. As Mukařovský wrote, "plot is not only contingent upon the quality of motifs but also upon their succession," for "if you change the sequence of motifs, you thereby also change the plot" (p. 107). In this respect, cinematic plot development resembles the consecutive revealment of space-signification. These two progressive semantic series, though concurrent, need not, however, be parallel. Indeed, the manifold relations between plot and the spaces in which it runs its course can be put to various uses. Even though plot is generally the film's fundamental semantic series, with space-signification serving as a "differentiating factor" (p. 107), this hierarchy may be turned upside down. As an example of a film where the plot, if any, is subservient to a dramatic array of interrelated spaces, Mukařovský cited Dziga Vertov's attempt in *The Man with a Movie Camera* (*Čelovek s kinoapparatom*, 1929), in which a single caption—say, "A Day in the Streets of Moscow"—could easily sum up the whole story. At the opposite pole is the primitive form of filmed theatre, where the story unwinds in front of a motionless camera, placing plot action into a static, semantically empty space. Recent experiments have gone further toward eroding this semantic plot-space foundation of cinema: abstract films, while teeming with kinetic imagery, forego both photographing reality and telling a story, thus producing a visual equivalent of noise; and Andy Warhol's experiments feature a static camera focused for hours on the equally immobile Empire State Building, seeking, it seems, to create a visual embodiment of boredom.

Between the two extremes of the "roving" and the "transfixed" camera runs the mainstream of contemporary cinema. To these nonabstract, narrative films applies Mukařovský's observation that the more a film relies on a temporal and causal joining of motifs, the more straightforward the story, the easier it is to exploit the semantic potential of space-signification. For a director eager to explore the uniquely cinematic dynamism of space, two main lines of approach offer themselves. Here is Mukařovský's description:

> . . . the dynamization of space is not a simple concept: shots function in the structure of cinema in a different way than do the changes in scene. It is thus possible to distinguish between plots which lend themselves easily to sharp breaks between individual shots—here plot motivation is moved chiefly into the interior of the dramatic characters, so that unusual transitions between shots can be interpreted as shifts in the field of vision of the characters themselves—and those plots susceptible to a frequent change in scene, which are grounded in the characters' external actions. (pp. 107–8)

As Mukařovský emphasized, this is a description, an epistemological investigation of the material of film, not a norm-setting prescription. As such, his account is as perceptive, accurate and valid today as it was forty years ago.

Mukařovský's brief supplementary study of film time has aged equally well. Indeed, this part of Mukařovský's contribution to film semiotics stands out just as sharply against the backdrop of the thirties, considering that the two leading contemporary theorists cited earlier, Erwin Panofsky and Rudolf Arnheim, a historian of art and a psychologist of perception, were rather one-sidedly preoccupied with spatial configurations, which, of course, tied cinema in with their respective fields, but which left little room for the consideration of cinematic time. The very fact that film is a time-art disassociates it from painting and sculpture, while bringing it into close alliance with theatre and epic narration. But despite their proximity as arts of plot, each stringing a group of events into a causally motivated sequence, film, drama and narrative fiction exhibit fundamentally different temporal structures. This special functioning of time, like that of space, guarantees each art its ineradicable specificity and autonomy and prevents the usurpation of one art's role by another.

Let us take another look at the kindred arts of cinema, theatre and narrative and ask how time works in each of them. If we recall the neoclassical idea of a threefold dramatic unity, we realize at once that, even if those normative principles are not adhered to, there are severe constraints in theatre on the artistic manipulation of the temporal dimension. To begin with, time in drama is unidirectional and nonreversible. It is as difficult to present two simultaneous actions on the stage as it is to find a way of staging an antecedent event with which to explain, retrospectively or in a theatrical flashback, so to speak, the current state of affairs. This is so because the time locus of the theatregoer and that of the play is always the present: the dramatic action takes place in the audience's presence even if the performance itself is of a historical play. Thus, although there are in the theatre two temporal levels, that of the plot and that of the audience, they necessarily run parallel to each other. This simultaneity or synchronism, however, does not exist in the reading of prose narrative. Readers can read the book at leisure, skip or interrupt their reading or speed-read. As far as epic narration goes, the readers' time, according to Mukařovský, is felt merely "as an indefinite present without temporal measure, detached from the elapsing past in which the story takes place" (p. 180).

The time of narration, in contrast to that of drama, is without any relation to the time of reading. The independence of the two time zones accounts for innumerable narrative strategies, unknown to theatre, for compressing the story into a time capsule, so that events spanning a generation may be told in a sentence or two.

Cinema offers a third alternative in artistic presentation of the time continuum. Film-time partakes of the attributes of both theatre- and narrative-time, adding a third level or dimension, that of screen-time, which mediates between the first two. Screen-time, given technically by the projection of twenty-four frames per second, has all the earmarks of stage-time: screen-time, too, is necessarily contemporaneous with the time of the spectator. There are similar limits in the live theatre and the movie theatre as to how long anyone can sit still, which only invites filmmakers like Erich von Stroheim in *Greed* (1923) or Hans-Jürgen Syberberg in *Hitler, a Film from Germany* (*Hitler, ein Film aus Deutschland*, 1977), to defy the extent of the audience's commitment and endurance.[36] This illustrates the fact that, in both theatre and cinema, audience-time is not an inert or neutral quantity as in reading but that, on the contrary, it is activated or deautomatized. Yet while sharing the physical circumscription of theatre-time, film-time also shares the boundlessness and bendability of narrative-time. In contrast to stage-play time, screen "play" time is not identical with the film story-time. In the theatre, as noted, the dramatic action takes place in the audience's presence, and the audience can participate in the play, should the stage direction call for it. This kind of involvement is impossible in cinema—or rather, it can happen only in the movies themselves, in a comedy like Buster Keaton's *Sherlock, Jr.* (1924), which parodies the hopelessness of the filmgoer's dream of joining the life on the screen, or in the Czech Laterna Magika, an ingenious mix of stage and film techniques. The film story-time, in other words, has its locus in the past. What filmviewers watch is a filmed "report" about events that happened some time before they entered the movie house. To put it differently, whereas the film story unreels in the viewers' presence, the viewers themselves are not present to it. Such, in brief, are the *differentia specifica* of film art.

Film story-time knows no bounds, for, like narrative-time, it is infinitely malleable. It can be stretched—in Michail Kalatozov's *The Cranes Are Flying* (*Letjat žuravli*, 1957) the hero's death, which in reality takes a few seconds, is shown in an extended sequence comparable to Ambrose Bierce's story of a man whose whole life, including his escape from execution, flashes before his eyes only moments before he is hanged; and it can also be condensed or telescoped in so-called bridging shots of falling calendar pages, newspaper headlines or changing seasons which (metonymically) abbreviate the duration of an action in much the same way as the terse but panoramic sentences of the epic.

In film, then, there are three strata of time: the story-time of the past and the screen- and audience-time, both located in the present. The resulting triple interplay of film-time generates a more complex structure than that of either the theatre or the literary narrative, one which combines, and transcends, the advantages of the other two modes of art.[37] As in the theatre, filmviewers can have a sensation of immediacy and verisimilitude, of events happening in front of their eyes. Yet at any moment the screen-time can frustrate the audience's identification with the story action. As in the narrative, the plot and the natural sequence of events may diverge and run along separate routes, so that in film, too, we should discriminate, with the help of Šklovskij's categories, between the *sjužet* (plot) and the *fabula* (story-stuff).[38] Thanks to screen-time, film is capable of portraying nearly static, atemporal configurations, as when one or several closeups of a figure or a room show us at length what could be seen at a glance. A good example here is the opening scene in Jiří Menzel's *Closely Watched Trains* (*Ostře sledované vlaky*, 1966) where a fumbling dispatcher trainee dons his new uniform, which the camera lovingly inspects, climbing slowly upward like some crawling insect until it reaches the young man's head, on which, in a timeless gesture of mock coronation, his mother places the official cap. The whole act, since it is all filmed in closeup, seems to take place outside of time, with both the unreal prolongation of action and the excessive enlargement of the camera's view making everything look truly hilarious. This filmic description is made possible because, even though the plot action is momentarily arrested, screen-time, which has all the continuity and mechanical regularity of clock-time, elapses coinstantaneously and in unison with audience-time. Moreover, in these interstices between screen-time, tightly overlapping with audience-time, and story-time, free to follow its own course, arise specifically filmic possibilities of slow, fast and reverse motion. Overcranking the camera, so that the film runs through it faster than the standard twenty-four frames a second, makes the projected movement take longer in screen-time than in reality; and the opposite holds for undercranking. The correlation between screen-time and story-time will appear still more paradoxical in reverse motion, since the progressive succession of screen- and audience-time collides head-on with the story-time running backward.

Small wonder that these sophisticated cinematic techniques have in turn begun influencing the artistic methods of the theatre in the use of rear projection and the like, as well as those of prose narrative, whether in elaborate descriptive vignettes (a kind of literary closeup prefaced by sentences like "Her eyes fell upon . . .") or in literary analogues of panning shots in which the verbal description follows the character's shifting field of vision or, finally, in the staccato style of verbal collage to be found in the prose of Šklovskij or the surrealists, which is a literary reenactment of montage.

To reiterate, then, the possibility of derailing or deforming the temporal procession of events discloses the singular feature of screen-time—that it alone is exempt from the tyranny of clock-time, from the relentless consecutiveness of chronology. Story-time, on the other hand, is the time of "real" events; and audience-time is similarly a projection of real-time into the structure of the work of film art, and thus captive to pure linearity. It is only by virtue of the screen-time that—to invoke an ancient distinction which Frank Kermode reintroduced into modern criticism—*chronos* is converted into *kairos*, that the interval of tick-tock becomes filled with significance.[39] But to divest this dichotomy of its theological overtones, we had best follow Mukařovský's suggestion and designate the time of the cinematic work of art itself—or, as Mukařovský put it, "the temporal span of the work . . . as a sign" (p. 183)—as semiotic time.

Sign-time is the time of artistic signification, not of physical reality. If so, the third stratum of semiotic time must exist in the other arts as well, or else they would be indistinguishable from nonartistic temporal processes. As Mukařovský observed, in both drama and narrative, semiotic time manifests itself as tempo, the pace of staged events, or as the swiftness or sluggishness of narration. In contrast to the cinema, where the screen-time—or we might also say projection-time—is measurable in duration or quantity, the tempo of theatrical performance or literary narration appears as an elusive quality coloring and nuancing the particular work. The overriding distinction between film, on the one hand, and theatre and narrative, on the other, is not that the former has more time levels than the latter two. Rather, to quote Mukařovský, "film is an art in which all three strata assert themselves equally" (p. 183), whereas in the rival arts of theatre and literature one layer of time comes to the fore, relegating the companion time levels to an ancillary role. While in the theatre, to repeat, audience-time holds sway over story-time, in narrative fiction it is story-time which predominates, with the cadence of re-presented actions, shown or told, molding the work's finished shape. Finally, rounding out the interassociation of the arts, there is the art which elevates into prominence semiotic time itself and nullifies the time of the audience as well as of the story: the art of lyric poetry. This salience of semiotic time—or, conversely, this independence from chronological time—explains why the structure of lyric is governed by and founded upon rhythm, the measured recurrence of the same phrase units. For it is with the help of rhythm, as Mukařovský rightly claimed, that the semiotic time of poetry ceases to be amorphous and unbounded and becomes, instead, a measurable quantity.

In this way, by contrast and comparison, the Prague School structural investigations of sign-time identify the distinctive characteristics of semiotic space and time not only in film but in the remaining arts as well, showing the similarities and differences of each.

‖●‖●‖●‖●‖●‖

This excursion into the cinema has not been a wasteful detour for the Prague structuralists (nor, I trust, for us). Jakobson and Mukařovský were not playing hooky, straying from their proper line of inquiry into the problems of verse and of poetic language. If, so long as the structuralists devoted their attention to poetry alone, they remained within a self-enclosed and seemingly self-referential world of verbal art, now the movie screen offered them, as it were, a window onto the outside world of everyday affairs. To be sure, not even in the case of film did Jakobson and Mukařovský subscribe to a naive version of realism, of a cinematically truthful and literal duplicate of the depicted reality. Rather, through their study of film signification, they conclusively proved that even this apparently perfect mimetic art is subject to semiotic conversion. For what generates meaning in cinema is not a principle of identity between the spatial, temporal, causal nexus of the world as we experience it in our day-to-day lives and the world as we observe it in our experience of the movies but precisely a principle of difference. In other words, it is only because people and objects and their experiential coordinates of time and space are free from the constraints of the physical universe that we can have an art of film, or, more precisely, an art of filmic signification.

It is scarcely a coincidence, then, that, once having solved the problem of film semiosis and explained the paradox of the reverse roles performed by verbal and visual signs, both Jakobson and Mukařovský ventured to define all art as a structure of signs.[40] The consequences of such a semiotic redefinition are revolutionary. The essence of this methodological breakthrough is effectively summed up in Roman Jakobson's well-known assertion from his paper "What Is Poetry?": "What we emphasize is not the separatism of art but the autonomy of aesthetic function" (p. 30).[41] (Interestingly, under "we" Jakobson here joins his fortunes with Tynjanov, Šklovskij and Mukařovský in an attempt to defend the "formalist study of literature." It is a touching, if somewhat anachronistic, gesture of allegiance, a way of stressing a continuity between the work of the Opojaz and that of the Prague Linguistic Circle, even though Tynjanov, Šklovskij and other formalists were forced to abandon literary theory altogether after

1930.)[42] This is how, echoing Tynjanov's joint manifesto of principles of 1928 with which this discussion of structuralism began, Jakobson amplified his forceful maxim: ". . . we do not proclaim the self-sufficiency of art but, rather, demonstrate that art is a component part of the social structure. Correlated with other component parts, art is constantly changing, since both the sphere of art and its relationship to other segments of the social structure are in dialectical flux" (ibid.).

Although no longer in strict isolation, cast out of the social domain, art does not lose its special identity, the aesthetic mode of existence. In terms of a dialectic of blindness and insight, we may say that Jakobson's reformulation retains the fundamental insight of formalism concerning the unique status and functioning of poetic art while removing much of formalism's methodological blindness. We can best understand the development of Jakobson's thought by juxtaposing two of his ingenious efforts, made a dozen years apart, at identifying the constitutive characteristics of poetry and literature in general. First, let us recall his polemical circumscription, so typical of orthodox formalism, of the subject of literary study, limiting it not to literature but to "literariness" (*literaturnost'*), that feature, or set of features, which turns a given work into a piece of literature. According to the young, combative Jakobson, we will not have a literary history, but merely a "conglomeration of home-grown disciplines," like the history of philosophy, of culture or of psychology, until we recognize the "device" as our sole concern. Poetry, he argued, is simply "language in its aesthetic function," that is, utterance produced solely "for the purpose of expression," one in which the communicative function, consequently, "has only minimal importance."[43] The formalist critic thus investigates the procedures that help render standard language literary, focusing attention on the laying bare of devices and the realization of verbal structures, but stays away at all cost from anything extraliterary—from biography, psychology, politics or philosophy—for fear of behaving, in Jakobson's provocative simile, like a policeman who arrests the culprit and all the innocent passersby into the bargain.

The change of Jakobson's position as articulated in "What Is Poetry?" is at once subtle and momentous. Now hardly a formalist but a bona fide structuralist, Jakobson claims that the poetic function or "poeticity" (*básnickost*), instead of being the exclusive preoccupation of the literary scholar, must be viewed as only one of the constituent parts of the poetic work's complex structure, just as poetry itself must be understood as one of the component parts of the manifold social structure. According to Jakobson's structural view, in contrast to his formalist stance, the difference between art and nonart, or between literary and nonliterary language, is one not of kind but of degree. Unlike "literariness," "poeticity" is not equated with the poetic work as a whole; it is identified merely as a part of that whole: the dominant part. As Jakobson puts it, "we can speak of poetry only when poeticity, the poetic function, attains decisive significance" (p. 30). In other words, aesthetic function is not coextensive with the whole of the poetic work, which, as Mukařovský first suggested in the essay "The Work of Poetry as a Complex of Values" (1932), also contains several nonaesthetic functions; conversely, aesthetic function is not restricted to the poetic work, manifesting itself, albeit in a subordinate position, in other genres of discourse, such as oratory, journalism, advertising and even ordinary conversations.

In another lecture—an important appendix to "What Is Poetry?"—Jakobson offers the most consequent definition of the poetic dominant.[44] "The dominant," he says, is the "focusing component of the work of art," which "rules, determines and transforms the remaining components. It is the dominant which guarantees the integrity of the structure" (p. 82). Definitional of poetry, the dominant, like Jakobson's ensuing understanding of poetry itself, is far from a fixed, immutable feature. According to the Prague School's dynamic conception of literary evolution, the dominant is historically variable—constantly inconstant. In late medieval Czech poetry, for example, the "mandatory and inalienable constituent dominating all the remaining elements" was rhyme rather than a compulsory number of syllables per line. The latter could fluctuate, whereas the former was indispensable: during this particular period, without rhyme a verse was not deemed to be verse at all. In Czech realist poetry, by contrast, rhyme was nonessential, but a regular syllabic scheme acquired prime importance. In modern Czech poetry, much of it in free verse, neither rhyme nor a syllabic patterning is synonymous with verse; instead, as Jakobson and Mukařovský repeatedly asserted, the compulsory and constitutive component is now intonational integrity.

Despite the dominant's historical changeableness, there is an underlying "poeticity," not so much a localizable feature as a function or orientation, which, Jakobson seems to suggest, remains universal. This transcendent poeticity comes into view anytime "the word is felt as a word and not merely as a stand-in for the designated object or as an outburst of emotion; when words and their organization, their signification, their external and internal form do not point indifferently to reality but rather acquire a weight and value of their own."[45]

"Why is it necessary to highlight that the sign does not coalesce with the thing" Jakobson goes on to ask. Indeed, why do we repeatedly have to break up the habitual forms and formulas that purport to attach words to things by "natural" contiguity? Here is Jakobson's semiotic answer:

Because besides the immediate awareness of the identity between sign and thing (A equals A_1), it is necessary that there be an immediate awareness of the inadequacy of that identity (A is not A_1). Such antinomy is vital because without contradiction there is neither movement of concepts nor movement of signs: the relationship between concept and sign becomes automatized, the process [of understanding—FWG] comes to a halt and the awareness of reality dies away. (pp. 30–31)

It is thanks to the path-breaking accomplishments of modern phenomenology, and implicitly of semiotics, Jakobson submits, that we recognize the profound, categorical distinction between the sign and the thing it stands for, "between the verbal meaning and the content at which this meaning is directed."[46] By excoriating "linguistic fictions" in politics as well as in art, phenomenology and semiotics help combat what Jakobson terms the "fetishism of the word." The reification of words culminated in the second half of the nineteenth century and made its appearance in positivistic philosophy and neogrammarian philology, as well as in novelistic realism and theatrical illusionism, everywhere fostering "faith in the paper word." In the twentieth century, in a revolutionary turnabout, not only semiotics and phenomenology but also avant-garde art disclose the special, distinct, autonomous functioning of the verbal domain. One art above all has produced irrefutable evidence that "language is merely one of the possible sign systems" (p. 29), and that, as we have seen, is the art of the film.

From the above statements, encapsulating the principles of the Prague School's semiotic reform or, better yet, revolution, the momentousness of Jakobson's new conception of poeticity should become clear beyond any doubt. For the formalists, including the Jakobson of the Chlebnikov study, poetic expression was "self-valuable": the purer, the less contaminated by nonpoetic values, the better. All that a formalist had to do was to dissect—and, one hopes, to delight in—the intricate web of poetic devices, oblivious to the fact that language, standard as well as poetic, is inextricably entwined with our workaday lives, our thinking, our most fundamental communicative exchange. In Jakobson's political (and, we may add, economic) metaphor, the formalists favored an attitude of segregation and protectionism, whereas the structuralists acknowledge the necessity of integration and of free trade. Indeed, Jakobson the structuralist descries to the fullest the vital importance of verbal art in its dialectical interaction with all the other modes of verbal behavior as much for the cognition of our mental landscape as for the perception of the physical world. For to the degree that, as Karcevskij observed, everyday discourse threatens to be frozen into a catalogue of fixed tags or to break down into a pile of deixes, the poeticity of poetry ensures the mobility of the ever-renewed matching of signs and things: if ordinary language (we may rephrase Karcevskij's view) gravitates toward stasis, poetic language—by underscoring the sign's asymmetric dualism, its noncoincidence with the signified thing—seeks to generate a dynamic disequilibrium imperative for both the evolution of language and the knowledge of reality. This is a far cry from the formalist *ostranenie*, that simple and simplistic stress on the fictionality and figurativeness of literary art, purportedly existing for its own sake.[47]

It would be apposite at this point to turn to Mukařovský's disquisition on the semiotics of art, which complements and bolsters Jakobson's analysis of the semiosis (or poeticity) of literature as his inquiry into film-time and film-space enhanced Jakobson's remarks on the semiosis of cinema. In doing so, however, it would be shortchanging Jakobson, as well as ourselves, to leave unmentioned the wealth of trenchant insights and illuminating examples with which "What Is Poetry?" abounds. René Wellek surely underrates the importance of this essay, as should be evident from the foregoing discussion, by calling it a "*boutade*" written to "*épater*" the audience.[48] Jakobson's aphoristic locutions and bon mots have, it seems, prevented Wellek from appreciating the true historical and theoretical value of "What Is Poetry?" Victor Erlich is much more on target when he pronounces this a "brilliant methodological essay," which moreover offers, as we shall see shortly, "one of the best extant treatments of the perennial problem of *Dichtung und Wahrheit.*"[49]

We have thus far seen the conclusion of Jakobson's argument; now we must retrace the route of how he got there. The gist of Jakobson's position has been that poeticity can be defined *only* functionally: poetry's principal task is to counteract the calcification of the concepts incorporated in signs. Poetry certainly cannot, Jakobson insisted, be defined thematically. While during the epochs of classicism and romanticism poetic themes may have been canonically proscribed, for the contemporary poet there is no taboo subject. Attempts at cataloguing artistic devices, poetic *Kunstgriffen*, are likewise bound to flounder, because the "history of art testifies to their changeability" (p. 20). Even were we to succeed in compiling an inventory of the poetic devices that characterize a given poetic school or movement, in doing so we would hardly weed out the artistic from the nonartistic, since instances of alliteration, euphony and various rhetorical tropes are likely to crop up in political speeches, in jokes, in colloquial conversations—even the "build-up of gossip," Jakobson remarks, "frequently follows the compositional rules of popular literature" (p. 21). Nor, according to Jakobson, can a search for poetic intention produce desirable results and help delineate the realm of the poetic. Alongside artistic intent, poets, especially the dadaists and surrealists, give free rein to chance in their works as a constructive device, for instance, like Chlebnikov, preserving accidental typographical errors. Small wonder, then, that some writers leave a deeper mark in literary history with their epistolary or diaristic artlessness than with their novelistic or poetic craft.

In other words, any endeavor to demarcate the province of art is about as futile as drawing borderlines between states in the shifting sands of a desert. This is the case not so much because artists unearth poetry in telephone directories, train schedules, menus and wine lists as well as in the lofty subjects of love, life and death. Rather, it is so chiefly because art and life, *Dichtung und Wahrheit*, overlap, amalgamate and interpenetrate. To illustrate the indivisibility within the poet's life and works of poetic fiction and biographical truth, Jakobson rehearses the exemplary case study of Karel Hynek Mácha, with side references to the Slovak romantic poet Janko Král' (1822–1876) and the Czech modernist Vítězslav Nezval (1900–1958), all three of whom, it turns out, in addition to being exceptional poets, shared a strong Oedipal complex.[50] Like Puškin, who could write a sublime love poem, "Pomnju čudnoe mgnoven'e" (I recall a wondrous moment), and then describe the same event and the woman in question in rather lewd terms in a letter to his friend, thereby presenting his biographer with an insoluble dilemma as to which account was "true" and which "stylized," Mácha celebrated the beauty of his beloved and, practically in the same breath, anatomized her in graphic and disfiguring detail in his diary. Does one genre of discourse, letter or diary, confer legitimacy on the given experience while another, lyric poetry, does not? No assumption could be more erroneous, avers Jakobson. Both versions are equally valid, equally authentic: they are but two "different facets of the identical object, of the identical experience," or, in the handy terminology of cinema, alternate takes of one and the same scene. Whether we confront statements in the form of an ode or in the form of a burlesque, we must grant them like claims to truth, for, as Jakobson asserts, they are simply "two modes of expression for one theme." In fact, Mácha's diary bears overwhelming resemblance to his poetry in that, in Jakobson's view, it evinces not the slightest "shade of utilitarianism." The diary, too, is written for its own sake, to give shape to experience, rather than to serve ulterior communication, to broadcast news: it is a form of "poetry for the poet" (p. 24). Conceivably, today Mácha might have attracted more admirers by publishing the sexually explicit diary, which would place him alongside such iconoclasts of modern literature as James Joyce or D. H. Lawrence, than by the dated romantic afflatus of his poems.[51]

Do not trust the teller, trust the tale. Or, when the actor sheds the mask, you will see the makeup. These adages pithily express the dangers and confusions lying in wait for the biographically minded critic. Jakobson attacks here the same *bête noire* that Mukařovský cornered in his review "The Artist's Personality in the Mirror of the Work" (1931), the simpleminded psychologism that apprehends relations among the most diverse phenomena, not excepting the relationship between the poet and his or her poetry, in the categories of causality instead of interpreting them in the (admittedly more daunting) terms of semioticity. Where the psychologistic view beholds a necessary balance, correspondence, even identity, between the work—an assembly of aesthetic signs—and its producer—the psycho-physical person of the author—the semiotic approach reckons that in any and all signs there is a disjunction, a slippage, an asymmetric imbalance between the sign itself, on the one hand, and the circumjacencies of producer, receiver and signified reality, on the other. "The artist is no less play-acting," Jakobson warns, "when he declares that this time he is abandoning *Dichtung* for naked *Wahrheit* than when he assures us that his work is nothing but sheer invention" (p. 22). When a writer like Tolstoj renounces as false and misguided his past *oeuvre* or art as a whole, he may, as Eichenbaum irreverently counseled, simply be searching for fresh, yet unexplored literary forms.[52] And when a critic inveighs against a rising new poet because his or her work is wanting in truth, conviction, credibility, verisimilitude or naturalness, the critic, as well, "in reality rejects one poetic trend, that is, one ensemble of means of deforming material, in the name of another poetic tendency, another group of alterant devices" (p. 22).

Life and art, of course, are phenomenally complexed notions which form a "dialectical alliance with ceaseless shifts and reversals," and the critics who confidently tell one from the other exhibit a self-defeating proclivity toward unriddling "equations with two unknowns" (p. 23). To the extent that art and life are knowable, they appear not as uniformly unequivocal but as intricately interchangeable. They stand, we could say, under the figure of chiasmus. On the one hand, because the "poeticity" of verbal expression emphatically announces that, in Jakobson's paradoxical rendition, "communication is not its goal, [preventive] censorship," which bears upon every speech act, "can be relaxed and suppressed" in poetry (p. 27). In other words, writers may disclose more of their anguish and, as the case may be, more of their psychological deviance when protected by the literary convention of fictitious genres or modes—wearing, so to speak, a poetic mask—than in other forms of discourse, the supposedly factual genres of letters, diaries, interviews and the like. Thus Majakovskij's suicide, to cite one example, was many times foretokened in his verse—to the disbelief of the reading public.[53] Or, to cite another of Jakobson's examples, the poetry of Janko Král' expresses still more blatantly than Mácha's—and the latter's poems bristle with lines like "Why is he my father? Why is he your seducer?"—a violent resentment of the father figure and an incestuous desire for a return to the womb, yet such erotically charged verses seem innocuous enough to be taught to adolescents.

On the other hand, we should not underestimate the likelihood of some poetic features' surfacing in the poet's life. In the case of Mácha, writes Jakobson, "the many-sided permeation of poetry and private life is evident not only in the heightened communicability [or divulgence—FWG] of Mácha's poetic work but also in the intimate thrusting of literary motifs into his life" (p. 26). Put more generally, just as every verbal act unavoidably becomes stylized (depending on the speaker's intention, the available repertory of expressive means, the particular communicative situation and the status of the interlocutor) and in turn stylizes the depicted event or experience, so a prevailing stylization (as embodied in the literature in vogue at the given time) exerts influence on the way the readers shape their experience. This possibility of living out one's life according to a literary model is exacerbated in writers, more careful and impressionable readers than most. In Mácha's day, the poets fancied that poetry was born out of pain, and Mácha himself was racked by self-lacerating, even self-annihilating, jealousy. How can a literary critic ever determine the extent to which Mácha's emotional torture was justified by facts or the extent to which it was motivated by a desire to act out in life the role of a suffering poet? Or, to take a contemporary example, how can a literary commentator decide when a writer like Norman Mailer is being almost psychotically belligerent and when he is merely imitating the heroes of his own works? Literary scholars have no way, really, of answering such questions. If the question of biographical fact or fiction can be answered at all, Jakobson submits, only forensic medicine, not literary criticism, should try to do so.

In time, the prevalent literary fashion may become the hallmark of the particular period of cultural history. A decade's major political elections, economic crises or criminal trials will eventually be forgotten, but a poet's work is still remembered. As Jakobson puts it, "only after the end of an era, once the close links among its individual components break down, only then are the poetic 'monuments' seen as standing above the miscellaneous pieces of archeological debris" (p. 32).[54] The significance of works of art emerges across the distance of time; contemporaries, as a rule, remain ignorant of the pervasive impact a poet may generate, even though his or her words shape the way they "joke with a friend, curse an enemy, express excitement, experience love or argue politics." Modern poets—practicing, like Nezval, the shock tactics of dada and surrealism—often provoke an entirely negative response, and yet—through the process of the sunken cultural taste or today's camp—"their motifs and intonations, their words and phrases spread ever further, forming the speech and the whole style of life" even of people who themselves may never have read a line of modern verse. The explanation of this phenomenon is simple, insists Jakobson:

Just as the poetic function organizes and controls a poetic work without necessarily leaping to the eye like a billboard, so, too, a poetic work substantially and purposefully organizes our ideological outlook without becoming conspicuous in the total complex of social values. It is precisely poetry which forestalls automatization, the corrosion of our formulas of love and hate, of resistance and reconciliation, of faith and renunciation. (p. 31)

We can, at this juncture, turn to Mukařovský's communication to the Eighth International Congress of Philosophy, "L'art comme fait sémiologique," and to its pendant, "La dénomination poétique et la fonction esthétique de la langue."[55] The two talks, although delivered on separate occasions, flow together as parts of the same comprehensive theory, the former discussing the semiotics of art as a whole and the latter applying these general principles to the particular case of verbal art. In what follows, therefore, no distinction is made between the two statements.

Defining art semiotically as an ensemble of signs, Mukařovský, like Jakobson, explores the two areas central to all semiotics, namely, semantics and sociology (or pragmatics, in Morris' sense: formalism, we recall, is essentially poetic syntactics). This expanded understanding of art as sign or signs—viewed not merely in terms of syntax but in terms of reference and social effect—yields several important propositions. One such semiotic proposition is that in any work of art, whether representational or abstract, thematic or devoid of theme, every constituent element is endowed with some meaning. This axiom reverses the formalist assumption that, in a literary work, every feature becomes an aspect of form and emphasizes that, on the contrary, every one of the work's structural components is a carrier of meaning—or, put more simply, that every particle of a work of art is capable of signifying. Once apprehended from the perspective of semiotics, the formalist position insisting on the autonomy of the verbal sign, on its holiday from reference, is logically insupportable. Since a sign, by any definition, is a "reality perceivable by the senses that has a relation to another reality which it is meant to evoke" (p. 5), a question naturally arises as to what kind of reality an autonomous sign of art is supposed to stand for or represent. As Mukařovský argues, implicitly criticizing the formalist stance, if the work of art was exclusively an autonomous sign, it would be "characterized solely by its serving as an intermediary among members of any one community" (p. 5). This would amount to saying that, though an intermediary, an inalienable part of social reality, art—in such self-contradictory defense of its unique status—is incapable of communicating information about any objects other than itself. Like aphasiacs who, even though still members of society, can no longer articulate anything about themselves or the surrounding world, a work of art, in this theory, simply exists, signifying nothing. While formalism, unaided by the semiotic conception, could brush aside the issue of artistic signification,

SEMIOTIC REFORMULATION ‖ 115

structuralism, now allied with semiotics, of necessity examines the relationships of artistic signs to the reality they inevitably represent.

To understand the import of the structuralists' semiotic reformulation of the nature of art, we must for the last time pit the Prague School's theory against its Opojaz precursor. As we have seen in the second chapter, adopting a formalist hypothesis, the Prague linguists' conception of language functions at first posed a basic antinomy between standard and poetic languages (or functional dialects). Poetic language, according to that early hypothesis, obstructs reference, in contrast to standard language, which facilitates it: the signs of the first linguistic subsystem are communicative; those of the second, autonomous. A sign which is absolutely autonomous, however, is an oxymoron, a contradiction in terms, because signs, in their very mode of existence, are dependent on the reality for which they stand, not independent of it. If art is an assembly of signs, if it is intrinsically semiotic, its signs must be partly *communicative*. From a semiotic perspective, the *Zweckmäßigkeit* of art, to recall Kant's aesthetic definition, cannot be completely without a *Zweck*.[56] The purpose of art is not, as Jakobson maintained, singularly inner-directed: in the *nexus finalis*, art's aesthetic self-purposiveness (or impracticality) must act as a dialectical counterweight to the communicative utility (or purposefulness) of nonaesthetic signs. The task of the semiotics of literary art, consequently, is to inquire into the principles of artistic communication, the kind of information verbal art conveys and the kind of acts of reference it performs.

When we look, with the aid of Mukařovský's semiotic optics, at an ordinary utterance made to impart information, we realize at once that the weight of the statement is directed to the referred-to reality. Hearing a sentence like "It's turning dark" and perceiving it as an informational utterance, we are inclined to test the validity of the assertion: Is it true that it is getting dark? Isn't it too early? Is the statement referring to a present, not a past or future, situation? Is the force of the sentence literal, pointing to an actual state of affairs, or is it figurative, making a metaphoric philosophical comment about general decline or decay? The answer to such questions, as Mukařovský points out, will be of considerable practical importance, since it "will determine the import of the communication for appropriate action" (p. 156). Our attitude to the selfsame utterance about the approaching dusk, however, changes the moment we sense that it is a poetic quotation. As much as in the first instance we wanted to establish the connection between the statement and the context of the reality in question, so in the second instance, in order to understand that poetic utterance on its own terms, we want to know the verbal, poetic *contexture* from which the citation has been taken. Where and in what text is the quotation to be found, in the beginning, the end, the refrain? (In addition, of course, we would wish to learn about the author of the poetic statement, who, unlike our immediate interlocutor, is absent and unknown.) Poetic reference, in short, is determined above all by the "way it is set into the verbal context," and "not by its relationship to the reality indicated" (p. 156). Indeed, "all the stylistic devices of poetry, for instance, various kinds of sound instrumentation [alliteration, euphony, rhyme—FWG] that elicit mutual semantic reactions among the words they bring together," as Mukařovský asserts following Tynjanov, "render service to the essential tendency of poetry, namely, to determine reference primarily by linkage in context" (pp. 156–57).

This focus on the poetic contexture, though it may blur, does not bar our perception of the context of reality. All that is involved in the switch from ordinary to poetic reference is, according to Mukařovský, a "shift in the center of [semantic] gravity" (p. 157). How, then, does poetic reference shed light on the reality of referents, which is the prime focus of ordinary reference? Here Mukařovský offers a bold speculative answer, and even if his thesis is ultimately unprovable, it nevertheless corresponds to our common experience of art and literature. The object of artistic reference, the referent of the aesthetic sign, is not a particular segment of reality, but the "total context of so-called social phenomena, for example, philosophy, politics, religion, economics and so on" (p. 5). The particular referent of a (relatively) autonomous, as opposed to a (relatively) communicative, sign is "not distinctly determinable," since, as we have seen, the centripetal movement of verbal contexture diverts our attention from the extraverbal referential context. To put it another way, the signs of poetic language draw attention to themselves, to their individual makeup (for instance, their striking sound shape or exceptional figurative application) and, even more important, to their reciprocal relationships (for example, their rhyme consonance, incantatory intonation, syntactic deviation such as enjambment, striking figuration and the like), thereby highlighting the ever-present process of choice among numerous linguistic options.

For this reason, in reading poetry—that is, in interpreting poetic reference—one is always made to sense the "potential presence of the entire lexical system of the language in question" (p. 160). Furthermore, by putting the factor of verbal choice in the forefront, poetic reference "makes manifest," Mukařovský writes, "the active intention of the author of reference" (p. 161), the maker of the particular lexical selection. A semantic, referential intention, to be sure, accompanies any verbal expression, but in poetic utterance—unlike in ordinary speech acts, where the informational reference is produced with a view to any number of disparate referents— "the intimate semantic coherence of verbal contexture" ensures that this intention "remains the same throughout the work." Instead of being renewed with every particular reference as in the case of purely informational locution, the work of poetic art, owing to its "unity of referential intention," assumes, Mukařovský holds, "the character of a global reference." Only this reference of a "higher order, represented by the work as a whole," he insists, then "enters into a strong relationship with reality" (p. 161). Yet the global reference is not the sole property of the autonomous signs of poetic language; it exists to some degree in "every linguistic performance" (p. 162). Mukařovský is not simply supplanting the old antinomy of standard and poetic languages with a new antinomy of the particular reference which pertains exclusively to one mode of language and the global reference which belongs to another mode. Much more dialectically, Mukařovský now proclaims that the two language styles are mutually counterbalancing: the strengthening of the immediate relationship of any particular reference to the denoted segment of reality weakens the global relationship of any poetic reference to the reality as a whole. As Mukařovský sums it up, "the informational function in all its aspects tends toward the pole of immediate relationship, the poetic function, contrariwise, toward the pole of global relationship" (p. 162).

Since the object of poetic reference is the whole social context and since this reference activates the entire lexicon, poetry, in this audacious theory, is an imaginative matching of two totalities—of the structure of reality and the structure of language.

Because of its global nature, the claim regarding the all-encompassing scope of poetic reference is not susceptible to proof or falsification. Mukařovský's brief illustration, however, drawing on Dostoevskij's *Crime and Punishment* (1866), convincingly shows why such a postulate can reasonably be entertained. In point of fact, Mukařovský's argument is far from new, since Aristotle had already made similarly far-reaching affirmation of the universal nature of art when he contended that "poetry is a more . . . serious business than history, since poetry speaks more of universals, history of particulars" (*Poetics*, 1451b). By portraying what is improbable but plausible, rather than reporting on what is possible or indeed actual, Dostoevskij, like every successful artist, carries the conviction that, even though the action described may be as remote from most readers' mundane experiences as Raskol'nikov's murder of the old woman, nevertheless each reader feels very intimately that "sua res agitur," that it is his or her personal business or concern which is being addressed. And so, despite the gap between languages, the cultural divide and the lapse of time, every reader discerns some aspects of the unified semantic intention which informs the whole of Dostoevskij's novel. And even if individual readers' reactions to the book and their subsequent life experiences will, as Mukařovský cautions, "only be partial symptoms of [Dostoevskij's] attitude toward reality," the stronger this reaction, the more intense their experience, "the stronger is the influence exerted by the work on the readers' conception of the world" (p. 161). It is as though, thanks to its extraordinary centripetal force, the work so totally absorbed readers into its alien world as to cast them back, in a centrifugal motion, into their own reality, seeing life in a new light.

Earlier we saw how Jakobson asserted that the influence of poetry is omnipresent, affecting the speech habits and cultural attitudes even of people indifferent to poetry. Mukařovský lends further credence to this view by suggesting that, in some cases at least, poetry and literature as a whole have a transforming power, one which can significantly alter the receptive reader's view of the world. Moreover, since the individual reader is a member of a wider community, and since "his conception of reality is modeled in broad outline on the system of values in force in that community," Mukařovský feels free to take the next logical step and assert that "through the mediation of the individual, poetry exerts an influence on the way the whole society conceives of the world" (pp. 161–62). Poetry, literature and art in general thus express and represent the values of the social and historical context which engenders them—and at the same time transcend that context. Again we recall Jakobson's contention concerning the permanence of works of art as against the evanescence of social, political or economic events. And Mukařovský, in turn, maintains that, because of its global reference, "art more than all other social phenomena is capable of characterizing and representing a given epoch" (p. 5). It is art's singular faculty—at once baffling and unquestionable—to represent the "age," which helps explain why art history is so often mixed with cultural history and why general history likes to base its periodization—for instance, Renaissance, classicism or Baroque—on the history of art.

Furthermore, just as Mukařovský refines the opposition between poetic language and standard language by assigning a similar capacity of global reference to both (though, of course, in the former mode global reference takes priority while in the latter it is usually subsidiary), so he insists that poetic language can successfully perform the main function of standard language—that of referring to particular objects rather than to global concepts. Signs of poetic language, being precisely signs, are both autonomous and communicative or informational. And since every sign is, in the classification of Karl Bühler mentioned in the preceding chapter, potentially a representation, an expression and an appeal, aesthetic signs, too, if they are to remain full-fledged signs, must be able to serve representational, expressive and appellant functions. In other words, aesthetic signs must communicate something not only about themselves, their inner structure, and not only about the general social context, but also about the particular segments of reality, about the producer of the artistic message as well as about the receivers of this message. Depending on which one of these practical communicative functions gains the upper hand—without, however, toppling the decisive aesthetic function—we can obtain different literary genres. In lyric poetry, for instance, it is the expressive function that asserts itself strongly, whereas prose fiction tilts the scales toward the referential and representational function. Moreover, depending on the varying degree of intensity with which these functions can manifest themselves, we can distinguish between so-called thematic or representational arts and nonthematic or abstract ones. On the one side, there are such "subjectless" arts as music and architecture, in which, according to Mukařovský, the informational function is "diffuse." The arts of dance and pantomime are, with respect to their communicative ability, somewhere near the middle of the semantic spectrum: their informational function is "veiled." On the other side, we have the representational arts of poetry, painting or sculpture, in which the practical referential function is clearly "evident" (p. 6). The presence of this function is undeniable, especially in genres such as the historical novel and the literary biography and their recent offshoots, called metafictions, "factions," novel-biographies and other fables of fact.

By now one might have formed the impression that Jakobson's and Mukařovský's semiotics of art goes so far in knocking down the insuperable barriers between art and social reality erected by early formalism as to raze them completely to the ground, obliterating any meaningful division between the realm of autonomous signs and the rival realm of communicative signs. Nothing, however, could be further from the truth. We remember how, notwithstanding the indistinguishability of "fiction" and "truth" within a poet's life and work, Jakobson roundly asserted that the autonomous signs of poetic language oppose and subvert the dominant tendency of ordinary language to regard the "sign and the object designated by it as monogamously and immutably bound to one another." [57] In contrast to communicative signs, then, aesthetic signs, to extend Jakobson's metaphor, appear promiscuous; in less figurative terms, they are ambiguous or, better still, polysemous. Similarly, Mukařovský puts forth two provisos which should help us avoid confusing art with nonartistic communication. Mukařovský's first proviso says that, no matter how extensive the role of extra-aesthetic practical functions, the "informational relationship between the work of art and the thing signified does not have *existential* value, even when such is asserted" (p. 7; emphasis mine)—that is, the mere existence of a phenomenon in the world of things is of no decisive consequence for the given work *qua* work of art.

We should forestall two possible misinterpretations at this point. One mistake would be the conclusion that theme, that highest translatable semantic unit, is the sole feature in a work of art which has a referential function. Mukařovský himself now upholds the opposite view—namely, that even nonthematic arts signify, albeit in a diffuse manner, by means of their formal constituents, all of which have a "virtual semiotic character" (p. 6). Thus, a patch of blue in an abstract painting can, if it is situated in the upper or lower part of the canvas, signify sky or sea, respectively. The other error would be the inference that, since theme is a mere axis of semantic crystallization, "*modifications* of the relationship to the thing signified are without importance for a work of art" (p. 7). On the contrary, states Mukařovský, these modifications, such as the "real" or "fictitious" status of the work's theme, characters or events, "function as factors of its structure." All the genres blending fact and fiction mentioned earlier are based on what Mukařovský describes as a "parallelism and counterbalance of a twofold relationship to a distinct reality, in one instance without existential value and in the other purely informational" (p. 7). Although hybrid "quasidocumentaries" and "unfictionalized narratives," even more than the nineteenth-century "realistic" or "naturalistic" novels, constantly invite us to take them at their word, as it were, our literary investigation of these works must never, Mukařovský warns, neglect the fact that the "essence of theme is to be a *unity of meaning* and not a passive copy of reality" (p. 7; emphasis mine). In other words, however conspicuous the informational factors of the literary work's semantic structure may be, this structure cannot be centrifugal, with single structural elements linking up referentially with particular segments of external reality, but is bound to be centripetal, with all its elements creating a series of internal semantic correlations, therein composing the work's contexture. Ultimately, if a literary work is to be viewed as a work of art, its aesthetic efficacy must without exception be judged by its structural coherence, not by its ostensible verisimilitude. In every work of art, in sum, composition holds sway over representation (as well as over expression or appeal).

Mukařovský's other proviso concerns the validity or reliability of the artistic work's global reference. This reference to the aggregate of social phenomena is performed by aesthetic signs which, no less than other types of signs, may have an indirect—metaphoric or otherwise figuratively oblique—relationship to signified reality. "It follows from the semiotic nature of art," Mukařovský argues, "that a work of art must never be utilized as a historical or sociological document without preliminary interpretation of its *documentary* value," by which he means the "quality of [the work's] relationship with the particular context of social phenomena involved" (p. 6; emphasis mine). For, besides official and publicly acclaimed works of art, there are numerous works which the public rejects as soon as they appear. The fate of Lautréamont and other *poètes maudits* is a good case in point. Thoroughly unappreciated by their contemporaries, these "accursed poets" were later found by the surrealists to be speaking intimately to another literary and social milieu. In this way, certain works of art or artistic movements may illuminate as much, if not more, the period which receives them as the period which, though it gives birth to them, ends up rejecting them. In fact, as Mukařovský suggests, the writings of Lautréamont and other maverick poets may have been so alien to the "contemporary system of values" that they "remained outside literature," or, more to the point, outside the cultural and literary mainstream. These works could not be accepted as literary by the reading community, Mukařovský claims, "until such time as, in the course of the evolution of the social context, they became capable of expressing it" (p. 5).

Before concluding this discussion of Mukařovský's art semiotics, however, we must note a serious shortcoming in his argument, all the more so since it has a direct bearing on the theory of reception history, which is one of the topics of the penultimate chapter. The source of Mukařovský's theoretical flaw seems to have been the ambitiousness of his semiotic enterprise. Investigating art within its social context, Mukařovský discovered that semiotics covers essentially the same ground as the traditional *Geisteswissenschaften* or the *sciences morales*, whose principal objects of study are social facts—or, in Mukařovský's description, those mental contents which exceed the "bounds of the individual consciousness" (p. 4). The emphasis on the transindividual character of linguistic and semiotic phenomena as ones which carry the stamp of collective approval derives, we remember, from the Saussurean concept of *langue*. Mukařovský, as he indicated in the 1932 interview and later in his analysis of *The Sublimity of Nature*, interpreted the mode of existence of these intersubjective phenomena in phenomenological terms, maintaining that the structure proper of the literary work lies not in the physical, material artifact (or *artis factum*) but in the corresponding aesthetic object embedded in the social consciousness. In chapter 3 we saw how Mukařovský failed to reconcile this phenomenologically framed theory with his structural and empirical practice. In "Art as Semiotic Fact" Mukařovský seeks to bring his phenomenological principles into alliance with the nascent semiotic doctrine. "The workthing," or the material datum, he now asserts, corresponds to Saussure's *signifiant*, while the "aesthetic object," or the immaterial signification, he identifies with Saussure's *signifié*. Unfortunately, this terminological reformulation further underlines the tension between Mukařovský's contending theoretical commitments. The problematic issue that Mukařovský skirts—at his peril—is the controversy concerning the arbitrariness as against the motivation of linguistic.and, by extension, all other signs. This is not the place to enter into that protracted debate. Suffice it to say that Mukařovský, by stressing the dynamic structure of the sign and the variable relationship of signs to reality, appears to advocate an interpretation of semiotic facts as arbitrary, whereas his own philosophic rigor and scientific ethos suggest that his position favors an understanding of signs as motivated.

Art as sign is motivated, or regulated, Mukařovský seems to say, by the norms located in the consciousness of a social collectivity. Nowhere in "Art as Semiotic Fact," however, does he inquire into the constitution or the particular properties of that consciousness. Granted, Mukařovský does conceive of it along structural lines: the collective's social consciousness, like works of literature, has a dominant component, here labeled the "central core," and, like literature itself, this consciousness is intrinsically dynamic and variable. There are distinct norms in different societies, and these norms also change within the same collective body over the course of time. A semiotician analyzing social facts, like the linguist or literary scholar, must pinpoint the dominant center of the consciousness and the range of "associative factors" in individuals' subjective reactions connected with it. A work of art objectified as an aesthetic object within the social consciousness is, for Mukařovský, akin to a word, which, as we saw at the beginning of this chapter, besides the semantic core has a host of auxiliary meanings. Consequently, the aesthetic object, the signification of the work of art, is given, Mukařovský says, by "what is common to subjective states of mind aroused in individuals of any particular community by the artifact" (p. 4). But two objections can be levied against this assertion. First, the analogy between the individual lexical unit and the whole work of art, though suggestive, is disturbingly vague, since we are dealing with two extremely different orders of complexity. While we can easily arrive at a consensus about the spectrum of meanings of a single word, such an agreement about the possible limits of a poetic work's signification is, by comparison, highly elusive, if not impossible. Second, in order to study the functioning of the social consciousness, we need a sociological or psychosociological theory of some kind, which Mukařovský does not even adumbrate (unless his conception of consciousness is phenomenological, as indicated in the previous chapter).

Mukařovský's two examples illustrating the regulatory mechanism which underlies the social consciousness confirm the suspicion that his theory, in this one crucial respect, does not quite hold. According to one of Mukařovský's examples, everyone's subjective perception of an impressionistic painting is apt to be wholly different in kind from that of a cubist painting. Though plausible, this statement requires corroboration either from—say, Gestalt—theory of perception or from empirical tests, for it is not entirely implausible that some reactions will have more features in common with respect to both styles of representation than they would with respect to each style separately. Mukařovský's second example, according to which the number of subjective associations elicited by a surrealist poem will differ quantitatively from those evoked by a classical poem, shows still more clearly how open to question his notion of the normative social consciousness really is. "The surrealist poem," according to Mukařovský, "makes it incumbent upon the reader to imagine virtually the entire contexture of the theme, whereas the classical poem all but precludes the freeplay of subjective associations due to its exactness of expression" (p. 4). The instances selected are, of course, extreme opposites of compositional styles, yet the assumption that the differences between them as reflected in the consciousness of their readers can be quantitatively ascertained is rather dubious. For one thing, Mukařovský does not propose a method of measuring such individual reactions, which, though varied, are supposedly strictly controlled by the core of the collective consciousness (nor, for that matter, does he advance any definition of what kind of uniformity of views constitutes a collective). For another thing, Mukařovský overlooks the important historical dimension of classical poetry, which exacts, particularly of modern readers, an extensive knowledge of mythology, religion, ancient history and philosophy, as well as a large set of poetic topoi, to decipher the wealth of classical allusions. Understanding Milton's *Lycidas* (1637), with its precise form of expression, may today require as much mental effort and give rise to as many subjective reactions as making sense of André Breton's *Les vases communicants* (1932), with its alogical associative composition. Finally, Mukařovský's explanation of the significance of the *poètes maudits* also leaves room for doubt, since he does not explain what changes in social values were needed for their literary reception. Did it take the shock of the Great War to make readers sensitive to poetic statements which the *belle époque* had deemed irrelevant? While dramatizing a methodologically challenging asynchrony between the evolution of the literary and social orders, Mukařovský does little to disentangle the intricacies of their interrelationships.

And so while failing, and failing as nobly as any extant theories, fully to come to grips with the complex dialectic interplay between art and society in their respective historical modes of existence, Mukařovský's semiotics at least provides the keys to such a dialectical understanding. We can do no better than to quote at length Mukařovský's optimistic prognosis:

. . . unless the semiotic character of art is adequately elucidated, the study of the structure of the work of art will remain necessarily incomplete. Without a semiotic orientation, the theorist of art will always be prone to regard the work as a purely formal construction or, on the other hand, as a direct reflection of its author's psychological, even physiological, dispositions or of the distinct reality conveyed by the work—or, as the case may be, of the ideological, economic, social and cultural situation of the given milieu. This train of thought will lead the theorist either to treat the evolution as a series of formal changes or to deny it completely (as is the case of certain current trends in aesthetic psychology) or, finally, to conceive of it as a passive commentary on an evolution exterior to art. Only the semiotic point of view allows the theorist to recognize the autonomous existence and essential dynamism of artistic structure and to understand the evolution of art as an immanent process but one in constant dialectical relationship with the evolution of other domains of culture. (p. 8)

‖●‖●‖●‖●‖●‖

After this milestone, the methodological reformulation enunciated in Jakobson's and Mukařovský's studies from the mid-1930s, semiotics became the dominant issue for the whole Prague Linguistic—or, better, Semiotic—Circle. The Prague School's great theoretical strides are nowhere more in evidence than in the programmatic editorial statement inaugurating the first issue of the Circle's own journal, *Slovo a slovesnost* (The Word and Verbal Art).[58] The signatories of this statement, the Circle's original founders—Bohuslav Havránek, Roman Jakobson, Vilém Mathesius, Jan Mukařovský and Bohuslav Trnka—were also, we recall, the principal authors of the 1929 "Theses," of which the new "Introduction" represents a worthy and innovative sequel. The "Introduction" breaks down into three sections, each reflecting a major semiotic concern. The first section addresses what the Prague scholars term "language culture." Under this heading, they subsume all those numberless instances in which language ceases to be a mere tool of communication, a stand-in for the material world, and becomes a self-sufficient object of the speakers' attention, contemplation or emotion. We know that such a change of attitude is commonly brought about by the relative "opacity" of poetic language, as when a rhyme juxtaposes two or more consonant words, thereby highlights their grammatical and semantic similarity or dissimilarity and in the process accords the constitutive verbal signs a degree of referential independence. Yet language becomes an autonomous phenomenon, a special world alongside the world of material things and ideas, just as often in linguistic analyses. While a conjunction cannot as a rule serve as a grammatical subject, the conjunction *and*, say, does acquire such a role in a sentence such as "*And* is a conjunction." Here the Prague semioticians seem to be looking ahead to the concept that Jakobson was later to label the "metalinguistic" or "glossing" function, that is, the focus on the linguistic code itself (cf. "Linguistics and Poetics," pp. 356 and 358). Interestingly, these two uses of language, poetry and metalanguage, are exact diametrical opposites: in poetry the principle of equivalence (of metrical similarity and dissimilarity or of semantic synonymity and antonymity) is projected into a sequence (as in rhyming couplets), whereas in metalanguage the sequence is used to build an equation (as in the sentence "A bachelor is an unmarried man"). In all these cases, language's referential or communicative function retreats into the background, since the language users' attention is concentrated on the constitution of language as a specific order of functional and semiotic values.

Language culture manifests itself daily in all sorts of ordinary social situations, whether we try to adopt our speech habits to the appropriate setting or take note of someone else's distinctive accent. In a democratic culture, as the language demands made by the new mass media increase, the editors assert that we witness a continual differentiation of verbal functions. Under these circumstances, society is obligated to devise ways of directing and planning various linguistic changes, thus promoting the systematic development of language. Besides the formal study of language as an abstract sign system, we need an ideological critique of language, that is, a conscious control of the relationship between signs and the objects signs designate. Time and again we must examine critically the precision, cogency and appropriateness of the signs employed, of their semiotic adequacy to the ends we want to pursue. And we must do battle, as Jakobson urged earlier, against the misuses and abuses of language—"against speech which illegitimately conceals or distorts its own message, against the kind of immaterial speech which is losing touch with reality, be it concrete or abstract" (p. 3). In the name of linguistic responsibility, the founders of *Slovo a slovesnost* call for the close cooperation of "linguists with educators and lawyers, philosophers and psychologists, psychiatrists and speech therapists, historians of literature and of art in general, experts in sociology, history, geography and ethnography" (p. 4). The journal's ultimate goal is to offer a "comprehensive description, critique and regulation of contemporary standard language in its diverse cultural tasks." Only in this way will society cease viewing language as a "chance accumulation of disparate elements" and treat it as a "totality whose individual components are tied by law-governed correlations" (p. 4)—in a word, as a structure, a systematic whole.

The second part of the "Introduction" moves from the affairs of language as a social institution to the business of poetry and its verbal material. Indeed, the contribution of poetry to our understanding of language as a whole is anything but nugatory. As the necessary antidote to the practical mandate of the language of communication, poetry "unceasingly sheds new light on the language system, charts unprecedented ways of using old tools, generates shifts in the hierarchy of linguistic elements, and replenishes the stock of stylistic formulas" (p. 5). We can detect here an echo of Jakobson's earlier argument; but Mukařovský's position regarding poetic reference can also be heard. In the eloquent formulation of the Circle's statement, besides the two interlocutors involved in any semiotic exchange, "there is in speech still a third solid point which pulls tight the fiber of the sign's internal texture, and that is the reality to which the sign points" (p. 5).

The sign's interior makeup is open for inspection in language much more radically than in any other semiotic medium, owing to our propensity for verbal expression: both spoken and written language are designed above all to articulate and mold the referential relationship between the sign and the signified reality. In art, we know, this referential relationship becomes attenuated. Hence the exemplary virtue of poetic art, its laying bare of the sign's inward construction, of the introverted referral of the external *signans* to the internal *signatum*. As the relationship between the sign and the particular referent grows more tenuous, the sign's dependence on overall social practices increases proportionately. "Although a work of art presents a world unto itself (or precisely because it does)," the Prague structuralists maintain, "it cannot be understood and assessed in any way other than in its relationship to the system of values upheld by the given community." Indeed, they go so far as the claim that "the whole dynamics of social development, the supersession and the strife among individual social strata and settings, the class, national and ideological struggle, all of this is intensely reflected in the relationship between art and society as well as in the evolution of art itself, even if the changes in the structure of art comprise a continuous and law-governed series" (p. 6). Semiotic investigation of literature must therefore inquire whether the writer's social background corresponds to that of his or her intended readership, whether the particular type of artistic creation satisfies the period's social demand and whether, as Mukařovský queried in the Polák study, all the available literary genres are destined for a single social group or, on the contrary, distinct genres appeal to specific social strata. As can be seen, literature, and by implication all the other arts, cannot be more firmly rooted in their social context than in the Prague School's nascent semiotic conception. In this comprehensive view, "the whole of reality, beginning with a sense percept and ending with the most abstract mental construct, emerges . . . as a vast, intricately organized empire of signs" (p. 5).

The "Introduction"'s brief third section deals with the questions of language history and historiography, since, from the semiotic viewpoint, "tradition is always one of the most acute constituent parts of every cultural edifice" (p. 6). Semiotic study of the past, consequently, is able to do even greater justice to historical events than that of the previous historicizing generation of neogrammarian philologists. The historical myopia of the neogrammarians, according to the structuralists, was painfully evident in their lack of regard for the "two most resplendent chapters in the development of medieval Czech culture and especially language" (p. 6). And the explanation of this shortsightedness is once again found in social history: in the 1890s, provincial Czech society, suffering from national and cultural repression, had to fight for elementary rights to its own nationhood and its own language and thus had little sympathy with the expansionist culture of medieval nobility. The first neglected chapter is that of the ninth century, the era of saints Cyril and Methodius, which witnessed the creation of Old Church Slavonic, the Slavs' standard literary language. The other disregarded period was the Gothic Middle Ages, when, under the enlightened reign of Charles IV, the Czech language became a language on a "world-class level and of imposing cultural amplitude" (p. 7) and, like Old Church Slavonic, deeply affected all Slavdom. It is this age of "magnanimous, self-confident and tenaciously purposeful" cultural creativity that the Prague scholars wish to claim as their true intellectual inheritance and glorious example.

Most linguists of the Prague Circle were in fact trained medievalists, yet none of them made Czech Gothic literature their province as much as Roman Jakobson. To observe the new semiotic theory in its practical application, we are, at the close of this chapter, compelled to take a look at Jakobson's historical analysis of Hussite poetry—despite the quaintness of this remote subject for the English-speaking reader. We could hardly find a more forceful proof of the deficiency of immanent historical analysis, although Jakobson himself framed the problem in somewhat different terms. While Jakobson's precursors in the study of Czech Gothic literature were largely guilty of investigative egocentrism, of imposing present-day aesthetic criteria on the poetry of another epoch, Jakobson himself committed the error of reverse historical foreshortening, of judging one period according to a scale of values inherited from the previous era. In his synoptic study "Old Czech Verse" (1934), Jakobson concluded that medieval epic verse reached full development by the second half of the fourteenth century, the golden age of Czech culture and society, and that the Hussite poetry of the fifteenth century, known as the "bronze age," was indeed marked by artistic decline, even decay—as is the literature of the romantic period, Jakobson notes, in the eyes of the orthodox classicist. In "Reflections on the Poetry of the Hussite Era," Jakobson therefore takes himself to task for overlooking the fact that new schools of artists have "fresh objectives, different systems, a modified hierarchy of values . . ." (p. 1).[59] To do justice to the innovations of Hussite poetry, one must, he affirms, broaden the scope of inquiry: "The development and differentiation of Czech poetic forms is contingent upon the expansion of the functions of the Czech poetic language: the history of poetry and of the language are closely interconnected here. Semantics, a basic aspect of poetic form, presents at the same time an epistemological problem: we must thus confront poetic structure with a comprehensive notion of the sign, which at this very time was undergoing substantial changes. From the word through the sign we proceed to a wider concentric circle: the social context in which a given sign system, linguistic and especially poetic, takes its effect" (p. 3).

From the standpoint of immanent analysis of verse, Hussite poetry exhibits a trend toward a sharp differentiation and circumscription of its three basic poetic kinds: sung verse (which replaced fourteenth-century Latin hymns); measured spoken verse (of which the most prominent genre in the previous epoch was the heroic epic); and measureless spoken verse, that is, a verse without a fixed syllabic scheme (which used to gravitate toward the measured epic verse). While, in the fourteenth century, sung verse was defined by an obligatory strophic division and an optional trochaic rhythm, and measured spoken verse by a mandatory trochaic pattern and a facultative strophic form, Hussite poetry throws into prominence the compulsory verse features and by and large discards the voluntary ones. Specifically, fifteenth-century sung verse seeks to suppress the trochaic tendency, which derives from the governing rhythm of Czech speech, and to replace it with an iambic construction. This iambic tendency, in turn, finds expression in religious and political songs, with their ability to signal the constitutive rising rhythm of iambs. In this way, Hussite sung verse becomes wholly dependent on music, since the musical rhythm here subdues the standard verbal rhythm. As a result, not only the rhythm of the Hussite song but its strophic form (which does away with rhyming pairs binding for the spoken type of versification) and its metric form (free of the otherwise necessary eight-syllable design) are stringently set off from the defining devices of spoken verse.

Measured spoken verse, on the other hand, intensifies its trochaic orientation and simultaneously disregards the earlier strophic segmentation. This formal rearrangement yields the Hussites' mixed lyric-epic genre, since sung verse took over the function of lyric poetry and measureless spoken verse supplanted the epic. The pronounced trochaic beat helps underline the declamatory, rather than musical, character of this verse, in which word boundaries are apt to coincide with the boundaries of the verse foot. In other words, in the measured spoken verse of the Hussite poets, just as, centuries later, in the Czech poetry of the Enlightenment and the second half of the nineteenth century, we observe the utmost approximation to the rhythmic ideal (although an ideal utterly alien to the preceding generation of versifiers as well as to the Baroque, romantic and modernist poets) according to which lines of verse follow one upon the other with the metronomic regularity of a perfect timepiece. Now, according to Jakobson, the reason why Hussite aesthetics sought to minimize the tension between the poetic form and the verbal material is that measured spoken verse, like unmeasured and sung verse, was used most of all as a "tool of party agitation" (p. 17). But propaganda by means of poetry, Jakobson remarks, can be conducted as a campaign with either lyrical and pathetic (in short, poetic) or epic and satiric (in short, prosaic) overtones—which accounts for the functional difference between measured and measureless verse, a difference fraught with political implications. For whereas the Hussites' revolutionary inspirational poetry favored verse narratives with a strong lyrical tint, the poetry of their adversaries, cast in measure-less spoken verse, was intent on mocking and belittling the more elevated style of measured verse. In terms of verse technique, fifteenth-century measureless spoken poetry loses its inclination toward the epic measure and, in order to distinguish itself from the lyrically flavored spoken verse, rejects in one swoop both the stable syllabic design and the octosyllabic rhythmic tendency typical of Hussite measured verse compositions.

Modernizing, or "egocentric," critics condemned the Hussites' "agit-prop" production as lacking artistic interest, and so did Jakobson, albeit because of the apparent stagnation in the development of versification dur-ing the fifteenth century. In Jakobson's revised, and historically rectified, view, the aesthetic function did not altogether disappear from Hussite po-etry but merely took second place to the general ideological dominant of the period. "Yet even such a minor and subordinate entity in the overall system of cultural values within this historical phase," Jakobson insists, "is a direct vehicle of the epoch's evolutionary pathos and eloquently testi-fies to its resoundingly innovative, radical character" (p. 21). When con-sidered in the larger context of the history of the Czech language, Hussite literature emerges as at once the culmination of the Gothic poetic tradition and its dialectical negation. We have surveyed the results of that negation: the severe reduction in the number of viable poetic kinds; their strict sepa-ration; the prevalent rhythmic monotony of spoken verse; the depreciation of poetry's formal effects; and, not least, the topical, uncompromisingly tendentious thrust of Hussite poetic output. At the same time, only during the Hussite era does the canon of Czech poetry attain its completion, for the literary language of all the genres practiced is Czech. Throughout the fourteenth century, the works in the highest poetic genre, sacred poetry, were still written in Latin. For the Hussites, Czech sung verse, as we have noted, assumes the function of Latin church songs—a shift whose evolu-tionary momentum cannot be underestimated. In Jakobson's argument— and here we are reminded of his analysis of the principles of linguistic di-achrony—"every such change in the interrelationship of poetic values in-exorably leads toward further disturbances of the [structural] equilib-rium" (p. 11).

The struggle for a Slavic national language, for *vulgare slavonicum*, goes back, we know, to the ninth century and the creation of Old Church Slavonic. Since the affairs of the church were at the center of medieval life, the demand to conduct the services in the Slavic vulgate (*"in lingua mea slavonica"*) inevitably had great political repercussions. Church Slavonic was from the first intended to stave off the influence of Rome and the ex-pansion of the Frankish German domain, both of which, according to Jakobson, "threatened to put the Czech lands into one-sided, slavish de-pendence on the West which would be contrary to their intermediate geopolitical location and their vital interests" (p. 4). Thanks to the success of the mission of saints Cyril and Methodius, the Great Moravian Empire oscillated culturally between Rome and Byzantium until the formal schism of 1054 between the Catholic and Orthodox churches, although its ties to the West, Jakobson notes, proved to be more decisive. Indeed, Church Slavonic, which prevailed from the last third of the ninth century until the end of the eleventh century, never quite managed to displace the Latin liturgy. At the turn of the twelfth century, the proponents of Latin very nearly destroyed all the Slavic documents (which is why the historians of the Enlightenment and modern Westernizers refuse to acknowledge the significance of Church Slavonic culture): with the exception of the eleventh-century manuscript known as *The Prague Fragments*, most Church Slavonic writings of Czech redaction survived only in Russian transcription. Glagolitic script, of *litterae slavonicae*, gave way to the Latin alphabet, just as Latin disestablished Church Slavonic as the standard literary language. Paradoxically, a century later, when new voices clamored for sacred rites *in proprio idiomate*, a language understood by the common folk, such calls for Slavic speech rights were made neither in Church Slavonic nor in Old Czech, its local offshoot, but in Latin. And this protracted fight for Czech language autonomy, for *bohemice nostre lingue*, was at last crowned with victory during the Hussite period.

The Hussite struggle for linguistic self-determination can also be interpreted semiotically: "The demand for divine services in the popular tongue is a demand for requisite comprehensibility" (p. 12). In medieval Gothic thought, however, the symbol defies elemental understanding. The symbol is taken to be a *mysterium*: "the interpenetration of diverse spheres of being is conceived of as miraculous, mystical cognition" (p. 12). The Gothic metaphor, too, is the manifestation of a symbol and is thus of considerable semantic, cognitive value. But toward the end of the Gothic Middle Ages there occur veritable "orgies of metaphor," and this (qualitative) overproduction inevitably leads to inflation and hence to (qualitative) devaluation. In Hussite poetry, the metaphor, like other poetic tropes, becomes divested of its untrammeled symbolic significance and is semantically downgraded to a mere "token" or "parable." Form in general is reduced to a plain and paltry envelope of content, since the Hussite authors are bent on rending "the dialectical unity of form and content, image and object, sign and signified thing" (p. 12), which lies at the heart of high medieval art and philosophy. We can now understand the Hussites' preference for simple, clearly delineated verse forms: the attraction of felicitous phrasing must not be allowed to detract from the communicated message. The Hussite reader cannot afford to pay more attention to the sensuous charm of verbal signs (such as that of poetic sound instrumentation) than to what is meant to be signified: "plus attendit ad signa sensibilia quam signata." Yet, despite the insistence on the minimal conspicuousness of poetic form, the aesthetic element does come through, after all, especially in Hussite sung verse: for even though verbally such poetry plays up its referential content to the fullest, musically it still acquires "artistic sanctification" (p. 20). Against keen Gothic nominalism ("universalia sunt nomina"), the Hussites put forth uncompromising realism. In religious matters the Hussites are similarly iconoclastic: they reject the doctrine of transubstantiation of bread and wine as the true body and blood of Christ, and treat communion in both kinds—that "precious mystery," says Jakobson—as a common occurrence: bread is only bread and wine is wine. This new realism, this "semioclastic" antinominalism which, in Jakobson's words, "proclaims the unequivocal and immutable property of the ideal substance of things unavoidably cancels out the dialectics of symbols" (p. 13). Ultimately, in a historically momentous dialectical reversal, a major epistemological turnabout, the Hussite movement stands the medieval mysticism on its head and, heralding the onset of the Reformation, submits all manifestations of life to strictly rationalistic considerations.

When seen in the social context of the time, the Hussites' need for elementary verse forms, like their zeal for liturgy in *publica voce*, reflects the movement's rationalistic bent. Politically this stance is articulated in a vigorous democratic platform—"a crucially meaningful element," according to Jakobson, "in the period's rich set of ambitions and aspirations" (p. 14). It is the third estate, the commons, who now become the chief consumers and often also producers of literature, whereas pre-Hussite poetry, written and patronized by the members of the higher social classes, sought to appeal to the ruling estates, the nobility and the clergy, of feudal Bohemia. In the fourteenth-century, we recall, one of the loftiest poetic genres was the heroic epic, whose heroes were either feudal lords (in the knightly epics) or saints of noble birth (in saints' lives) and whose anti-heroes—subjects of scorn and ridicule—were the burghers, artisans and peasants, the rank and file of the Hussite movement. Not surprisingly, in Hussite poetry, "the knight and the saint, the two leading figures of feudal mythology, lose their claim to heroic parts" (p. 16). Exhausted formally at the close of the fourteenth century after a series of stylistic transformations and deprived thematically of its ideological legitimacy, the epic—that aristocratic genre for the sophisticated reader—cedes the pride of place to the cruder verse forms accessible to the Hussite masses. As Jakobson impartially observes, "in the conditions of a civil war, the propaganda effectiveness becomes the main impulse behind literary creation" (p. 14).

Like its poetic activity, the whole Hussite trend can be interpreted, Jakobson asserts, as the apogee of the Gothic era and simultaneously as its total historical inversion. The Hussites' strenuous efforts to reform, to remedy the social wrongs and theological errors of Catholicism, give rise to

the Reformation. In what Jakobson sees as a typical illustration of the dialectical change of quantity into quality, the reformers' super-Catholicism
turns into fervid revolutionary anti-Catholicism: the Hussite protest against
the abuses of the church establishment becomes a revolt against all powers
that be. Moralizing doggerel such as "I vy, páni, znamenajte / A své chu-
diny nechajte! / Což na nich viece žádáte, / Než-li uložené jmáte, / Proti
bohu to činíte / A svú dušiu tiem viníte" (Take note, o ye lords / And
leave your poor folk be! / Why demand more of them / than has been allotted to you? / You are acting against God / And so bring guilt upon your
soul) starts out as metaphor (for instance, the lord as a drone) but soon
engenders myth, and "myth, even if not completely realized, becomes a
moving force of history" (p. 2). The end result is the emergence of "modern methods for contesting traditional authorities" (p. 2). In Hegelian categories, the Hussite phase is the negation of a negation, since the Hussites
are engaged in a fight against "the debasement, adulteration, negation of
the original Christian tradition" (p. 2). Yet such a double negation, in Jakobson's view, is never a true return to the positive original. The fruit of
the Hussite uprising is the very opposite of its authentic intent: although
conceived in medieval spirit, it ends up giving birth to the temper of modern times (cf. p. 3). Because religion is the dominant component of medieval ideology, and because other domains such as art, economy or science
are all profoundly interdependent, the Hussite revolution undermines the
church monopoly in spiritual matters and brings about a secularization of
religion itself, which in its turn is a "decisive step toward the secularization of culture as a whole" (p. 2).

As with any historical turning point, it is useless to try to determine
whether the new radical movement was actually incited by the rejection of
the contemporary social and political order or by the memory of a better
past, the era of saints Cyril and Methodius—just as it is futile to argue
whether language or literature played a key part in the cultural flowering
of Czech. When assessing the importance of the Hussite period, its comprehensive qualitative transformation, historians therefore can neither de-
duce the movement's initial motives from the achieved results nor project
the eventual ends from the incipient causes. As we know from linguistics,
Jakobson submits, every social value, just like language, is both *energeia*
(activity) and *ergon* (product), which, though inseparably intertwined, are
far from identical. What one can say—dialectically, or evenhandedly—is
that "the unruly destructive spirit of the revolutionary era is at the same
time a creative spirit which within itself inexorably carries the symptoms
of a new order" (p. 21). Under these circumstances, once the whole system
of cultural values is set in motion, poetry, even if it is ostensibly conservative or retrogressive, is bound to experience extensive change and trans-
valuation. We can hardly conclude with a more appropriate statement than

Jakobson's striking methodological analogy, which, besides testifying to his staggering scholarly versatility, helps tie together the various parts of this chapter:

Although poetry is a totality set apart by a series of specific signs and determined as a totality by its own dominant—namely, poeticity—it is at the same time a part of the higher totalities of culture and of the overall system of social values. Each of these self-governing, integral components is ruled by immanent laws of self-motion, while simultaneously depending on the other parts of the pertinent system: if one component changes, its relationship to the other components also changes, and so do the components themselves. With the invention of photography, the tasks and structure of painting are altered—as are the tasks and structure of theatre with the invention of cinema. We are merely recording the *interrelationship* [my emphasis] between two facts, but we do not insist on ascertaining at all costs which fact is prior and then look for an express causal relationship between them. We could say that with the invention of photography comes a revision of the tasks and thus of the structure of painting; but we could just as well say that painting, in the course of its internal development, had reached a stage at which its tasks were so sharply delineated and restricted that photography had to come into existence . . . to take care of the remaining tasks. Both formulations are equally legitimate and equally one-sided. (p. 3)

NOTES

1. The convergence of the views of the Prague Circle and the Bachtin group is particularly evident in V. N. Vološinov, *Marxism and the Philosophy of Language*, trans. Ladislav Matejka and I. R. Titunik, and P. N. Medvedev/M. M. Bakhtin, *The Formal Method in Literary Scholarship: A Critical Introduction to Sociological Poetics*, trans. Albert J. Wehrle. (Tzvetan Todorov offers a synthetic account of this trend in *Mikhaïl Bakhtine: Le principe dialogique*.) In one of his major studies, "O jazyce básnickém" (1940), Mukařovský in fact refers specifically to Vološinov's article "Konstrukcija vyskazyvanija" (The Construction of the Utterance), *Literaturnaja učeba* 1 (1930): 65–87 (cf. "On Poetic Language," *WVA*, p. 50). On the other hand, Prague school theory of poetic language had considerable influence on Michail Bachtin's older brother, Nicholas Bachtin, a classicist at the University of Birmingham. See the latter's "English Poetry in Greek: Notes on the Comparative Study of Poetic Idioms," *The Link: A Review of Mediaeval and Modern Greek* 1 (1938): 77–84 and 2 (1939): 49–63, esp. 50–58.

2. Quoted from *The Confessions of St. Augustine* (ca. 397–400), trans. John K. Ryan (Garden City, N.Y.: Image-Doubleday, 1960), p. 51.

3. See Karel Svoboda, "La théorie gréco-romaine du signe linguistique," *Časopis pro moderní filologii* 26 (1939): 38–49, for more details concerning the parallel between St. Augustine's semiotic teachings, a synthesis of the ancient views on the subject, and those of Saussure. We still lack a history of semiotics, but the volumes by Gérard Genette, *Mimologiques: Voyage en Cratylie*, and Tzvetan Todorov, *Théories du symbole*, as well as *Symbolisme et interprétation*, build much-

needed foundations for such a project (the two books by Todorov exist in English).

4. Cf. *Course*, pp. 15–17, 66–67, 77–78 (in English translation). The correspondence between Durkheim's and Saussure's thought has been examined in several articles—see, for example, "Quelques remarques sur les rapports de la sociologie et de la linguistique: Durkheim et F. de Saussure," *Journal de psychologie* 30 (1933): 82–91, by Witold Doroszewski (1899–1976), a one-time collaborator of the PLC: cf. his contribution "Autour de 'phoneme'" to *Travaux* 4 (1931): 61–74.

5. For the state of the art in the 1950s and 1960s, see Stephen Ullmann, *Semantics: An Introduction to the Science of Meaning*, and John Lyons, "Semantics: General Principles," in *Introduction to Theoretical Linguistics*, pp. 400–481; or consult Lyons' two-volume study, *Semantics*, published by Cambridge University Press in 1977.

6. "Semasiologie a její význam pro jazykozpyt," *Časopis pro moderní filologii* 13 (1926–1927): 40–45, 121–33. See also two essays by the Circle's František Oberfalcer (1890–), "Hlavní problémy semantiky" (The Main Problems in Semantics) and "O příčinách změn ve významu slov" (On the Causes of Changes in Verbal Meaning), *Listy filologické* 54 (1927): 103–12, 218–33, and 55 (1928): 92–102, 211–16.

7. *Travaux* 1 (1929): 88–93; cf. "The Asymmetric Dualism of the Linguistic Sign," trans. Wendy Steiner, in *PS*, pp. 49–54. For biobibliographical information concerning Karcevskij, a seldom-mentioned figure in current linguistic discussion, see the commemorative issue of *Cahiers Ferdinand de Saussure* 14 (1956).

8. It may be useful to indicate here the difference between the meaning and value of the linguistic sign. Saussure's handy example shows that while the French *mouton* means the same as the English *sheep*, the value of the two words is not equal, as in English there is an additional term *mutton* for which French has no equivalent (*Course*, pp. 115–16).

9. Consult also "O potencionálnosti jazyka" (On the Potentiality of Language), *Sl. sl.* 1 (1935): 148–51, a lecture to the Circle by the Ukrainian scholar Agenor Artymovič (1879–1935). In this argument, language necessarily exists *in potentia* as a requisite norm subsequently to be realized by various speakers of the language group. The dichotomy "potential norm"–"actual realization" corresponds to Saussure's opposition *langue-parole* but not, as Artymovič cautioned, to that between *energeia* and *ergon*; while the *parole* is, in actual fact, a *Tätigkeit*, the *langue*, rather than a "thing," is the permanent possibility underlying the speech event. The first Prague scholar to address this issue was Vilém Mathesius in his lecture "O potencionálnosti jevů jazykových," *Věstník Král. české společnosti nauk* (1911): 1–24, translated by Josef Vachek as "On the Potentiality of the Phenomena of Language," in *A Prague School Reader in Linguistics*, pp. 1–32.

10. As students of literature will recognize, this plight of the truly authentic expression snared in an unremitting pattern of repetition and difference has been a major theme in modern writing at least since Flaubert, who, in *Madame Bovary* (II, 12, p. 196 in the Garnier ed.), put it this way: "He could not distinguish, this experienced man, the dissimilarity of sentiment beneath the sameness of expression. . . . As if the fullness of feelings did not sometime spill out through the emptiest of metaphors, since no one, ever, can give the exact measure of his needs, or concepts, or sorrows . . ." It is doubtful, however, that linguists, as technicians of

language, would endorse Flaubert's artistic or metaphysical lament: "[and since] human speech is like a cracked cauldron on which we beat out tunes to set bears dancing, when we wish to mollify the stars."

11. This term is Edward Sapir's; cf. chapter 7 of *Language: An Introduction to the Study of Speech*, which bears the title "Language as a Historical Product: Drift." Interestingly, Sapir also uses the metaphor of an incline upon which the temporal passage of language is said to take place: ". . . our language has a 'slope' [and] the changes of the next few centuries are in a sense prefigured in certain obscure tendencies of the present. . . . Our very uncertainty as to the impending details of change makes the eventual consistency of their direction all the more impressive" (p. 155).

12. For an overview of Karcevskij's career, see N. S. Pospelov, "O lingvističeskom nasledstve S. Karcevskogo" (The Linguistic Legacy of S. Karcevskij), *Voprosy jazykoznanija* 6 (1957): 46–56, and Wendy Steiner, "Language as Process: Sergej Karcevskij's Semiotics of Language," in *SSM*, pp. 291–300.

13. Vladimír Skalička's article "Asymetrický dualismus jazykových jednotek" (The Asymmetric Dualism of Language Units), *Naše řeč* 19 (1935): 296–303, is, in terms of theory, no more than a footnote.

14. Two recent studies help situate Karcevskij's work vis-à-vis that of Mukařovský and Jakobson: Peter and Wendy Steiner, "The Relational Axes of Poetic Language," a postscript to Jan Mukařovský's *On Poetic Language*, trans. and ed. John Burbank and Peter Steiner, pp. 71–86, and Linda R. Waugh, *Roman Jakobson's Science of Language*, esp. pp. 37–63. Moreover, Peter Steiner attempts to develop Karcevskij's ideas in such essays as "In Defense of Semiotics: The Dual Asymmetry of Cultural Signs," *New Literary History* 12 (1981), 415–35, and "The Semiotics of Literary Reception," in *SLP*, pp. 503–20.

15. For a detailed examination of this issue, see Lubomir Doležel, "Mukařovský and the Idea of Poetic Truth," *Russian Literature* 12 (1982): 283–97.

16. This is a rewording of the terms *osnovnoj priznak značenija* and *vtorostepennyj priznak značenija* (the basic and secondary semantic features) by Jurij Tynjanov, the presiding spirit over Mukařovský's semantics; cf. *Problema stichotvornogo jazyka* (Leningrad: Academia, 1924), pp. 49–50. Two sections of this book, "Rhythm as the Constructive Factor of Verse" and "The Meaning of the Word in Verse," have been translated well by M. E. Suino in *RRP*, pp. 126–45, and ineptly in *The Problem of Verse Language*, in the translation of the whole book by Michael Sosa and Brent Harvey (Ann Arbor: Ardis, 1981).

17. The first quotation comes from Aristotle's *Rhetoric* 1404*b* (in Richard Claverhouse Jebb's translation) and the second from *Poetics* 1458*a*.

18. A more faithful translation of "večerní máj" is "an evening May"; it is less suitable for our purpose, however, since such a combination of two nouns would complicate the issue, even though in set expressions like "evening star" the term clearly functions as an adjectival modifier. Other translated examples similarly depart from the literal in order to drive the point home a little more explicitly.

19. Cf. his entries "Metafora" and "Metonymie" in *Masarykův slovník naučný* (The Masaryk Encyclopedia), vol. 4 (Praha: Československý kompas, 1929), pp. 896, 905. Compare also Tomaševskij's discussion of poetic vocabulary in the first part of *Teorija literatury (Poetika)*, 4th ed. (Moskva: Gos. izd-vo, 1928).

20. *The Rhetoric* 1405*b*.

21. See, for instance, Monroe C. Beardsley, "The Metaphorical Twist," *Philosophy and Phenomenological Research* 22 (1962): 293–307. Of the more recent studies, see especially Samuel R. Levin, *The Semantics of Metaphor*, and the issue entitled *The Scandal of Metaphor* of *Poetics Today* 4 (1983).

22. Mukařovský's own example of metaphor is the line "Pak v pláních hloh vzplá červený a bílý" (Then in the plains the hawthorn flares up red and white), in which "flares up" replaces "blooms," the marginal meanings shared by the two verbs connoting the lively colors of flowers and flames.

23. "Co je poezie?" (What Is Poetry?), *Volné směry* 30 (1933–1934): 229–39; quoted from *SVA*, p. 29. (An English translation is in *SA*, pp. 164–75; rpt. in *SW* 3, pp. 740–50.)

24. It may be this principle that Roland Barthes had in mind when trying to settle the question of what he termed a "signifying practice," which, he thought, "is first of all a differentiated signifying system, dependent on a typology of significations (and not on a universal matrix of the sign [as Barthes himself had held earlier]). This requirement of differentiation was laid down by the Prague School; it implies that signification is not produced in a uniform way, but according to the material of the signifier (this diversity founds semiology). . . ." ("Theory of the Text" [1978], trans. Ian McLeod, in *Untying the Text: A Post-Structuralist Reader*, ed. Robert Young, p. 36).

25. "Úpadek filmu?" (Is the Film in Decline?), *Listy pro umění a kritiku* 1 (1933): 45–49. (An English translation is in *SA*, pp. 145–52; rpt. in *SW* 3, pp. 732–39.) Compare also Tynjanov's restatement of Béla Balázs' notion about what constitutes the basis of the movies: "The visible man and the visible thing appear as elements of film art only when they are presented as meaningful signs" ("Ob osnovach kino" [On the Foundations of Cinema], *Poetika kino* [The Poetics of Cinema], ed. Boris Eichenbaum [Leningrad: Kinopečat', 1927]; quoted from the bilingual version in *Poetica* 3 [1970]: 520). It is worth mentioning that another distinguished formalist theorist of film, Boris Eichenbaum, discerned how motion pictures turn upside down the procedures of verbal art, noting that, while the reader moves from the printed word to evocation or visualization of the described objects, the viewer moves from the "object[s], from comparison of successive shots, to their comprehension, to naming them. . . ." ("Literatura i kino" [Literature and Cinema], in *Literatura: Teorija, kritika, polemika* [Leningrad: Priboj, 1927], p. 297).

26. Compare Jakobson's analysis in "On Realism in Art" (see chapter 2, note 26, above) with his remarks on cinema in "The Metaphoric and Metonymic Poles," in *Fundamentals of Language*, 2nd rev. ed. (The Hague: Mouton, 1971), pp. 90–96, esp. p. 92.

27. Jakobson sketched only the barest outlines of the two basic kinds of cinematic structure without illustrating the workings of filmic metaphor. Still, this formalist-structuralist approach to film found a worthy successor in Jurij Lotman, *Semiotics of Cinema*, trans. Mark E. Suino; *Semiotika kino i problemy kinoestetiki* first appeared in 1973. Starting from the observation that "the verbal arts . . . strive to construct from the material of conventional signs a verbal image whose iconic nature is clearly manifested," while, at the same time, "the propensity of graphics and painting for narration is a paradoxical but continual tendency of the

visual arts" (p. 8, cf. p. 37), Lotman demonstrates why filmic sequences tend to be grounded in metonymic shot conjoinings. See also Jakobson's comments in "Visual and Auditory Signs" and "On the Relation between Visual and Auditory Signs" (1964), rpt. in *SW* 2, pp. 334–44.

28. Unless otherwise indicated, all references to particular films, whether from the silent or sound era, are mine.

29. Panofsky's magisterial "Style and Medium in the Motion Pictures" (1934) and representative portions of Arnheim's writings on film (1933–1934) have been collected in *Film Theory and Criticism: Introductory Readings*, ed. Gerald Mast and Marshall Cohen.

30. "K diskusi o řeči ve filmu" (A Discussion on Speech in Film), *Sl. sl.* 1 (1936): 38–42 (the first quotation comes from p. 41 and the second from p. 39). Although successful as filmmakers, Vančura is better known as an experimental novelist and Honzl as an innovative stage director. It may be no coincidence that Vančura's novels inspired two of the most ambitious Czech films of the 1960s, František Vláčil's *Markéta Lazarová* (1967) and Jiří Menzel's *Capricious Summer* (*Rozmarné léto*, 1968).

31. This point forms the centerpiece of Maurice Merleau-Ponty's lecture "The Film and the New Psychology" (1945), in his *Sense and Non-Sense*, trans. Hubert L. Dreyfus and Patricia Allen Dreyfus, pp. 48–59.

32. See André Bazin, *What Is Cinema?*, trans. Hugh Gray.

33. "K estetice filmu" (A Note on the Aesthetics of Film) appeared together with Jakobson's "Is the Film in Decline?" in *Listy pro umění a kritiku* 1 (1933): 100–108. "Čas ve filmu" (Time in Film), although written in the 1930s, appeared only in *SE*, pp. 179–83. Both are translated in *SSF*, pp. 178–90 and 191–200. I discuss them in the order of their appearance.

34. Cf. Eichenbaum's "Problemy kinostilistiki" (The Problems of Film Stylistics) in *Poetika kino*, pp. 13–51.

35. In Mukařovský's view, this absence of a limit, more precisely of the fixed frame, is a feature distinguishing the depiction of space in cinema from that of most illustrations. Mukařovský evidently overlooked the comic strip, which, in America at least, was then in its heyday. Alex Raymond's action strip *Flash Gordon*, one of the most successful specimens of the genre, began appearing in 1934, the year of Mukařovský's venture into film theory. No less an authority than Erwin Panofsky considered the comic strip, which possesses such expressive devices as detail or special angle "shots," a rich source of film art. And then, only animation separates the comic strip from the film cartoon, which, in Disney's early work, represented a chemically purified essence of the possibilities of cinema (cf. Panofsky, "Style and Medium in the Motion Pictures," pp. 153, 160).

36. Cf. the screenplay *Hitler, a Film from Germany*, trans. Joachim Neugroschel, preface by Susan Sontag (New York: Farrar, 1982).

37. Although drawing on different methodological premises, Käte Hamburger arrives at a similar conclusion in her analysis of cinematic fiction: "The motion-picture as such is the reason why the film is both drama rendered epic and epic rendered drama. The factor of motion in cinematic photography turns the latter into a narrative function. . . . In the film dramatic and epic techniques mesh, resulting in a special form of dramatized epic and epically rendered drama, both in

one—a blend wherein in a peculiar but nevertheless structurally and epistemologically well-founded manner each of these two factors is at once enlarged upon and restricted" (*The Logic of Literature* [1957], trans. Marilynn J. Rose, pp. 229–30).

38. Cf. Šklovskij, *Teorija prozy* (Moskva: Federacija, 1925), passim. Incidentally, in one respect only—that is, in subscribing to Jakobson's opinion that the soundtrack diminishes film's flexibility in changing temporal planes to the point where the artistic plot and the real story-stuff are one—Mukařovský's own analysis appears anachronistic. A shift from a present to a past action, in this view, is supposed to be especially difficult: a dead man cannot come alive in the next scene. This is exactly what happens in Billy Wilder's *Sunset Boulevard* (1950), which is narrated by the man whose corpse we see floating in the swimming pool as the film opens; yet this clumsy dramaturgy produces such a mildly incongruous effect that, perhaps because of the dream-logic of the movies, only a few spectators notice that something is amiss. Moreover, Mukařovský seems not to have contemplated that the seeming irreversibility of film-time could be put to tremendous advantage, as in Claude Lelouch's *The Crook* (*Le voyou*, 1970), where the action moves back into the past without any hint; not until near the end, when those past events link up again with the present, do viewers realize that they have been hoodwinked—and then they have to see the movie again to find out how and at what point they were duped. In a later film, *Happy New Year* (*La bonne année*, 1972), not wishing to repeat the same trick, Lelouch signals the plot's return to the past by switching from black and white to color. This circular serpent-biting-its-tail structure has also been used effectively in literature, most notably in Vladimir Nabokov's short story "The Circle" (1936; English translation in the collection *A Russian Beauty and Other Stories* [New York: McGraw-Hill, 1973], pp. 253–68). Here, tellingly, the opening sentence says "In the second place . . ." and the last sentence "In the first place. . . ." As the quoted sentences plainly show, however, such a verbal "commodius vicus of recirculation" (as Joyce described the structure of *Finnegans Wake*) cannot, for the reason described above, achieve the surprise effect of the cinema.

39. *The Sense of an Ending: Studies in the Theory of Fiction*, esp. pp. 46–52.

40. Actually, the first Prague School scholar to address the issue of general semiotics—though not the semiotics of art—was Miloš Weingart (later, as we have seen in the preceding chapter, one of Mukařovský's opponents) in his contribution to the Mathesius *Festschrift* "Semiologie a jazykozpyt" (Semiotics and Linguistics), in *Charisteria*, pp. 5–13. Weingart recognized the importance of semiotics for the study of natural languages and proposed, following the example of Wilhelm Wundt, a synchronically conceived typology of the gestures which accompany everyday speech.

41. "Co je poezie?" quoted from Jakobson, *Studies in Verbal Art: Texts in Czech and Slovak* (*SVA*), pp. 20–32 (unless otherwise indicated, this and all the subsequent quotations are from p. 30). Jakobson delivered this paper as a lecture to the organization of Prague artists called Mánes in 1933.

It is curious to note that the anthology I use is a reprint of *Slovesné umění a umělecké slovo* (Verbal Art and the Artistic Word), ed. Miroslav Červenka (Praha: Československý spisovatel, 1969), which precedes by four years a similar collection of Jakobson's essays entitled *Questions de poétique*, ed. Tzvetan Todorov (Paris: Seuil, 1973). Unfortunately, the original Czech collection, although printed and bound, was subsequently banned by the government and destroyed. In this way it ironically, and lamentably, repeats the fate of the first collection of Russian formalist essays ever to be published outside the Soviet Union, *Teória literatúry*, ed. Mikuláš Bakoš (Trnava: Urbánek, 1941), which was withdrawn from circulation by the pro-Nazi Slovak government; the second edition finally came out in 1971.

42. See Erlich, "Repercussions," in *RF*, pp. 140–53.

43. Quoted from *Novejšaja russkaja poezija: Nabrosok pervyj* (Praha: Politika, 1921), p. 10, rpt. in *SW* 5, pp. 299–354; in English translation, "Modern Russian Poetry: Velemir Khlebnikov [Excerpts]," in *Major Soviet Writers: Essays in Criticism*, ed. and trans. E. J. Brown (London: Oxford University Press, 1973), pp. 62–63.

44. This lecture, delivered at Masaryk University in Brno, where Jakobson taught Russian and Slavic linguistics and medieval Czech literature from 1933 until 1939, has never been published in the original Czech; it first appeared as "The Dominant," translated by Herbert Eagle, in *RRP*, pp. 82–87; rpt. in *SW* 3, pp. 751–56. This concept had been crucial, as Jakobson himself remarked, to the elaboration of the formalist theory, where it underwent numerous redefinitions. For a discussion of some aspects of the formalists' approach to the dominant, see Erlich, *RF*, esp. pp. 199ff.

45. Some twenty-five years later, this is how Jakobson restated his notion of the poetic function: "This function, by promoting the palpability of signs, deepens the fundamental dichotomy of signs and objects" (*Style in Language*, p. 356). Jakobson formulated this idea for the first time, though a little less clearly, in his monograph on Chlebnikov in 1921: "In emotional language and poetic language, the verbal representations (phonetic as well as semantic) concentrate on themselves greater attention; the connection between the aspect of sound and that of meaning is tighter, more intimate, and language is accordingly more revolutionary, insofar as habitual associations by contiguity (*smežnost'*) retreat into the background" (*Major Soviet Writers*, p. 62; in the original, *Novejšaja russkaja poezija*, p. 10). As can be seen, over the years Jakobson's views evolved toward greater lucidity but remained fundamentally unchanged. Gérard Genette, however, has sought to tease out, unconvincingly to my mind, various inconsistencies in Jakobson's definitions of poetic language: see Genette, "Formalisme et langage poétique," *Comparative Literature* 28 (1976): 233–43, a reprint of a section from *Mimologiques* (pp. 302–14).

46. For an extensive discussion of the place of phenomenology in Jakobson's semiotics, see Elmar Holenstein, *Roman Jakobson's Approach to Language: Phenomenological Structuralism*, trans. Catherine and Tarcisius Schelbert; consult also the review article by Peter and Wendy Steiner, "Structures and Phenomena," *PTL: A Journal for Descriptive Poetics and Theory of Literature* 3 (1978): 357–70.

47. In "Vers une science de l'art poétique," a preface to *Théorie de la littérature: Textes des Formalistes russes*, ed. Tzvetan Todorov (Paris: Seuil, 1966), Jakobson himself railed against the talk of *ostranenie* (i.e., defamiliarization) as fraught with the early formalism's, and particularly Šklovskij's, "inept platitudes on the professional secret of art"; rpt. in *SW* 5, p. 542.

48. In a review of *SA*, *Dispositio* 1 (1976): 362.

49. A review of the same volume, *Comparative Literature* 30 (1978): 274.

50. Jakobson returned to the work of his favorite Czech and Slovak poets later in his career, proving an extraordinary dedication to the poetry of his adopted country: "Stroka Machi o zove gorlici" (Mácha's Verse on the Call of the Turtledove), *International Journal of Slavic Linguistics and Poetics* 3 (1960): 89–108, rpt. in *SW* 5, pp. 486–504, and "The Grammatical Structure of Janko Král's Verses," *Sborník Filozofickej fakulty Univerzity Komenského* 16 (1964): 29–40, rpt. in *SW* 3, pp. 482–98.

51. Jakobson's plea for an unexpurgated edition of Mácha's diary was at last answered in 1980 by the exile publishing house *68 Publishers* of Toronto. At home, Mácha has been turned into a national hero, and the official veneration combined with official prudery is not very conducive to publishing Mácha's private jottings in Czechoslovakia even some century and a half after his death (born in 1810, Mácha died in 1836).

52. Boris Eichenbaum, "Literaturnaja kar'era L. Tolstogo," in *Moj vremennik* (Leningrad: Izdatel'stvo pisatelej, 1929), pp. 109–14; translated as "The Literary Career of Lev Tolstoi" by Gary Kern in Eichenbaum's *The Young Tolstoi* (Ann Arbor: Ardis, 1972), pp. 136–41.

53. See Jakobson's impassioned analysis of this motif in "O pokolenii, rastrativšem svoich poetov," *Smert' Vladimira Majakovskogo* (Berlin: Petropolis, 1931), pp. 7–45, rpt. in *SW* 5, pp. 355–81; translated as "On a Generation That Squandered Its Poets" by E. J. Brown in his anthology *Major Soviet Writers*, pp. 7–32.

54. This and the following passages have been omitted from the abbreviated English version of "What Is Poetry?" (in the original, they are on pp. 31 and 32).

55. The first essay is *Actes du Huitième Congrès international de philosophie à Prague 2–7 septembre 1934*, ed. Emanuel Rádl and Zdeněk Smetáček (Praha: Oranizační komitét kongresu, 1936), pp. 1065–72, and the second contribution is in *Actes du Quatrième Congrès international des linguistes tenu à Copenhague du 27 août au 1er septembre 1936*, ed. Louis Hjelmslev et al. (Copenhagen: Munksgaard, 1938), pp. 98–104. Both essays have been translated into English twice, respectively, in *SSF*, pp. 82–88, *WVA*, pp. 65–72, and *SA*, pp. 3–9, 155–63. The two sets of translations vary in several places, since the former are based on the Czech version while the latter follow the French originals. Under the circumstances I have found it unnecessary to offer yet another translation: I use, with slight modification, the renditions by I. R. Titunik and Susan Janacek in *SA*, references to which are given below.

56. Cf. "The Third Moment" of Immanuel Kant's *Analytic of the Beautiful*, trans. Walter Cerf (Indianapolis: Bobbs-Merrill, 1963). The complete *Kritik der Urteilskraft* first appeared in 1790.

57. "What Is Poetry?" p. 22.

58. "Úvodem," *Sl. sl.* 1 (1935): 1–7; cf. "By Way of Introduction," in *Recycling the Prague Linguistic Circle*, ed. and trans. Marta K. Johnson, pp. 32–46.

59. "Úvahy o básnictví doby husitské" (Reflections on the Poetry of the Hussite Era), *Sl. sl.* 2 (1936): 1–21; parts subsumed under the title of the third section, "Signum et signatum," translated by Michael Heim, in *SA*, pp. 176–87. This essay grew out of Jakobson's presentation before the Circle on 29 April 1935.

5 | Readers' Reception History and the Individual Poetic Talent

Those masterful images because complete
Grew in pure mind, but of what began?
A mound of refuse or the sweepings of a street,
Old kettles, old bottles, and a broken can,
Old iron, old bones, old rags, that raving slut
Who keeps the till. Now that my ladder's gone,
I must lie down where all the ladders start,
In the foul rag-and-bone shop of the heart.

W. B. YEATS

We could not find a better starting point for this next to last chapter than a statement by Mukařovský which graphically epitomizes the development of Prague structuralism at its final stage:

The inner unity of structuralism in literary theory rests in its conception of structure as an assembly of forces balancing each other in dialectical tensions. Structure is not merely the construction of a single poetic work but also the work's relationships to all that surrounds it and with which it comes in contact. For structuralism, a sequence of works in time appears to be a structure in motion. The ties of literature with the other arts, even with the more distant realms of culture such as science, religion, politics and the like, and, finally, the relationship of literature to society, are understood as reciprocal tensions among structures. A poet's individuality is a structure; and the group of poets living in a given era also constitutes a structure in which individuals represent dynamic parts whose efficacy is conditioned not only by their personal dispositions (the degree of talent, special propensities) but also, to a certain extent, by the relationship of each poet to others and to the group as a whole. Indeed, for structuralism no question of literary theory is beyond its fundamentally integral, and at the same time dialectical, understanding—and in this lies its inner unity.[1]

Looking back at the Jakobson-Tynjanov manifesto which began this exposition, we see how impressive a distance the Prague School has traveled since its early days, for the entire theoretical position of Jakobson and Tynjanov, and hence of incipient structuralism, is summed up in the first half of Mukařovský's paragraph. Jakobson and Tynjanov merely argued that, analogous to Saussurean *langue*, literature is a system of norms which underlie every work of poetic art or *parole*; that the literary system or structure retains its systemic character even while undergoing changes in time; and that the direction and frequency of the changes of the literary system are in some measure contingent on the transformations in the overall social and cultural context. Yet, for the Russian theorists, the "system of systems" (and, of course, each particular subsystem) appeared as a free-floating abstraction without moorings in the elemental communicative situation, cut loose from the producers as well as receivers of artistic and nonartistic messages. In Mukařovský's statement, by contrast, structuralism embraces, in an integral and dialectical fashion, all the vital agents—both the artists and, as we shall see in the second part of this chapter, their audience—indispensable for any communicative exchange. Moreover, as means and products of human communication, artistic structures, in Mukařovský's new conception, are no longer self-referring formal relationships but, rather, hierarchical correlations invested with meaning. In this phase of structuralism, structures are, first and last, referential, semantic—in short, semiotic.

The complicated issues posed by the developing semiotic theory, as we observed in chapter 4, pushed the problem of literary history into the background, propelling the research interest of the Prague scholars more toward literary semantics and the sociology of literature and art.[2] The concern for literary history, however, returned to the fore in the Circle's discussions with the imminent outbreak of World War II. As *The Contribution of Czechoslovakia to Europe and to Humanity*, a beautifully produced anthology edited by Vilém Mathesius, shows, in the late 1930s the structuralists rose to the defense of the national values embodied in Czech literature and culture.[3] The first essay, describing "The Czech Share in the Church Slavonic Culture," came from the pen of Roman Jakobson; but it appeared under the sobriquet Olaf Jansen, since Jakobson, after nearly twenty years in Czechoslovakia (he had arrived there in July 1920 at the age of twenty-four), was forced to flee before the encroaching Nazis in March 1939.[4] His departure, needless to say, marked the end of the central chapter in the Circle's history. But even under the trying circumstances of the German occupation, the Prague linguists and critics continued along the lines of their previous research, seeking, as we shall see, in the history of Czech literature and culture the *raison d'être* of their country's existence as a nation.

The grave political and ideological considerations, however, did not overshadow the structuralists' preoccupation with theoretical—linguistic, literary and semiotic—problems. The remarks by Mukařovský from the opening quotation made in 1944 during a heated debate with another Prague scholarly group, the Society for Literary History, testify to the Circle's enduring theoretical spirit. The impetus for this debate, in a way a repeat of the controversy surrounding Mukařovský's study of *The Sublimity of Nature*, arose out of a programmatic piece entitled "Literary History: Its Problems and Its Tasks," written by a junior member of the Circle, Felix Vodička.[5] The two polemical exchanges concerning a structural theory of literary history, which took place ten years apart, point up a curious fact about the reception of structuralism among scholars committed to the more traditional approaches to literature and history. These polemics suggest above all that while the structuralists' numerous analyses of specific texts proved unassailable, their attempts to move beyond the formalist *explication de texte* into the wider realm of literary, and then social, history have invariably given rise to alarm. What literary historians seemed to find most unpalatable was the claim that the study of changes in literary evolution lends itself to the same systematic elucidation as the treatment of concrete literary works. They preferred to emphasize the uniqueness both of historical material and of the historian's own understanding. In this respect, the debate reenacted the quarrel between personalizing *Geistesgeschichte* and objectifying *Literaturwissenschaft*.

The reconciliation of the contending and oftentimes contradictory claims of the two viewpoints—one focusing on the unique and the individual, the other highlighting the systemic and the social—has been one of the chief goals of the structural theory of literary history from the start. As the structuralists insisted, there is always repetition in difference and uniformity in transformation: it is the system, they argued time and again, that provides the solution. The Prague structuralists' predilection for the system at the expense of the individual resulted, however, in a sort of *Literaturgeschichte ohne Namen*, a depersonalized, almost anonymous literary history which, though both literary and historical, still threatened to dissolve itself—as the Marxist critics pointed out—into unwarranted abstractions. On the other hand, traditional historians' orientation toward the unrepeatable and the exceptional, whether in individual artists or in individual epochs, placed a premium on psychology to the detriment of art's specificity and autonomy. The career of Felix Vodička, discussed in the following section, offers a textbook example of the fundamental conflicts rending traditional and structural approaches to literary history and, more important, shows a way of resolving such conflicts.

In an interesting methodological turnabout, Vodička, working at the outset in the traditional historical mold, gradually embraced structuralism, only to veer later toward more and more detailed—one might almost say, formalist—readings of specific texts, though from a unified historical perspective. Vodička's scholarly development thus reverses the evolution of Mukařovský's and Jakobson's theories, which, having at first concentrated on literary texts to the exclusion of everything else, eventually integrated literature into the broadest possible context of the life of individual writers, readers and, ultimately, the society as a whole. Moreover, Vodička's conversion to structural theory after casting his lot with conventional literary history demonstrates that structuralism's own development gives the lie to the received notion of historical progress as a harmonious passing of the torch from one critic to another in smooth succession—that "literary history of the generals," each standing on the shoulders of predecessors. Without a doubt Mukařovský's most faithful disciple but never directly his student, Vodička had to shed many of his initial preconceptions and, so to speak, reeducate himself in mid-career.[6] Therefore, let us now examine Vodička's prestructuralist writings—and then contrast them with his structural investigations of the reception of literary works.

‖●‖●‖●‖●‖●‖

Since most of the Circle's founders, like most Russian formalists, were of the generation of the 1890s, Felix Vodička (1909–1974) can be said to belong to the second generation of structuralists. Vodička also differs from his structuralist forerunners in his academic background. Whereas Mukařovský and Jakobson were trained principally in aesthetics and in linguistics, respectively, Vodička specialized in Czech literature and in history. It may not be an exaggeration to suggest in this connection that structuralist literary theory and criticism came into being precisely because its protagonists were unencumbered by traditional concepts of literary study. Vodička, by contrast, steeped in established literary scholarship, discovered structuralism, and with it the need for methodological reflection, only after a series of unmemorable exercises in literary history.

Vodička's early essays would be of scant interest today if they did not so well exemplify the attitude toward literature against which the structuralists, and later Vodička himself, reacted. This is the attitude of academic eclecticism which, though ostensibly devoted to verbal art, turns the literary work into a *res nullius*, all the while drawing inspiration from psychology, social history, philosophical or religious thought and the like. Between 1933, when still at the university, and 1941, when his first structuralist study appeared, Vodička wrote five extended historical studies, none of which shows the least interest in poetic theory. Although dedicated to literary topics, these studies do not question the status of literature and of literary language; they deal instead with extraliterary phenomena which the works of literature are, as Vodička believed, meant to illustrate or document.

Taken together, three of Vodička's earliest essays comprise a sketch of Franco-Czech literary and cultural relations during the second half of the nineteenth century.[7] Vodička begins by examining the influence of Charles Baudelaire on the decadent Czech poets of the nineties, then moves chronologically backwards to Théodore de Banville's effect on the poets of the eighties and finally traces Pierre-Jean de Béranger's reception in Bohemia during the sixties and seventies. In particular, the first two comparative studies, "Březina and Baudelaire" and "Vrchlický and Banville," are marred by Vodička's overriding concern for psychological typology.[8]

The basic premises of this typology remain unexamined throughout, and its results are undistinguishable from vulgar biographism. In Vodička's opinion, a philological analysis of shared motifs or themes—not to speak of formal and linguistic similarities[9]—discloses a merely external dependence of one poet on another in an exercise smacking of what he views as positivistic *Stoffgeschichte*. Far more relevant for him is the question of the spiritual or "inner affinity" between poets, in this case between the symbolist Otokar Březina (1869–1929) and Baudelaire, which, as he says, must be discernible within the poetic texts themselves. Yet at the same time, Vodička makes such frequent use of biographic, extratextual material (correspondence, diaries and reminiscences) that he is compelled to conclude that, even though—as he himself admits—the primary lessons the Czech poet learned from the French were in versification, rhyme and metaphor, the presumed all-important psychological resemblance between Březina and Baudelaire failed to manifest itself in Březina's poetry. Vodička's final statement curiously disproves his original methodological assumption: only biographical, not textual, features of what Vodička considers to be Březina's "inborn spiritual disposition" account for his sympathetic response to Baudelaire.

Vodička gets caught up in a similar contradiction when discussing Banville's contribution to the development of Jaroslav Vrchlický, a protean poet who has been described as an "analogue to Hugo, Carducci, and Tennyson, combined."[10] Once again, Vodička's stated aim is to reduce the problem of poetic influence to that of the common psychological, artistic types of the examined poets. To the extent that Vrchlický welcomed the challenge of rendering into Czech, through either translation or original poetic composition, the formally recalcitrant modes of the rondeau, the odelette and the ballad, which the *parnassien* Banville reintroduced into modern French poetry, formal analysis would seem eminently called for. No matter—Vodička remains engrossed in the charting of the poets' "internal relationships," their spiritual similarities and differences. Among the cardinal disparities between Banville and Vrchlický, for example, Vodička lists the fact that in their erotic poetry the former expressed passion for women in general, whereas the latter's poetic ardor was always incited by a particular lady. One prevailing similarity, on the other hand, is the two poets' shared fascination with women's hair, a recurrent motif in their respective *oeuvres*. Although Vodička is well aware that such thematic emulation is often prescribed by the complicated, stringent formal patterns of the ballad, he nevertheless must probe into the poets' private lives in order to uncover evidence of their poetic kinship.

In this approach, despite Vodička's claims that he is dealing with the "essence" of poetry, a work is simply looked through for its subject matter, usually conceived in psychological terms, or is altogether overlooked.

Even when on occasion Vodička explores literary rather than private concerns of the poets in question, his explanations once again derive from purely thematic, not formal or compositional, aspects of their poetry. As if Vrchlický's desire, for example, to bring modern Czech literature onto a par with that of France, Italy or England were not sufficient proof of his preoccupation with poetic forms, Vodička finds it necessary to call upon Vrchlický's poems with such thematically explicit titles as "A Ballad on Ballad." Or, in a similar vein, he tells us about Vrchlický's special interest in literary history, of which the poems devoted explicitly to other Czech poets and writers are the all-revealing indication.

While the Baudelaire and Banville essays focus on the relationship of individual Czech poets of subsequent generations to their respective French models, the third study, "The Echo of Béranger's Poetry in Czech Literature," sets the problem of comparative literary study in a sociological perspective.[11] Vodička no longer attributes the source of Béranger's appeal to his poetic output, let alone his typical personal traits, but to the success with which he fulfilled the demands made on poetry by a specific historical moment. In matters of form, Béranger was far from an innovator. In this instance, therefore, Vodička's indifference to textual analysis of poetry seems less of a drawback. What Vodička endeavors to show this time is the complex set of elements, both literary and social, which determine the role a given poet's work will play in national literature.

Such factors as the local political situation and social structure help clarify, in Vodička's view, the failure among poets of several generations to create a Czech equivalent of Béranger's *chanson* with its immediate mass appeal. In the 1830s, at the close of Béranger's own career, Czech readership turned a deaf ear to the political stridency in Béranger's poetry. A further factor, having to do with the sociology of genre, hampered Béranger's early reception: his poetry drew its inspiration from urban life, but Czech popular poetry grew out of folk songs. Only after the revolutionary events of 1848 could Béranger make his mark on the Czech scene, for then the need for politically effective poetry became quite acute. That no Czech "citizen-poet" emerged in the fifties should be explained, according to Vodička, by the fact that most poets felt torn between two contradictory stances. As citizens committed to a liberal national program, the members of the "May" group, though taking their name from Mácha's celebrated lyric-epic poem, wished to produce tendentious and hortatory verse that would move the common reader to political action. But under the sway of Byron no poet—except for Vítězslav Hálek, the leading literary artist of the *Máj* generation—could suppress the subjective inclinations at odds with most readers' everyday experience. In this Czech quest for efficacious poetic journalism, Béranger's often flippant poetry was transformed into a rather earnest poetic undertaking. As a result, the generation of the seventies, the group "Ruch" (Rush) began writing utilitarian poetry with a vengeance, churning out slogans rather than poetic verse. But by the 1880s, Vrchlický and other "Lumírians" (i.e., contributors to the journal *Lumír*) vehemently rejected this downgrading of poetic creation geared to serve overt political goals. Now, at last, the Czechs were ready to appreciate not Béranger but Hugo, the Parnassians, Baudelaire . . .

Unlike the first two essays, Vodička's extensive historical survey of Béranger's reception is not spoiled by *ad hoc* psychological explanations of the artists' personal proclivities. In examining literary conventions and their interaction with social and political changes instead of individual poetic texts, Vodička put his thorough historical knowledge to good use and, in the process, hit upon the fertile methodological problem of reception, which he was later to elaborate. Still, the Béranger piece lacks proper focus, does not establish a hierarchy of relationships in literary evolution and haphazardly registers various changes instead of explaining them systematically. In the end, it strikes one as diffuse and prolix, falling squarely into what has been aptly called the portmanteau school of history, which, in its eclecticism, favors comprehensiveness over selectivity.

Another study from this period, treating the topic of regional literature in Moravia, once more displays the strength of Vodička's painstaking historical approach.[12] Following the twists and turns of the career of Jan Herben (1857–1936) as a prose writer, from his romantic admiration of the *Volk* to his critically realistic assessment of it, Vodička leaves no stone unturned. His study is little handicapped by the fact that Herben's literary accomplishments—since the journalist and the chronicler in him got the better of the artist—were undistinguished. This effort, in short, belongs more appropriately to cultural than to literary history. The subject of Vodička's other two studies, Karel Hynek Mácha, had to be handled in a radically different manner, however. Indeed, sensitized to aesthetic, formal matters, Vodička now adopts several theoretical premises framed by the scholars associated with the Linguistic Circle: Mukařovský, Jakobson, F. X. Šalda and Otakar Zich. In "Mácha as Playwright," Vodička continues to see the key point as the struggle between an individual's psychological makeup and the unbending requirements of form.[13] For Mácha, the struggle is between his propensity for self-expression in portrayal of emotional states or lyrical descriptions and the dramatic demands for action in historical plays. But in the next study, "The Period and the Work," Vodička takes the driving force of literary history to be the conflict between the prevalent poetic canon and the ever-renewed necessity on the part of many up-and-coming poets to alter that canon.[14] The latter essay shows Mácha's endeavors, whether in the domain of poetic language, versification, literary genre or the conception of beauty, against the background of the conceptions valid for the preceding period. Here Vodička is on the threshold of the structuralist understanding of literary evolution. His analysis of Mácha's *oeuvre*, however, remains excessively thematic and psychologistic.

‖●‖●‖●‖●‖●‖

Vodička's breakthrough toward structuralism occurs in his contribution to the *Festschrift* in memory of the major historian of Czech literature, Arne Novák (1880–1939).[15] Published in 1940 in occupied Czechoslovakia, Vodička's article reflects the cardinal concerns of the time in its anxiety over the fate of Czech culture. Every culture, affirms Vodička, is an "individual totality" following its own "evolutionary curve given by its internal requirements . . . and by its ability to respond in a typical way to outside stimuli" (p. 197). The decisive characteristic of Czech culture throughout history has been its steadfast orientation toward Western Europe—not only Germany, but, as a counterbalance to the overwhelming German pressure, also England and France. What aspect of Western culture, asks Vodička, did the Czechs find most worthy of imitation and appropriation? The emphatic answer, sharply contradicting his previous beliefs, is: "the formal [*tvarové*] values or accomplishments . . . that have augured new ways in the realization of artistic tasks" (p. 202).

Thus Mácha, in Vodička's new argument, was not really under the spell of Byron's titanism; rather, what Mácha sought to learn from the English master was the mixed lyric-epic form of the romantic tale. Similarly, Béranger's petty-bourgeois world view did not intrigue the Czechs so much as the *chanson*'s supple and succinct means of embodying revolutionary pathos. Finally, the Parnassians as well as the symbolists were appreciated most of all for their "artistic, rather than ideological, solutions to literary problems" (p. 203). Indeed, the West—particularly France—has all along set an example of how to integrate the "telltale signs of new [formal] possibilities that crop up at random into a complete aesthetic system, a structure of mutually dependent elements" (p. 204). And Czech literature inevitably followed suit, while at the same time pursuing its own path of development. In this account of the nature of literature, clearly, Vodička drops all psychologically grounded explanations and supplants them with a structural view of the history of art forms as belonging to a (relatively) autonomous realm guided by concerns and principles of its own.

Jan Mukařovský, too, was among the contributors to the volume commemorating Arne Novák. His article, "The Tradition of 'Form,'" expresses views which complement and buttress those of Vodička in a way reminiscent of the earlier Mukařovský-Jakobson collaborations.[16] We have seen how the Prague structuralists untiringly strove to identify the distinguishing characteristics of poetic language as opposed to ordinary language and how, in their comparisons with the other arts, they endeavored to locate those aesthetic features which differentiate, for example, literature from film. In the Novák contribution, Mukařovský attempts to define the distinctive traits of a national (in this instance, Czech) literature which determine its place among other (European) literatures. We recall that, when discussing the nature of cinematic norms, Mukařovský remarked that every art faces a single limitation: it cannot lose its identity even when it assimilates aesthetic impulses from the neighboring arts. But Mukařovský also noted that the threat of any art's foregoing its distinctiveness is not very serious, since each art is bound to attain the same effect by different means and since, by using the same means, it is bound to produce different effects. A similar principle, according to Mukařovský, holds true for a national literature, which, if it is to preserve its sense of independence and self-direction, "must transform foreign incentives and influences to suit its own needs" (p. 245).

Consequently, the development of European literature cannot be determined by one or two national centers that exert influence on the rest of the literatures of the Continent in ever-widening gyres. Such a notion of comparative literature as consisting of a "handful of active national subjects and numerous passive objects" (p. 248) is false, Mukařovský argues, because every literature, dependent as it is on the specific tongue, "addresses in its own manner the tasks posed by the evolution of European literature" (p. 247). Thus, on the one hand, the function of a given metre or rhyme must vary in relation to the different linguistic materials of individual languages. The Czech iamb of necessity differs from the German iamb, since in Czech there is a dearth of ascending or alternating word units, which, however, abound in German. Similarly, masculine rhymes in Czech and English are not at all alike: in Czech masculine rhymes constantly vie for dominance with feminine rhymes, whereas in English masculine rhymes predominate, at times completely excluding the two-syllable feminine ones from rhymed verse. On the other hand, when Czech poetry seeks to reproduce effects achieved in the poetry of another nation, it cannot rely on the same means: the Lumírians, wishing to emulate the alexandrine of Hugo and Parnassians with its flowing, lineal intonation, were forced to recast standard word order, a syntactic change the French poets themselves did not find necessary. Closely bound up with the character of a language, even entire literary movements, such as symbolism or futurism, acquire quite dissimilar characteristics in the artistic expressions of different countries, for every national literature must pursue a path charted by its own linguistic principles.

In this essay, animated by patriotism and a profound feeling for Czech literature, Mukařovský goes so far as to replace the term *struktura*, with its Latin derivation, by a term *tvar*, a Slavic word etymologically related to expressions for shaping or creating (*tvar, utváření, tvořivost*). The Czech equivalent of the German term *Gestalt, tvar* is a near synonym of *forma* and is comparable to the English word *shape*. We shall, however, keep the category of *structure* to avoid needless complications. Both *tvar* and *struktura* are holistic concepts which subsume "form" as well as "content."[17] As Mukařovský maintains, from the perspective of the aesthetic function, not only the form but the work as a whole is seen to comprise a structure. Individual elements composing the work—for instance, rhythm, euphony, lexical selection or sentence construction—are partial structures subordinate to the total holistic structure of the work; and the work's holistic structure, in turn, is subordinate to the hierarchically higher structure of the given genre.

What are the distinguishing structural properties of a national literature? These are of two kinds, according to Mukařovský, one set of properties being contingent on the structural makeup of the pertinent language, the other on the vital poetic tradition. Both sets serve the same main functions: first, to ensure that some structural features of a nation's literature remain unchanged throughout its development, and second, to secure a continuous, uninterrupted evolution of the overall structure of that literature. The two structural sets, of course, are equally indispensable for the preservation of the particular literature's identity and self-determination. In the now familiar argument, the structure of a literature evolves in accordance with its own inner laws, and "outside influences can function only as accidents that are sufficiently strong to enhance the evolutionary movement, yet weak enough not to disrupt the intrinsic continuity" (p. 246).

The permanent features characterizing Czech poetry of all periods—the stress on the first syllable of the word, the independence of quantity or syllabic length from verbal stress, the relatively free word order—derive directly from the structure of the Czech language. The poetic tradition, likewise, generates lasting structural values. One such structural accomplishment of more than passing or period importance is the freeing of verse intonation from the domination of poetic rhythm. We remember that the principal achievement of Polák's *Sublimity of Nature* was its discovery of a rhythmic syncopation which invigorated the monotonous, mechanical verse of the Puchmajerians with its full realization of the metre. Several generations later, the Lumírians once more had to combat a similar tendency toward strict rhythmic regularity in their own poetry and to discover, or partly rediscover, means of creating an aesthetically effective tension between rhythm and verse intonation. Having turned intonation into an independent structural element through the frequent use of enjambment, the Lumírians paved the way for Nezval and other modernists who, as we know, subsequently elevated intonational integrity into the poetic dominant, displacing the syllabic scheme (as the syllabic scheme had earlier displaced rhyme) from the top of the structural pyramid. The liberation of verse intonation from subservience to metre and its promotion to the place of decisive structural significance was motivated, in Mukařovský's view, by two factors: internally, by the need for greater rhythmic variation, and, externally, by the desire to follow the example of contemporary French versification. Still, the poetic achievement of the Lumírians in a way transcends these temporal determinants, for the *Lumír* poets finally found an answer to a problem faced by Czech poets as early as the fourteenth century and only half-successfully solved by Polák and his successors of the first part of the nineteenth.

As Mukařovský points out, a structural solution of this sort has a durable value, because the new structure becomes part of the historical repertory or reservoir of poetic structures. A new generation of poets can fall back at will on the existing, though temporarily submerged, structure and turn it to uses other than those originally intended for it. Once a particular structure is created, it does not disappear as a viable possibility even when it is left behind in the evolution of the given poetic genre, if for no other reason than that it serves as a prerequisite for a dialectical negation by the poetic generation that immediately follows. More importantly, as Mukařovský reasons, a literature's reserve of structures contributes to that literature's future refinement: "the longer the evolutionary road taken by a certain literature and the greater and more differentiated the reserve of its structures, the more subtle and complex are the ways in which it responds to new historical stimuli" (p. 249). It is the variety of developmental changes that enriches the literature's store of structures. The literature's historical continuity, which must be maintained at all costs—even in an attenuated fashion, as when Czech Baroque literature nearly disappeared from the historical scene of the Counter Reformation, only to make its impact much later on the poetry of national revival and on that of Mácha—in turn guarantees that the literature's development will follow its own characteristic course. As Mukařovský insists, there is no structure without continuity: "Material and form are transient, but structure, an energy binding all of the work's components into a unity, flows continuously through time" (p. 252).

When compared with his notion of literary evolution as spelled out in the Polák study, Mukařovský's latest conception displays a number of important theoretical advances. To start with, the process of historical change no longer appears as a straightforward linear sequence but, rather, as an involuted reversible pattern: poetic structures are never utterly automatized and finite—on the contrary, they are historically renewable. Indeed, each structural model, instead of serving ends prescribed by the needs of a single period, in the long run enlarges the fund of vital poetic "forms" valid for all time. Most importantly, poetic values created during the evolution of a literature are not all historically relative as Mukařovský argued in "Polák's *Sublimity of Nature*"; some structural solutions, whether those dictated by the material of the language or those generated from within the given poetic tradition, earn a place of permanent and historically transcendental significance.

We can attribute much of Mukařovský's change of outlook—from historical relativism toward a structural universalism—to his growing understanding of the semiotic model of art. In his, and Jakobson's, first semiotic ventures, the Prague structuralists reasserted the Aristotelian claim of the universality of art. The theoretical challenge from that point on has been the identification of those structural factors of poetry that endure and can thus become "universal" at least for the literature in question, despite the onslaughts of historical changes, be they linguistic, aesthetic or ideological. "The Tradition of 'Form'" richly indicates, albeit once more on the level of versification alone, the important turn of direction in Mukařovský's developing theory. Vodička's inaugural lecture to the Prague Linguistic Circle, "Methodological Remarks on the Study of the Literary Work's Reception," however, appears to have been inspired by the earlier phase of Mukařovský's semiotic understanding.[18] As a consequence, Vodička's conception of literary reception, although considerably advancing the structural notion of literary evolution, suffers from a theoretical time lag, again putting a premium, as we shall see, on historical variability instead of on historical invariants.

Nevertheless, on this very lecture rests Vodička's claim to fame as a structuralist literary theorist. For what Vodička accomplished here, in spite of the one-sided emphasis on the relativity of historical transformations of literature, was to think through the implications of the hitherto partly neglected aspect of the semiotic model at the heart of the Prague School's theory—the aspect which in Charles Morris' terminology goes under the label of pragmatics[19]—in order to present a new theory of reception of literary works.

We know that as a sign any literary work, like any verbal expression, is situated in a communicative circuit which without exception contains the context of the referred-to reality, the producer, the receiver and, of course, the message itself. Just as any utterance is capable of performing four basic functions—namely, the referential, expressive, conative and poetic—depending on what aspect of verbal communication it is set toward, so we can obtain four distinct critical orientations, commonly known as the mimetic, expressive, pragmatic and formalist.[20] While, in the history of criticism, classical literary theory was predominantly concerned with the issue of representation, romantic with expression and formalist with poetry's internal construction, Vodička proposed to tackle the problem of literature's impact on and reception by the reading public. In contrast to traditional pragmatic approaches derived from classical rhetoric, Vodička's theory, far from being in any way prescriptive or normative, focuses on the readers' constitutive role in the creation of the literary work's meaning.

In articulating his critical proposals, Vodička, much like René Wellek before him, attempted to combine—and cross-pollinate—the ideas of Jan Mukařovský with those of Roman Ingarden. From Mukařovský's writings, Vodička adopted the seminal notions regarding the structural evolution of literature. The first of these is the conception of the unceasing conflict between the automatized, stylistically stale verbal means of standard language and their ever-renewed actualization (or deautomatization) in poetic language. Next comes the model of structure as a hierarchically ordered whole consisting of the structural dominant and numerous subdominant elements which, endowed with dynamic and energic qualities, are interlocked in a state of fragile equilibrium. A third basic concept is the principle of continual permutation in the function and significance of individual elements during the structure's diachronic evolution, which results in altered correlations of super- and subordination. Last, and most important for Vodička's receptional theory, is Mukařovský's elaboration of the semiotic nature of art, particularly of the dynamic organization of the Janus-like sign, which, in the case of art, is comprised of the work's material vehicle (or the *signifiant*) and its immaterial analogue in the aesthetic object (or the *signifié*).[21]

From Ingarden, Vodička borrowed the category of "concretization."[22] Put simply, this designation means in the context of Ingarden's phenomenological theory what aesthetic object does in Mukařovský's structural theory, namely, to quote Vodička, "the concrete shape of a work which has become the object of aesthetic perception" (p. 117). For Ingarden, we remember, the literary work is a multilayered formation which, besides the strata of sound and meaning, consists of the stratum of represented objects and that of schematic aspects through which the represented objects manifest themselves.[23] The four general strata and their temporal extension build up the work's basic (intentional) scheme, a rough blueprint containing many so-called *Unbestimtheitsstellen* or "spots of indeterminacy." Because the work as such, according to Ingarden, is a mere schematic formation, its numerous gaps must be filled through individual concretizations in the readers' aesthetic experience. In studying concretizations, the readers' aesthetic addenda, one does not so much analyze and describe the defining properties of the literary artifact as explore the changing appearances the given work assumes in the perception of the literary public. By extension, a *Rezeptionsgeschichte*, a history of concretizations, instead of following up historical connections between contemporaneous or successive literary works, traces the ensuing permutations which all works undergo as they are assimilated by distinct groups of readers over the course of time.

Unlike Ingarden, Vodička does not locate the conditions for concretization in the ontological status of the literary work, in its "essential" skeleton which is brought to "life" only in the readers' aesthetic experience, but in the circumstances in which, as a sign, a single work typifies only one component part of a larger literary system.[24] As we know, according to the structural theory of language, every speech act or *parole* presupposes the existence of an underlying, immaterial system of norms or *langue*, so that no individual act of expression can be comprehended without regard to the linguistic code, the intersubjective set of rules, of that language. Similarly, according to the structuralists, any discrete work is in some way nothing more than a material instantiation of the overall, intangible literary structure. To grasp adequately the meaning of the literary work of art, one must, just as in a relationship of figure to ground, come to grips with the body of aesthetic norms underpinning it. Moreover, since the system of such norms is not a static, motionless construct but a vital, dynamic structure, literature, like language, can forever change. The grounds for concretization, in Vodička's view, are discovered in the continuous regrouping of norms, against the shifting background of which the literary public responds to every literary work. For this reason, in contrast to Ingarden, Vodička circumvents the problem of the work's status and identity, whether phenomenological or empirical, on the level of the material artifact, since for him every work becomes a potentially endless series of concretized aesthetic objects.

The prodigious variability of the literary work as an aesthetic object, then, is directly dependent on the ongoing change of the literary norms or conventions upheld by the reading community. These norms together comprise what we may call the literary consciousness; and this in turn forms an integral part of the all-comprehensive collective ideology. Therefore, to complete the picture of the "life" of literary works within social praxis, the reception theory confronts, as Vodička shows, such a range of issues as "how the work is perceived; what values are ascribed to it; in what form it appears to those who experience it aesthetically; what semantic connections it evokes; in what social milieu it exists and in what hierarchical order" (p. 114). In short, Vodička's main theoretical concern—and also his main contribution to structuralism—is the investigation of the literary and social norms which motivate the reception of poetic works in various periods of history.

Above all, the readers' active responses—whether of approval, indifference or dismissal—to literary works define the problematics of reception. Admittedly, the public's attitude to any given work is likely to vary greatly during its subsequent reception, but then not all critical reactions—recorded as they are not only in reviews, essays and literary histories but also in diaries, correspondence, memoirs and interviews—are equally valid. It is thus imperative, when undertaking a study along the lines of reception, "to winnow out subjective elements and to determine what in the particular concretization has demonstrable historical validity" (p. 122). This means that we must at the start face the problem of what Ingarden describes as "the literary atmosphere" and Vodička dubs "context": "the state of events facilitating the given work's aesthetic perception and evaluation" (p. 123).

This context, in terms of which all pronouncements on works as aesthetic objects are made, incorporates the group of critical assumptions, postulates, habits and expectations prevalent in a certain historical period. Of course, within every critical paradigm there is, thanks to the dynamism of norms, always room for a broad scale of values. It follows that the unity of a historical period derives not from the uniformity of value judgments but from the consistency of the context. For example, as Vodička remarks, despite several discordant valuations at the turn of the century of the poetry of Jan Neruda (1834–1891), a major writer spanning the "May" and "Lumír" generations, all concretizations were rooted in one and the same psychologistic conception of the artistic personality. Conversely, even though there may be a congruence of judgment in two distinct periods, the judgments themselves are apt to be derived from various critical norms and, consequently, to refer to different, aesthetically actualized features of the same work. This is to say that with every alteration of the normative context, the work's interpretation moves to "an entirely new semantic plane, even if the text itself offers no incentive for such a shift," as, for example, in the theological exegesis of *The Song of Songs* (p. 124).

In every literary and cultural epoch, the context of normative postulates is intimately bound up with the literary production of the time, since both arise from and react to the same literary tradition. Nonetheless, the system of literary norms does not run quite parallel to the structure of existing literary works. Conservative at most times, the general norm tends to lag behind the contemporary poetic output. Less often, during a fallow season, criticism can anticipate and press for novel, norm-setting works of art. On occasion, the exacting precepts of avant-garde manifestos may be impossible to put into practice, as in the case of the surrealist novel. In any event, this energizing interplay between norms and works infuses new life into literary production as well as consumption. Furthermore, viewed structurally, the literary norms do not operate in a vacuum but, rather, intersect with the whole nexus of social, political and intellectual values. The interrelationships with the sphere of social action further condition the structural dynamism of literary change. In the final analysis, the context of norms, both aesthetic and nonaesthetic, furnishes the regulating framework within which, unavoidably, the reception or rejection of every artistic creation takes place.

For the historical reconstruction of the readers' response, the views of the critics of a given period represent concretizations in their most crystallized shape. Vodička writes:

. . . literary history is not so much concerned with individual readings as with those which stabilize or at least advance the stability of a particular concretization. The literary work does not become part of a literary tradition—that is, an assembly of prevailing aesthetic norms and values—by merely existing, but largely through the stability of its concretization. Practically speaking, this means that after some hesitation due to the novelty of the work, it is accepted into the literary canon in this concretized form. To be sure, the stabilized concretization retains its validity for a limited time only—after which the work takes on a different form when a new concretization is registered, published and, having attained a degree of consensus, introduced into the period's system of literary values. It is possible, of course, to have two or three concretizations side by side; this, however, stems from the literature at that moment being governed by two or three norms divided, say, along generational lines. (p. 118)

The literary historian's task is indeed formidable. On the one hand, several disparate concretizations may coexist at any time; on the other, no single concretization really lasts. In one instance, a recent concretization rapidly supersedes the preceding one; in another, ruptures and sharp discontinuities occur between successive concretizations. And then, with its concretization firmly established, the new, or the newly concretized, work itself becomes norm-instituting. The setup of norms thus modified subsequently puts all other works into a new perspective, from which they in turn can receive further concretizations.[25] Granted, not every concretization is norm-breaking or norm-setting; concretizations run the whole gamut of norm-preparing, -initiating, -intensifying, -fulfilling, -justifying or -repeating; still, the production of concretizations and the ensuing circulation of norms is a highly dynamic, interminable process. As a result, instead of simply following an "evolutionary curve," which is how Vodička describes it, the diachrony of literary reception more resembles an undulating line, oft-broken and doubled back on itself.

As if historians' efforts to impose order on the enormous flux of critical response were not difficult enough, they must also cope with the inadequacy of critics' testimonies. In the history of every literature there are works initially ignored because they disappointed or surpassed the readers' expectations that nevertheless exerted a profound influence on later artists or entire movements. But even if no concretizations materialize in public, "the work's qualities," as Vodička argues, "affect the immanent evolution of literary structure" (p. 119). Lingering underground, as it were, such works surface and insert themselves into the period's system of values once the context of norms in the literary consciousness has suitably evolved to absorb the earlier radical experiment. As literary history amply shows, the rebirth of previously neglected works frequently accompanies the emergence of a new poetic generation, with or without assistance from the critics. (In the history of English literature, the fate of Blake's Prophetic Books or the revival of the school of Donne come to mind.) All of this underlines once more the fact that, despite their close interdependence, the structures of norms and those of literary forms are not totally isomorphic and that, as a consequence, historians are obliged to pursue two fields of research.

Just as the absence of critical acknowledgment does not necessarily spell the work's demise, so, too, the solidified concretization does not guarantee its vitality. Textbooks often perpetuate in vain the reputation of so-called classics which for all intents and purposes are dead. Concretizations, like automatized elements of language, tend to lose their appeal through unremitting repetition. Obviously, a startling reinterpretation, as well as a number of other diachronic events, actualizing the work's hitherto dormant or worn-out qualities, can bring the dated masterpiece to its former prominence. For these reasons, the need to discriminate between vital and moribund concretizations will inescapably figure among the problems plaguing the receptional inquiry.

At this crossroads, a sociologically oriented analysis comes to the historians' aid. It supplements the historical scrutiny of the structural opposition of automatization and actualization and the dialectical interchange of text and context with a survey of the changing cultural taste among respective social classes. Sociological analysis can do various things: it helps shed light on the relation of highbrow and lowbrow literature and on the way popular forms such as epistles, travelogues, family albums or crime stories eventually penetrate into the more sophisticated literary genres. It can also account for the historically often decisive effect of such heteronomous factors as the market mechanism of book publishing and distribution and, last but not least, for politically motivated upheavals in the social structure. Furthermore, sociological study can clarify how literary protagonists, from Goethe's Werther to Kerouac's "dharma bums," stand as models for social behavior or how literary works (Emile Zola's, for example) act as catalysts in the resolving of social inequities. All the while, however, structuralist historians must heed the maxim according to which literary facts, albeit social in nature, are (to use the Greek term that the Czechs liked to employ) aesthetic phenomena *kat' exochen*. In the end, they must look for the explanation of literary changes above all within the movement of the literary structure itself.

Even so, any study of literary impact and reception, though supported by sociological data, remains incomplete as long as it fails to consider, besides individual works, two other components of literary history—the author and the literary period.

With respect to the creative personality, too, Vodička's structuralist position is poles apart from the naive, outmoded psychological taxonomies of his early essays. The poet's personal identity dissolves altogether, for Vodička now understands the author in "the metonymic sense, as a unity created by the works of an author in their totality" (p. 126). In other words, his attention has moved from the actual writer to the body of what he or she has written. Here is Vodička's central argument:

> Like certain constants in the author's approach to the execution of his material, individual works make up parts of [the author's] structure, which is likewise subject to different evaluations and also requires concretization. This structure, too, is influenced by the general character of the period norm and . . . must be situated in the period context. . . . analogous to the structure of an individual work, the structure of the author is not to be apprehended as a sum of its elements but as a dynamically organized system with a dominant tendency. This organization, however, is not firmly established but comes into being through concretization. We can reconstruct the structure of the author by projecting it into the appropriate moment in literary evolution; but we can see its true concretization in evolving literature only when we have testimonies of this concretization at hand. (pp. 126–127)

It follows that "writers" affect the unfolding of structural history in complex ways. In time, their individual works experience an ebb and flow of reception, a different facet of their *oeuvre* assuming the place of esteem in the readers' eyes. And if the author, like Jan Neruda, practices several genres at once, he or she may variously be identified as preeminently a poet, short-story writer or journalist. In short, the total structure of the author exhibits the same traits which, in their changeability, characterize literary evolution in general.

In Vodička's view, this principle extends *ipso facto* to the concept of literary period. Traditionally, art periods have proved extremely resistant to an unambiguous definition of both their temporal span and their content. Conventional attempts to encase a period between a pair of dates taken over from social history have, in their application to art history, been notoriously unsatisfactory. Only infrequently has the articulation of aesthetic forms been in step with greater historical events. Literary periods, it would seem, are more convincingly represented by certain artistic tendencies and concepts typical of a circumscribed sequence of works. Indeed, from the fixed vantage point of one era—say, of the present—such period concepts appear fairly coherent and homogenous. But a closer look at the historical fortunes of the concept of a given period reveals a very different picture.

Let us take Vodička's example of classicism. Boileau, in the seventeenth century, perceives classicism through the precepts of Horatian theory, with Homer as the embodiment of the eternal rules of art. But for

Perrault, the playwrights of the era of Louis XIV show a firmer grasp of these principles. Early romantics such as Herder associate the concept of literary antiquity with Homer, the national bard. And later romanticism equates classicism almost exclusively with Sophoclean tragedy. At various stages of history, each theorist places divergent aspects of a period's global structure in the foreground and nearly obliterates others, each of necessity judging the period's complex of norms from the standpoint of his or her own time. Understandably, the image of the period being an extrapolation from its preserved works, the complications of reception increase, since, as Vodička points out, what we witness every time is "an encounter between two totalities, both marked by variability, boundlessness and ambiguity" (p. 131).

As can be seen, Vodička's conception of literary reception echoes closely Mukařovský's structural theory of literature and its history in all key points. Like Mukařovský, Vodička privileges structural relations rather than separate terms, the background of norms rather than the foreground of single works, the social rather than individual character of literary facts, the dynamism and change of structure rather than its stasis and fixity and, finally, the intrinsic tension rather than the stable harmony of the literary work (as well as the author and the period) viewed as a sign. In fact, all that Vodička's reception history does is to switch the focus of inquiry away from the immanent order of literary development toward the literary and social consciousness which contains the works of literature when they are perceived as aesthetic objects. Vodička thus explores the very area that Mukařovský himself, at least at the time of "Polák's *Sublimity of Nature*" and his first semiotic probes, left undefined. And although considerably improving our understanding of the functioning of the social consciousness, that repository of aesthetic objects, Vodička's reception history unfortunately brings out the central weakness in Mukařovský's theory, one we have already noted several times. For despite his intentions, Vodička's study of literary reception gives the impression that the relationship between the work's *signifiant* and *signifié*, the material vehicle and its corresponding aesthetic object, is arbitrary, even though it is motivated by the norms engrafted in the literary consciousness of a certain reading community.

More precisely, the character of those aesthetic objects which are historically representative is motivated by the literary norms comprising the core of the collective consciousness of the reading public at a particular time. Vodička situates this normative core in the activity and testimony of literary critics. Following Mukařovský, he strains greatly to separate the wheat from the chaff, that is, the semiotically typical from the merely subjective. Yet the aesthetic object typical of one period of reception, founded upon one set of norms, may, according to Vodička, seem unrecognizable in another period, borne as it is by a different set of norms. In other words, to the extent that Vodička, by investigating the context of norms, refines upon Mukařovský's semiotic opposition between the work's *physicum* and the intangible aesthetic object, he does so only synchronically, not diachronically: the context motivates the work as sign in one period, but it leaves arbitrary and unmotivated the changes to which the aesthetic object is prey during literary evolution. It would appear that one aesthetic object—the aesthetic shape the work acquires at a particular stage in the history of reception—is as valid historically as any other (cf. p. 57 above), even though the disparate aesthetic objects may not even be comparable, for Vodička does not show what the basis for such a comparison between or among diverse aesthetic objects might be. While successfully avoiding the twin traps of aesthetic dogmatism, which holds that there is an ideal model that all art must approximate, and aesthetic subjectivism, which claims that all aesthetic judgments are ultimately personal and lacking general validity, Vodička falls into a third snare of historical relativism, which perceives the process of change as chaotic and uncontrollable. Unwittingly, he returns us to Saussure's original dilemma of changes that seem to defy the system of which they are parts.

One of the major causes of Vodička's theoretical difficulties is his hasty dismissal of Ingarden's concept of the work as an incomplete scheme which requires completion, in individual concretizations, of the unfinished or indeterminate places—and of those places only. As Vodička sees it, "not just the schematic part[s] but the work's entire structure is subject to concretization since it [the structure of the work] is projected against the background of the given literary tradition and so acquires, in the changing temporal, spatial, social and, to some degree, individual circumstances, ever-new characteristics" (p. 117). Vodička's solution, however, demands too steep a price for an explanation of historical changes, in that he arrives at this explanation at the expense of the literary work's structural unity. If any and all structural components of a particular work can eventually be reshuffled according to the expectations of the readers, it may well happen that the various critical testimonies, the very stuff of reception history, will not be referring to the same work of art. For Vodička, the aesthetic object swallows up, as it were, the work's material vehicle: incessant changing of its guises obliterates the work's underlying identity.

This conclusion is more than a little ironic, and for two diametrically opposite reasons. On the one hand, Ingarden as a phenomenological philosopher works *von oben*, as his project concerns issues of general ontology, a correction of certain of Husserl's investigations, using the literary work of art merely as a particular instance of a larger phenomenological problematics. Ingarden's literary work is itself an abstraction, a concept of an object of a special (intentional) kind; it is not the concrete individual work which literary critics scrutinize in their daily practice. Yet it is Ingarden who proposes a theory of the literary work of art which, though far from static, insisting as it does on the necessary process of concretization, nevertheless preserves intact the work's identity, its essential selfsameness in all aesthetically possible variants. On the other hand, Vodička as a structural literary critic and historian works *von unten*, examining the fluid, historically and socially conditioned character of particular literary works, in this case those of Jan Neruda, as he takes stock of their fluctuating reception and then attempts to frame a theory to account for that fluctuation. The irresistible momentum of literary change, however, that most commonplace empirical fact of every literary historian's study, overwhelms Vodička's theory to the point where he can theoretically justify the numerous reasons for the changes in literary reception but is unable to explain the nature of the work of art which itself undergoes those changes. The crux of Vodička's problem is the same paradox we detected earlier in Mukařovský's conception of immanent evolution—namely, that the structuralists' practice, capable of producing seemingly irrefutable analyses, descriptions and categorizations of literary texts, is at odds with their own theory, which suggests that their critical readings, too, are individual concretizations to be discarded by the next generation of readers adhering to a new set of literary norms. Analytic empiricism and theoretical relativism collide head-on—paradoxically, to the loss of the Prague scholars' scientifically (statistically, diagrammatically, linguistically) based practical criticism, whose validity is undermined from within by its "supporting" theory.

The Prague School's theory of literary history, in the version Vodička inherited, is, we might say, at once overelaborate and not elaborate enough. It bristles with dialectical antinomies—ordinary and poetic language, practical and autotelic functions, communicative and aesthetic signs, the sign's two-tiered structure of material vehicle and aesthetic object—all of which are designed to elucidate the internal and external dynamism of literary mutations. At the same time, this highly sophisticated theory itself gets caught in the maelstrom of the incessant flux of historical changes which it seeks to understand and to which it also contributes. This is where Vodička's concept of the history of readers' reception is not sufficiently elaborated: captivated by the changes in the views of literature over the course of time, Vodička at a crucial stage of analysis ultimately fails to discriminate between genuine literary and theoretical norms and the passing trends of literary taste. The former are no doubt contestable and thus subject to different interpretive inflections, but the theories they imply remain essentially unchanged, as is the case with Aristotle's *Poetics*, the widely divergent interpretations of which—say, from the neo-classical revival to the present—can at least be compared, contrasted and debated.

But changes in literary taste, like changes in fashion, though obligatory in one season, are completely irrelevant in another. Consequently, what Vodička and other students of reception may end up mapping is not the systemic alteration of literary norms but the "whirligig of taste," a chaos of critical views which I. A. Richards eloquently depicts as "a few conjectures, a supply of admonitions, many acute isolated observations, some brilliant guesses, much oratory and applied poetry, inexhaustible confusion, a sufficiency of dogma, no small stock of prejudices, whimsies and crotchets, a profusion of mysticism, a little genuine speculation, sundry stray inspirations, pregnant hints and random *aperçus*."[26] In other words, in measuring the high and low tides of the literary work's reception, Vodička reveals new features not of the particular work of art itself, nor yet of the principles of literary theory and of the mechanism of norms, but of what Northrop Frye calls the "vacillations of fashionable prejudice."[27] Too much a historian, Vodička seems to respect all historical facts equally and lacks the theoretical stringency to make the necessary discrimination between two classes of literary documents, between theories and critical opinions. As Frye acerbically puts it, the "literary chit-chat which makes the reputations of poets boom and crash in an imaginary stock exchange . . . cannot be part of any systematic study, for a systematic study can only progress: whatever dithers or vacillates or reacts is merely leisure-class gossip" (p. 18).

These words may be too harsh to castigate Vodička's literary reception, since they run counter to his avowed goal of investigating the changing background of norms against which the literary public experiences a given work or works. Nevertheless, although made in a context of different arguments, the polemical strictures of Richards and Frye highlight the fact that, just as evolutionary value cannot be disengaged from aesthetic value in the study of literary history, evolutionary value cannot be divorced from intellectual value in the study of the history of literary theory.[28] A historian or a critic cannot just collect, collate and classify facts from literary history or from the history of literary theory; willy-nilly, he or she must select, evaluate, in short, interpret them. But the truth is that when Vodička describes how the three extant concretizations of Jan Neruda's poetry from around 1901 sprang from a psychologistic understanding of poetic personality, whereas three other concretizations from about 1895 issued from an objective approach to problems such as those of national literature, the simplicity or artificiality of poetic style and the relationship between style and content (cf. p. 123 above), he is not telling us very much about Neruda's *oeuvre*, or why one notion of literature replaced another or the theoretical validity of the discordant concretizations, some of which could conceivably be of value to structuralist critics while others definitely could not. Vodička is mainly collecting memorabilia of literary milieux, of special interest neither to the student of Neruda's works (since works by any number of other writers could exemplify the same kind of period concretization) nor to the student of literary theory (since such mementos are by and large devoid of theoretical concepts not spelled out elsewhere, in poetic treatises, theoretical discussions, artists' programmatic statements and the like).

The saving point of Vodička's notion of readers' reception, as he made plain in his inaugural lecture to the Circle, "Methodological Remarks on the Study of the Literary Work's Reception"—and plainer still in his synoptic study "Literary History: Its Problems and Its Tasks"[29]—is that it is *not* a self-sufficient theory of literature which would pretend to illuminate the complex nature of literary works and literary history in their entirety. Instead, it forms part of a larger tripartite theory. This comprehensive literary theory is spearheaded, as is always the case in structuralism, by the examination of the immanent series of the literary works themselves. The second component part of the overall structural theory is the study of the works' genesis, of the literary, linguistic and semantic sources of their creation. These sources and influences are, according to Vodička, the means, not the causes, for the production of literary works of a given genre at a particular stage of evolution. Genetic structuralism, in other words, explores above all the aesthetic norms, and only secondarily the biographic or social circumstances, which fomented or hampered the execution of literary tasks of the period. And the final component of this general theory of literary structuralism is that of readers' reception. All three components operate on the same premise, namely, that we must first come to grips with the structure of the artistic norms before we can grasp the structure of the individual work of art. Since it is the literary works comprising the order of the received tradition which are the primary bearers of these norms, genetic and receptionist inquiries are merely auxiliary, though frequently invaluable, aspects of the global structural theory of literature.

In the last analysis, its apparent novelty notwithstanding, Vodička's history of readers' reception emerges as a rather old-fashioned critical undertaking. Bypassing the analysis of the works themselves, the study of the works' reception by the reading public simply reverses the direction of traditional investigations of literary influence. Whereas the study of genesis centers on the influenced work, the study of reception centers on the influencing work: the former examines the conditions for the conception and birth of the work, the latter the conditions for its afterlife. It is a matter of shifting perspective, not of distinct approach, which indicates the kind of enterprise the critic happens to be engaged in. When Vodička surveys the impact of the translation of Chateaubriand's *Atala* (1801; 1805) on the nascent prose fiction of the Czech literary revival, only with difficulty can one determine whether he is in fact describing Chateaubriand's influence on or his reception by the struggling Czech belletrists of the early nineteenth century.[30] It is perhaps this mixture of methodological novelty, conventional literary scholarship and incomplete theoretical foundations in Vodička's project that explains why today, a quarter-century after Vodička's first attempts, the theories of readers and *Rezeptionsgeschichte*, though widespread and influential, still remain largely unsatisfactory. The roots of contemporary failures at developing the reader-oriented literary theory go back to Vodička's, and in part Mukařovský's, lack of success at extending Saussure's notion of *langue* (or, in current linguistic parlance, of *competence*) to the study of literature. Unaware of the troubling theoretical impediments besetting the investigation of literary norms, especially since, for the most part, the influence of the Prague School has been either indirect or nonexistent, the contemporary reader-based theory moves along two separate routes, both first foreseen by René Wellek in his critique of Mukařovský's structural methodology. One trend, particularly prevalent in Germany, seeks to identify the type of norms governing literary reception and consumption by means of sociological analyses, all the while risking the danger of arriving at the consensually held truism, the lowest denominator common to the survey respondents. The other trend, gaining considerable critical popularity in North America, follows Wellek's original, ill-advised prescription (upon which Wellek, as we know, did not act) by claiming that, through a kind of dialectical volte-face, the most competent reader's reading becomes the paradigm case which other, less competent readers should strive to duplicate. It does not seem troublesome under the circumstances that the "ideal" or "super" readers invariably turn out to be the very critics proposing this latest "theory."[31] (There is admittedly a third reader theory, deriving from psychoanalysis, but, like its precursors in literary psychology, it does not even begin to attack the problem of literary consciousness but simply shifts a type of inquiry that the Prague structuralists sought to discredit from writer to reader.) When all is said and done, the nature of literary competence remains as elusive as ever. But Vodička at least deserves plaudits, unlike the more modern theorists of reader and reception, for uncovering a fecund and previously little-explored area of historical inquiry, even if this area still awaits its proper theoretical grounding.[32]

‖●‖●‖●‖●‖●‖

Another irony attendant on Vodička's sketchy plan for a theory of reception history is that, albeit an attentive disciple, he does not adequately represent Mukařovský's position regarding the nature of the aesthetic norm, which remains universal even though it is constantly violated—just as he does not do full justice to Ingarden's theory of the literary work as a schematic formation, certain parts of which remain of necessity stable, others mutable. It may be another instance of an insight obtained at the cost of methodological blindness, for while investigating the context of norms, as we have observed, Vodička makes no reference to Mukařovský's theory of norm in his "Methodological Remarks" and mentions that theory in passing, only to stress the aesthetic norm's historical fragility, not its enduring universality, in "Literary History: Its Problems and Its Tasks." Beginning with the monograph "Aesthetic Function and Norm as Social Facts,"[33] Mukařovský realized, however, that his dynamic structural theory of the historical circulation of functions and norms (and soon also values) could be exploded by its own dynamism if he presented a conception of perpetual historical motion without a single point of rest. Although it is indubitably true, Mukařovský notes, that throughout the history of art there is a stronger tendency toward subverting, rather than preserving, the prevalent aesthetic norm of the period—to this extent Vodička's stress on the ever-shifting background of norms squares with the facts—the norm in art does retain its normative character. In order to understand the character of this norm which survives repeated challenges and attacks, we must, Mukařovský insists, take a lesson from linguistics. As linguistics teaches us, we should always "distinguish a norm from that regulation which is its codification" (p. 74). In language there are numerous instances of uncodified norms. Many regional dialects, for instance, are perfectly binding for the members of the particular speech community without ever having been explicitly formulated. Other language norms, though similarly binding, resist formulation altogether: witness those stylistic or compositional rules which are in force even if they cannot be sufficiently spelled out in any handbook of style. Its uncodified character, then, is a fundamental feature of the norm in language—and even more so in literature. Here, more than in other domains, the norm is a "regulatory energic principle . . . rather than a [codified] regulation" (p. 74).

As a dynamic regulatory principle, the aesthetic norm oscillates between two contending normative principles: it claims general validity, for otherwise it could not function normatively, yet at the same time it is subject to synchronic limitations (there being always several competing norms) and diachronic alterations (norms superseding one another without cessation). This intrinsic fragility, or limited universality, sets human norms apart from natural laws valid for all time. According to Mukařovský, "the norm is grounded in a basic dialectical antinomy between binding validity which admits no exception and a mere regulatory . . . potentiality which implies the possibility of transgression" (p. 28). Depending on whether a norm gravitates toward the pole of enforced validity or the pole of permissible vitiation, we are able to situate legal, linguistic and aesthetic norms within this spectrum—and hence better comprehend the norm in general and the aesthetic norm in particular. We immediately observe that legal "laws" and aesthetic norms will move toward the respective ends of the spectrum, with language norms in the middle. As a law, the norm in jurisprudence leans toward strict, unexceptional validity, whereas the norm in literature and art usually provides a mere backdrop for the constant infractions every new work of art unavoidably causes. In principle, however, every concrete application of a norm, whether legislative or aesthetic, necessarily alters it, since the norm, like the linguistic sign, must always fit new realities. The drawn-out process of lower and higher court appeals testifies to the sometimes extraordinary difficulty of matching law and deed.[34] The conformity between an aesthetic norm and a work of art is more problematic still, for art puts a far greater premium on "making it new," that is, on the deviation from rather than the fulfillment of the reigning norm.

The continual modification and turnover of the established artistic norm is only a liminal case of a general process of normative change. No norm, precisely because it is a norm, can withstand changes. In law, however, major restatements of the norm are comparatively rare: laws are by definition codified, and their stability—as well as the occasional enactment of a new law—is enforced by the courts and the legislature. Language changes, be they grammatical, lexical or stylistic, also tend to be rather slow; as a rule, they are almost imperceptible to the community of speakers and seem to occur in spite of a community's will, as the interest of its members lies in the protection of the existing system of language rules, not in any tinkering with that system. Only art, exhibiting a low tolerance for repetition, for derivative imitation, generates a need for constant reform. Its development, consequently, is marked by a ceaseless revolt against the prevailing convention, against the omnipresent code of protocol and precedence. Although there are periods—for instance, classicism—in which artists are pledged to convention, more often—as during periods of romanticism and modernism—the heritage of earlier art, rather than being honored, is exposed, refigured, extended or violated. Even if to some extent norm-abiding—or else it would have no history, only chaotic past—art, unlike law or language, is inherently nomoclastic. In sum, while in all norms there is perpetual struggle between a normative inertia and historical motion, aesthetic norms, in contradistinction to all other norms, incline principally toward the latter.

One reason why the evolution of art, in contrast to the steady, gradual development in legal and linguistic realms, is so tumultuous is that art permits, even demands, competition among diverse norms. In a given society there can be but one system of laws; only a legal monopoly ensures that all the separate laws within the legal system are reciprocally commensurable, so that a particular law can be applied positively and directly without fear

of contradiction. A particular language community, in contrast, effort-
lessly accommodates several distinct language systems, such as various regional dialects or functional dialects. Yet, because of this numerousness of
norms, language wavers between a simultaneous tendency toward preservation and violation of the norm: standard language, the unmarked form,
tends toward preservation, while poetic language, the marked form, tends
toward violation. What a given community does not condone, its tolera-
tion of difference notwithstanding, is a jumbling together of, say, standard
language with one of the local dialects. But in art a mixing of disparate
norms is not only desirable, it is often the key to the aesthetic effect of a
work of art. Indeed, as Mukařovský argues, every art work appears as

a complex knot of norms: fraught with inner agreements and disagreements, the
work represents a dynamic equilibrium of heterogeneous norms, which are applied
in part positively and in part negatively. This equilibrium is inimitable in its
uniqueness, even though at the same time it takes part, precisely due to its instability, in the continuous immanent movement of the art in question. (p. 75)

In Mukařovský's view, there are five principal categories of norms
which, upon entering the work of art, occupy all kinds of positions and
oppositions, thereby producing ever-new aesthetic stresses and "distresses"
or discords (for a uniform concordance of diverse norms would lead to a
structure that is stable, hence repeatable, hence epigonic). The first category consists of norms ingrained in the artistic material. In poetry these
are the norms, in themselves aesthetically indifferent, of ordinary language
which—through a deformation of a certain grammatical feature, for instance—acquire the status of aesthetic norms. To the second category belong technical norms, sediments of earlier stages in the development of
art, such as metrical schemes and other formulas, which must be aug-
mented by later generations of artists in order to achieve the desired aesthetic effect. Third, there are various practical—ethical, religious, political—norms embodied in the theme of the work which, though essentially
extra-aesthetic, can play an artistic role in the work's composition, as does
the breach of a moral imperative in Greek tragedy. The fourth category is
comprised of aesthetic norms proper, of the genre and style memory of the
preceding epochs in the history of art. Every genre is itself an ensemble of
norms: thus the heroic epic is defined not only by its theme but by its verse
form—the Greek hexameter, for instance—and by lexical selection, like
the Homeric *epitheton*. Several genres, of course, exist at one and the same
time and, as long as they remain effective, are all open to subsequent modifications. It is the distinctive modifications of one or several norms wrought
by the individual artist which constitute the fifth and final category. By
offering an individual variation of the dominant setup of period norms, a
new balance of their intricate interrelationships, this last category bears

the impress of the artists' personalities, their unique artistic signatures. Every new work of art thus oscillates between past, present and future states of artistic norms: being a point of articulation in the immanent evolution of art, the work is perceived as a tension between the past norm and its current transgression, which in turn is destined to become the background for the creation of the future norm. So while contemporaries may sense the work's juxtaposition of earlier norms with the newly designed ones as strained and jarring, future readers may well view it as harmonious reconciliation of aesthetic clashes.

This brief survey, in which emphasis repeatedly falls on the individual departure from and alteration of the norm, confirms that aesthetic norms have had a shaky and tenuous existence throughout most of their history. If they are so readily broken, can we still speak of them as norms? (It is this question that Vodička brushed aside, much to the disadvantage of his receptionist project.) Mukařovský counters possible skepticism on this point with a two-pronged answer. One is that, even though in art itself the aesthetic norm is constantly assaulted by every inventive artist, this norm asserts itself with considerable coercive power in the extra-aesthetic sphere, where the aesthetic function is secondary: not in the sphere of art but in that of social taste, in fashion, furnishings, social ceremonies and the like. Here a slight break with convention is often considered a grave faux pas, so much so that it may result in the ostracizing of the guilty party: as we know, the force of a norm, whether codified or not, is never felt as strongly as at the moment when it is infringed upon. The spheres of art and taste are intimately connected. Much of art reviewing, for instance, straddles the borderline between them. In general, as Mukařovský writes, "practical life unceasingly provides artistic creation with its aesthetic norms, and artistic creation returns these norms in a rejuvenated form." "In this way," Mukařovský continues, "aesthetic function fully acquires the authority in practical life which is again and again denied to it in art" (p. 77).

But it is Mukařovský's second answer which is laden with significance, displaying his full realization of the dangers of relativism, of the incessant changeability which threatens the very existence of the aesthetic norm. "It is therefore necessary," he writes, "to find a *constant* from which we could derive the authority of the aesthetic norm and which, because of its constancy, could stand as the unchanging center through all of the norm's possible mutations" (p. 77; emphasis mine). Mukařovský locates this much-needed constant in the human physical and also, in part, mental constitution, which stays the same in different social milieux at different times. In other words, "it is the human attitude to the world which is in the last instance the source of aesthetic, as all other, norms" (*CPE*, p. 44). This is another way of stating that aesthetic efficacy does not so much inhere in the objects of perception but, rather, requires for its realization certain necessary features in the constitution of the perceiving subjects. Such necessary anthropological preconditions are, for the temporal arts, the regularity of rhythm—which is founded, according to Mukařovský, upon the periodicity of blood circulation and of breathing—and, for spatial arts, the constituents of symmetry such as the right angle, the vertical and the horizontal—which arise from the upright position of the human body.

These anthropological principles, which demonstrate a vital connection between the aesthetic norm and our psychophysical foundation, are not, Mukařovský warns, ideal or transcendental norms. In fact, total observance of such principles—for instance, in mechanical rhythm or in geometric diagrams—is likely to produce aesthetic indifference. Rather, these principles should be taken as "mere anthropological prerequisites for one thesis in the dialectical antinomy of the aesthetic norm whose coequal antithesis is the negation (and therefore contravention) of the constitutive principles" (p. 28). Although far from "ideal," the anthropological postulates nevertheless succeed in motivating concrete aesthetic norms, so that the whole development of art alternates between periods which aspire to their full realization ("classicisms") and those which strive for their maximum disruption ("romanticisms"). The enormous importance of such anthropological constants, as Mukařovský well understood, is that they help bring the great variety of aesthetic norms down to a common denominator, the constitutive characteristics of the human species. While increasing the intrinsic dynamism of norms—since, rather than a single set, artists can upset both the norms of the preceding period and the universal anthropological ones—these constants at the same time provide a measure against the background of which every departure can be felt as a violation of a norm. As Mukařovský puts it, "anthropological constants . . . serve as a standard by which to judge, at each moment of the evolution, the aesthetic divergence, that angle at which [the work—FWG] touches the primordial human foundation: they are points of orientation and thus principles of order in the evolution of norms" (*CPE*, p. 45).

The anthropological constants are also crucial for the identification of the universal value in art.[35] Now, in Mukařovský's aesthetics, function, norm and value are the three conceptual cornerstones. Function, according to the Prague School's definition, is the relation between a "thing" and the end the thing usually serves. Norm, in turn, is the criterion with the aid of which we can estimate the capacity of the thing to carry out the appropriate function. And value is the thing's utility, its success, with respect to the goal of that function. We have seen that at the outset, in the Circle's "Theses," the notion of function suffered from a sociological relativism, since new functional dialects could be multiplied *ad hoc*. But, as we have also observed, the Bühlerian Organon-model reduced the number of language functions to their communicative essentials. The Prague School's concept of norm, as we have examined it, especially Vodička's study of reception, similarly suffered from historical relativism: in the historical merry-go-round of norms—the top, dominant norm being forever upset by the rising norm—one norm seemed as valid as any other, and their circulation in time seemed just that—an aimless, and senseless, yet interminable process. Only the axiom of the anthropological constant introduced a principle of order in the evolution of norms. The conception of value, as well, appeared purely relative. In his analysis of *The Sublimity of Nature*, Mukařovský, able to investigate change but not permanence, sought—without success—to sever evolutionary value from aesthetic value. Thanks to the anthropological constant, however, Mukařovský could advance the claim not only that a true work of art undergoes changes in time and space but that it is also capable of resisting them. Indeed, "the universal value of the artistic work," according to Mukařovský, rests in its capacity to "retain its semantic import and its aesthetic efficacy" in environments which are widely divergent socially by appealing to what is "universally human in people," that is, to their anthropological foundation (pp. 82–83).

In Mukařovský's view, the benefit deriving from the earlier stage of axiological relativism was the discovery of the continuous line in the evolution of artistic structures. The task of axiological universalism is to determine not the qualities demanded by the evolutionary momentum of the given art but the qualities which transcend that momentum, those features which permit the work to exert its influence long after it has played out its "evolutionary" role. After all, from the moment of its creation, the work as a sign aims at an audience, and each artistic act, according to Mukařovský, is "always accompanied by the artist's intention to win unconditional approval," (p. 18), even if, as is the case with symbolist and post-symbolist art, the audience consists of a small group of devotees. Since every artist creates with the thought of attracting an audience—the work of art is a sign, not the artist's private expression—artistic creation preserves, despite the continuous fluctuations of aesthetic values, "the character of an implacable search for perfection" (p. 79), without which, just as without the postulate of "ideal" norm, the history of art would appear to be lacking direction and purpose. No artist, however, can readily pinpoint this universal aesthetic value and then hold up his or her work as a model for others. The universal value in art is not irrevocably vested in particular works, not even in those which resonate across cultures and centuries. This value cannot be static, solidly established for all and at all times. On the contrary, it must, Mukařovský avers, maintain the characteristics of "continual live energy" (p. 79) capable of renewing itself time and again. Art must in principle as much follow the pattern of tradition as it must heed the requirements of the present, and only the "universal value with its features of live energy can make way for the synthesis of these two anti-nomial imperatives: because of precisely this variability, it can draw the artist's attention to those among his precursors whose works best correspond to current artistic trends" (pp. 79–80).

Mukařovský's concern for the universals of art brought about an important methodological change of heart, enabling him to integrate into the structural and semiotic theory two factors he had hitherto kept out of it, namely, the material artifact of the work and the work's receiver, the perceiving subject. The work as aesthetic object is by definition changeable and is therefore poor proof of the durable qualities of the given work of art. The fact that some works outlast the storms of fickle taste gives sufficient ground for assuming that their unfading value is bound up not with the transitory aesthetic object but, rather, with the aesthetic makeup of the material artifact. Thus Mukařovský grants that the relationship between the dual semiotic facets of the work is highly motivated by the manner of the work's artistic making (although he does not specify what manner), so that the aesthetic object now appears as the "result of the meeting of the impulses arising from the artifact with the vital aesthetic tradition which is the property of the whole collective" (p. 80). And the collective—in another significant theoretical advance—no longer presents itself, to Mukařovský, as an impersonal and in great measure indiscriminate juggernaut which rolls over the individual's will. As Mukařovský cedes, "the place of the confluence [between the artifact and tradition] is the consciousness of the . . . individual" (p. 82). The aesthetic value, therefore, cannot repose exclusively in the material substratum of the work, because, according to Mukařovský, "people alone can establish the relation between the material artifact and the value directed at the immaterial aesthetic object" (p. 82). In other words, there can be no universal aesthetic value within the work which would not touch upon some essential trait constitutive of humanity as a whole.

Of the three main criteria for the assessment of permanent artistic value—the effectiveness of the work in different social environments, its resistance to the corrosion of time and the evidence of the individual aesthetic judgment—the first two, since they help us measure only the more or less transient aspects of the work's value, are of secondary relevance. The criteria of time and space are necessarily relative and have, in Mukařovský's opinion, "only indirect relation to the development of art: they merely set up examples to be followed" (p. 81). It is the third criterion of "evidence," that is, "the aesthetic judgment derived from previous experience, whether one's own or borrowed," which aspires toward universality. This criterion is Mukařovský's redefinition of the Kantian concept of *a priori* aesthetic judgment, except that it is not transcendental as it is in Kant but is, on the contrary, itself an agent in the history of art, simultaneously under the influence of and in turn influencing the course of artistic development. This is to say that the evidence of individual aesthetic judgment is inescapably subjective, and its "aspiration toward unlimited validity is," according to Mukařovský, "a mere postulate with which an individual addresses the collective" (p. 81). Unlike the other two criteria, however, the criterion of evidence is directly implicated in the evolution of art, since it "mediates between the subjective intention of the artist and the objective historical tendency which manifests itself through the work and also becomes influenced by it in the future" (p. 81). The third criterion, then, consisting of the recurrent aspiration toward universality, is also historically determined and thus variable. Yet this is because the universal aesthetic value is not in any way solidified or ossified but is, instead, "continually arising" (p. 83). Mukařovský, as a matter of fact, resolutely rejects the idea, dear to traditional aesthetics, of some metaphysical essence, of transcendental Beauty. As he argues, the universal aesthetic value does not get used up in the aesthetic effects of the work of art. A successful work of art, as Mukařovský first suggested when discussing the impact of Dostoevskij's *Crime and Punishment*, must touch the innermost core of the readers' own being and connect intimately with their own experiences of the world. Aesthetic value, we know, is only one among the many values constituting the readers' world, just as, on the other hand, the work of art does not consist of the aesthetic value alone but entails any number of ethical, philosophical, social and other values. And so it may well be, Mukařovský daringly speculates, that aesthetic value is in its very mode of existence nothing more than a "mere index of a reciprocal balance among the manifold values which the work entails" (p. 83).[36]

If the quest for art universals strikes one as exceedingly arduous, perhaps even belabored, it is because Mukařovský is seeking to identify not the *langue* but the *langage* of art. Structuralism, of course, begins with the premise that art is a system, in synchronic cross-section as well as in diachronic evolution. What structural theory must establish next are the preconditions for the existence of such a system. *Langage*, according to Saussurean understanding, is the general human faculty for communicating by means of language and other sign systems. Since this faculty exists in and is characteristic of people in general, modern linguistics, like Prague structural aesthetics, tries to locate universal "deep structures" in the human constitution, specifically in the mind. Yet the practice of art, though widespread, is—in comparison with language—restricted to specially creative individuals, the artists, a restriction which carries within itself the advantage of "permitting far more leeway and far less uniformity than the normal use of speech" (p. 83). Nevertheless, art does possess certain universal "archetypes," observable less in high art than in primitive, folk or children's art. Even literature for children seems, as Mukařovský notes, "to acquire a value independent of the passage of time and the crossing of space" (p. 83). Like the norms of languages, the archetypal principles of art cannot be prescriptive; they exist on such an abstract level of generality, Mukařovský insists, that they cannot possibly be contravened. This abstraction, or indefiniteness, guarantees that, just as there are numerous *langues*, so there will be "new and previously untrodden ways which art can take in its quest for the anthropological human foundation" (p. 83). As Mukařovský sees it, any time a work of art makes close contact with that universal human base, what we have is an artistic victory, a work of supreme art. Yet, by itself, the anthropological constant is, in Mukařovský's view, devoid of aesthetic qualities, which leads him to conclude that "between [the constant] and its aesthetic realizations there is a *qualitative* tension and that each realization discloses a new view of the basic human constitution" (p. 84). In this way, by positing the anthropological constant as the necessary pivot in the development of art, Mukařovský attempts to redress the shortcomings of his earlier structural and sociological relativism. The foregrounding of the human subject, the full repercussions of which we shall examine in the final section of this study, henceforth came to occupy the center of Mukařovský's structural and semiotic inquiry.

Several reasons prompted this venture into the territory of general aesthetics and philosophy of art. In Mukařovský's conception, there is no categorical division but a hierarchical interdependence between the general theory of art and the theory of literature, just as there is no logical separation but a deep-seated interpenetration between his literary theory and historical poetics—so much so that their forced severance for purposes of analysis—the narrowing of the inquiry to one or the other aspect of Mukařovský's global structural theory—is likely to falsify the theory as a whole as well as in its various aspects.[37] In particular, what I have tried to show is that Mukařovský, unlike Vodička, realized the unsupportable implications of his immanent, historically relativistic approach to literary history. It is not immediately clear, however, how Vodička could have applied Mukařovský's universalist tenets to the study of reception. The universals of language and literature resist ready-made specification. We can only observe that Mukařovský's grounding of rhythm in the human biological constitution helps make intelligible why the whole history of Czech versification, as we have noted on several occasions, is marked by perpetual oscillations between a strict realization of the metre and its repeated deregulation. But even if the concrete application of universal aesthetic principles to reception aesthetics remains uncertain, what is beyond dispute is the fact that Vodička's type of inquiry solely lacks a principle of order. Such inquiry could perhaps profit most from a theory of interpretation which would assist the historian of reception in arbitrating the validity of various critical statements under examination, to help determine what might have been individual or even period aberrations and what were genuine contributions to our understanding of the historical process of understanding literature. Moreover, by postulating the anthropological constant as the standard of value underlying the evolution of all art, Mukařovský rectified the failure of his attempt in the Polák study to disengage aesthetic from historical value, for which Wellek had taken him to task. However, Wellek himself, we recall, proved unable to define the nature of that value inextricably present in art history. It was left to Mukařovský to show the way. Most importantly, having followed the reasons behind Mukařovský's inclusion of the perceiving subject as an indispensable part of the semiotics of art, we shall be able to explain the next stage in the development of his theory, which may otherwise seem methodologically eclectic, arbitrary, even erratic—his leanings toward phenomenology.

‖●‖●‖●‖●‖●‖

The last phase in the development of Mukařovský's structuralism is rather hard to reconstruct. All of the essays discussed in the remaining pages were delivered as lectures to the Prague Circle during the turbulent years of World War II, but because of the German ban on Czech publications—including the journal of the Circle, *The Word and Verbal Art*—could not be published at that time. After the war, Mukařovský, who in the interim had begun converting to Marxism, republished in *Chapters in Czech Poetics* most of his major essays that had previously seen print, omitting the studies from the period of the occupation. It was not until 1966, upon the publication of Mukařovský's *Studies in Aesthetics*, that these remarkable essays reached the reading public.[38] Without these late phenomenological probes into the role of the individual in the development of art any account of Prague structural theory would be incomplete and seriously distorted. Their delayed publication is symptomatic of the fate of structuralism in the 1950s, when, after Stalin's perorations on "Marxist" linguistics, structural theory became anathema in all areas of research. Only the political thaw of the mid-1960s brought about a full rehabilitation of the Prague Linguistic Circle and a resurrection of Mukařovský's forgotten works. Yet the period of the Prague Spring was too brief for the younger structuralists to absorb all the implications of Mukařovský's philosophical revisions of his previous methodological stance. With structuralism once again taboo in Czechoslovakia, the phenomenological aspect of Mukařovský's theory is still in need of detailed clarification after more than thirty years.

Mukařovský himself is partly responsible for the uncertainty about the place of phenomenology in his theoretical evolution. For one thing, he never explicitly criticized his previous stance, even though, understandably enough, he continually revised, and refined, his theoretical principles. Whenever making mention of an earlier, now untenable, position of his own, Mukařovský couched such criticism in the most general terms, as in the essay "Can There Be a Universal Value in Art?": "Humanity, which has lately experienced a period, not yet finished, of axiological relativism, now seeks to introduce the idea of permanent value . . ." (p. 78). Moreover, perhaps in reaction to the totalizing attempts of idealistic aesthetics, Mukařovský at no time tried to write a structuralist *summa* which would bring his various partial efforts—in linguistics, poetics, semiotics, aesthetics—under the roof of a single unified theoretical construction.

The disjointedness, if not discrepancy, between the separate parts of his theory is particularly patent in "The Place of the Aesthetic Function among the Other Functions," in which he proposed a new, phenomenologically conceived, typology of functions. Yet, even though he had earlier worked with the Bühlerian scheme of functions, also phenomenologically derived, Mukařovský made no attempt at correlating Bühler's typology with his own; nor did he ever again refer to the new typology once he had produced it. Paradoxically, the essay which defined the place of the aesthetic function in the world of functions itself remained without a specific place allotted to it within the overall framework of Mukařovský's theory. Nevertheless, this essay performed, even if only implicitly, an inestimable role in the elaboration of his concept of the position of the individual vis-à-vis the development of art.

The essay on functions is Mukařovský's one work expressly committed to the phenomenological method. Allusions to phenomenology, however, are interspersed throughout the writings of the Prague scholars practically from the beginning. We have seen how, in the 1932 interview, Mukařovský claimed that structure is not an empirical reality but a phenomenological model embedded in the social consciousness of a collective, and how Jakobson, in the 1934 lecture, praised phenomenology for disclosing what we may call the fundamental semiotic asymmetry of language. Mukařovský's first references to Husserl and his type of analysis date to 1935,[39] the year Husserl, at the invitation of the Kant-Gesellschaft and Brentano-Gesellschaft as well as the Cercle Philosophique and Cercle Linguistique, delivered a series of lectures in Prague on the relationship between philosophy and history, "Die Krisis der europäischen Wissenschaften und die Transcendentale Phänomenologie."[40] Mukařovský's forthright espousal of phenomenology in his reflections on the nature of the aesthetic and other functions, consequently, was not a sudden about-face but, rather, the culmination of a growing acquaintance with Husserlian philosophy. The *point d'appui* for Mukařovský's analysis of functions is the belief that only the phenomenological *Wesensschau*, a deduction from the nature of function itself, can provide a clue to an authentic comprehension of the ways in which humans react to and act upon the universe.

Accordingly, function must not be simply and unilaterally projected onto the object of analysis, since it is the human subject who is the prime source, the fount of all functions. From the standpoint of the subject, every action addressed to the surrounding world can simultaneously perform several tasks or functions. The incertitude concerning the motives and aims of human actions springs from the fact that "for people, in all of their acts, various functions necessarily enter into relationships of reciprocal tensions: they arrange themselves hierarchically, crisscross and merge with one another" (p. 68). Every human deed is polyfunctional, just as numerous functions are inexorably present in everything we do. This innate polyfunctionality reveals itself only from the vantage point of the subject; when looked at from the vantage point of the object, function appears to be directed toward a specific goal and thus seems monofunctional. Yet as "modes" or "methods" or "ways" of "human self-realization vis-à-vis the world," functions are, Mukařovský insists, fundamentally and ineradicably "polyfunctional" (p. 69).

Since people can realize themselves in respect to the world either directly (that is, by means of tools) or through the mediation of signs (which are no mere instruments but representations on equal footing with the reality they signify), functions divide themselves into two basic categories: the unmediated and the semiotic. Each of these categories splits into two subcategories, depending on whether it brings to the fore the object or the subject. In Mukařovský's typology, the two unmediated functions are the practical and the theoretical: the first foregrounds the object, for "the realization of the subject aims at transforming the object, that is to say, reality," while the second foregrounds the subject, for its goal is to "project reality into the consciousness of the subject" (pp. 69–70), leaving unchanged the object of the function, the reality itself. In turn, the two semiotic functions are the symbolic and the aesthetic. The former, according to Mukařovský, thrusts the object to the forefront. The focus of attention here is on the effectiveness with which the symbolizing sign can signify the symbolized thing: both the sign and the signified reality appear as objects: "either reality is affected by the sign," Mukařovský explains, "or it [reality] operates by means of the sign" (p. 70). When the relationship between the symbol and the symbolized is effective, the flag, for instance, can represent the country, and insulting the symbol is tantamount to insulting what it stands for; when their relationship is ineffective, as when a drawing of the heart is meant to connote love, the symbol deteriorates to a mere "allegory." Finally, the second semiotic function, the aesthetic, puts in the forefront the human subject. This fourfold typology can be diagrammed in the following way:

```
                    UNMEDIATED
              Practical │ Theoretical
                        │
OBJECT IN     ──────────┼──────────────          SUBJECT IN
FOREGROUND              │                         FOREGROUND
                        │
              Symbolic  │ Aesthetic
                    SEMIOTIC
```

Curiously enough, it is the subject who, until the postulation of universal anthropological constants, was largely absent from Mukařovský's aesthetic and semiotic theory. Mukařovský, following Jakobson and the formalists, defined art as the domain in which the aesthetic function predominates; and the aesthetic function, in this view, manifests itself by diverting attention from the object of reference and riveting it to the sign itself, so that the sign with the aesthetic function dominant tends to refer not to particular items but to the social reality as a whole. Now Mukařovský reaffirms his older view, but with a radical modification. The aesthetic sign continues, in the modified theory, to reflect within itself the whole of reality. The art work's ability to typify a certain era stems from the fact that, "as a pure aesthetic sign, the work of art demonstrates on the basis of one particular all other particulars as well as their totality— the reality as such" (p. 70). But here is the modification: "The reality which as a whole is reflected in the aesthetic sign is also unified in this sign in accordance with the image of the unified subject" (p. 80). As can be seen, in its mediateness or semioticity aesthetic function resembles symbolic function, and in its emphasis on the subject it approaches theoretical function, yet it is quite distinct from both. In contrast to symbolic function, which mediates between a symbol and a particular facet of reality, aesthetic function mediates between the sign and the whole of reality. And in contrast to theoretical function, which strives to produce a unified picture of reality, aesthetic function incites a unified attitude toward it.

More importantly, for aesthetic function, reality is a mediated, not unmediated, object: the unmediated object here is the aesthetic sign. According to Mukařovský, the hallmark of the aesthetic sign is that it "projects into reality as a general law the subject's attitude as it manifests itself in the structure of that sign . . ." (p. 70). While for aesthetic function sign is the unmediated object in which it must be realized, for theoretical function sign is only an instrument, a means toward the knowledge of reality, which is its unmediated object. Put differently, for theoretical function a sign becomes a sign-instrument, whereas for aesthetic function, as for symbolic function, it becomes a sign-object—except that, in distinction to the symbolic sign, which must affect some part of reality, the aesthetic sign merely projects itself, and hence the subject's attitude, into that reality as a whole.

The one function which we have put aside, the practical function, is, as it was in the earliest version of the Prague School theory, the very antinomy of aesthetic function: it neither foregrounds the subject nor is mediated. Yet it is the basic, the unmarked, function: providing the fundamental means of human existence, it is closest to reality. Indeed, as Mukařovský points out, we should be speaking of practical functions, not of the practical function, since there are so many subtle shades of this type of function—as many, in fact, as there are shades of reality with which this function comes into contact. But even though acting as the elemental function, it is not hierarchically superior: without becoming subordinate, different functions enter into combinations with the practical function, thus creating further functional nuances, such as the magical, which, according to Mukařovský, is a blend of the symbolic and the practical functions.

No function can thus be reduced to another, Mukařovský maintains, just as no function can be *a priori* superordinate. Assigning a priority would fly in the face of the phenomenological endeavor to create a basic typology whose validity transcends the bounds of time. The typological categories must therefore remain unchanged; only the relationships among the categories can undergo constant alterations. "Although such interrelationships, the reciprocal ties among functions, cannot be hierarchical," Mukařovský writes, "they may become, in evolution, the tracks along which the shifts in hierarchies take place" (pp. 72–73). The typological divisions provide the main lines of possible combinations and groupings between functions. The practical and the theoretical functions go together, as we know, because they are unmediated; the symbolic and the aesthetic, because they are mediated. The practical and the symbolic, on the other hand, are alike in their foregrounding of the object; the theoretical and the aesthetic in their foregrounding of the subject. Two more possible functional groupings are left to be accounted for: that of the practical with the aesthetic and that of the theoretical with the symbolic. Indeed, such couplings occur quite frequently, as when the practical and the aesthetic functions commingle as they do in theatre or architecture or when, as in the mystical philosophy of the Baroque, there is a symbiosis of symbolism and epistemology.

Nevertheless, phenomenologically, the members of these last pairs remain furthest apart. As Mukařovský explains, the practical function is directed outward (toward the transforming of reality), while the aesthetic function is inner-directed (that is, toward the self-purposiveness of the act or thing in which it realizes itself). In the second pair, the theoretical function deliberately reduces the sign's effectiveness to that of a mere "signal," fixed and singular as the ciphers of logic or mathematics, whereas the symbolic function, if it is to retain its impact on reality, must resist the sign's downgrading to an allegory. Consequently, such opposing functions must be, as Mukařovský concludes, linked together precisely because of their polarization. Thus, the practical function and the aesthetic function are so profoundly antithetical that—were we to confront the aesthetic function with the group of nonaesthetic functions—all functions, the theoretical included, would emerge as apparently "practical." What, Mukařovský asks, is the outcome of this antagonism? "It is," he answers, "that wherever the practical function retreats by a step, the aesthetic function immediately follows after it as its negation, so that these functions frequently enter into conflict with each other, contesting the same thing or act" (p. 73). As is especially clear in the case of language, if we recall Jakobson's argument concerning the indispensability of the poetic function (or poeticity), the tension between and among functions is vital for the requisite mobility of signs. On the one hand, only the potential presence of the symbolic function, as Mukařovský shows, alerts us to the intensity of the referential relation between sign and thing (since it maintains the sign's hold on the referred-to aspect or part of reality); on the other, only the potential effect of the aesthetic function fastens our attention to the sign's independence from a particular reality (since the autotelic—aesthetic—sign refers to the reality as a whole). But this mobility of signs and versatility of functions no longer exists for the sake of language alone, as it appeared before, but, rather, for the self-realization of the subject, at once the source and the destination of all signs in their varied functions.

The purest way for the subject's self-realization is through the creation of art. As Mukařovský comments in the essay "Intentionality and Unintentionality in Art," employing a principal phenomenological category without at any point directly evoking phenomenology or the name of its founder, "the work of art stands out among human products as the archetypal example of intentional creation" (p. 89). Intention, in phenomenological theory, is what distinguishes human acts and artifacts from natural ones. While everything we do is informed to one degree or another by our intention to perform such and such a deed or create such and such an object, only within the work of art can every detail and facet become saturated with intention: we know that as an aesthetic sign the work functions as an indivisible whole. The nature of intention, in other words, depends on the subject and the goal of his or her action or creation. In practical actions, the most quotidian manifestations of intentionality, intention is directed both toward the author or performer of intention and toward the desired end. The basic questions here are whether the individual's goal is indeed a desirable one and whether he or she has the capacity to attain it. In art both terminal points of intention, author and aim, acquire different status. We know that, in the (structural, semiotic, phenomenological) theory of Mukařovský, artistic creations do not serve any goal or goals exterior to them but, instead, are ends in themselves. Similarly, the decisive subject, who in the case of practical actions is solely the author of intention, is in art not so much the "author as the subject to whom the work is addressed, that is, the *perceiver*" (p. 91). Mukařovský explains this paradox of art according to which the perceivers (readers, listeners or spectators) gain preference over the authors (the creative artists) by saying that the authors themselves, when looking at their creations as the expression of pure intentionality rather than as products meant to implement some practical task—whether as commercial items or as propaganda pieces— approach the works precisely from the standpoint of the hypothetical perceivers to whom they are appealing. These perceivers, of course, are phenomenological subjects, not concrete individuals, just as intentionality is a phenomenological, and not a psychological, phenomenon.

Intentionality itself comes to the fore in a work of art because, as we have noted, the two terminal points, crucial in practical actions, forfeit much of their claim to the perceiver's attention in art. In Mukařovský's view, the reason for the diminished importance of the author and external aim is that, since both lie outside the work, they stand in the way of our efforts at reconstructing the unity of the work, the unity which defines it as a work of art. As Mukařovský enjoins,

> The unity of the artistic work which theorists of art so often sought . . . either in the artist's personality or in experience conceived of as a unique encounter of the artist's personality with reality, and which the formalist movements unsuccessfully explained as a total harmony of all of the work's parts and elements (one which in reality never exists)—this unity can rightly be found only in intentionality, that force active within the work which strives to resolve the contradictions and tensions among its constituent parts and elements, thereby imposing a unified meaning on their ensemble and defining the specific relation of every part to the rest. (p. 93)

Intentionality in art is above all a semantic energy which binds the seemingly incongruous component parts of the work into a meaningful whole. It is intentionality with which the artists, when approaching their work as pure communication addressed to perceivers, infuse the entire creation of works of art. And it is intentionality which the perceivers, during the act of perception, are determined to re-create as the works' constitutive unity.

The phenomenological focus on the perceivers tacitly recasts the relationships among the main categories of Mukařovský's theory of art. As before, the work of art signifies in its entirety, not through its individual parts. But unlike the first version of Mukařovský's semiotics, where the work as a whole reflected the total context of social phenomena, in the phenomenologically grounded version, the whole of the work, well-suited to affect or relate to any facet of the perceiver's personalities "'signifies' the experiences of the perceivers, his mental world" (p. 92). (We should note that Mukařovský states the new possibility of the work's signified only parenthetically, perhaps aware of contradicting his previous position, but the contradiction may be avoidable if the subject, identified as the anthropological constant, mediates between the work of art as a social fact and the experiential reality of humanity. As we have observed, Mukařovský himself, however, never tried to conjoin the disparate parts of his theory.) In other words, the perceivers, through reconstituting the structure of the work's parts, activate the global meaning of the work which, Mukařovský avers, is present neither in any one of its parts nor in their mechanical addition. Even though the resulting unity is largely prescribed by the work—as an intentional object, it must exhibit the marks of intentionality etched by the author—the perceivers play no small part in choosing a particular component of the work as the fundamental organizing part and in coordinating the remaining parts with it. Yet intentionality, like the anthropological constant, is not a fixed and localizable trait of art in general; nor can it be firmly implanted in a concrete work of art. Its existence, too, is dynamic and historically labile. The outcome of the perceivers' encounter with the structure of the work, the intentionality of a work is vulnerable to interpretive shifts—contingent on such historical factors as period, generation, social milieu and the like—so that different components may become the carriers of the intentionality: elements which at first appeared neutral, devoid of specific intention, may later seem to be endowed with intentionality, as do expressive means common to the period language of an older poetic work which affect the modern reader as if they were deliberate archaisms. In short, intentionality in art, much like aesthetic norm and value, is live (semantic) energy, omnipresent yet inherently unstable.

As a sign, the work of art necessarily manifests an intentional unity. But, as Mukařovský asserts, the work is not a pure sign, and its unity is not absolute. Put differently, besides intentionality, the work of art necessarily also manifests aspects of unintentionality. Any of the work's intentional aspects—intentional, that is, from the standpoint of the author—may be interpreted as unintentional by the perceiver: for instance, a poet's consciously irregular realization of metre can strike the reader as deficient skill. Genuine unintentionality, conversely, may have the effect of calculated intentionality, as is the case with ancient statues whose fragmentary torsos convey the impression of aesthetic completeness. In principle, intentionality creates, as we know, the impression of a semantically unified (mediated) object, the opposite of "natural" (unmediated) reality, but the work of art, as long as it connects with the perceivers' experience of the world, simultaneously gives the impression of an immediate reality. In the performing arts especially, viewers experience moments of great empathy, of nearly total identification with the world as depicted on the stage or the screen, oblivious to the staged (that is, intentional) artificiality (that is, semioticity) of the artistic proceedings. Thus, the work of art ceases to function as an intentional autonomous sign and becomes transmogrified in the audience's mind into the real (that is, artistically "unintentional") thing. Yet insofar as viewers respond to the work as just another experience of the familiar world, they shut their eyes to the work's intentional unity.

Such confusion between the natural and the intentional in art arises not only because the audience may misinterpret the intentionality of the work but also because of certain elements within the work which act as obstacles to the perceivers' efforts at semantic unification. In other words, the work of art affects, and moves, the audience as a sign and as a thing at one and the same time. As Mukařovský explains,

The internal unification [of the sign—FWG] induced by intentionality evokes a particular relation to the work and forms the axis around which can cluster [the perceivers'] associations and feelings. On the other hand, as a semantically indefinite thing (which it is owing to its unintentionality), the work acquires the capacity to elicit the most varied associations and feelings, which need not have anything in common with its semantic makeup. The work is thus able to connect with the wholly personal experiences, associations and feelings of any perceiver. . . . The perceiver's entire *individual* attitude to reality, whether active or contemplative, will henceforth be more or less altered due to this influence. The work of art has such an immense impact on people, not because—as standard opinion has it—it offers the imprint of the author's personality and his experiences, but because it affects the *personality and the experiences of the perceiver.* And this it can accomplish thanks to the fact that an element of unintentionality is contained and felt within it. (p. 98)

Unintentionality is indispensable for the viewers' perception of the work as not purely a sign but a thing as well.[41] As a pure sign, possessing the faculty of global reference, the work would reach such heights of abstraction and be so removed from the perceivers' world of experience as to be of little or no relevance at all. As Mukařovský argues, "to the extent to which we perceive it as an autonomous aesthetic sign, the work of art appears deprived of any *direct* contact with reality, and not only with external reality but also—above all—with the reality of the perceiver's mental life" (p. 105).

Mukařovský's suggestion that, as an intentional sign and not an unintentional thing, the work of art is really a *res nullius*, a property common to all but without relation to anything individual, leads to quite an astounding conclusion (cf. p. 98 above). It was the battle cry of the formalists that extrinsic literary theories (some of which Vodička personified early in his career) disregard the specific nature of art and so void art works of their existence. According to the formalists, the specificity resided in the forms of art, but, according to the structuralists, it rests in the peculiar semantic quality of global reference. But just as the work as a mere thing is not a work of art, so, following Mukařovský's argument, as a pure sign it does not sufficiently relate to the world of things, our daily habitat. To function fully as a work of art, therefore, the work must have both the semiotic and "realistic" effect: its impact must be at once that of the mediating sign and the immediate thing. "Only unintentionality," Mukařovský insists, "can render the work as mysterious in the eyes of the perceiver as is the object whose purpose is unknown." And he goes on to say:

> Only unintentionality, with its resistance to semantic unification, is able to incite the perceiver's active attention; and only unintentionality, which due to its indeterminacy opens the way for the most diverse associations, can, through the contact between perceiver and work, set in motion the whole of the perceiver's life experience. . . . In this manner, unintentionality helps integrate the work into the sphere of the spectator's existential interests and endows it with an urgency beyond the reach of a mere sign, behind whose every feature the perceiver would sense an intention of someone other than himself. (p. 105)

It is the task of the perceiver to keep a delicate balance between the intentionality and unintentionality, between the semiosis and materialness, of the work of art, a balance which must be restored with every fresh act of perception. Although such an equipoise is historically fragile, continually renewable, it is not altogether unpredictable. On the one side, the perceiver is, of course, a member of society; on the other, the work is a part of the evolving structure of art. And inasmuch as artistic structures are intentional structures, the renewal of intentionality falls in line with the development of art. The renewal of unintentionality occurs sporadically, however, only on those occasions when there is a disaccord between the received structure of art and the mode of construction of new works of art. Any time novel artistic trends profess that they are revivifying the sense of reality numbed by previous forms of art, they are in fact, as Mukařovský states, reclaiming the unintentionality which their works must have in order to be of consequence to the intended receivers. The proportion and relative significance of intentionality and unintentionality in the perception of art constantly fluctuate during the history of art, for their dialectical interrelation admits practically inexhaustible variations, both of quantitative preponderance of intentionality over unintentionality (and vice versa) and of qualitative gradation between them.

Thus, thanks to the notion of intentionality and unintentionality, Mukařovský in one stroke dramatically improves upon the structural semantics of art, placing artistic creations more firmly in the world of everyday experience, and elaborates a conception of the perceiving subject with which any sophisticated semiotic theory of art—and of art's reception—will have to grapple.

||●||●||●||●||●||

At last we come to a point in Mukařovský's development which is a terminus rather than a junction. In this final stage, Mukařovský's structuralism swings full circle and incorporates into its theory the one semiotic factor—that of the individual artistic personality—whose import Mukařovský has all along strained to invalidate or at least to deflate. Mukařovský's disinclination to tackle the problem of the creative subject in art has been motivated in part by the Saussurean legacy of exiling the speaking subject from the structural study of language. Analogous to the methodological bifurcation of synchrony and diachrony, Saussure, we recall, also insisted on cleaving *langue* from *parole*. Investigative focus on individual utterance thwarts, Saussure believed, the researcher's recognition of the regularity of the language system. Like the seeming fitfulness of diachronic changes, the capriciousness of individual speech acts appeared to Saussure as inimical to the structural uniformity of the language system as it exists in synchronic cross-section. Moreover, Mukařovský's other specialty, aesthetics (and by extention literary theory), concentrated, in the hands of the preceding generation of scholars, wholly on the problematics of the individual artist, demoting aesthetics to an appendage of psychology, a mere *ancilla psychologiae*. Thus, as an aesthetician and literary theorist, Mukařovský found himself in a double bind at the outset of his career: structural linguistics, his methodological model, renounced any concern for the individual, while aesthetics, his field of research, felt no need for a system. Under these conditions, the prospect of structural aesthetics—that is, of the systematic study of individual artists and their works—must have seemed more like an impossible vision of opposites meeting. But perhaps the strongest reason for Mukařovský's recoiling from the questions of individual creativity was the general trend of modernism, of the art of his contemporaries, which, as a reaction to romantic and symbolist afflatus—the notion of the artist as a genius, a sage or an outcast—sought to place the creative talent in a more sober perspective. In this respect, art and scholarship alike rebelled against the domination of psychology, the spiritual matrix of the nineteenth century, both trying, from the beginning of the twentieth century onward, to proclaim their autonomy as domains *sui generis*. The development of Prague linguistic and literary structuralism, especially as represented by the career of Mukařovský as well as Jakobson,

far from being unique or erratic, thus appears (along with pure phenomenology, philosophical axiology or normative jurisprudence) as part
and parcel of the modern paradigm.

So far we have traced two converging curves of Mukařovský's theoretical evolution, that of his ever-tighter lodging of art and literature in
the social context as well as in the experiential context of the individual
and that of his progressive semantization of the work of art as a sign signifying those contexts. We must now draw the third line of Mukařovský's
thought—one, as we have seen, largely inspired by phenomenology—
concerning the role of the individual in art. For Mukařovský, phenomenology served as a catalyst in the search for artistic universals, the permanent facet of art and, if we recall Lukács' argument, the proper subject
of the aesthetic part of literary history; in addition, phenomenology was
instrumental in Mukařovský's foregrounding of the subject, and of the
perceiving subject in particular. In the examination of the individual artist,
phenomenology enabled Mukařovský, as we shall see, to stipulate two important sets of distinctions with the support of which he managed even
here to cede little ground to (mechanistic) psychology.

The first of these distinctions is that between sundry historically conditioned views of the nature of creative personality and the unconditional
and invariable aspect of the artistic subject. In the lecture "Personality in
Art," Mukařovský has no trouble showing how drastically the idea of the
artist changes from one epoch to another.[42] The notion of individual artistic expression was, as Mukařovský points out, completely foreign to the
Middle Ages: artists could not give free vent to impulses and instincts—
such psychological categories were unheard of at the time—since their
task was to imitate, however imperfectly, the Beauty of the Divine. During
the Renaissance, the order of nature replaced the divine order as the object
of imitation, and although artists took considerable pride in skill and individual craft, their works expressed their understanding of nature, not personal dispositions. But in the Romantic Movement, the work of art materi-
alized as an external replica of the artists' internal spiritual states: the
cultivation of artistic genius became the acme of art. Symbolism further
exacerbated the paradox of according the place of esteem more to artists
than to their art, turning art into an esoteric cult—the obverse of the general accessibility of medieval art—with secrets communicable only to the
initiated few. The advent of modernism marks yet another twist in the understanding of the relation of artists to art: no more a spontaneous expression of the artists' souls, the works are once again detached from the artists, and the possible connections between the artistic creators and their
works appear at best tangential and multiform.

In the second part of the lecture, however, Mukařovský turns around
and asserts that all of the views of artists he has just described are histori-

cally relative opinions. Allowing that the literary scholar is apt to endorse the prevailing view of the day, Mukařovský nevertheless argues that one must "unmask everything that is historically relative as merely transitory" and attempt, instead, "to disclose the unchanging essence of the thing itself" (p. 240). Once again, phenomenology offers a solution. As Mukařovský declares, the definition of the artist as the creator of an artistically intentional work (cf. *CPE*, p. 169) transcends all temporal determinants and applies equally well to artists of all periods. There cannot be a work of art, Mukařovský affirms, which has not been created by an artist. As an object devoid of intentionality, the work would be indistinguishable from a natural object. Being the exact opposite of natural objects, works of art, intentional objects par excellence, are without exception all created by artists with a view to eventual perceivers. The work of art of necessity mediates between two parties, artists and their audience. Like a conversation, which cannot take place without a speaker and a listener, art—for instance, literature—cannot exist without a creator and a perceiver. According to Mukařovský, dialogue can in fact serve as a model for art—in art, too, the "speaker" can take turns with the "listener." Folkloric art vividly illustrates the fact that, as in a conversational exchange, the artist and the listener or spectator cannot be easily sorted out—not only because each artist can become a member of the audience but also because each member of the audience is potentially a folk artist. More importantly, the dialogic model provides yet one more proof that, like a language utterance, the work of art is a sign mediating between two (or more) "conversational" partners and that, as a sign, it is understood by both. As Mukařovský observes, "during the act of creating, every artist has a perceiver on his mind and takes him into account, while the perceiver, on the other hand, understands the work as the utterance of an author and senses the author behind it" (p. 241). This dialogic conception of artistic intercourse finds itself at loggerheads with the received—psychologistic—view of art as a direct expression of the artist, to which the receiver has only indirect and incomplete access. If we understand art as dialogue, Mukařovský argues,

we no longer see . . . the author as indissolubly bound to the work, nor do we see the spectator as merely incidental and without an essential relation to it; rather, we acknowledge that the author's relation to the work does not fundamentally differ from that of the spectator; that they are simply two parties between whom the work mediates; and that the work, because of its mediating faculty, is a *sign* and not an expression. (p. 241)

As an intentional sign, the work bears within it, we remember, the marks of intentionality. The source of that intentionality is, of course, the "artist" or, better still, the author's subject. From the point of view of the work as an intentional sign, the authorial subject is to be found within, not outside of, the work. The traces of this subject are scattered in every facet of the work, appearing more explicitly in some of the work's features than in others. The subject is implicitly present in the selection of each of the work's components, from the choice of a word to that of the theme. It manifests itself explicitly—in a work of verbal art, for instance, through personal, possessive and demonstrative pronouns and the point of view these imply, through verbal tenses and their temporal perspective and through other verbal deictics. At its most explicit, the subject is incarnated in the lyrical "I." But even at its most explicit, the subject remains within the work as the organizing principle of the work's unity. As such, the subject is present even where, as in drama, it seems invisible, dispersed as it is in several personae. It is at this point, in explaining dramatic dialogue, that the dialogic model displays its explanatory value. Put simply, the *dramatis personae* are not autonomous individuals who converse for themselves (if they were, we might, as Mukařovský notes, just as well erect a fourth wall in front of the stage [cf. *CPE*, p. 83]) but are instead vehicles for the dialogue between the author and the audience—or more precisely, between two subjects. In a stage play, individual characters are merely projections of the subject "who has calculated [the characters'] words and their effect," addressing these words not to the characters but to "another subject" (p. 242). As Mukařovský maintains, in drama, as in all arts, there are actually not "two separate subjects but only a single subject." The sole distinction here is that "at a certain time the subject is embodied in someone we call the author and at another in someone we call the perceiver" (p. 242). If this paradox sounds familiar, it is because Mukařovský repeats the argument first put forth in the analysis of intentionality: in creating an intentional sign, which is a work of art, the artist considers his or her work above all from the standpoint of the receiver.

Just as the author is indistinguishable from the perceiver when contemplating a work, so the creative and perceiving subjects become one within the work. As Mukařovský claims, "there is only one subject contained within the work, and that subject is provided by the work's intentionality" (p. 242). Rather than a concrete individual, then, the subject is a "mere epistemological prerequisite" or "an abstract point" (*CPE*, p. 54), which can be filled by the perceiver as much as by the author. Whether this point is at a particular time filled by someone who projects intentionality onto the work or by someone who perceives it in the completed work is, as Mukařovský points out, a matter external to the work itself. In other words, the subject, as the carrier of intentionality, is the centripetal force of structural coherence, binding together and reconciling the dissonant elements that compose the work's structure, and it is the force of this unity which the perceiving subject feels during the act of perception. In this way, the perceiving subject, the receiver of the sign, discerns in every work the creating subject, the creator of the sign, as the principal stimulus of the percipient's current mental state. In Mukařovský's argument, the authorial subject, or we can say the implied author, is nothing more than a *semiotic construct* corresponding to the reader's state of mind. The subject, to repeat, is but a focal point of the work, whose place within the overall structure of the work is given by the fact that "all [the work's] elements converge upon the subject and, in so doing, *signify* it" (*CPE*, p. 84). Thus, as traditional aesthetic theory demanded, the subject does, in the final analysis, safeguard its uniqueness—not, however, because it relates to a unique individual (as we have seen, it can, on the contrary, be filled by any number of individuals) but because it is the "single point of convergence of all of the work's significations" (*CPE*, p. 84).[43]

Before proceeding with this discussion, we should—to prevent possible confusion—briefly retrace our steps. As noted earlier, Mukařovský, in working out his theory of artistic personality, proposed two sets of qualifying distinctions. The first such distinction established a way of discriminating between a variety of historically conditioned, and thus impermanent, views on the nature of the artist and the phenomenological definition of the artist, universally valid. The second distinction, in turn, helps us distinguish the phenomenological subject, the hypothetical point or postulate existing outside of time, from the concrete being existing in history. If the first distinction sorts out the permanent aspect of artists from transient conceptions of them, the second marks the permanent aspect common to all artists—the authorial subject—from the individual psychophysical personalities. So far Mukařovský succeeded in securing the autonomy of the subject without making any concessions to psychology, but only at the cost of excluding the real author from his analysis. After all, the authorial subject does not divulge any information about the creative individual which we could not glean from the work itself. We are still, in other words, within the bounds of immanence, treating the text as a manifestation of pure intentionality. But just as Mukařovský argued that the work of art exhibits at once traits of intentionality and unintentionality, that it is both a sign and a thing, so he now claims that personality, in addition to the authorial subject, expresses itself in art through the concrete person of the author. In "The Individual and Literary Development" and related essays, he goes so far as to assert that literary theory, if it is to do justice to the complexities of literary history, "cannot pass over the individual [author] with impunity" (p. 226).

However, the main reason behind Mukařovský's attempts to debar the artistic personality from structuralism was not so much a fear of the incursion of psychology into the domain of aesthetics and literary theory—the notion of the work of art as an intersubjective sign, not a subjective expression, proved a strong enough defense—as a recognition, inherited from Saussure, that the individual was apt to play havoc with the systemic evolution of (literary) structure. As long as Mukařovský explored the immanent literary order, which includes intentionality and subject as its integral parts, the development of literature appeared orderly, systematic and law-governed. Yet, as Mukařovský realized, the moment we step outside the boundaries of immanence, we are compelled to admit that literary history does not conform to any principles of prevenient necessity. Once we look at the evolution of the literary order from the point of view of the individual artist, the fallacy of the belief in a kind of algebra of change, of totally predictable or governable modulations of the literary system, becomes self-evident. Indeed, as Mukařovský reminds us, the structuralists never subscribed to a naive, single-cause view of history.[44] Nevertheless, he points out, implicitly refuting his argument from the study of *The Sublimity of Nature*, the structuralists' conception was not entirely free of causal determinism. Here is his argument:

As long as we see only the immanent [literary—FWG] development and next to it the other series [political, ideological, cultural] as intervening at exactly the moment and in exactly the manner required by this development, there is always the danger that the word *regularity* [*zákonitost; Gesetzmäßigkeit*], even if the scholar himself understands it teleologically, will contain a latent element of mechanical causality and lead to a scheme in which causes produce their effects in an obligatory and unequivocal fashion. But once we recognize that behind this regularity is the constant possibility of hidden chance represented by the individual (by the individual as genus), which operates without interruption as the obverse of such regularity, the notion of the lawlike development becomes divested of the last traces of causality. Chance and necessity cease being mutually exclusive and instead become integrated into a genuine, always dynamic and energizing, dialectic opposition. (p. 234)

In other words, the personality of the author, the irreducible accident of history, is the crucial—yet because of its individuality largely unpredictable—factor in determining what particular path of evolution the given literature will take at a specific moment of its development. If the literature in question has, after stage A, reached, say, stage B_1, this stage will be only one of several options: stages B_2, B_3 or B_4 could also have resulted, given the possibilities inherent in stage A. In principle, the state of literature at one time can, in its evolution, give rise to numerous evolutionary alternatives. But the fact that one of the alternate choices becomes implemented (in our case, B_1), while others (B_2, B_3, B_4) remain unrealized, is, from the standpoint of the evolving literary series, a matter of accident. Still, the development of stage B_1 is not wholly fortuitous. On the one hand, the number of possible alternatives is limited by the makeup of the literary structure of the period. On the other hand, literature develops not completely of its own accord but in the context of other social and cultural series. Therefore, what may appear to be an accidental occurrence from the standpoint of the literary series may prove to be a necessary consequence from the standpoint of the wider historical context.

For example, to return for a moment to the period of the Czech literary revival mentioned in chapter 3, one of the attempts at reforming the monotonous (syllabo-tonic) verse of the Puchmajerians, we recall, came in the form of the proposal for the quantitative metric system (*časomíra*). Though an unaccountable development in terms of the immanent literary order, this proposal was nevertheless motivated by two historical circumstances: in the context of European literature, by the wave of neoclassicism that favored quantitative versification and, in the specifically Czech context, by the humanistic tradition of Czech Protestantism. Still these circumstances, while pointing toward an answer, do not offer a conclusive solution. What was the particular connection between the Protestant tradition and quantitative versification? As Mukařovský demonstrates, such a connection was possible only because two influential Czech poets with a scholarly interest in metrics, František Palacký (1798–1876) and Pavel Josef Šafařík (1795–1861), had come under the influence of foreign (German and Hungarian) quantitative poetry. Similarly, the efforts of Milota Zdirad Polák at disrupting the rhythmic monotony of the Puchmajerians' verse by means of tetrasyllabic words and, when these were unavailable, by elongated neologisms could not have been foretold by examining only the structure of Czech language and literature. To understand why Polák resorted to that particular metrical strategy, one must seek the explanation in Polák's biography, in the fact that, having spent most of his life abroad, he had a rather uncertain knowledge of the Czech language (cf. *CPE*, pp. 165–66). Such, then, is the irreducible residue of personality, equally inexplicable from the standpoint of the literary or any other series. As Mukařovský concedes, echoing the point the Marxist critics made in criticizing "Polák's *Sublimity of Nature*," "it is the individual who is, in the final analysis, the agent of every historical change in the given culture" (*CPE*, p. 52).

Individual artists, thanks to their "unique, unconditional and unalterable" (p. 228) features, thus stand in opposition to the immanent literary, and every other, series they affect. Yet the actions of the individual personalities are not capricious or destructive of the series upon which they have impact. We must remember that, in Mukařovský's argument, the relationship between artists and the immanent structure of literature is not fortuitous but dialectical. Although, from the point of view of the affected series, the artists' acts often appear to be interruptions of the temporal continuity of the evolving structure, these acts at the same time press forward the structure's inner motion. We come back to the concept which Mukařovský first formulated when defending his method in the Polák study. "To evolve," he said, "means always to become something different, but without impairment of identity."[45] The evolving structural series must preserve its identity, or else we could not grasp its temporal continuity; yet without a disturbance of its identity, the series could not evolve. As Mukařovský affirms, "the disturbance of identity maintains evolutionary movement and its preservation secures a regularity of this development" (p. 229). As we know, according to the fundamental structuralist tenets, while the evolving literary series itself tends toward the preservation of its identity, the incentives for disturbance of the series arise from the other (heterogeneous) series comprising the given culture—from another art, from philosophy, politics, science and the like. In the version articulated in the Polák study, however, these cultural series were seen in direct contact with one another. In "The Individual and Literary Development," Mukařovský offers a far-reaching correction: the sole outside factor affecting literature directly is the individual person, for all the series of culture and society can enter into contact with literature, and with each other, only through the mediation of the individual. "Personality," Mukařovský asserts, "is the point of intersection on which converge all the external influences that can affect literature and, simultaneously, the point of departure from which they penetrate literary evolution" (p. 229). Consequently, the abstract thesis concerning the preservation and negation of the identity of the literary series emerges, in Mukařovský's revised theory, as the concrete conflict between literature and personality. In this dialectical antinomy, "the individual stages in the immanent literary evolution constitute the thesis. The personalities which intervene in literary evolution at a given stage operate as the antithesis: they present the antithesis because from them stems the negation of literature's identity, that tendency to transform it into something other than what it has hitherto been" (pp. 229–30).

As part of the dialectical antinomy, personality, rather than being outside of literary evolution, is very much inside it: "it is its negative aspect" (p. 230). This is another way of saying that, although personalities are the most unpredictable, because least determined, factor in literary history, the randomness of their impact—their sequence, intensity and utilization—is significantly controlled by the literary structure's internal requirements. Even strong artistic personalities could not exert influence on the literary scene if the immanent evolution of literature itself had not set the stage for their entrance. Thus, the extraordinary impact of Mácha's presence in the history of Czech literature stands out all the more against the backcloth of the aborted attempts, like that of Polák, at creating elevated or monumental genres which would restore to Czech poetry some of its lost luster after the poetic bleakness of the Baroque religious verse. Moreover, historically speaking, the artist, even a major one like Mácha, seldom performs solo (to extend the theatrical metaphor) but is, rather, accompanied by an ensemble, the artistic generation. Just as the literature of a period is a structure which contains numerous, if restricted, evolutionary possibilities, so, too, the generation is a structure which, though open-ended, holds a limited number of available places, especially at the summit of the structural hierarchy. Thus, the strongest poets of a generation are likely to be adversaries or, better still, antipodes and to be closely bound together precisely because of their antagonism.[46] At times the bond of their interdependence may be so tight—as was the tie between Mácha and his chief poetic rival, Karel Jaromír Erben (1811–1870)—that the peculiarity of one poet's *oeuvre* cannot be fully grasped unless confronted with the *oeuvre* of the other. The two poets carry out two antithetical structural tendencies: Mácha toward the suppression of the semantic motivation linking the poem's ingredient parts, Erben, on the contrary, toward their intensive motivation. And if two poets of a generation lay claim to the same position of structural and evolutionary prominence, one of them is bound to lose in the ensuing contest: while one plays the leading role, the other must be contented with a supporting part. Thus, in the "May" generation, one poetic trend, tending toward spontaneous and free-flowing lyricism, found voice in the poetry of Vítězslav Hálek; the opposing trend, tending toward muted and emotionally repressed poetic utterance, found expression in the work of Jan Neruda. This left the third strong poet of the generation, Adolf Heyduk (1835–1923), without a major part; as a result, Heyduk eventually turned to a secondary or substitute evolutionary line and became a regional poet of Moravia and Slovakia. As Mukařovský concludes, the relationships among artistic contemporaries are to a considerable degree "given not by the poets' personal propensities, but by their reciprocal ties as . . . representatives of different evolutionary trends" (p. 232).

If, on the other hand, the poets' individual talents and proclivities set them at odds with the prevalent tendencies of literary history, they may seek other forms of expression or they may simply never reach the level of art that they might have under more propitious evolutionary conditions. Strong talents, of course, will follow their instincts and, though "accursed" by their coevals, they will, much like Stendhal, go on addressing future, more sympathetic readers. The *inadaptés* are extreme instances of the conflict between individual artists and the structure of artistic evolution. At the other extreme are the epigones, whose personal dispositions conform totally to the prevailing structural requirements. Successful artists, therefore, discern the direction of artistic development but deflect and bend it to suit their needs. Although they cannot reverse the trend of events, they can at least give a twist, or even put a check, to the immanent forces of literary evolution. Their works will not interrupt the evolutionary flow: though shaping the momentary state of the evolving structure, the individual artists' works cannot be without antecedence or consequence, and even the partial disaccord between the artists' predispositions and the predominant tendencies of art is in some measure preconditioned. Still, Mukařovský states with conviction, there is no danger of determinism in this theory. He writes:

Just as literary structure constitutes a unity from the standpoint of which the interventions of personality appear as accidents violating the [structure's] immanent regularity, personality, too, constitutes a self-contained unity from the standpoint of which the regularity of the immanent evolution, which compels the personality to adapt to it, appears in turn as an accident violating the immanent order of the personality. Every component part of the literary work can be observed both in its relation to the work's structure—that is, we can determine the degree to which [the given part] is law-governed—and in its relation to the poet's personality—that is, we can determine the degree to which it is accidental vis-à-vis the preceding phase of literary development. And, conversely, every aspect of the poet's personality can be observed both in its necessary relation to that structure of the individuality of which it is a part and in its relation to the work, in which, however, it must yield to the external pressure [of the literary order—FWG]. The history of literature is a struggle between the inertia of the literary structure and the forcible impingements of personalities, while the history of poetic personality, the poet's biography, amounts to the artist's struggle with the inertia of the literary structure. (pp. 232–33)

In short, every constituent part, as well as the whole of the literary work, can in principle be determined as much by the evolution of the structure as by the individual poetic personality. As a result, literary evolution, the interplay of the causal and the accidental, rather than following a straightforward evolutionary line as it had in Mukařovský's previous view, now exhibits a multilinear pattern of simultaneous advances and retreats, of anticipations and delays, of leaps and falls, of consolidations and dead ends and, above all, of amalgamated extremes. As Mukařovský rightly claims, "the antinomy between literature and personality is the most fundamental of all the possible antinomies of literary history: it is, to be sure, also the most complex one, since it implicates all the others" (p. 230).

If we take one last glance at the Jakobson-Tynjanov theses that set the plan for the future structural theory, we see that Prague School structuralism, especially in the hands of Mukařovský, fulfilled that program far beyond the initial expectations: from a consistently functional point of view, Prague structural and semiotic theory arrived at a synthesis of synchronic and diachronic approaches, healed the rift between *langue* and *parole* and, in so doing, not only situated art in the context of social affairs but also brought it into firm alliance with the vital interest of artists and their audience.

NOTES

1. From a 1944 talk at the Circle, "K methodologii literární vědy" (On the Methodology of Literary Theory), first published in *CPE*, pp. 189–90.

2. Concerning the first research area, see especially Mukařovský, "Genetika smyslu v Máchově poesii" (The Genesis of Meaning in Mácha's Poetry), in *Torso a tajemství Máchova díla* (The Torso and the Mystery of Mácha's Work), ed. Jan Mukařovský (Praha: Borový, 1938), pp. 13–110, "Sémantický rozbor básnického díla: Nezvalův *Absolutní hrobař*" (The Semantic Analysis of a Poetic Work: Nezval's *Absolute Gravedigger*), *Sl. sl.* 4 (1938): 1–15, and "O jazyce básnickém" (On Poetic Language), *Sl. sl.* 6 (1940): 113–45; and Jakobson's "Poznámky k dílu Erbenovu" (Notes on the Work of Erben), *Sl. sl.* 1 (1935): 152–64, "Randbemerkungen zur Prosa des Dichters Pasternak," *Slavische Rundschau* 7 (1935): 357–74, "Socha v symbolice Puškinově" (The Statue in Puškin's Poetic Symbolism), *Sl. sl.* 3 (1937): 2–24, and "K popisu Máchova verše" (Toward a Description of Mácha's Verse), in *Torso a tajemství*, pp. 207–78. Concerning the second area, see Mukařovský, "Dialektické rozpory v moderním umění" (Dialectical Contradictions in Modern Art), *Listy pro umění a kritiku* 3 (1935): 344–57, "Poznámky k sociologii básnického jazyka" (Notes on the Sociology of Poetic Language), *Sl. sl.* 1 (1935): 29–38, and *Estetická funkce, norma a hodnota jako sociální fakty* (Aesthetic Function, Norm and Value as Social Facts) (Praha: Borový, 1936). (Almost all of these essays now exist in English translation.) A further discussion of the structuralists' extensive investigations in these two interrelated fields would carry us away from the principal theme; besides, these studies refined and extended, without substantially revising, the principles of semiotic analysis, the groundwork for which had been laid in the works examined in the preceding chapter.

3. *Co daly naše země Evropě a lidstvu* (Praha: Sfinx, 1939).

4. "Český podíl na cirkevněslovanské kultuře," pp. 9–20; Jakobson's second contribution to this volume dealt with "The Czech Influence on Medieval Polish Literature" ("Český vliv na středověkou literaturu polskou"), pp. 48–51. The accomplishments of Jakobson in the study of medieval Czech literature, which because of its highly specialized nature is hardly touched upon here, are summarized in František Svejkovský, "Roman Jakobson and Old Czech Literature," *Roman Jakobson: Echoes of His Scholarship* (*RJ*), ed. Daniel Armstrong and C. H. van Schooneveld, pp. 453–69. (See also Miroslav Renský, "Roman Jakobson and the Prague School," pp. 379–89, and Thomas G. Winner, "Roman Jakobson and Avantgarde Art," pp. 503–14.) The English reader may consult Jakobson, "Medieval Mock Mystery (The Old Czech *Unguentarius*)," in *Studia Philologica et Litteraria in Honorem L. Spitzer*, ed. A. G. Hatcher and K. L. Selig (Berne: Francke, 1958), pp. 245–65. We must similarly omit the work of two of Jakobson's students of medieval Czech language and literature, Karel Horálek (b. 1908) and Josef Hrabák (b. 1912), who, after Jakobson's departure, became prominent members of the Circle.

5. "Literární historie, její problémy a úkoly," in *CJP*, pp. 209–400. Mukařovský, we should note, originally delivered his "polemical remarks" at one of the Circle's sessions, most likely on 7 July 1944.

6. It was Vodička who wrote the lead essay, "Celistvost literárního procesu"

(The Integrity of the Literary Process), a synopsis of Mukařovský's career in structuralism, for Mukařovský's *Festschrift, Struktura a smysl literárního díla*, pp. 87–107. (Another version of this paper can be found in English in *Poetics* 4 [1972]: 5–15.) And it was Vodička who provided the foreword to Mukařovský's seminal volume *Studie z estetiky* (*SE*, pp. 9–13).

7. For a fuller account of this and other periods, see Arne Novák, *Czech Literature* (1932), trans. Peter Kussi (Ann Arbor: Michigan Slavic Publications, 1976), esp. pp. 161–254. (Novák also devotes a long chapter to the earlier period of national revival, pp. 113–60.) One may consult René Wellek's review of the English translation of Novák's history: "Propagace české literatury" (The Dissemination of Czech Literature), *Proměny* 15 (1978): 28–33.

8. "Březina a Baudelaire," *Časopis národního musea* 107 (1933): 86–104; and "J. Vrchlický a Th. de Banville," *Sborník Společnosti Jaroslava Vrchlického* 11 (1932–33): 84–112.

9. A footnote (p. 89) in the Březina and Baudelaire paper indicates that Vodička had access to Mukařovský's unpublished lecture investigating the semantic properties in the poetry of another symbolist, Jaroslav Kvapil. But Vodička, unimpressed by this type of analysis, thought reference to the poet's life experience of greater explanatory value.

10. René Wellek, "Czech Literature: East or West?" in *Czechoslovakia Past and Present*, ed. Miloslav Rechcígl, Jr., vol. 2 (The Hague: Mouton, 1968), p. 900.

11. "Ohlas Bérangerovy poesie v české literatuře," *Listy filologické* 62 (1935): 301–66.

12. "Moravské beletristické studie Jana Herbena" (Jan Herben's Moravian Fiction Studies), *Časopis Matice moravské* 62 (1938): 201–30, 343–60. The ethnographer Petr Bogatyrev also studied the culture in this part of Czechoslovakia. See *The Functions of Folk Costume in Moravian Slovakia*, trans. Richard G. Crum (The Hague: Mouton, 1971), which first appeared in 1937.

13. "Mácha jako dramatik," in *Karel Hynek Mácha: Osobnost, dílo, ohlas* (Mácha: Personality, Work, Echo), ed. Arne Novák (Praha: Družstevní práce, 1937), pp. 133–41.

14. "Doba a dílo," in *Věčný Mácha: Památník českého básníka* (The Eternal Mácha: Memorial of a Czech Poet), ed. Antonín Hartl et al. (Praha: Čin, 1940), pp. 73–97.

15. "Západní orientace v nové české literatuře" (The Western Orientation in the New Czech Literature), in *Strážce tradice: Arne Novákovi na památku* (The Guardian of Tradition: In Memory of Arne Novák) (Praha: Borový, 1940), pp. 197–204. All quotations come from this text. Although not a structuralist, Novák counted among the members of the Circle.

16. "Tradice tvaru," *Strážce tradice*, pp. 265–77; quoted from *KCP* 1, pp. 245–52.

17. In order to distinguish between the concepts of the whole in Gestalt psychology and in linguistic and literary structuralism, Mukařovský himself was soon compelled to stop equating *tvar* with *struktura*. Gestalt wholes like melody or verse dispose toward closure, as do the compositions (compositional wholes) of spatial arts and the contextures of temporal arts. Structures, on the other hand, understood as dynamic fields of energy moving through time and inscribed in the social

consciousness, are intrinsically open-ended. Cf. Mukařovský's "Pojem celku v teorii umění" (The Concept of the Whole in the Theory of Art) (1945), in CPE, pp. 85–96; English translation in *SSF*, pp. 70–81.

18. Delivered on 3 March 1941, Vodička's lecture came out under the title "Literárně historické studium ohlasu literárních děl: Problematika ohlasu Nerudova díla" (The Historical Study of the Reception of Literary Works: The Problematics of Jan Neruda's Reception), *Sl. sl.* 7 (1941): 113–32. All references are to this text; cf. "The Concretization of the Literary Work: Problems of the Reception of Neruda's Works," translated by John Burbank, in *PS*, pp. 105–34.

19. Cf. chapter 3, note 32, above.

20. M. H. Abrams put forward a similar analytic scheme in *The Mirror and the Lamp: Romantic Theory and the Critical Tradition* (esp. pp. 6–29), drawing on Charles Morris' semiotic model.

21. In point of fact, this antinomy seems to have been common to much of early twentieth-century aesthetics. Compare Broder Christiansen, *Philosophie der Kunst*, or Wolff Dohrn, *Die kunstlerische Darstellung als Problem der Ästhetik*.

22. See especially the section "The 'Life' of a Literary Work," in Ingarden, *The Literary Work of Art*, pp. 331–55 (cf. chapter 3, note 34, above).

23. The father of this conception may actually be Aristotle. Cf. Ingarden's paper "A Marginal Commentary on Aristotle's *Poetics*," *Journal of Aesthetics and Art Criticism* 20 (1961–1962): 163–73 and 273–85.

24. The relationship between Ingarden and Vodička has been discussed by Herta Schmid in "Zum Begriff der ästhetischen Konkretisation im tschechischen Strukturalismus," *Sprache im technischen Zeitalter* 36 (1970): 290–318, and by Rolf Fieguth in "Rezeption contra falsches und richtiges Lesen? Oder Mißverständnisse mit Ingarden," *Sprache* 38 (1971): 142–59. Also see John Fizer, "Ingarden's and Mukařovský's Binominal Definition of the Literary Work of Art: A Comparative View of Their Respective Ontologies," *Russian Literature* 13 (1983): 269–90.

25. T. S. Eliot's conception of European literature as forming a simultaneous order suggests that, in this respect at least, he might be thought of as a "proto-structuralist." See his observation: ". . . what happens when a new work of art is created is something that happens simultaneously to all the works of art which preceded it. The existing monuments form an ideal order among themselves, which is modified by the introduction of the new (the really new) work of art among them. The existing order is complete before the new work arrives; for order to persist after the supervention of novelty, the *whole* existing order must be, if ever so slightly, altered; and so the relations, proportions, values of each work toward the whole are readjusted; and this is conformity between the old and the new" (*Selected Essays*, p. 5). "Tradition and the Individual Talent" originally appeared in 1919.

26. *Principles of Literary Criticism*, p. 6.

27. *Anatomy of Criticism*, p. 9.

28. Cf. the argument on p. 58, above.

29. A section of this study which summarizes Vodička's findings in the area of reception exists in two English translations under the title "The History of the Echo of Literary Works," in *A Prague School Reader on Esthetics, Literary Structure*

and Style, ed. and trans. Paul L. Garvin, pp. 71–81, and "Response to Verbal Art" in SA, pp. 197–208.

30. "Překlad Chateaubriandovy Ataly" (The Translation of Chateaubriand's Atala), in Počátky krásné prózy novočeské: Příspěvek k literárním dějinám doby Jungmannovy (The Beginnings of Modern Czech Prose Fiction: A Contribution to the Literary History of Josef Jungmann's Era) (Praha: Melantrich, 1948), pp. 49–122. It should be clear that, as was the case with Mukařovský, the critique of Vodička's reception theory in no way belittles his signal attainments as a literary critic and historian. Indeed, The Beginnings of Modern Czech Prose Fiction is in many ways a critical triumph that convincingly displays the formidable strength of structural and historical analysis of literary texts. Reexamining the same period of Czech literature as Mukařovský's study of The Sublimity of Nature, Vodička's book on early Czech prose is a fair match in analytic subtlety and historical penetration for Mukařovský's "analysis and evolutionary ordering" of poetry. It appears that during the war years Mukařovský and Vodička were planning a comprehensive history of Czech prose, a counterpart to Mukařovský's and Jakobson's history of Czech verse: just as the structuralists took the verse line as the basic structural unit in the study of poetic evolution, so they hoped to develop a theory of the sentence as the basic structural unit in the evolution of prose. The project was never realized, partly because of the inadequacies of the Prague researchers' narrative theory. Yet the results of Vodička's examinations of early Czech prose and of Mukařovský's studies of contemporary Czech prose fiction, particularly that of Karel Čapek and Vladimír Vančura, are most impressive; only the specifically Czech nature of the Prague structuralist material makes access to their work difficult for the foreign reader, and, like the Jakobson-Mukařovský venture into the history of Czech verse, these first-rate examples of practical structural criticism have to be omitted from this discussion. A German translation of the Chateaubriand chapter, however, can be found in a volume of Vodička's writings, Die Struktur der literarischen Entwicklung, ed. Frank Boldt, pp. 227–305; it also includes the two essays by Vodička mentioned above. One may also profitably consult Miroslav Drozda, "Vodička's The Beginnings of Modern Czech Prose (Počátky krásné prózy novočeské) in the Light of the Theory of Fiction," translated by Peter Petro, as well as the second part of Lubomir Doležel, "The Conceptual System of Prague School Poetics," in SLP, pp. 127–35 and 115–23, respectively.

31. This is a burgeoning field of study, but the following two anthologies offer very useful surveys: The Reader in the Text: Essays on Audience and Interpretation, ed. Susan R. Suleiman and Inge Crosman, and Reader-Response Criticism: From Formalism to Post-Structuralism, ed. Jane P. Tomkins. One may also consult the well-informed study Reception Theory: A Critical Introduction by Robert C. Holub, especially the section on Mukařovský and Vodička as precursors of today's Rezeptionsgeschichte (pp. 29–36). A collection of essays by the members of the Konstanz School, whose approach resembles the Prague School's views most closely, is New Perspectives in German Literary Criticism, ed. Richard E. Amacher and Victor Lange.

32. Another critical account of Vodička can be found in Miloš Sedmidubský, "Literary Evolution as a Communicative Process," in SLP, pp. 483–502. For sur-

vey accounts of Vodička's career as a structuralist literary historian, see Miroslav Červenka, "O Vodičkově metodologii literárních dějin" (On Vodička's Methodology of Literary History), an afterword to Vodička's selected essays, *Struktura vývoje* (The Structure of Development), pp. 329–50, and Jurij Striedter, "Zu Felix Vodičkas Theorie der 'Konkretisation' als Teil einer strukturalistischen Literaturgeschichte," the second part of a longer introduction to the German translation of *Struktura vývoje, Die Struktur der literarischen Entwicklung*, ed. Frank Boldt, pp. lix-ciii. The impact of Vodička's work on the later generation of Prague structuralists is especially evident in Jiří Levý, "Geneze a recepce literárního díla" (The Genesis and the Reception of the Literary Work), in *Bude literární věda exaktní vědou?* (Will Literary Study Be an Exact Science?), pp. 77–146.

33. "Estetická funkce a norma jako sociální fakty," *Sociální problémy* 4 (1935): 89–104, 197–213, 284–94; quoted from the expanded version, "Estetická funkce, norma a hodnota jako sociální fakty" (1936), in *SE*, pp. 17–54, esp. pp. 27–40. The following discussion also draws on Mukařovský's communication "La norme esthétique," in *Travaux du IXe Congrès international de philosophie*, vol. 12/3, ed. Raymond Bayer (Paris: Hermann, 1937), pp. 72–79, quoted from the Czech translation in *SE*, pp. 74–77; and on the public lecture "Problémy estetické normy" (The Problems of the Aesthetic Norm), first delivered during the second half of the 1930s but published only in *CPE*, pp. 35–48, in 1971. To avoid confusion, the abbreviation *CPE* precedes page references to the last article. For an English translation of the first study, see *Aesthetic Function, Norm and Value as Social Facts*, trans. Mark Suino (Ann Arbor: Department of Slavic Languages, 1970), and of the second, "The Aesthetic Norm," in *SSF*, pp. 49–56. One may also consult Mukařovský's essay "Estetika jazyka" (The Aesthetics of Language), *Sl. sl.* 6 (1940): 1–27, rpt. in *KCP* 1, pp. 41–77, which analyzes the nature of aesthetic and linguistic norms.

34. Mukařovský was alert to the legal aspects of the problem of norm thanks to the work of the so-called Brno Normative School of Law composed of František Weyr, Jaroslav Kallab, Karel Engliš and other jurists and economists. These scholars were followers of the legal theories of Hans Kelsen, the author of the Austrian Constitution, whose major theoretical statement is to be found in *Reine Rechtslehre* (Wien: Deuticke, 1934), now in English translation, *The Pure Theory of Law*, trans. Max Knight.

35. See Mukařovský's essay "La valeur esthétique dans l'art peut-elle être universelle?" in *Les conceptions modernes de la raison*, vol. 3, *Raison et valeur* (Paris: Institut international de collaboration philosophique, 1939), pp. 17–29; quoted from *SE*, pp. 78–84 (English translation in *SSF*, pp. 57–69); compare also an earlier version, "Problémy estetické hodnoty" (The Problems of Aesthetic Value) (1935–1936), first published in *CPE*, pp. 11–48, esp. pp. 27–32.

36. In "Aesthetic Function, Norm and Value," Mukařovský first advanced the idea that "the work of art emerges, in the final analysis, as a genuine ensemble of extra-aesthetic values and as nothing else than exactly such an ensemble," because, as he put it, "aesthetic value dissolves into the particular extra-aesthetic values and is but a global designation for the dynamic integration of their reciprocal relationships" (*SA*, p. 51). A challenging hypothesis, it accords perfectly with the

basic structural premise which assigns priority to differential relations rather than to independent terms, entities or essences.

37. For a comprehensive discussion of the Prague School's semiotic aesthetics, see the following articles: Peter Steiner, "The Conceptual Basis of Prague Structuralism," in *SSM*, pp. 351–85, "Jan Mukařovský's Structural Aesthetics," in *SSF*, pp. ix–xxxiv, and "The Roots of Structuralist Esthetics," in *PS*, pp. 174–219; Jiří Veltruský, "Jan Mukařovský's Structural Poetics and Aesthetics," *Poetics Today* 2 (1980–1981): 117–57, and "Comparative Semiotics of Art," in *Image and Code*, ed. Wendy Steiner, pp. 109–32; and Thomas G. Winner, "Jan Mukařovský: The Beginnings of Structural and Semiotics Aesthetics," in *SSM*, pp. 433–55, and "On the Relation of the Verbal and the Nonverbal Arts in Early Prague Semiotics: Jan Mukařovský," in *The Sign: Semiotics around the World*, ed. R. W. Bailey et al. pp. 227–37.

38. For our purposes, the most germane articles are "Místo estetické funkce mezi ostatními" (1942), "Záměrnost a nezáměrnost v umění" (1943), "Osobnost v umění" (1944) and "Individuum a literární vývoj" (1943–1945), in *SE*, pp. 65–73, 89–116, 236–44 and 226–35. We shall discuss them in the order of their listing. English translations—"The Place of the Aesthetic Function among the Other Functions," "Intentionality and Unintentionality in Art" and "Personality in Art"—can be found in *SSF*, pp. 31–48, 89–128 and 150–68; the last essay, "The Individual and Literary Development," is in *WVA*, pp. 161–79.

39. Cf. Mukařovský's university lecture "Problems of Aesthetic Value," in *CPE*, p. 32 as well as pp. 11 and 17.

40. This, Husserl's last published work, appeared in the Belgrade journal *Philosophia* 1 (1936): 77–176; the English translation is "Philosophy and the Crisis of European Man," in *Phenomenology and the Crisis of Philosophy*, trans. Quentin Lauer, pp. 149–92. Husserl's talk to the Linguistic Circle on 18 November 1935, "Phänomenologie und Sprachenwissenschaft," however, was probably given extempore, and no text or record of it now exists. The phenomenological movement was strongly represented in Prague in the 1930s by Ludwig Landgrebe and Jan Patočka, professors, respectively, in the German and Czech parts of Charles University; see Landgrebe, "Erinnerungen eines Phänomenologen an den *Cercle Linguistique de Prague*," in *SSM*, pp. 40–42, and Patočka, "Husserlův pojem názoru a prafenomén jazyka" (Husserl's Notion of Intuitive Idea and the Primal Phenomenon of Language), *Sl. sl.* 29 (1968): 17–22.

41. It is interesting to note that the slipperiness of Mukařovský's evolving concepts on occasion shows up in the slippage of his terms. For instance, in the definition of 1934, the term *work-thing* designated the signifying side of the artistic sign—the artifact whose constitution Mukařovský never properly elucidated. Now the same term stands for the *nonsemiotic* aspect of aesthetic communication. For more on this unresolved contradiction, see Miroslav Červenka, "The Literary Artifact," in *The Sign in Music and Literature*, ed. Wendy Steiner, pp. 86–102, esp. p. 87.

42. In addition to the works listed in note 38 above, two related essays by Mukařovský are taken into account in what follows: "Básník a dílo" (The Poet and the Poetic Work) and "Problémy individua v umění" (The Problems of the Indi-

vidual in Art) in *CPE*, pp. 161–74 and 49–84. Delivered as university lectures shortly after the war, these articles bear witness to the fact that, until the moment of his conversion to Marxism in the late forties, Mukařovský continued his structural investigations of artists and their place in the history of art. For more on this aspect of the Prague School theory, see Thomas G. Winner, "The Creative Personality as Viewed by the Prague Linguistic Circle: Theories and Implications," in *American Contributions to the Seventh International Congress of Slavists*, vol. 1, *Linguistics and Poetics*, ed. Ladislav Matejka, pp. 242–57.

43. This aspect of Mukařovský's theory has inspired the work of Miroslav Červenka, a leading theorist of the postwar generation of Prague structuralists. See especially his "Literární dílo jako znak," *Orientace* 4 (1969): 58–64, the last chapter of a book entitled *Významová výstavba literárního díla* (The Semantic Structure of the Literary Work). Červenka's book has unfortunately not yet been published in the original Czech, as structuralism has once again been banished from Czech literary studies, but it exists in German translation: *Der Bedeutungsaufbau der literarischen Werks*, ed. Frank Boldt and Wolf-Dieter Stempel, pp. 163–83. The last chapter, "The Literary Work as Sign," appeared in English, in my translation, in the collection *Language, Literature and Meaning II: Current Trends in Literary Research*, ed. John Odmark, pp. 1–25, and another chapter, "A Contribution to the Semantics of the Literary Work," in *Papers in Slavic Philology*, vol. 1, *In Honor of James Ferrell*, ed. Benjamin A. Stolz, pp. 27–35.

44. In fact, as early as 1934, in a fascinating preface to the posthumous publication of Karel Hlaváček's *Psalms* ("Předmluva k vydání Hlaváčkových *Žalmů*," rpt. in *KCP* 2, pp. 219–34), Mukařovský reasoned: "That trend of psychologistic aesthetics which holds that poetic composition is an unmediated expression of the dispositions and proclivities of the poet as a psychophysical personality likes to construct an opposition between the poet and reality: it interprets poetic creativity as the poet's struggle with reality and for reality. Today it is clear, however, that wedged between the poet and the reality to be transformed is the *artistic structure* which is borne by the collective and which is evolving from within itself, albeit under the constant pressure from external factors. The poet's approach to reality is necessarily mediated by this structure, whose every embodiment in a concrete work of art takes place thanks to a dialectical synthesis of the poet's subjective tendencies and the objective evolutionary preconditions, both internal and external. Every distinctly individual poetic system thus always puts limits on the freedom of its creator, even where the poet's dispositions nearly coincide with the organization of his own poetic structure" (p. 219–20; emphasis mine). And Jakobson, in a splendid postscript to the Czech translation of Boris Pasternak's autobiographical prose *Ochrannaja gramota* ("Kontury Glejtu" [1935], translated by Jarmila Veltruský as "The Contours of *The Safe Conduct*," in *SA*, pp. 188–96; the expanded version, "Randbemerkungeng zur Prosa des Dichters Pasternaks," rpt. in *SW* 5, pp. 416–32), argued along similar lines: "If many individual traits of Pasternak's poetry are in harmony with the characteristic features of his personality and the social environment, his work necessarily also contains those qualities which the poetry of the period stringently imposes (as the indispensable mainstay of its total structure) on every one of its poets, regardless of his individual or social propensities, so that any poet who refused to comply would automatically find

himself ejected from the mainstream of this poetry. The poet's artistic mission never enters his biography without a struggle, just as his biography is never entirely absorbed in his artistic mission" (*SA*, p. 195; cf. *SW* 5, p. 431). Earlier still, as we have noted, in what is perhaps his most intensely personal and compassionate study ("how is it possible to write about Majakovskij now, when the paramount subject is not the rhythm, but the death of the poet?"), Jakobson ruefully observed, "Is there anyone of us who doesn't share the impression that the poet's volumes are a kind of scenario in which he plays out the filmed story of his life?"—for in Majakovskij's writings "the suicide theme transcends literature and is already in the 'realm of literature of fact'" ("On a Generation That Squandered Its Poets," in *Major Soviet Writers*, pp. 7, 22, 23). As can be seen, Mukařovský's and Jakobson's essays from the mid-1930s—which, along with their works discussed in chapter 4, to my mind represent Prague structuralism at its very best—display in passing the most trenchant insights into the interaction among art, artist and artistic experience, but the full elaboration of this problematics unfolded only a decade later.

45. See p. 75, above.

46. Cf. Jan Mukařovský, "Protichůdci: Několik poznámek o vztahu Erbenova básnického díla k Máchovu" (Antipodes: Some Remarks on the Relationship of Erben's Poetic Works to Mácha's), *Sl. sl.* 2 (1936): 33–43, and Roman Jakobson, "Poznámky k dílu Erbenovu" (Notes on the Work of Erben), *Sl. sl.* 1 (1935): 152–64 and 218–29.

6 | A Summary Conclusion

I must Create a System, or be enslav'd by another Mans

. . . .

Striving with Systems to deliver individuals from those Systems

WILLIAM BLAKE

It is time to bring this story of the Prague School literary history, and of its structural and semiotic theory, to an end. Reflecting on the shape this work has assumed, we recognize once again the immense usefulness of Charles Morris' semiotic categories. When looked at through the lens of semiosis, the development of the Prague School theory, and hence this account of it, refracts into three distinct stages: those of syntactics, semantics and pragmatics. Thus chapter 2 shows that, following closely on the heels of formalism, the Prague School's approach, notwithstanding the protestations of the Circle's scholars, at first remained confined to syntactics, to the study of the internal, intertextual relationships of language and literature viewed as immanent systems. Pursuing the idea of the system to its ultimate conclusions, Jakobson, as we have seen, succeeded in demonstrating that language preserves its homeostatic character in diachronic motion as much as in the momentary synchronic stasis of the system: it is the system's own intricate mechanism that maintains internal stability and adjusts itself to any inside or outside disturbance. At the same time, Jakobson and his colleagues convincingly displayed the limits of the idea of a self-enclosed system, namely, the impossibility of determining the velocity and future course of structural changes. In turn, Mukařovský, extending the concept of immanent evolution from linguistics to the study of literary history, proved the theoretical insufficiency of the view that a literary work, much like an event in language history, is but one link in a self-fueling chain reaction, obeying without appeal, so to speak, the unrelenting laws of the system of literature. According to these laws, as the formalists initially framed them, literature, or rather poetic language, must undo the dullness of ordinary language. Since the effectiveness of language is always being flattened on the anvil of custom by the hammer of repetition—or as the formalists would have it, since poetry must exempt things from the perils of familiarity—it is the business of poetic actualization to renew language's expressive potency, its systemic flexibility.

In chapter 3, increasingly dissatisfied with the formalists' attempts to rope off literature behind a *cordon sanitaire*—a sterile precinct uncontaminated by anything "inartistic" such as politics, philosophy or biography—Jakobson and Mukařovský found it imperative to enlarge the scope of inquiry beyond syntactics in the direction of semantics. Rather than being immanently self-reflexive, as if made without human agency or reference to concrete historical experience, literature now appeared, rightfully, in the full context of social reality, bound to it by many direct and indirect ties. As the Prague Circle's scholars discovered, the emergence of a particular work at a particular time could not be adequately explained unless the evolution of literature became correlated with the larger social and historical trends, literature's *tertium comparationis*. While in chapter 3, subscribing to the notion of automatization and actualization as the *causae internae* of literary evolution, Mukařovský examined the place of literature in the social setting from outside, leaving unexplored the way in which art itself signifies or embodies that setting, in chapter 4, thanks to the semiotic conception of art, Mukařovský and Jakobson were afforded a view from inside. The work of art, instead of being opaque and unyielding, at that point emerged as exceptionally transparent—exceptionally so because signifying not separate sections of reality but the total organization of the social structure. As an aesthetic sign, the literary work, by drawing attention away from single referents and toward the process of semantic contexture, assures that the perceiver realizes that—just as everyday discourse may give the impression that the sign is identical to the thing it represents—the discourse of art constantly calls this identity into question. Only such dialectical questioning guarantees the mobility of signs, those consummate instruments that sharpen our awareness of reality thanks to the tension between their aesthetic (poetic) and communicative (referential) functions: for just as signs cease being signs without their referential (or allotelic) functions, without representing objects, so, on the other hand, to represent objects as their proxies, signs themselves have to come into prominence and become palpable, which is precisely the mission of the aesthetic (autotelic) function. Even in film, the referential transparency of art is not total, as Jakobson and Mukařovský established, for in order to signify at all, cinematic representations must diverge semantically from reality, not coincide with it.

Semantics, throwing into relief the relationship of signs to the things they signify, underlined the importance of artistic semiosis for our understanding and interpretation of reality. In chapter 5, consequently, semantics gave way to pragmatics, its indispensable complement. In the Prague

204 II HISTORIC STRUCTURES

School pragmatic theory, the work of art, a sign serving communication among the members of the literary community, acquired the guise of different aesthetic objects depending on the normative background against which it is perceived. As Vodička proposed, a full-fledged structural study of literary history must investigate, besides the sequence of works as they supersede one another in time, the changing appearances of individual works as they are assimilated by subsequent generations of readers. Vodička's pragmatics, as we have noted, was resolutely sociological, emphasizing historical and social modifications in the background of norms. In contrast, Mukařovský's pragmatic theory strove to identify an underlying constant which would introduce a principle of order into the apparent randomness of historical changes. Mukařovský located this constant in the human constitution and—with the aid of phenomenology—in the human subject. This methodological refocusing on the perceiving subject, instead of on the work or the social context in which the work is embedded, enabled Mukařovský to equate the mode of existence of the aesthetic function with the foregrounding of the creative subject, of the subject's intentional activity. Finally, coming full circle, Mukařovský's structuralism admitted the significance of the role played by the concrete individual, not just the phenomenological subject, in the history of art, an admission which resulted in a revised, and much improved, notion of literary history as an interplay of (causal) literary evolution and (casual) interventions of creative human individualities.

Yet despite its comprehensiveness—in the end the work of the Prague scholars does indeed contain all three semiotic modalities—Prague structuralism, probably due to Jakobson's departure, remained a project for, rather than a finished version of, a theory of literary history. This incompleteness shows up in three different ways. First, in Mukařovský's unwillingness, or perhaps inability, to integrate the disparate and seemingly incompatible proposals, some inspired by structuralism and some by phenomenology, into a unified theoretical framework. Second, even though significantly compensating in theory for the earlier exclusion of the perceiving subject and the creative individual, Mukařovský—owing, it seems, largely to the adverse circumstances of the war and the subsequent political turmoil—did not put his refurbished theory into practice. There is no study testifying to the final stage of Mukařovský's pragmatic theory in the way in which *Mácha's "May"* had represented his first formalist, largely syntactic, stage of pure immanence and "Polák's *Sublimity of Nature"* exemplified the transition to the second stage, the introduction of semantics into the projected general semiotic theory of art. The Prague School pragmatics only existed, on the one hand, in the practical historical criticism of Vodička—which, however, lacked a firm theoretical foundation—and, on the other, in the far-reaching theoretical postulates of Mukařovský—

which, however, missed the support of concrete criticism. And third, the merely preparatory character of the Prague School theoretical scheme manifests itself most clearly in the fact that, though writing a host of articles and historical monographs, neither Mukařovský nor any of his collaborators ever produced that envisioned structural and semiotic history of Czech literature.

In the absence of such a work of literary historiography, it is perhaps understandable why, while scrutinizing the complex dialectics of literary evolution, Mukařovský did not dwell much on the difficulties attending the writing of history. Mukařovský, of course, took notice of the fact that, with the passing of time, works of historical scholarship frequently become appreciated for their literary and artistic qualities. Still, at no point did he analyze the place of fictional elements in the patterns of emplotment which are imposed on any historiographic composition. Moreover, surprising as it may be in the light of present-day structuralist and semiotic speculation, Mukařovský, Jakobson and other Prague savants paid little attention to the more philosophical or metaphysical aspects of language. In comparison with "poststructuralism," the Prague School writings are free of anxiety or aporia that language may be a constricting grid which conceals reality as much as it reveals it, stifling as much as stimulating individual expression.[1] For Prague linguists, language presented itself as an object of technical study; and for Prague literary scholars, it appeared, in its aesthetic function, as a perpetually renewable source of the perceiver's ever more finely calibrated perception of and ever more subtle orientation in the world. The Prague School, in short, retained its scientific, and scientifically optimistic, spirit throughout. But in the end, meditating about the role of the artist in the scheme of things, Mukařovský and the other structuralists came to realize that—as writing, as language—all our knowledge as humans, and of humanity, is historical and that, like the sea, it is (in the words of Elizabeth Bishop) always the "same" and yet forever "flowing, and flown."

NOTE

1. For an exemplary statement of this view of language as a coercive power, see Roland Barthes, "Lecture in Inauguration of the Chair of Literary Semiology, Collège de France, January 7, 1977," trans. Richard Howard, *October* no. 8 (1979): 4–16; rpt. in *A Barthes Reader*, ed. Susan Sontag, pp. 457–78. If, to invoke an ancient distinction, current structuralists resemble Platonic exegetes or ideologues in their approach to language and literature, the Prague structuralists appear as thoroughgoing Aristotelians, believing with Aristotle that it is the task of poetics, as of any analytic discipline, to "look for precision in each class of things just so far as the nature of the subject admits" (*Nichomachean Ethics*, 1094b).

Appendix 1. A List of Lectures on Poetics, Aesthetics and Semiotics Given in the Prague Linguistic Circle, 1926–1948

Wherever possible, the following list includes bibliographic references to published lectures; many lectures, however, remained unpublished, and several others could not be located. Information on first publication follows the equation sign. For a complete compilation, which also includes talks on linguistic topics, see "List of Lectures Given in the Prague Linguistic Circle (1926–1948)," in *SSM*, pp. 607–22.

1926–1927

17 MAR. Mukařovský, Jan. "O motorickém dění v poesii" (On Motor Action in Poetry).

1928

3 FEB. Mukařovský, Jan. "Zvukosled v Máji a jeho souvislost s jinými složkami básně" (Sound-Sequences in *May* and Their Relation to Other Elements of the Poem). Cf. his *Máchův Máj. Estetická studie*. Praha: Filosofická fakulta University Karlovy, 1928, pp. 1–75.

7 FEB. Tomaševskij, Boris. "La nouvelle école d'histoire littéraire en Russie" = "Nová ruská škola v bádání literárně-historickém." Trans. Jan Mukařovský. *Časopis pro moderní filologii* 15 (1928): 12–15.

30 MAR. Mukařovský, Jan. "Trojí řešení subjektivace epiky v Máji, Alfredu a Satanele" (Three Solutions in Subjectivizing the Epic in *May*, *Alfred* and *Satanela*). Cf. his *Máchův Máj. Estetická studie*, pp. 110–53.

16 DEC. Tynjanov, Jurij. "Problema literaturnoj evoljucii" (The Problem of Literary Evolution). Cf. "O literaturnoj evoljucii." In his *Archaisty i novatory*. Leningrad: Priboj, 1929, pp. 30–47.

1929

11 JAN. Fischer, Otokar. "O rýmech Březinových" (On Březina's Rhyme) = "Březinův rým." *Tvar* 3 (1929): 55–72.

8 FEB. Sedlák, Jan V. "Literární historie a literární věda" (Literary History and Literary Study) = *Literární historie a literární věda*. Praha: Fr. Borový, 1929.

8 NOV. Fischer, Otokar. "O znělce Kollárově" (On Kollár's Sonnet) = "Kollárův sonet." In his *Duše a slovo*. Praha: Melantrich, 1929, pp. 238–62.

1930

25 MAR. Jakobson, Roman. "Jazykové problémy v Masarykově díle" (Language Problems in Masaryk's Work). Mukařovský, Jan. "Masaryk jako stylista" (Masaryk as a Stylist) = *Masaryk a řeč*. Praha: Pražský linguistický kroužek, 1931.

16 OCT. Fischer, Otokar. "Erbenova Kytice" (Erben's *Bouquet*) = "Karel Jaromír Erben." In *Kytice z pověstí národních*. Ed. with notes by Otokar Fischer. Praha: Státní nakladatelství, 1930, pp. 5–9, 93–116.

1931

13 FEB. Mukařovský, Jan. "Sémantika básnické řeči Březinovy (I)" (The Semantics of Březina's Poetic Language—I).

5 MAR. ———. "Sémantika básnické řeči Březinovy (II)" (The Semantics of Březina's Poetic Language—II).

26 MAR. Jirát, Vojtěch. "O Máchově rýmu" (On Rhyme in Mácha) = "Hudebnost Máchova rýmu." *Časopis pro moderní filologii* 18 (1932): 24–34.

4 MAY Fischer, Otokar. "Konrád Wallenrod" = "Zur Ideengeschichte des 'Konrad Wallenrod.'" *Germanoslavica* 1 (1931–1932): 55–76.

18 JUNE Jirát, Vojtěch. "Rým u Viktora Dyka" (Rhyme in Viktor Dyk) = "Rýmové umění Viktora Dyka." *Lumír* 57 (1931).

1932

4 JAN. Fischer, Otokar. "Ohlas písní ruských" (The Echo of Russian Songs) = "K Ohlasu písní ruských." *Práce Učené společnosti Šafaříkovy v Bratislavě* 10 (1932): 3–24.

8 FEB. Mukařovský, Jan. "Básnictví a spisovný jazyk" (Poetry and Standard Language) = "Jazyk spisovný a jazyk básnický." In *Spisovná čeština a jazyková kultura*. Ed. Bohuslav Havránek and Miloš Weingart. Praha: Melantrich, 1932, pp. 123–256.

15 MAR. Trubeckoj, N. S. "Dostoevskijs humoristische Erzählungen." Cf. his *Dostoevskij als Künstler*. The Hague: Mouton, 1964.

6 DEC. Bém, A. L. "Osobní jména u Dostojevského" (Personal Names in Dostoevskij) = "Ličnye imena u Dostoevskogo." In *Sbornik' v' čest' na prof. L. Miletič'*. Sofia: Makedonskija naučen' institut', 1933, pp. 409–34.

1933

17 JAN. Zich, Otokar. "Tempo básnické řeči" (Tempo of Poetic Language).

13 FEB. Mukařovský, Jan. "Milota Zdirad Polák" = "Polákova *Vznešenost přírody*. (Pokus o rozbor a vývojové zařadění básnické struktury)" (Polák's *Sublimity of Nature*: An Attempt at an Analysis and Historical Ordering of a Poetic Structure). *Sborník filologický* 10 (1934–1935): 1–68.

13 MAR. Kožešník, Karel. "Formální rozbor morálky v Lafontainovych bajkách" (A Formal Analysis of Morals in La Fontaine's Fables).

24 MAY Jirát, Vojtěch. "Sluchová a zraková sféra v obrazech lyriky Platenovy" (The Auditory and Visual Spheres in the Images of Platen's Lyric) = "Zrakový a sluchový prvek v motivech i obrazech Platenovy lyriky." *Časopis pro moderní filologii* 20 (1934): 53–62.

14 DEC. Siebenschein, Hugo. "Překladatelské problémy (Na okraj Fischerova Viléma Busche)" (The Problems of Translation: Apropos Fisher's Wilhelm Busch).

1934

29 JAN. Bém, A. L. "K otázce literárních vlivu" (On the Question of Literary Influence).

12 MAR. Wellek, René. "Šklovského teorie prósy" (Šklovskij's *Theory of Prose*) = "Šklovskeho 'Teorie prózy.'" *Listy pro umění a kritiku* 2 (1934): 111–15.

15 OCT. Seidel, Eugen. "Zum Problem der Sprache H. Heines."

10 DEC. Bém, A. L., and Wellek, René. "Na okraj Mukařovského studie o M. Z. Polákovi" (A Discussion of Mukařovský's Study of Miroslav Zdirad Polák) = Wellek, René. "'Dějiny českého verše' a metody literární historie" (*The Development of Czech Verse* and the Methods of Literary History). *Listy pro umění a kritiku* 2 (1934): 437–45; and Bém, A. L. "Methodologické poznámky ke studii Jana Mukařovského 'Polákova *Vznešenost přírody*'" (Methodological Comments on Mukařovský's Study). *Časopis pro moderní filologii* 21 (1935): 330–34.

1935

14 JAN. Becking, Gustav. "Das Musikwerk als Zeichen."

18 MAR. Čiževskyj, Dmytro. "Die Barockdichtung." Cf. "Příspěvek k symbolice českého básnictví náboženského" (A Contribution to the Symbolism of Czech Religious Poetry). *Sl. sl.* 2 (1936): 98–105.

30 MAR. Wollman, Frank. "Věda o slovesnosti a její poměr k vědám sousedním" (The Study of Verbal Art and Its Relation to Adjacent Disciplines) = "Věda o slovesnosti. Její vývoj a poměr k sousedním vědám." *Sl. sl.* 1 (1935): 193–202.

8 APR. Mukařovský, Jan. "Vítězslav Hálek" = "Vítězslav Hálek." *Sl. sl.* 1 (1935): 73–87.

29 APR. Jakobson, Roman. "Básnictví husitské doby" (The Poetry of the Hussite Era) = "Úvahy o básnictví doby husitské." *Sl. sl.* 2 (1936): 1–21.

6 MAY Utitz, Emil. "Sprache als Kultur" = "Kultur und Sprache." *Travaux* 6 (1936): 147–59.

3 JUNE Jakobson, Roman, and Mukařovský, Jan. "Metodologická diskuse o Grundově knize o Erbenovi" (A Methodological Discussion of Grund's Book on Erben) = "Poznámky k dílu Erbenovu: I. O mythu a II. O verši" (Notes on Erben's Work: I. On Myth; II. On Verse). *Sl. sl.* 1 (1935): 152–64, 218–29; and "Protichůdci. Několik poznámek o vztahu Erbenova básnického díla k Máchovu" (Antipodes: Some Remarks on the Relationship of Erben's Poetic Works to Mácha's) *Sl. sl.* 2 (1936): 33–43.

1936

3 FEB.   Bém, A. L. "Metoda drobných pozorování v literární vědě" (A Method of Close Observations in Literary Study).

22 FEB.   Václavek, Bedřich. "České zlidovělé písně" (Czech Folk Songs) = "České světské písně zlidovělé." In his *O lidové písni a slovesnosti*. Praha: Československý spisovatel, 1963, pp. 129–42.

29 FEB.   Mráz, Andrej. "Lev Tolstoj a Slováci (K problému literárních vlivů)" (Leo Tolstoy and the Slovaks [On the Problem of Literary Influences]). Cf. his *L. N. Tolstoj u Slovákov*. Bratislava: Slovenská akadémia vied a umení, 1950, 51 pp.

30 MAR.   Trost, Pavel. "Sprache des Romans von Céline (=   Strukturální rozbor Célinova románu *Voyage au bout de la nuit*)."

27 APR.   Novák, Arne. "O českém slohu kritickém" (On Style in Czech Criticism) = "Český sloh kritický let sedmdesátých a osmdesátých." *Sl. sl.* 2 (1936): 145–56.

25 MAY   Fischer, Otokar. "Symbol matek v Goethově *Faustu*" (The Symbol of Mothers in Goethe's *Faust*) = "Le symbole des mères dans le *Faust* de Goethe." *Travaux* 6 (1936): 207–21.

4 JUNE   Hrabák, Josef. "Srovnávání verše staročeského a staropolského" (A Comparison between Old Czech and Old Polish Verse) = *Staropolský verš ve srovnání se staročeským*. Praha: *PLC*, 1937 (= Studie Pražského linguistického kroužku, no. 1), 71 pp.

22 JUNE   Helfert, Vladimír. "K otázce hudebnosti v poesii" (On the Question of Musicality in Poetry) = "Poznámky k otázce hudebnosti řeči (Několik námětů k diskusi)." *Sl. sl.* 3 (1937): 99–105.

16 NOV.   Šalda, F. X. "Máchova próza" (Mácha's Prose) = "O krásné próze Máchově." In *Torso a tajemství Máchova díla*. Ed. Jan Mukařovský. Praha: Fr. Borový, 1938, pp. 181–200.

23 NOV.   Rippl, Eugen. "Humor lidové češtiny" (The Humor of Colloquial Czech).

1937

3 FEB.   Horák, Jiří. "Puškin a Mickiewicz."

8 FEB.   Jakobson, Roman. "K Puškinově symbolice" (On Symbolism in Puškin) = "Socha v symbolice Puškinově." *Sl. sl.* 3 (1937): 2–24.

26 APR.   Mukařovský, Jan. "Památce F. X. Šaldy" (In Memory of F. X. Šalda) = "F. X. Šalda." *Sl. sl.* 3 (1937) 65–78.

31 MAY   Eisner, Pavel. "Zrození básnického překladu" (The Birth of Poetic Translation).

1 OCT.   Wellek, René. "Vývoj anglické literární vědy" (The Development of English Literary Scholarship) = "Vývoj anglické literární vědy." *Sl. sl.* 4 (1938): 95–105.

18 OCT.   Utitz, Emil. "K jazykové estetice" (On the Aesthetics of Language).

1938

14 FEB.   Florovskij, Antonij. "České prvky v staroruské literature" (Czech Features in Old Russian Literature) = "Vliv staré české literatury v oblasti ruské." In *Co daly naše země Evropě a lidstvu*. Praha: Bohumil Janda, 1939, pp. 139–43.

7 NOV.   Mukařovský, Jan. "Poznámky k významové výstavbě Máchova díla" (Notes on the Semantic Construction of Mácha's Work) = "Genetika smyslu v Máchově poesii." In *Torso a tajemství Máchova díla*. Ed. Jan Mukařovský. Praha: Fr. Borový, 1938, pp. 13–110.

1939

22 MAY   Mukařovský, Jan. "Významová skladba a komposiční osnova Čapkovy prózy" (The Semantic Construction and Compositional Frame of Čapek's Prose) = "Významová výstavba a komposiční osnova epiky Karla Čapka." *Sl. sl.* 5 (1939): 113–31.

12 JUNE   Průšek, Jaroslav. "O významové výstavbě čínské povídky" (On the Semantic Construction of the Chinese Short Story) = "O struktuře čínského románu a povídky." *Sl. sl.* 5 1939: 195–209.

19 JUNE   Bogatyrev, Petr. "Lidové divadlo u Čechů a Slováků" (The Popular Theater of the Czechs and Slovaks). Cf. introductory chapter of his *Lidové divadlo české a slovenské*. Praha: F. Borový, 1940.

23 OCT.   Mukařovský, Jan. "O významové výstavbě Vančurově" (On the Semantic Structure in Vančura) = "Dvě studie o Vladislavu Vančurovi." In his *KCP*, vol. 2. Praha: Melantrich, 1941, pp. 403–21.

1940

15 JAN.   Mukařovský, Jan. "Problémy estetiky jazyka" (Problems of the Aesthetics of Language) = "Estetika jazyka." *Sl. sl.* 6 (1940): 1–27.

4 MAR.   Vašica, Josef. "Liturgická povaha Kyjevských listů, pokus o nové řešení" (The Liturgical Character of the Kyev Letters: An Attempt at a New Solution) = "Slovanská liturgie nově osvětlena Kyjevskými listy." *Sl. sl.* 6 (1940): 65–77.

27 MAY   Heidenreich, Julius. "O tradici a tradicionalismu u A. Nováka" (On Tradition and Traditionalism in Arne Novák) = "Tradice a tradicionalismus u Arna Nováka." In *Morava Arnu Novákovi: Sborník básní, studií a vzpomínek*. Ed. Ivo Liškutín. Praha: Miroslav Stejskal, 1941, pp. 48–102.

1 JULY   Honzl, Jindřich. "Jevištní dílo jako soubor znaků" (The Scenic Work as an Assembly of Signs) = "Pohyb divadelního znaku." *Sl. sl.* 6 (1940): 177–88.

16 SEPT.   Mukařovský, Jan. "Dialog a monolog" (Dialogue and Monologue) = "Dialog a monolog." *Listy filologické* 76 (1940): 139–60.

4 DEC.   Havránek, Bohuslav. "Základní problematika stylu a stylistiky" (Basic Problems of Style and Stylistics) = "Stylistika." In *Ottův slovník naučný nové doby*, vol. 6/1. Praha: Novina, 1940–1943, pp. 471–73.

16 DEC.   Florovskij, Antonij. "Česká bible v dějinách východoslovanské kultury a písemnictví" (The Czech Bible in the History of East Slavic Culture and Litera-

ture) = "Češskaja Biblija v istorii russkoj kul'tury i pis'mennosti." *Sborník filologický* 12 (1940–1946): 153–258.

1941

13 JAN. Žilka, František. "O způsobech překládání Písma" (On Translating the Bible). Cf. "Starý a nový překlad Nového zákona" (The Old and New Translation of the New Testament). *Sl. sl.* 2 (1936): 106–12.

3 FEB. Mukařovský, Jan. "Mezi literaturou a výtvarnictvím" (Between Literature and the Visual Arts) = "Mezi poesií a výtvarnictvím." *Sl. sl.* 7 (1941): 1–16.

17 FEB. Trnka, Bohumil. "Individuálnost a kolektivnost ve stylu" (The Individual and the Collective in Style) = "K otázce stylu." *Sl. sl.* 7 (1941): 61–72.

3 MAR. Vodička, Felix. "Metodické poznámky k studiu ohlasu literárních děl" (Methodological Remarks on the Study of the Reception of Literary Works) = "Literarněhistorické studium ohlasu literárních děl. Problematika ohlasu Nerudova díla." *Sl. sl.* 7 (1941): 113–32.

24 MAR. Mukařovský, Jan. "O básníku" (The Poet) = "Básník." In his *SE*, pp. 144–52.

21 APR. Kalista, Zdeněk. "Česká legenda baroková" (Czech Baroque Legends) = "Legendická tvorba." In *České baroko: Studie, texty, poznámky*. Ed. Zdeněk Kalista. Praha: Evropský literární klub, 1941, pp. 313–16.

5 MAY Veltruský, Jiří. "Dramatický tekst jako divadlo" (The Dramatic Text as the Theatre) = "Dramatický tekst jako součást divadla." *Sl. sl.* 7 (1941): 132–44.

1942

23 FEB. Horálek, Karel. "Rozbor staročeského verše a povaha přízvuku" (An Analysis of Old Czech Verse and the Nature of Stress) = "Rozbor verše a staročeský přízvuk." *Sl. sl.* 8 (1942): 57–80.

27 APR. Mukařovský, Jan. "Přísloví jako součást kontextu" (The Proverb as a Component Part of the Context) = "Přísloví jako součást kontextu." In his *CPE*, pp. 277–359.

21 SEPT. Nováková, Julie. "Kvantita v českém verši přízvučném" (Quantity in Czech Accentual Verse) = "Kvantita v českém verši přízvučném." *Sl. sl.* 10 (1947–1948): 96–107.

30 NOV. Mukařovský, Jan. "Situace estetické funkce mezi funkcemi ostatními" (The Place of the Aesthetic Function among the Other Functions) = "Místo estetické funkce mezi ostatními." In his *SE*, pp. 65–73.

1943

11 JAN. Heidenreich, Julius. "K thematické výstavbě básnického díla" (On the Thematic Construction of the Poetic Work) = "O tvaru motivů." *Sl. sl.* 9 (1943): 68–96.

15 JAN. Mukařovský, Jan. "O pojmu vývoje v umění" (On the Notion of Evolution in Art) = "Individuum a literární vývoj." In his *SE*, pp. 226–35.

5 MAY Nováková, Julie. "Souhláskové skupiny v českém verši" (Consonantal

Groups in Czech Verse) = "Souhláskové skupiny v českem verši." *Sl. sl.* 12 (1950): 19–32.

26 MAY   Mukařovský, Jan. "Záměrnost a nezáměrnost v umění" (Intentionality and Unintentionality in Art) = "Záměrnost a nezáměrnost v umění." In his *SE*, pp. 89–108.

21 SEPT.   Nováková, Julie. "Český verš pod vlivem časomíry" (Czech Verse under the Influence of Quantitative Versification).

22 DEC.   Horálek, Karel. "Řecká předloha staroslověnského překladu evangelia" (The Greek Model of the Old Slavic Translation of the Gospel). Cf. resumé in *Sl. sl.* 9 (1943): 218–19; and his *Evangeliáře a čtveroevangeliáře. Příspěvky k textové kritice a k dějinám staroslověnského překladu evangelia.* Praha: Státní pedagogické nakladelství, 1954, 290 pp.

1944

26 JAN.   Honzl, Jindřich. "Mimický znak a mimický příznak" (Gestural Sign and Gestural Signal) = "Mimický znak a mimický příznak." *Otázky divadla a filmu* 3 (1947–1948): 29–35.

21 FEB.   Vodička, Felix. "Jungmannova účast na vývoji české prózy" (Jungmann's Role in the Development of Czech Prose) = "Jungmannova účast na vývoji české prózy." In his *Počátky krásné prózy novočeské.* Praha: Melantrich, 1948, pp. 19–47.

7 JULY   Jedlička, Alois. "Jungmannova účast při tvoření české terminologie literárně vědné a linguistické" (Jungmann's Role in the Creation of Czech Literary and Linguistic Terminology) = *Josef Jungmann a obrozenská terminologie literárně vědná a linguistická.* Praha: Česká akademie věd a umění, 1948, 94 pp.

1945

26 MAR.   Nováková, Julie. "Český časoměrný hexametr" (Czech Syllabic Hexameter) = Chapters 1 and 2 in "Tři studie o českém hexametru." *Věstník královské české společnosti nauk. Třída filosoficko-historicko-filologická* no. 5 (1947), 85 pp.

27 JULY   Mukařovský, Jan. "Věta Vančurovy prózy" (The Sentence in the Prose of Vančura) = *O Vladislavu Vančurovi. Dvě přednášky.* Praha: Opatrný, 1946, 36 pp.

10 DEC.   ———. "Strukturalismus" = "Strukturalismus v estetice a ve vědě o umění" (Structuralism in Aesthetics and Art Theory). In his *KCP*, vol. 1, pp. 13–16.

1946

14 JAN.   Nováková, Julie. "Český přízvučný hexametr" (Czech Accentual Hexameter) = Chapter 4 in "Tři studie o českém hexametru" (see above).

28 JAN.   Sychra, Antonín. "Hudba a slovo v lidové písni vokálního typu" (Music and Text in Folk Music) = *Hudba a slovo v lidové písni: Příspěvek k strukturální analyse vokální hudby.* Praha: Svoboda, 1948 (= Studie Pražského linguistického kroůku no. 5), 83 pp.

4 MAR.   Vodička, Felix. "Období Jungmannovo ve vývoji a periodisaci české literatury" (Jungmann's Era in the History of Czech Literature and Its Periodization) = "Preromantismus v české literatuře a vliv jeho evropských vzorů na českou prózu." In his *Počátky krásné prózy novočeské*, pp. 125–48.

11 JUNE   Nováková, Julie. "Indické rozměry v tvorbě Jungmanna a jeho školy" (Indian Features in the Work of Jungmann and His School) = "Indické rozměry v českém básnictví." *Věstník královské české společnosti nauk. Třída filosoficko-historicko-filologická* no. 8 (1952): 1–31.

1947

6 OCT.   Sychra, Antonin. "Materiál hudby s hlediska fonologického" (Musical Material from a Phonological Point of View). Cf. "Lidová píseň z hlediska semiologického" (Folk Song from a Semiotic Point of View). *Sl. sl.* 11 (1948–1949): 7–23.

1 DEC.   Mayenowa, Maria Renata. "Pokus o vymezení jazyka básnického a jiných typů jazyka" (An Attempt at Distinguishing Poetic Language and Other Language Types). Cf. resumé in *Sl. sl.* 12 (1950): 54–55.

1948

19 JAN.   Cejp, Ladislav. "Cambridgská škola" (The Cambridge School) = "Cambridgská škola." *Časopis pro moderní filologii* 31 (1948): 197–201, 278–87.

26 APR.   Nováková, Julie. "Problém stříbrné latiny" (The Problem of Silver Latin). Cf. resumé in *Sl. sl.* 12 (1950): 55–56; and *Devět kapitol o t. zv. stříbrném věku římské slovesnosti. Pokus o třídní výklad* (The So-Called Silver Epoch of Roman Letters: An Attempt at a Class Interpretation). Praha: Československá akademie věd, 1953, 141 pp.

Appendix 2. A List of Secondary and Related Sources

Lists of primary sources can be found in several places. My compilations of Mukařovský's and Vodička's writings are, respectively, in *SSF*, pp. 251–66, and *SLP*, pp. 599–607. Jakobson's bibliography covering the Prague School years can be found in *To Honor Roman Jakobson: Essays on the Occasion of His Seventieth Birthday* (The Hague: Mouton, 1967), pp. xi–xxxiii; and René Wellek's partly in his *Concepts of Criticism*, ed. Stephen G. Nichols, Jr. (New Haven: Yale University Press, 1963), pp. 365–77, and in his *Essays on Czech Literature* (The Hague: Mouton, 1963), pp. 11–16. A selected bibliography of works in linguistics is appended to *The Linguistic School of Prague*, pp. 166–78, and in poetics to *A Prague School Reader on Esthetics, Literary Structure, and Style*, pp. 153–63.

THE PRAGUE SCHOOL

Angioni, Giulio. "Il 'circolo linguistico di Praga' e la considerazione funzionale del folklore." *Lingua e stile* 6 (1971): 487–98.

Bachtin, Nicholas. "English Poetry in Greek (Notes on the Comparative Study of Poetic Idioms)." *The Link: A Review of Mediaeval and Modern Greek* 1 (1938): 77–84 and 2 (1939): 49–63.

Bailey, R. W. et al., eds. *The Sign: Semiotics around the World*. Ann Arbor: Michigan Slavic Publications, 1978.

Bakoš, Mikuláš. "Historische Poetik und Literaturgeschichte." In *Formalismus, Strukturalismus und Geschichte*. Ed. Aleksandar Flaker and Viktor Žmegač. Kronberg: Scriptor, 1974, pp. 145–54.

Bělič, Oldřich. "Les principes méthodologiques du structuralisme estétique tschécoslovaque." *La pensée* no. 154 (1970): 52–61.

Bielfeldt, Sigrun. "Konkretisation der Konkretisation? Zum Verhältnis von čechischem Strukturalismus und 'Rezeptionsästhetik.'" In *Slavistische Studien zum VIII. internationalen Slavistenkongreß in Zagreb 1978*. Ed. Johannes Holthusen et al. Köln: Böhlau, 1978, pp. 27–50.

Bierwisch, Manfred. "Strukturalismus, Geschichte, Probleme und Methoden." *Kursbuch* 5 (1966): 77–152.

Boldt, Frank, ed. *Literaturwissenschaftliche Arbeiten von Prager Strukturalisten (1935–1970)*. (*Postilla Bohemica* nos. 4–5 [1973]).

Broekman, Jan M. *Strukturalismus: Moskau-Prag-Paris*. Freiburg: Alber, 1971, pp. 67–105.

Brousek, Marketa. *Der Poetismus: Die Lehrjahre der tschechischen Avantgarde und ihre marxistischen Kritiker*. München: Hanser, 1975.

Brown, Edward J. Rev. of *WVA*, by Jan Mukařovský. *Structuralist Review* 2 (1979): 108–9.

———. "Roman Osipovich Jakobson: 1896–1982." *Russian Review* 41 (1983): 91–99.

Bruss, Elizabeth W. Rev. of *WVA*, by Jan Mukařovský. *Comparative Literature* 31 (1979): 170–74.

Bulygina, T. B. "Pražskaja lingvističeskaja škola." In *Osnovnye napravlenija strukturalizma* (The Basic Trends of Structuralism). Ed. M. M. Guchman. Moskva: Nauka, 1964, pp. 46–126.

Bundálek, Karel. "Probleme der Dialektik in der Kunst vom Standpunkt Bertolt Brechts und Jan Mukařovskýs." *Otázky divadla a filmu* 2 (1971): 63–79.

Červenka, Miroslav. "O Vodičkově metodologii literárních dějin" (On Vodička's Methodology of Literary History). Afterword to *Struktura vývoje*, by Felix Vodička. Praha: Odeon, 1969, pp. 329–50.

———. "Die Grundkategorien des Prager literaturwissenschaftlichen Strukturalismus." In *Zur Kritik literaturwissenschaftlicher Methodologie*. Ed. Viktor Žmegač and Zdenko Škreb. Frankfurt: Athenäum, 1973, pp. 137–68.

———. "A Contribution to the Semantics of the Literary Work." Trans. F. W. Galan. In *Papers in Slavic Philology*, vol. 1, *In Honor of James Ferrell*. Ed. Benjamin A. Stolz. Ann Arbor: Department of Slavic Languages, University of Michigan, 1977, pp. 27–35.

———. *Der Bedeutungsaufbau der literarischen Werks*. Ed. Frank Boldt and Wolf-Dieter Stempel. München: Fink, 1978.

———. "New Perspective on Czech Structuralism." Rev. of *SSM*. *PTL: A Journal for Descriptive Poetics and Theory of Literature* 4 (1979): 359–70.

———. "The Literary Work as Sign." Trans. F. W. Galan. In *Language, Literature and Meaning II: Current Trends in Literary Research*. Ed. John Odmark. Amsterdam: Benjamins, 1980, pp. 1–25.

———. "Der versologische Band von Jakobson's *Selected Writings*: Bemerkungen eines Bohemisten." Rev. of *SW* 5. *Wiener Slawistischer Almanach* no. 7 (1981): 259–75.

———. "The Literary Artifact." In *The Sign in Music and Literature*. Ed. Wendy Steiner. Austin: University of Texas Press, 1981, pp. 86–102.

———. "'Foničeskaja linija' Mukařovskogo i intonacionnyj analiz sticha." *Russian Literature* 12 (1982): 227–66.

Chlumský, Milan. "Les problémes d'une nouvelle esthétique." *Lire* (*Revue d'esthétique* nos. 2–3, 1976). Paris: 10/18, 1976, pp. 249–93.

Chvatík, Květoslav. *Strukturalismus und Avantgarde*. München: Hanser, 1970.

———. "Die Strukturalistische Auffassung des Verhältnisse von Kunst und Gesellschaft." In *Proceedings of the Sixth International Congress of Aesthet-*

ics. Ed. R. Zeitler. Uppsala: Acta Universitatis Uppsaliensis, 1972, pp. 163–65.

———. "J. L. Fischer—The Founder of Dialectical Structurology in Czech Philosophy." In *Semiotics and Dialectics: Ideology and the Text*. Ed. Peter V. Zima. Amsterdam: Benjamins, 1981, pp. 223–41.

———. "Semiotics of a Literary Work of Art: Dedicated to the 90th Birthday of Jan Mukařovský (1891–1975)." *Semiotica* 37 (1981): 193–214.

———. *Tschechoslowakischer Strukturalismus: Theorie und Geschichte*. Trans. Vlado Müller. München: Fink, 1981.

———. "Die ästhetische Einstellung." *Semiotik* 5 (1983): 229–42.

———, and Zdeněk Pešat, eds. *Poetismus*. Praha: Odeon, 1967.

Čivikov, G. "Das ästhetische Zeichen der Prager Strukturalisten und das Peircesche Zeichenmodel." *Neophilologus* 65 (1981): 321–42.

Clark, W. H., Jr. Rev. of *SA*. *Journal of Aesthetics* 35 (1977): 363–65.

Danek, Danuta. "Obrona prozy: Wokół koncepcji poetyckości praskiej szkoly strukturalnej" (A Defense of Prose: On the Prague Structural School's Notion of Poeticity). In her *O polemice literackiej w powieści* (Literary Polemic in the Novel). Warszawa: Państwowy institut wydawniczy, 1972, pp. 13–69 and 161–81.

Deák, František. "Structuralism in Theatre: The Prague School Contribution." *Drama Review* 20 (1976): 83–94.

DeGeorge, Fernande M. "From Russian Formalism to French Structuralism." *Comparative Literature Studies* 14 (1977): 20–30.

De Paz, Alfredo. "Semiologia e sociologia nell'estetica di Mukařovský." *Lingua e stile* 16 (1975): 531–70.

Doležel, Lubomir. "Zur statistischen Theorie der Dichtersprache." In *Mathematik und Dichtung*. Ed. Helmut Kreuzer and Rul Gunzenhäuser. München: Nymphenburger Verlag, 1965, pp. 275–93.

———. "The Prague School and the Statistical Theory of Poetic Language." In *Prague Studies in Mathematical Linguistics*, vol. 2, 1967, pp. 97–104.

———. "Russian and Prague School Functional Stylistics." *Style* 2 (1968): 143–58.

———. "Prague School Stylistics." In *Current Trends in Stylistics*. Ed. B. B. Kachru and H. F. W. Stahlke. Edmonton: Linguistic Research, 1972, pp. 37–48.

———. "Narrative Composition: A Link between German and Russian Poetics." In *Russian Formalism*. Ed. Stephen Bann and John E. Bowlt. Edinburgh: Scottish Academic Press, 1973, pp. 73–84.

———. *Essays in Structural Poetics and Narrative Semantics*. Prepublications of the Toronto Semiotic Circle no. 3. Toronto: Victoria University, 1979.

———. Rev. of *WVA*, by Jan Mukařovský. *Style* 15 (1981): 64–68.

———. "The Conceptual System of Prague School Poetics: Mukařovský and Vodička." In *SLP*, 109–26.

———. "Mukařovský and the Idea of Poetic Truth." *Russian Literature* 12 (1982): 283–97.

Drozda, Miroslav. "Vodička's *The Beginnings of Modern Czech Prose* (*Počátky Krásné Prózy Novočeské*) in the Light of the Theory of Fiction." Trans. Peter Petro. In *SLP*, 127–36.

Eagle, Herbert. "The Czech Structuralist Debate on the Role of Intonation in Verse Structure." In *SSM*, 521–41.

———. "The Semiotics of Art: A Dynamic View." Rev. of *SA*. *Semiotica* 19 (1977): 367–96.

———. "Verse as a Semiotic System: Tynjanov, Jakobson, Mukařovský, Lotman Extended." *SEEJ* 25 (1981): 47–61.

Eco, Umberto. "The Influence of Roman Jakobson on the Development of Semiotics." In *RJ*, p. 39–58.

Effenberger, Vratislav. "Roman Jakobson and the Czech Avant-Garde between Two Wars." Trans. Iris Urwin. *American Journal of Semiotics* 2 (1983): 13–21.

Eimermacher, Karl. "Zum Verhältnis von formalistischer, strukturalistischer und semiotischer Analyse." In *Methodische Praxis der Literaturwissenschaft: Modelle der Interpretation*. Ed. Dieter Kimpel and Beate Pinkerneil. Kronberg: Scriptor, 1975, pp. 259–83.

Erlich, Victor. Rev. of *SA*. *Comparative Literature* 30 (1978): 274.

Faye, Jean Pierre, and Léon Robel, eds. *Le Cercle de Prague*. Paris, 1969 (= *Change* no. 3).

Felice, Emilio de. "Storicismo e strutturalismo." *Lingua e stile* 2 (1967): 259–76.

———. "O 'historismu' a 'strukturalismu'" (On "Historicism" and "Structuralism"). *Česká literatura* 16 (1968): 651–56.

Filosofický časopis 17 (1969) (issue on structuralism).

Fizer, John. "Ingarden's and Mukařovský's Binominal Definition of the Literary Work of Art: A Comparative View of Their Respective Ontologies." *Russian Literature* 13 (1983): 269–90.

Fokkema, Douwe Wessel. "Continuity and Change in Russian Formalism, Czech Structuralism, and Soviet Semiotics." *PTL: A Journal for Descriptive Poetics and Theory of Literature* 1 (1976): 153–96.

———, and Elrud Kunne-Ibsch, eds. *Theories of Literature in the Twentieth Century: Structuralism, Marxism, Aesthetics of Reception, Semiotics*. New York: St. Martin's Press, 1978.

Frank, Joseph. "The Master Linguist." Rev. of *Dialogues* by Roman Jakobson and Krystyna Pomorska. *New York Review of Books*, 12 April 1984: 29–33.

Freeman, Donald C. Rev. of *WVA* and *SSF*, by Jan Mukařovský. *Journal of Aesthetics and Art Criticism* 38 (1979): 95–97.

Galan, F. W. "Literary System and Systemic Change: The Prague School Theory of Literary History, 1928–48." *PMLA* 94 (1979): 275–85.

———. "Nedožité jubileum" (A Posthumous Anniversary of Felix Vodička). *Proměny* 17 (1980): 87–88.

———. "Roman Jakobson in Memoriam." *Premeny* 19 (1982): 92–95.

———. "Cinema and Semiosis: The Prague School View (I) and The Missing Frame (II)." *Semiotica* 44 (1983): 21–53.

Garvin, Paul L., ed. and trans. *A Prague School Reader on Esthetics, Literary Structure, and Style*. Washington, D.C.: Georgetown University Press, 1964.

———. "The Prague School of Linguistics." In *Linguistics Today*. Ed. Archibald A. Hill. New York: Basic Books, 1969, pp. 229–38.

———. "Linguistics and Semiotics." *Semiotica* 20 (1977): 101–10.

Grande, Maurizio. "Il problema della lingua poetica nella scuola di Praga." *Nuova corrente* 56 (1971): 375–95.

Grebeničková, Růžena. "Cesty marxistické literární vědy a léta třicátá" (The Paths of Marxist Literary Theory in the Thirties). *Československá rusistika* 6 (1961): 88–101.

Grygar, Mojmír. "Vývojové napětí literárních a mimoliterárních jevů" (The Developmental Tension between Literary and Extraliterary Phenomena). *Česká literatura* 14 (1966): 367–92.

———. "Pojetí literárního vývoje v ruské formální metodě a v českém strukturalismu" (The Concept of Literary Evolution in the Russian Formal Method and in Czech Structuralism). *Česká literatura* 16 (1968): 266–88.

———. "The Possibilities of a Structural Analysis of the Literary Process." *Russian Literature* 12 (1982): 331–400.

———. "The Role of Personality in Literary Development." Trans. Jitka Kaufman. In *SLP*, pp. 187–210.

Günther, Hans. "Tschechischer Strukturalismus und materialistische Literaturtheorie." *Alternative* no. 82 (1972): 38–41.

———. "Funktionsanalyse der Literatur." In *Neue Ansichten einer Kunftigen Germanistik.* Ed. Jürgen Kolbe. München: Hanser, 1973, pp. 174–84.

———. *Struktur als Prozeß: Studien zur Ästhetik und Literaturtheorie des tscheschischen Strukturalismus.* München: Fink, 1973.

———. "Geschichtliche Positionen: Russischer Formalismus, Marxismus, tschechischer Strukturalismus." In *Literaturwissenschaft: Grundkurs 2.* Ed. Helmut Brackert and Jörn Stückrath. Reinbeck bei Hamburg: Rowolt, 1981, pp. 319–28.

Halle, Morris. "Roman Jakobson's Contribution to the Modern Study of Speech Sounds." In *SSM*, pp. 79–100.

———, ed. *Roman Jakobson: What He Taught Us.* Supplement to vol. 27 (1983) of *International Journal of Slavic Linguistics and Poetics.*

Haman, Aleš. "Einige Bemerkungen zu Mukařovský's Auffassung des Wertes." *Wiener Slawistischer Almanach* no. 8 (1981): 117–24.

Holenstein, Elmar. *Linguistik, Semiotik, Hermeneutik.* Frankfurt: Suhrkamp, 1976.

———. *Roman Jakobson's Approach to Language: Phenomenological Structuralism.* Trans. Catherine and Tarcisius Schelbert. Bloomington: Indiana University Press, 1976.

———. "The Structure of Understanding: Structuralism versus Hermeneutics." *PTL: A Journal for Descriptive Poetics and Theory of Literature* 1 (1976): 223–38.

———. "Jakobson's Contribution to Phenomenology." In *RJ*, pp. 145–62.

———. "Prague Structuralism—A Branch of the Phenomenological Movement." Trans. John Odmark. In *Language, Literature and Meaning I: Problems of Literary Theory.* Ed. John Odmark. Amsterdam: Benjamins, 1979, pp. 71–97.

———. "On the Poetry and the Plurifunctionality of Language." In *Structure and Gestalt: Philosophy and Literature in Austria-Hungary and Her Successor States.* Ed. Barry Smith. Amsterdam: Benjamins, 1981, pp. 1–43.

———. "Five Jakobsonian Principles of Poetics." Trans. Catherine Schelbert. *American Journal of Semiotics* 2 (1983): 23–34.

Holmes, Wendy. "Prague School Aesthetics." Rev. of *SA. Semiotica* 33 (1981): 155–68.

Hrušovský, Igor. "Struktura a dialektika" (Structure and Dialectics). *Filosofický časopis* 13 (1965): 193–203.

Ihwe, Jens. *Linguistik in der Literaturwissenschaft.* München: Bayerischer Schulbuch Verlag, 1972.

Innis, Robert E. *Karl Bühler: Semiotic Foundations of Language Theory.* New York: Plenum, 1982.

Jankovič, Milan, ed. *K interpretaci uměleckého literárního díla* (Toward the Interpretation of the Literary Work of Art). Praha: Ústav pro českou literaturu, 1970.

———. "Perspectives of Semantics Gesture." *Poetics* 4 (1972): 16–27.

———. "The Individual Style and the Problem of *Meaning* of the Literary Work." Trans. F. W. Galan. In *Language, Literature and Meaning II: Current Trends in Literary Research.* Ed. John Odmark. Amsterdam: Benjamins, 1980, pp. 27–53.

———. "Die Inhaltsfunktion der künstlerischen Form als offenes Problem." In *SLP*, pp. 243–85.

———. et al., eds. *Struktura a smysl literárního díla: Janu Mukařovskému k 75. narozeninám* (The Structure and the Sense of the Literary Work: On Jan Mukařovský's 75th Birthday). Praha: Československy spisovatel, 1966.

———, and Miroslav Procházka. "Vorläufiger Bericht über den literarischen Nachlaß Jan Mukařovský's." *Wiener Slawistischer Almanach* no. 8 (1981): 9–12.

Jechová, Hana. "Le poétisme tchèque entre le cubisme et le surréalisme." *Revue de littérature comparée* 51 (1977): 202–11.

Johnson, D. Barton. "The Role of Synesthesia in Jakobson's Theory of Language." In *Slavic Linguistics and Poetics: Studies for Edward Stankiewicz on His 60th Birthday.* Ed. Kenneth E. Naylor et al. Special issue of *International Journal of Slavic Linguistics and Poetics* 25–26 (1982): 219–32.

Johnson, Marta K., ed. and trans. *Recycling the Prague Linguistic Circle.* Ann Arbor: Karoma, 1978.

Kačer, Miroslav. "Mukařovského termín 'sémantické gesto' a Barthesův 'rukopis (écriture)'" (Mukařovský's Category "Semantic Gesture" and Barthes' "Ecriture"). *Česká literatura* 16 (1968): 593–97.

———. 'Der Prager Strukturalismus in der Ästhetik und Literaturwissenschaft." *Welt der Slaven* 13 (1968): 64–86.

Kalivoda, Robert. "Die Dialektik des Strukturalismus und die Dialektik der Ästhetik." In his *Der Marxismus und die moderne geistige Wirklichkeit.* Frankfurt: Suhrkamp, 1970, pp. 9–38.

Karbusický, Vladimír. *Widerspiegelungstheorie und Strukturalismus.* München: Hauser, 1973.

———. "The Experience of the Indexical Sign: Jakobson and the Semiotic Phonology of Leoš Janáček." Trans. Thomas G. Winner. *American Journal of Semiotics* 2 (1983): 35–58.

Kautman, František. "Strukturalismus v díle Jana Mukařovského" (Structuralism in the Work of Jan Mukařovský). *Filosofický časopis* 15 (1967): 494–512.

Kevelson, Roberta. "Reversals and Recognitions: Pierce and Mukařovský on the Art of Conversation." *Semiotica* 19 (1977): 281–320.

Kosík, Karel. *Dialectics of the Concrete: A Study on the Problem of Man and World.* Dordrecht: Reidel, 1976.

Krampen, Martin, "A Bouquet for Roman Jakobson." Rev. of *RJ. Semiotica* 33 (1981): 301–5.

Krámský, Jiří. *The Phoneme: Introduction to the History and Theories of a Concept.* München: Fink, 1974.

Křesálková, Jitka. "Per una storia delle idee strutturali e semiotiche in Cecoslovacchia." In *La semiotica nei paesi slavi: Programmi, problemi, analisi.* Ed. Carlo Prevignano. Milano: Feltrinelli, 1979, pp. 487–93.

Landgrebe, Ludwig. "Erinnerungen eines Phänomenologen an den *Cercle Linguistique de Prague.*" In *SSM*, pp. 40–42.

Lenhoff, Gail. "The Aesthetic Function and Medieval Russian Culture." In *SLP*, pp. 321–40.

Lepschy, Giulio C. "The Prague School." In his *A Survey of Structural Linguistics.* London: Faber, 1970, pp. 53–64.

Levinton, G. A. "Iz marginalij k poetike pražskoj školy—Opredelenie metra u N. S. Trubeckogo" (Marginalia on the Poetics of the Prague School: N. S. Trubeckoj's Definition of Metre). *Russian Literature* 10 (1981): 67–78.

Levý, Jiří. "The Meanings of Form and Forms of Meaning." In *Poetics-Poetyka-Poetika.* Ed. Roman Jakobson et al. Vol. 2. The Hague: Mouton, 1966, pp. 45–59.

———. *Die literarische Übersetzung: Theorie einer Kunstgattung.* Trans. Walter Schamschula. Frankfurt: Suhrkamp, 1969.

———. "Generative Poetics." In *Sign-Language-Culture.* Ed. A. J. Greimas et al. The Hague: Mountin, 1970, pp. 548–57.

———. *Bude literární věda exaktní vědou?* (Will Literary Studies Become an Exact Science?). Praha: Československý spisovatel, 1971, pp. 77–146.

———. "Genesi e ricezione dell' opera d'arte." *Strumenti critici* 5 (1971): 39–66.

Linhartová, Věra. "La place de Roman Jakobson dans la vie littéraire et artistique Tchécoslovaque." In *RJ*, pp. 219–35.

Martens, Günter. "Texstrukturen aus rezeptionsästhetischer Sicht: Perspektiven einer Textästhetik auf der Grundlage des Prager Strukturalismus." *Wirkendes Wort* 23 (1973): 359–79.

Matejka, Ladislav. "Crossroads of Sound and Meaning." Rev. of *SW* 1–2, by Roman Jakobson. *Journal of Slavic Linguistics and Poetics* 20 (1975): 93–120.

———. "Le formalisme taxinomique et la sémiologie functionnelle pragoise." *L'Arc* no. 60 (1976): 22–28.

———. "Postscript: Prague School Semiotics." In *SA*, pp. 265–90.

———. "Preface." In *SSM*, pp. ix–xxxiv.

———. "Literary History in a Semiotic Framework: Prague School Contributions." In *SLP*, pp. 341–70.

Mayenowa, Maria Renata. "Analyza doktryny stylistycznej Praskiego koła" (Analysis of Prague School Stylistics). In *Praska szkola strukturalna w latach 1926–*

1948: Wybór materiałów. Ed. Maria Renata Mayenowa. Warzawa: Państwowe wydawnictwo naukowe, 1966, pp. 26–40.

———. "Classic Statements of the Semiotic of Art: Mukařovský and Morris." In *SSM*, pp. 425–32.

Motschmann, Jochen. "Zum Strukturbegriff im russischen Formalismus und Prager Strukturalismus." In *Strukturalismus: Ideologie und Dogmengeschichte.* Ed. Wulf D. Hund. Darmstadt: Luchterhand, 1973, pp. 349–77.

Nebeský, Ladislav. "On the Potentially Poetic Aspects of Artificial Languages: Notes on the Development of Theoretical Thought in J. Mukařovský's Work." *Poetics* 2 (1971): 87–90.

Newman, Lawrence W. "Towards a Prague School Theory of Semantics." *Semiotica* 19 (1977): 341–54.

Nobis, Helmut. "Literarische Evolution, Historizität und Geschichte." *LiLi* 4 (1974): 91–110.

Osolsobě, Ivo. "Czechoslovak Semiotics Past and Present." *Semiotica* 9 (1973): 140–56.

O'Toole, L. M. Review of *SSF*, by Jan Mukařovský. *British Journal of Aesthetics* 19 (1979): 377–80.

Patočka, Jan. "Roman Jakobsons phänomenologischer Strukturalismus." *Tydschrift voor Filosofie* 38 (1976): 129–35.

Pešat, Zdeněk. "K teorii a metodologii literárního vývoje" (On the Theory and Methodology of Literary History). In *Československé přednášky pro VI. mezinárodní sjezd slavistů.* Praha: Academia, 1968, pp. 309–16.

———. "Die Identität des literarischen Werks in seiner Veränderlichkeit." *Wiener Slawistischer Almanach* no. 8 (1981): 125–32.

Philippi, Klaus-Peter. "Formalismus-Strukturalismus." In *Methodendiskussion.* Ed. J. Hauff. Frankfurt: Athenäum, 1971, pp. 101–26.

Polák, Josef. "Ke vzniku českého literárněvědného strukturalismu" (On the Origin of Czech Structuralism in Literary Study). *Sborník prací filozifické fakulty Brněnské Univerzity* 22 (1973): 41–53.

Pomorska, Krystyna. "Roman Jakobson and the New Poetics: Notes on the Jakobsonian Method in the Analysis of Slavic Poetry and Prose." In *RJ*, pp. 363–78.

Popovič, Anton, ed. *Štrukturalizmus v slovenskej vede, 1931–1949* (Structuralism in Slovak Scholarship). Martin: Matica Slovenská, 1970.

Pospelov, N. S. "O lingvističeskom nasledstve S. Karcevskogo" (The Linguistic Legacy of S. Karcevskij). *Voprosy jazykoznanija* 6 (1957): 46–56.

Prague poésie, Front gauche. Paris, 1972. (= *Change* no. 10).

Radway, Janice A. Rev. of *SSF*, by Jan Mukařovský. *Southern Humanities Review* 13 (1979): 267–68.

Rappaport, Gilbert. "Distinctive and Redundant Contrasts in Jakobsonian Phonology." Rev. of *The Sound Shape of Language*, by Roman Jakobson and Linda R. Waugh. *SEEJ* 25 (1981): 94–108.

Reeves, Charles Eric. "Poetics and Dialectics." Rev. of *WVA*, by Jan Mukařovský. *Semiotica* 39 (1982): 115–24.

———. Rev. of *PS*. *Poetics Today* 4 (1983): 177–80.

Renský, Miroslav. "Roman Jakobson and the Prague School." In *RJ*, pp. 379–89.

Riquelme, John Paul. Rev. of *SSF*, by Jan Mukařovský. *Clio* 8 (1979): 443–46.

Rudy, Stephen. "Jakobson's Inquiry into Verse and the Emergence of Structural Poetics." In *SSM*, pp. 477–520.

Schamschula, Walter. Rev. of *SA*. *PTL: A Journal for Descriptive Poetics and Theory of Literature* 2 (1977): 401–2.

Schmid, Herta. "Zum Begriff der ästhetischen Konkretisation im tschechischen Struckturalismus." *Sprache im technischen Zeitalter* 36 (1970): 290–318.

———. "Entwicklungsschritte zu einer modernen Dramentheorie im russischen Formalismus und im tschechischen Strukturalismus." In *Moderne Dramentheorie*. Ed. Aloysius van Kestern and Herta Schmid. Kronberg: Scriptor, 1975, pp. 7–40.

———. "Anthropologische Konstanten und literarische Struktur." In *Maurice Merleau-Ponty und das Problem der Struktur in den Sozialwissenschaften*. Ed. Richard Grathoff and Walter Sprondel. Stuttgart: Enke, 1976, pp. 36–60.

———. "Aspekte und Probleme der ästhetischen Funktion im tschechischen Strukturalismus." In *SSM*, pp. 386–424.

———. "Der Funktionsbegriff des tschechischen Strukturalismus in der Theorie und in der literaturwissenschaftlichen Analyse am Beispiel von Havels *Horský hotel*." In *SLP*, pp. 455–81.

Schmid, Wolf. *Der ästhetische Inhalt: Zur semantischen Funktion poetischer Verfahren*. Utrecht Slavic Studies in Literary Theory no. 1. Lisse: Peter de Ridder, 1976.

Schwarz, Ullrich. *Rettende Kritik und antizipierte Utopie: Zum geschichtlichen Gehalt ästhetischer Erfahrung in den Theorien von Jan Mukařovský, Walter Benjamin und Theodor W. Adorno*. München: Fink, 1981.

Sedmidubský, Miloš. "Literary Evolution as a Communicative Process." In *SLP*, pp. 483–502.

Simmons, Sarah. "Mukařovský, Structuralism, and the Essay." *Semiotica* 19 (1977): 335–40.

Slawiński, Janusz. "Jan Mukařovský—Programm einer Strukturalen Ästhetik." In his *Literatur als System und Prozeß*. Ed. Rolf Fieguth. München: Hanser, 1975, pp. 203–17.

Stankiewicz, Edward. "Structural Poetics and Linguistics." In *Current Trends in Linguistics XII*. The Hague: Mouton, 1974, pp. 625–59.

———. "Poetics and Verbal Art." In *A Perfusion of Signs*. Ed. Thomas A. Sebeok. Bloomington: Indiana University Press, 1977, pp. 54–76.

———. "Roman Jakobson (A Commemorative Essay)." *Semiotica* 44 (1983): 1–20.

Steiner, Peter. "The Conceptual Basis of Prague Structuralism." In *SSM*, pp. 351–85.

———. "Jan Mukařovský and Charles W. Morris. Two Pioneers of the Semiotics of Art." *Semiotica* 19 (1977): 321–34.

———. "Jan Mukařovský's Structural Aesthetics." Introduction to *SSF*, pp. ix–xxxiv.

———. "'Formalism' and 'Structuralism': An Exercise in Metahistory." *Russian Literature* 12 (1982): 290–330.

———. "In Defense of Semiotics: The Dual Asymmetry of Cultural Signs." *New Literary History* 12 (1982): 415–35.

————. "The Roots of Structuralist Esthetics." Afterword to *PS*, pp. 174–219.

————. "The Semiotics of Literary Reception." In *SLP*, pp. 503–20.

————, and Sergej Davydov. "The Biological Metaphor in Russian Formalism: The Concept of Morphology." *Sub-stance* 17 (1977): 149–58.

————, and Wendy Steiner. "Structures and Phenomena." Rev. of *Roman Jakobson's Approach to Language: Phenomenological Structuralism*, by Elmar Holenstein. *PTL: A Journal for Descriptive Poetics and Theory of Literature* 3 (1978): 357–70.

————, and Wendy Steiner. "The Axes of Poetic Language." In *Language, Literature and Meaning I: Current Trends in Literary Research*. Ed. John Odmark. Amsterdam. Benjamins, 1979, pp. 35–70.

————, and Bronislava Volek. "Semiotics in Bohemia in the 19th and Early 20th Century." In *The Sign: Semiotics around the World*. Ed. R. W. Bailey et al. Ann Arbor: Michigan Slavic Publications, 1978, pp. 206–26.

Steiner, Wendy. "Language as Process: Sergej Karcevskij's Semiotics of Language." In *SSM*, pp. 291–300.

Striedter, Jurij. "K. H. Mácha als Dichter der europäischen Romantik." *Zeitschrift für Slawische Philologie* 31 (1963): 42–90.

————. "Zu Felix Vodičkas Theorie der 'Konkretisation' als Teil einer strukturalistischen Literaturgeschichte." Introduction to *Die Struktur der literarischen Entwicklung*, by Felix Vodička. Ed. Frank Boldt. München: Fink, 1975, pp. lix–ciii.

————. *From Formalism to Structuralism*. Cambridge, Mass.: Harvard University Press (forthcoming).

Strohschneider-Kors, Ingrid. *Literarische Struktur und geschichtlicher Wandel*. München: Fink, 1971.

Sus, Oleg. "Anfänge der semantischen Analyse in der tschechischen Poetik (J. Durdík und seine Theorie der dichterischen Sprache)." *Zagadnienia rodzajów literackich* 7 (1964): 42–56.

————. "Predystorija čēsskogo strukturalizma i russkaja formal'naja škola" (The Prehistory of Czech Structuralism and the Russian Formal School). *Československá rusistika* 12 (1967): 229–35.

————. "Příspěvek ke strukturní teorii estetické normy" (A Contribution to the Structural Theory of Aesthetic Norm). *Estetika* 3 (1966): 300–318.

————. "O struktuře (K pojmosloví českého strukturalismu v díle Jana Mukařovského)" (Structure: Notes toward a Terminological Category in the Work of Jan Mukařovský). *Česká literatura* 16 (1968): 657–66.

————. "Les traditions de l'esthétique tchéque moderne et du structuralisme de Jan Mukařovský: Du 'formisme' au structuralisme." *Revue d'esthétique* 24 (1971): 29–38.

————. "Die Genese der semantischen Kunstauffassung in der modernen tschechischen Ästhetik." *Welt der Slaven* 17 (1972): 201–24.

————. "Die Wege der tschechischen wissenschaftlichen Ästhetik (J. Mukařovský)." *Welt der Slaven* 17 (1972): 155–74.

————. "On the Genetic Preconditions of Czech Structuralist Semiology and Semantics: An Essay on Czech and German Thought." *Poetics* 4 (1972): 28–54.

————. "On the Origin of the Czech Semantics of Art: The Theory of Music and Poetry in the Psychological Semantics of Otakar Zich." *Semiotica* 9 (1973): 117–39.

————. "On Some Structural-Semantic Problems in Mukařovský's Theory of Aesthetic Norm." *Zagadnienia rodzajów literackich* 19 (1976): 35–52.

————. "Zwischen 'Formalismus' und 'Strukturalismus': Zur Kritik am sog. slavischen Formalismus und zu den Problemen des Übergangs von der 'Prager ästhetischen Schule' zur strukturalen Literatur- und Kunsttheorie." *Welt der Slaven* 22 (1977): 401–31.

————. "Die ersten Ansätze zu einer Kunstsemiotik im alten tschechishcen Formalismus bei Josef Durdík (Ein Kapitel aus der Geschichte der tschechischen Ästhetik)." *Wiener Slawistischer Almanach* no. 5 (1980): 71–115.

————. "Fragezeichen zum Problem der literarischen Entwicklung." *Wiener Slawistischer Almanach* no. 8 (1981): 133–57.

————. "From the Pre-history of Czech Structuralism: F. X. Šalda, T. G. Masaryk and the Genesis of Symbolist Aesthetics and Poetics in Bohemia." Trans. Peter Petro. In *SLP*, pp. 547–80.

Svejkovský, František. "Roman Jakobson and Old Czech Literature." In *RJ*, pp. 453–71.

Sziklay, László. "The Prague School." Trans. S. Simon. In *Literature and Its Interpretation*. Ed. Lajos Nyirö. The Hague: Mouton, 1979, pp. 69–111.

Titunik, I. R. "Between Formalism and Structuralism: N. S. Trubetzkoy's *The Journey beyond the Three Seas* by Afonasij Nikitin as a Literary Monument.'" In *SSM*, pp. 303–19.

Todorov, Tzvetan. "Sémiologie du théâtre." *Poétique* 8 (1971): 515–38.

————. "Jakobson's Poetics." *Theories of the Symbol*. Trans. Catherine Porter. Ithaca, N.Y.: Cornell University Press, 1982, pp. 271–84.

Tomčík, Miloš. "Mukařovského prínos do súčasnej estetiky" (Mukařovský's Contribution to Contemporary Aesthetics). *Slovenské pohľady* 83 (1967): 56–63.

"Tschechische Strukturalismus: Ergebnisse und Einwande." *Alternative* no. 80 (1971).

Vachek, Josef, ed. *A Prague School Reader in Linguistics*. Bloomington: Indiana University Press, 1964.

————. Rev. of *A Prague School Reader on Esthetics, Literary Structure, and Style*, ed. Paul L. Garvin. *Linguistics* 6 (1965): 103–6.

————. *The Linguistic School of Prague: An Introduction to Its Theory and Practice* Bloomington: Indiana University Press, 1966.

————. *Written Language: General Problems and Problems of English*. The Hague: Mouton, 1973.

————. *Selected Writings in English and General Linguistics*. Prague: Academia; The Hague: Mouton, 1976.

————. "An Eloquent Plea for the Binaristic Conception." Rev. of *The Sound Shape of Language*, by Roman Jakobson and Linda R. Waugh. *Semiotica* 33 (1981): 301–5.

————. "Prague Linguistic School: Its Origins and Present-Day Heritage." *Wiener Slawistischer Almanach* no. 7 (1981): 217–41.

————. "Written Language as a Heterogeneous System." In *Language Form and Linguistic Variation: Papers Dedicated to Angus McIntosh*. Ed. John Anderson. Amsterdam: Benjamins, 1982, pp. 485–96.

Van der Eng, Jan. "The Effectiveness of the Aesthetic Function." In *SLP*, pp. 137–60.

Veltruský, Jiří. *Drama as Literature*. Atlantic Highlands, N.J.: Humanities Press, 1977.

————. "Jan Mukařovský's Structural Poetics and Aesthetics." *Poetics Today* 2 (1980–1981): 117–57.

————. "Comparative Semiotics of Art." In *Image and Code*. Ed. Wendy Steiner. Ann Arbor: Michigan Studies in the Humanities, 1981, pp. 109–32.

————. "The Prague School Theory of Theater." *Poetics Today* 2 (1981): 225–35.

Vlašín, Štěpán et al., eds. *Avantgarda známá a neznámá*. 3 vols. Praha: Svoboda, 1970–1972.

Vodička, Felix. "The Integrity of the Literary Process." *Poetics* 4 (1972): 5–15.

Volek, Emil. Rev. of *SA*. *Clio* 8 (1979): 439–42.

Waugh, Linda R. *Roman Jakobson's Science of Language*. Lisse: Peter de Ridder, 1976.

————. "The Poetic Function and the Nature of Language." *Poetics Today* 2/1a (1980): 57–82.

————. "Illuminating the Grammar of Poetry and the Poetry of Grammar: An Essay Commemorating the Publication of 'Russian and Slavic Grammar.'" *American Journal of Semiotics* 2 (1983): 131–39.

Wellek, René. Rev. of *A Prague School Reader on Esthetics, Literary Structure, and Style*, ed. Paul L. Garvin. *Language* 31 (1955): 584–87.

————. "Czech Literature: East or West." In *Czechoslovakia Past and Present*. Ed. Miloslav Richcígl, Jr. Vol. 2. The Hague: Mouton, 1968, pp. 893–902.

————. "The Literary Theory and Aesthetics of the Prague School." In *Discriminations: Further Concepts in Criticism*. New Haven: Yale University Press, 1971, pp. 275–303.

————. Rev. of *SA*. *Dispositio* 1 (1976): 361–63.

————. "Vilém Mathesius (1882–1945), Founder of the Prague Linguistic Circle." In *SSM*, pp. 6–14.

Winner, Thomas G. "The Aesthetics and Poetics of the Prague Linguistic Circle." *Poetics* 8 (1973): 77–96.

————. "The Creative Personality as Viewed by the Prague Linguistic Circle: Theories and Implications." In *American Contributions to the Seventh International Congress of Slavists*. Vol. 1., *Linguistics and Poetics*. Ed. Ladislav Matejka. The Hague: Mouton, 1973, pp. 242–57.

————. "Genre Theory in the Light of Structural Poetics and Semiotics." In *Theories of Literary Genres*. Ed. Joseph Strelka. Vol. 8 of *Yearbook of Comparative Literature*. University Park: Pennsylvania State University Press, 1976, pp. 254–68.

————. "Grandes thèmes de la poétique jakobsonienne." *L'Arc* no. 60 (1976): 55–63.

————. "Jan Mukařovský: The Beginnings of Structural and Semiotics Aesthetics." In *SSM*, pp. 433–55.

————. "Roman Jakobson and Avantgarde Art." In *RJ*, pp. 503–14.

————. "On the Relation of the Verbal and the Nonverbal Arts in Early Prague Semiotics: Jan Mukařovský." In *The Sign: Semiotics around the World*. Ed. R. W. Bailey et al. Ann Arbor: Michigan Slavic Publications, 1978, pp. 227–37.

————. "Some Fundamental Concepts Leading to a Semiotics of Culture: An Historical Overview." *Semiotica* 27 (1979): 75–82.

————. "Czech Poetics and Semiotics in the 1960's." In *Czech Literature since 1956: A Symposium*. Ed. William E. Harkins and Paul J. Trensky. New York: Bohemica, 1980, pp. 119–33.

————. *Aesthetic Semiotics: East and West: Essays on Semiotic Theory in the Creative Arts*. San Diego: Schlacks (forthcoming).

Zadražil, Ladislav. "Mezi poetikou a dějinami literatury: Poznámky k aktuálnímu významu meziválečného vývoje sovětske literárněvědné metodologie" (Between Poetics and Literary History: Notes on the Significance of the Development of Soviet Literary Methodology between the Two Wars). *Československá rusistika* 22 (1977): 167–74.

Zima, Pierre V. "De la structure textuelle à la structure sociale." *Lire* (*Revue d'esthétique* nos. 2–3 [1976]). Paris: 10/18, 1976, pp. 186–223.

Zumr, Josef. "Některé otázky českého herbartismu" (Some Questions concerning the Influence of J. F. Herbart in Bohemia). In *Filosofie v dějinách českého národa*. Praha: Československá akademie věd, 1958, pp. 166–85.

————. "Teoretické základy Hostinského estetiky (Hostinský a Herbart)" (The Theoretical Basis of Hostinsky's Aesthetics: Hostinský and Herbart). *Filosofický časopis* 8 (1958): 311–14.

OTHER RELATED SOURCES

Aarsleff, Hans. "Bréal, 'la sémantique,' and Saussure." In his *From Locke to Saussure: Essays on the Study of Language and Intellectual History*. Minneapolis: University of Minnesota Press, 1982, pp. 382–98.

Abrams, M. H. *The Mirror and the Lamp: Romantic Theory and the Critical Tradition*. Oxford: Oxford University Press, 1953.

————. *Natural Supernaturalism: Tradition and Revolution in Romantic Literature*. New York: Norton, 1971.

Althusser, Louis. *For Marx*. Trans. Ben Brewster. New York: Pantheon, 1969.

————, and Etienne Balibar. *Reading Capital*. Trans. Ben Brewster. New York: Pantheon, 1970.

Amacher, Richard E., and Victor Lange, eds. *New Perspectives in German Literary Criticism: A Collection of Essays*. Princeton: Princeton University Press, 1979.

Arac, Jonathan. "History and Mystery: The Criticism of Frank Kermode." *Salmagundi* no. 55 (1982): 135–55.

Arato, Andrew, and Eike Gebhardt. *The Essential Frankfurt School Reader*. New York: Urizen Books, 1978.

Aristotle. *Aristotle's Theory of Poetry and Fine Art*. Trans. S. H. Butcher. New York: Dover, 1951.

————. *The Rhetoric and the Poetics*. Trans. W. Rhys Robert and Ingram Bywater. New York: Modern Library, 1954.

————. *La poétique*. Ed. and trans. Roselyne Dupont-Roc and Jean Lallot. Preface by Tzvetan Todorov. Paris: Seuil, 1980.

Auerbach, Eric. *Mimesis: The Representation of Reality in Western Literature*. Trans. Willard R. Trask. Princeton: Princeton University Press, 1953.

Augustine, Saint. *The Confessions*. Trans. John K. Ryan. Garden City, N.Y.: Image Books, 1960.

Bachtin, M. M. *Voprosy literatury i estetiki: Issledovanija raznych let* (The Problems of Literature and Aesthetics: Investigations from Various Years). Moskva: Chudožestvennaja nauka, 1975.

————. *Estetika slovesnogo tvorčestva* (The Aesthetics of Verbal Creation). Ed. S. G. Bočarov. Moskva: Iskusstvo, 1979.

————. *The Dialogic Imagination: Four Essays in the Philosophy of Language and Theory of the Novel*. Ed. Michael Holquist. Trans. Caryl Emerson and Michael Holquist. Austin: University of Texas Press, 1980.

Baran, Henryk, ed. *Semiotics and Structuralism: Readings from the Soviet Union*. White Plains, N.Y.: International Arts and Sciences Press, 1976.

Barthes, Roland. "History or Literature." In his *On Racine*. Trans. Richard Howard. New York: Hill and Wang, 1964, pp. 153–72.

————. *Critique et vérité*. Paris: Seuil, 1966.

————. *Elements of Semiology*. Trans. Annette Lavers and Colin Smith. London: Jonathan Cape, 1967.

————. *Image-Music-Text*. Trans. Stephen Heath. New York: Hill and Wang, 1977.

————. "Lecture in Inauguration of the Chair of Literary Semiology, Collège de France, January 7, 1977." *October* no. 8 (1979): 4–16. Rpt. in *A Barthes Reader*. Ed. Susan Sontag. New York: Hill and Wang, 1982, pp. 457–78.

————. *New Critical Essays*. Trans. Richard Howard. New York: Hill and Wang, 1980.

————. "Theory of the Text" (1978). Trans. Ian McLeod. In *Untying the Text: A Post-Structuralist Reader*. Ed. Robert Young. Boston: Routledge, 1981.

Bate, W. Jackson. *The Burden of the Past and the English Poet*. New York: Norton, 1970.

Bateson, Gregory. *Steps toward the Ecology of Mind: Collected Essays in Anthropology, Psychiatry, Evolution, and Epistemology*. San Francisco: Chandler, 1972.

————. *Mind and Nature: A Necessary Unity*. New York: Dutton, 1979.

Bauman, Richard. "Conceptions of Folklore in the Development of Literary Semiotics." *Semiotica* 39 (1982): 1–20.

Bazin, André. *What Is Cinema?* Trans. Hugh Gray. 2 vols. Berkeley: University of California Press, 1967 and 1971.

Beardsley, Monroe C. "The Metaphorical Twist." *Philosophy and Phenomenological Research* 22 (1962): 293–307.

Beckner, Morton. *The Biological Way of Thought*. New York: Columbia University Press, 1959.

Bělehrádek, Jan. "Holismus." *Biologické listy* 22 (1937): 169–79.

Benjamin, Walter. "Literaturgeschichte und Literaturwissenschaft." In his *Angelus Novus*. Frankfurt: Suhrkamp, 1966, pp. 450–56.

————. "Theses on the Philosophy of History." In his *Illuminations*. Ed. Hannah Arendt. New York: Schocken, 1968, pp. 253–64.

Bennett, Tony. *Formalism and Marxism*. London: Methuen, 1979.

Benoist, Jean-Marie. *The Structural Revolution*. New York: St. Martin's Press, 1978.

Benveniste, Emile. *Problems in General Linguistics*. Trans. Mary Elizabeth Meek. Coral Gables: University of Miami Press, 1971.

Berlin, Isaiah. *Vico and Herder: Two Studies in the History of Ideas*. New York: Random-Vintage, 1977.

————. "The Hedgehog and the Fox." In his *Russian Thinkers*. Ed. Henry Hardy and Aileen Kelley. New York: Viking, 1978, pp. 22–81.

Bertalanffy, Ludwig von. *General Systems Theory: Foundations, Development, Applications*. Rev. ed. New York: Braziller, 1968.

————. "Cultures as Systems: Toward a Critique of Historical Reason." In *Phenomenology, Structuralism, Semiology*. Ed. Harry R. Garvin. Lewisburg: Bucknell University Press, 1976, pp. 151–61.

Blanchard, Marc Eli. "Literary Semiotics, Stylistics, and Historical Models." *Semiotica* 40 (1982): 139–61.

Bloom, Harold. *The Anxiety of Influence: A Theory of Poetry*. New York: Oxford University Press, 1973.

Bouissac, Paul. "A Compass for Semiotics." Rev. of *Contributions to the Doctrine of Signs*, by T. A. Sebeok. *Ars Semeiotica* 2 (1979): 205–21.

Bruford, W. H. *Literary Interpretation in Germany*. Cambridge: Cambridge University Press, 1952.

Bruss, Elizabeth W. "Peirce and Jakobson on the Nature of the Sign." In *The Sign: Semiotics around the World*. Ed. R. W. Bailey et al. Ann Arbor: Michigan Slavic Publications, 1978, pp. 81–98.

————. "Signs and Practices: An Expanded Poetics." *Poetics* 7 (1978): 263–72.

Bühler, Karl. *Sprachtheorie: Die Darstellungsfunktion der Sprache*. Jena: Fischer, 1934.

Burke, Kenneth. *Language as Symbolic Action: Essays on Life, Literature, and Method*. Berkeley: University of California Press, 1966.

Burkhardt, Richard W., Jr. *The Spirit of System: Lamarck and Evolutionary Biology*. Cambridge, Mass.: Harvard University Press, 1977.

Burns, Elizabeth, and Tom Burns, eds. *Sociology of Literature and Drama*. Harmondsworth: Penguin, 1973.

Buyssens, Eric. *Linguistique historique: Homonymie, stylistique, sémantique, changements phonétiques*. Bruxelles: Presses Universitaires de Bruxelles, 1965.

Canary, Robert H., and Henry Kozicki, eds. *The Writing of History: Literary Form and Historical Understanding*. Madison: University of Wisconsin Press, 1978.

Carnap, Rudolf. *Meaning and Necessity: A Study in Semantics and Modal Logic*. 2nd ed. Chicago: University of Chicago Press, 1956.

Cassirer, Ernst. "Structuralism in Modern Linguistics." *Word* 1 (1945): 99–120.

————. *The Philosophy of Symbolic Forms*. Vol. 1, *Language*. Trans. Ralph Manheim. New Haven: Yale University Press, 1955.

Cavell, Stanley. *Must We Mean What We Say? A Book of Essays*. Cambridge: Cambridge University Press, 1976.

Chatman, Seymour, ed. *Literary Style: A Symposium*. London: Oxford University Press, 1971.

———, ed. *Approaches to Poetics*. New York: Columbia University Press, 1973.

Christiansen, Broder. *Philosophie der Kunst*. Hanau: Clauss, 1909.

Cohen, G. A. *Karl Marx's Theory of History: A Defence*. Princeton: Princeton University Press, 1979.

Cohen, Ralph, ed. *New Directions in Literary History*. Baltimore: Johns Hopkins University Press, 1974.

Collingwood, R. G. *Essays in the History of Philosophy*. Ed. William Debbins. Austin: University of Texas Press, 1965.

Culler, Jonathan. *Structuralist Poetics: Structuralism, Linguistics and the Study of Literature*. Ithaca: Cornell University Press, 1975.

———. *Ferdinand de Saussure*. Harmondsworth: Penguin, 1976.

———. *The Pursuit of Signs: Semiotics, Literature, Deconstruction*. Ithaca, N.Y.: Cornell University Press, 1981.

Curtis, James M. "Bergson and Russian Formalism." *Comparative Literature* 28 (1976): 109–21.

Danto, Arthur C. *The Transfiguration of the Commonplace: A Philosophy of Art*. Cambridge, Mass.: Harvard University Press, 1981.

de Man, Paul. "Form and Intent in the American New Criticism." In his *Blindness and Insight: Essays in the Rhetoric of Contemporary Criticism*. New York: Oxford University Press, 1971, pp. 20–35.

———. "Semiology and Rhetoric." In his *Allegories of Reading: Figural Language in Rousseau, Nietzsche, Rilke, and Proust*. New Haven: Yale University Press, 1979, pp. 3–19.

Derrida, Jacques. *Of Grammatology*. Trans. Gayatri Chakravorty Spivak. Baltimore: Johns Hopkins University Press, 1976.

———. *Writing and Difference*. Trans. Alan Bass. Chicago: University of Chicago Press, 1978.

Dessoir, Max. "Art History and Systematic Theories of Art." *Journal of Aesthetics and Art Criticism* 19 (1961): 463–69.

———. *Aesthetics and Theory of Art*. Trans. Stephen A. Emery. Detroit: Wayne State University Press, 1970.

Dijk, Teun van, and János S. Petöfi, eds. *Theory of Metaphor. Poetics* 4 (1975).

Dilthey, Wilhelm. *Pattern and Meaning in History: Thoughts on History and Society*. Ed. H. P. Rickman. New York: Harper, 1962.

Dohrn, Wolff. *Die kunstlerische Darstellung als Problem der Ästhetik*. Hamburg: Voss, 1907.

Doležel, Lubomir. "Eco and His Model Reader." Rev. of *The Role of the Reader: Explorations in the Semiotics of Text*, by Umberto Eco. *Poetics Today* 1 (1980): 181–88.

Donoghue, Denis. *Ferocious Alphabets*. Boston: Little, Brown, 1981.

Doroszewski, Witold. "Quelques remarques sur les rapports de la sociologie et de la linguistique: Durkheim et F. de Saussure." *Journal de psychologie* 30 (1933): 82–91.

Doubrovsky, Serge. *The New Criticism in France*. Trans. Derek Coltman. Chicago: University of Chicago Press, 1973.

Dray, William H., ed. *Philosophical Analysis and History*. New York: Harper, 1966.

Ducrot, Oswald, and Tzvetan Todorov. *Encyclopedic Dictionary of the Sciences of Language*. Trans. Catherine Porter. Baltimore: Johns Hopkins University Press, 1979.

Eaton, Howard O. *The Austrian Philosophy of Values*. Norman: University of Oklahoma Press, 1930.

Eco, Umberto. *The Role of the Reader: Explorations in the Semiotics of Texts*. Bloomington: Indiana University Press, 1979.

Ehrenfels, Christian von. "Über 'Gestaltqualitäten.'" *Vierteljahrsschrift für wissenschaftliche Philosophie* 14 (1890): 249–92.

Eliot, T. S. "Tradition and the Individual Talent" (1919). In his *Selected Essays*. New ed. New York: Harcourt, 1950, pp. 3–11.

Engliš, Karel. *Teleologie jako forma vědeckého poznání* (Teleology as a Form of Scientific Knowledge). Praha: Topič, 1930.

———. "O hodnotě a hodnocení" (On Value and Evaluation). *Filosofický časopis* 15 (1967): 117–31.

Erlich, Victor. "Some Pitfalls of Literary Structuralism." *Modern Occasions* 2 (1971): 518–26.

———. *Russian Formalism: History-Doctrine*. 3rd ed. New Haven: Yale University Press, 1981.

Even-Zohar, Itamar. *Papers in Historical Poetics*. Tel Aviv: Porter Institute for Poetics and Semiotics, 1978.

———. "Polysystem Theory." *Poetics Today* 1 (1979): 287–310.

Falk, Eugene H. *The Poetics of Roman Ingarden*. Chapel Hill: University of North Carolina Press, 1981.

Fayerabend, Paul. *Against Method: Outline of an Anarchistic Theory of Knowledge*. London: Verso, 1978.

Fechner, Gustav Theodor. *Vorschule der Aesthetik*. 2nd ed. Leipzig: Breitkopf, 1897.

Fieguth, Rolf. "Rezeption contra falsches und richtiges Lesen? Oder Mißverständnisse mit Ingarden." *Sprache im technischen Zeitalter* 38 (1971): 142–59.

Fleisher, Helmut. *Marxism and History*. Trans. Eric Mosbacher. New York: Harper, 1973.

Fodor, Jerry A., and Jerrold J. Katz, eds. *The Structure of Language: Readings in the Philosophy of Language*. Englewood Cliffs, N.J.: Prentice-Hall, 1964.

Foucault, Michel. *The Order of Things: An Archeology of the Human Sciences*. New York: Random House, 1970.

———. *The Archeology of Knowledge*. Trans. A. M. Sheridan Smith. New York: Harper, 1972.

———. *Language, Counter-Memory, Practice: Selected Essays and Interviews*. Ed. Donald F. Bouchard. Trans. Donald F. Bouchard and Sherry Simon. Ithaca, N.Y.: Cornell University Press, 1977.

Frank, Joseph. *The Widening Gyre: Crisis and Mastery in Modern Literature*. Bloomington: Indiana University Press, 1968.

Frye, Northrop. *Anatomy of Criticism: Four Essays*. Princeton: Princeton University Press, 1957.

———. "New Directions from Old." In his *Fables of Identity: Studies in Poetic Mythology*. New York: Harcourt, 1963, pp. 52–66.

————. "On Value-Judgements." In his *The Stubborn Structure: Essays on Criticism and Society*. Ithaca: Cornell University Press, 1970, pp. 66–73.

————. "Spengler Revisited." In his *Spiritus Mundy: Essays on Literature, Myth and Society*. Bloomington: Indiana University Press, 1976, pp. 179–98.

————. "Literature, History, and Language." *Bulletin of the Midwest Modern Language Association* 12 (1979): 1–7.

————. *The Great Code: The Bible and Literature*. New York: Harcourt, 1982.

Gablik, Suzi. *Progress in Art*. New York: Rizzoli, 1976.

Gadamer, Hans-Georg. *Truth and Method*. Trans. Garrett Barden and John Cumming. New York: Seabury, 1975.

————. *Philosophical Hermeneutics*. Trans. and ed. David E. Linge. Berkeley: University of California Press, 1976.

Galan, F. W. Rev. of *Structuralist Poetics: Structuralism, Linguistics and the Study of Literature*, by Jonathan Culler. *Clio* 5 (1976): 371–74.

————. Rev. of *A Theory of Semiotics*, by Umberto Eco. *Canadian Review of Comparative Literature* 4 (1977): 354–58.

————. Rev. of *Literature and Semiotics: A Study of the Writings of Yu. M. Lotman*, by Ann Shukman. *Canadian Review of Comparative Literature* 7 (1980): 468–73.

————. "Eichenbaum and Structuralism." Letter. *Times Literary Supplement*, 31 July 1981: 877.

————. Rev. of *Literary Criticism and the Structures of History*, by Geoffrey Green. *World Literature Today* 57 (1983): 519.

————, ed. *Poetics of Cinema: Readings in the History of Film Theory*. New York: Columbia University Press (forthcoming).

Gardiner, Patrick, ed. *Theories of History*. New York: Free Press, 1959.

————. *The Nature of Historical Explanation*. London: Oxford University Press, 1961.

Garson, Judith. "Literary History: Russian Formalist Views, 1916–1928." *Journal of the History of Ideas* 31 (1970): 399–412.

Gay, Peter. *Style in History*. New York: Basic Books, 1974.

Geertz, Clifford. *The Interpretation of Cultures: Selected Essays*. New York: Basic Books, 1973.

Gelley, Alexander. "Toward a Theory of History in Literature: Merleau-Ponty and Gadamer." *PTL: A Journal for Descriptive Poetics and Theory of Literature* 1 (1976): 357–66.

Gellner, Ernest. "What Is Structuralism?" *Times Literary Supplement*, 31 July 1981: 881–83.

Genette, Gérard. *Mimologiques: Voyage en Cratylie*. Paris: Seuil, 1976.

————. *Palimpsestes: La littérature au second degré*. Paris: Seuil, 1982.

Glowiński, Michal. "Theoretical Foundations of Historical Poetics." *New Literary History* 7 (1976): 237–45.

————. "Reading, Interpretation, Reception." *New Literary History* 11 (1979): 75–81.

Godel, Robert, ed. *A Geneva School Reader in Linguistics*. Bloomington: Indiana University Press, 1969.

Goldmann, Lucien. *Toward a Sociology of the Novel*. Trans. Alan Sheridan. London: Tavistock, 1975.

Goodman, Nelson. *Languages of Art: An Approach to a Theory of Symbols*. Indianapolis: Bobbs-Merrill, 1968.

Gould, Stephen Jay. *Ontogeny and Phylogeny*. Cambridge, Mass.: Harvard University Press, 1977.

Greenberg, Joseph H., ed. *Universals of Language*. Cambridge, Mass.: MIT Press, 1963.

———. "Synchronic and Diachronic Universals in Phonology." *Language* 42 (1966): 508–17.

Greimas, A. J. "Structure et histoire." In his *Du sens: Essais sémiotiques*. Paris: Seuil, 1970, pp. 103–16.

———. *Sémiotique et sciences sociales*. Paris: Seuil, 1976.

———, and J. Courtés. *Semiotics and Language: An Analytical Dictionary*. Trans. Larry Crist et al. Bloomington: Indiana University Press, 1982.

Guillén, Claudio. *Literature as System: Essays toward the Theory of Literary History*. Princeton: Princeton University Press, 1971.

———. "Literary Change and Multiple Duration." *Comparative Literature Studies* 14 (1977): 101–18.

Günther, Hans, ed. *Marxismus und Formalismus*. München: Hanser, 1973.

———. "Exakte Literaturwissenschaft und Kultursemiotik: Zwei Tendenzen im sowjetischen Strukturalismus." *LiLi* 4 (1974): 137–46.

———. "Literarische Evolution und Literaturgeschichte: Zum Beitrag des russischen Formalismus." In *Der Diskurs der Literatur- und Sprachgeschichte*. Ed. B. Cerquiglini and H. U. Gumbrecht. Frankfurt: Suhrkamp, 1983, pp. 265–79.

Habermas, Jürgen. *Communication and the Evolution of Society*. Trans. Thomas McCarthy. Boston: Beacon Press, 1979.

Halliday, Michael A. K. *Learning How to Mean: Explorations in the Development of Language*. London: Edward Arnold, 1975.

Hamburger, Käte. *The Logic of Literature*. Trans. Marilynn J. Rose. Bloomington: Indiana University Press, 1973.

Hansen-Löve, Aage A. *Der russische Formalismus: Methodologische Rekonstruktion seiner Entwicklung aus dem Prinzip der Verfremdung*. Wien: Verlag der Österreichischen Akademie der Wissenschaften, 1978.

———. "Semantik der Evolution und Evolution der Semantik: Ein Forschungsbericht zu I. P. Smirnovs Model einer diachronen Semiotik." *Wiener Slawistischer Almanach* no. 6 (1980): 131–90.

Harari, Josue V., ed. *Textual Strategies: Perspectives in Post-Structuralist Criticism*. Ithaca, N.Y.: Cornell University Press, 1979.

Harris, Zellig S. *Methods in Structural Linguistics*. Chicago: University of Chicago Press, 1951.

Hartman, Geoffrey. "Structuralism: The Anglo-American Adventure." In his *Beyond Formalism: Literary Essays, 1958–1970*. New Haven: Yale University Press, 1970, pp. 3–23.

———. *The Fate of Reading and Other Essays*. Chicago: University of Chicago Press, 1975.

———. *Criticism in the Wilderness: The Study of Literature Today*. New Haven: Yale University Press, 1980.

Hawkes, Terence. *Structuralism and Semiotics*. London: Methuen, 1977.

Hayden, Donald E., E. Paul Alworth, and Gary Tate, eds. *Classics in Linguistics*. New York: Philosophical Library, 1967.

Hempel, Carl G. "The Function of General Laws in History" (1942). In his *Aspects of Scientific Explanation*. New York: Free Press, 1965, pp. 231–43.

Hexter, J. H. *The History Primer*. New York: Basic Books, 1971.

Hirsch, David H. "Signs and Wonders." *Sewanee Review* 87 (1979): 628–38.

Hirsch, E. D., Jr. *The Aims of Interpretation*. Chicago: University of Chicago Press, 1976.

Hjelmslev, Louis. *Prolegomena to a Theory of Language*. Trans. Francis J. Whitfield. Madison: University of Wisconsin Press, 1969.

———. *Language: An Introduction*. Trans. Francis J. Whitfield. Madison: University of Wisconsin Press, 1970.

Hohendahl, Peter U. "Beyond Reception Aesthetics." *New German Critique* no. 28 (1983): 108–46.

Holub, Robert C. "The American Reception of Reception Theory." *German Quarterly* 55 (1982): 80–96.

———. *Reception Theory: A Critical Introduction*. London: Methuen, 1984.

Howard, Roy J. *Three Faces of Hermeneutics: An Introduction to Current Theories of Understanding*. Berkeley: University of California Press, 1982.

Hoy, David Couzens. *The Critical Circle: Literature and History in Contemporary Hermeneutics*. Berkeley: University of California Press, 1978.

Hrushovski, Benjamin. "Poetics, Criticism, Science: Remarks on the Fields and Responsibilities of the Study of Literature." *PTL: A Journal for Descriptive Poetics and Theory of Literature* 1 (1976): iii–xxxv.

———. "The Meaning of Sound Patterns in Poetry." *Poetics Today* 2 (1980): 39–56.

———. "The Structure of Semiotic Objects: A Three-Dimensional Model." *The Sign in Music and Literature*. Ed. Wendy Steiner. Austin: University of Texas Press, 1981, pp. 11–25.

Husserl, Edmund. "Philosophy and the Crisis of European Man." In his *Phenomenology and the Crisis of Philosophy*. Trans. Quentin Lauer. New York: Harper, 1965, pp. 149–92.

———. *Ideas: General Introduction to Pure Phenomenology*. Trans. W. R. Boyce Gibson. New York: Humanities Press, 1968.

Ingarden, Roman. *The Cognition of the Literary Work*. Trans. Ruth Ann Crowley and Kenneth R. Olson. Evanston: Northwestern University Press, 1973.

———. *The Literary Work of Art*. Trans. George G. Grabowicz. Evanston: Northwestern University Press, 1973.

Jacob, François. *The Logic of Life: A History of Heredity*. Trans. Betty E. Spillman. New York: Pantheon, 1973.

Jameson, Fredric. *The Prison-House of Language: A Critical Account of Structuralism and Russian Formalism*. Princeton: Princeton University Press, 1972.

Janik, Allan, and Stephen Toulmin. *Wittgenstein's Vienna*. New York: Simon and Schuster, 1973.

Jauss, Hans Robert. *Aesthetic Experience and Literary Hermeneutics*. Trans. Michael Shaw. Minneapolis: University of Minnesota Press, 1982.

———. *Toward an Aesthetics of Reception*. Trans. Timothy Bahti. Minneapolis: University of Minnesota Press, 1982.

Jonas, Hans. "Change and Permanence: On the Possibility of Understanding History." *Social Research* 38 (1971): 498–528.

Kahler, Erich. *The Meaning of History*. New York: George Braziller, 1964.

———. *Out of the Labyrinth: Essays in Clarification*. New York: George Braziller, 1967.

Keiler, Allan R., ed. *A Reader in Historical and Comparative Linguistics*. New York: Holt, 1972.

Kelsen, Hans. "The Pure Theory of Law and Analytic Jurisprudence." *Harvard Law Review* 55 (1941): 44–70.

———. *The Pure Theory of Law*. Trans. Max Knight. Berkeley: University of California Press, 1970.

Kermode, Frank. *The Sense of an Ending: Studies in the Theory of Fiction*. London: Oxford University Press, 1967.

King, Robert D. *Historical Linguistics and Generative Grammar*. Englewood Cliffs, N.J.: Prentice-Hall, 1969.

Kloepfer, Rolf. "Escape into Reception: The Scientistic and Hermeneutic School of German Literary Theory." *Poetics Today* 3 (1982): 47–75.

Koffka, Kurt. *Principles of Gestalt Psychology*. New York: Harcourt, 1935.

———. "Problems in the Psychology of Art." In *Art: A Bryn Mawr Symposium*. Bryn Mawr College, 1940, pp. 180–273.

Kohler, Wolfgang, *The Task of Gestalt Psychology*. Princeton: Princeton University Press, 1969.

Korpan, Barbara D. "Literary Evolution as Style: The 'Intrinsic Historicity' of Northrop Frye and Juri Tynianov." *Pacific Coast Philology* 2 (1967): 47–52.

Kracauer, Siegfried. *History: The Last Things before the Last*. New York: Oxford University Press, 1969.

Kraus, Oskar. *Die Werttheorien: Geschichte und Kritik*. Brünn: Rohrer, 1937.

———. "Wert, Norm und Recht." In *Travaux du IXe Congrès international de Philosophie*. Ed. Raymond Bayer. Paris: Hermann, 1937, pp. 16–21.

Kristeva, Julia. *Semeiotikè: Recherches pour une sémanalyse*. Paris: Seuil, 1969.

———. *Desire in Language: A Semiotic Approach to Literature and Art*. Ed. Leon S. Roudiez. New York: Columbia University Press, 1980.

Kubler, George. *The Shape of Time: Remarks on the History of Things*. New Haven: Yale University Press, 1962.

Kuhn, Thomas S. *The Structure of Scientific Revolutions*. 2nd ed. Chicago: University of Chicago Press, 1970.

———. *The Essential Tension: Selected Studies in Scientific Tradition and Change*. Chicago: University of Chicago Press, 1977.

Kurzweil, Edith. *The Age of Structuralism: Lévi-Strauss to Foucault*. New York: Columbia University Press, 1980.

Labov, William. *Sociolinguistic Patterns*. Philadelphia: University of Pennsylvania Press, 1972.

Lacan, Jacques. *The Language of the Self: The Function of Language in Psychoanalysis*. Trans. Anthony Wilden. New York: Dell, 1968.

———. "On Jakobson." *Gradiva* 1 (1977): 152–60.

LaCapra, Dominick, and Steven L. Kaplan, eds. *Modern European Intellectual History: Reappraisals and New Perspectives*. Ithaca, N.Y.: Cornell University Press, 1982.

Lakatos, Imre, and Alan Musgrave, eds. *Criticism and the Growth of Knowledge*. London: Cambridge University Press, 1970.

Landesman, Charles, ed. *The Problem of Universals*. New York: Basic Books, 1971.

Landgrebe, Ludwig. *The Phenomenology of Edmund Husserl: Six Essays*. Ed. Donn Welton. Ithaca, N.Y.: Cornell University Press, 1981.

Langer, Susanne K. *Philosophy in a New Key: A Study in the Symbolism of Reason, Rite, and Art*. Cambridge, Mass.: Harvard University Press, 1942.

———. *Feeling and Form*. New York: Scribner's, 1953.

Lass, Roger, ed. *Approaches to English Historical Linguistics: An Anthology*. New York: Holt, 1969.

Lehmann, Winfred P. *Historical Linguistics: An Introduction*. 2nd ed. New York: Holt, 1973.

———, and Yakov Malkiel, eds. *Directions for Historical Linguistics: A Symposium*. Austin: University of Texas Press, 1968.

Levin, Harry. "Literature as an Institution" (1946). Rpt. in *Literary Opinion in America*. Vol. 2. Ed. Morton Dauwen Zabel. New York: Harper, 1962, pp. 655–66.

Levin, Samuel R. *The Semantics of Metaphor*. Baltimore: Johns Hopkins University Press, 1977.

Lévi-Strauss, Claude. *Structural Anthropology*. Trans. Claire Jakobson and Brooke Grundfest Schoepf. New York: Basic Books, 1963.

———. "History and Dialectic." In his *The Savage Mind*. Chicago: University of Chicago Press, 1966, pp. 245–69.

———. *Structural Anthropology*. Vol. 2. Trans. Monique Layton. New York: Basic Books, 1976.

Linsky, Leonard, ed. *Semantics and the Philosophy of Language: A Collection of Readings*. Urbana: University of Illinois Press, 1952.

Lodge, David. *Working with Structuralism: Essays and Reviews on Nineteenth- and Twentieth-Century Literature*. London: Routledge, 1981.

Lotman, Jurij. *Semiotics of Cinema*. Trans. Mark E. Suino. Ann Arbor: Michigan Slavic Contributions, 1976.

———. *The Structure of the Artistic Text*. Trans. Ronald Vroon. Ann Arbor: Michigan Slavic Contributions, 1977.

———. "The Text and the Structure of Its Audience." *New Literary History* 14 (1982): 81–87.

Lucid, Daniel P., ed. *Soviet Semiotics: An Anthology*. Baltimore: Johns Hopkins University Press, 1977.

Lukács, Georg. *History and Class Consciousness: Studies in Marxist Dialectics* (1923). Trans. Rodney Livingstone. Cambridge, Mass.: MIT Press, 1971.

———. "Zur Theorie der Literaturgeschichte." *Text + Kritik* nos. 39–40 (1973): 24–51.

Luria, S. E. "What Can Biologists Solve?" *New York Review of Books*, 7 February 1974: 27–28.

Lyons, John. "Semantics: General Principles." In his *Introduction to Theoretical Linguistics*. Cambridge: Cambridge University Press, 1968, pp. 400–481.

———. *Semantics*. 2 vols. Cambridge: Cambridge University Press, 1977.

Macherey, Pierre. *A Theory of Literary Production*. Trans. Geoffrey Wall. London: Routledge, 1978.

Macksey, Richard, and Eugenio Donato, eds. *The Structuralist Controversy: The Languages of Criticism and the Sciences of Man*. Baltimore: Johns Hopkins University Press, 1970.

Mandelbaum, Maurice. *The Problem of Historical Knowledge: An Answer to Relativism*. New York: Harper Torchbooks, 1967.

Mannheim, Karl. "Structural Analysis of Epistemology." In his *Essays on Sociology and Social Psychology*. Ed. Paul Kecskemeti. New York: Oxford University Press, 1953, pp. 15–73.

Marcus, Steven. "Limits of Literary History." In his *Representations: Essays on Literature and Society*. New York: Random House, 1975, pp. 129–36.

Martin, Wallace. "The Epoch of Critical Theory." *Comparative Literature* 31 (1979): 321–50.

Martinet, André. "Structural Linguistics." In *Anthropology Today*. Ed. A. L. Kroeber. Chicago: University of Chicago Press, 1953, pp. 574–86.

———. *Elements of General Linguistics*. Trans. Elisabeth Palmer. Chicago: University of Chicago Press, 1966.

Martínez-Bonati, Felix. "Roman Jakobson's Conception of the Poetic Function of Language." In his *Fictive Discourse and the Structures of Literature: A Phenomenological Approach*. Trans. Philip W. Silver with the author. Ithaca, N.Y.: Cornell University Press, 1981, pp. 141–52.

Masaryk, Thomas G. *Versuch einer concreten Logik (Classification und Organisation der Wissenschaften)*. Rpt. of the 1887 ed. Osnabrück: Biblio, 1970.

Mast, Gerald, and Marshall Cohen, eds. *Film Theory and Criticism: Introductory Readings*. New York: Oxford University Press, 1974.

Matejka, Ladislav. "On the First Russian Prolegomena to Semiotics." In V. N. Vološinov, *Marxism and the Philosophy of Language*. Trans. Ladislav Matejka and I. R. Titunik. New York: Seminar Press, 1973, pp. 161–74.

———. "The Roots of Russian Semiotics of Art." In *The Sign: Semiotics around the World*. Ed. R. W. Bailey et al. Ann Arbor: Michigan Slavic Publications, 1978, pp. 146–72.

Mayenowa, Maria Renata. *Poetyka teoretyczna: Zagadnienia języka* (Theoretical Poetics: The Questions of Language). 2nd ed. Wroclaw (Breslau): Zaklad Narodowy imienia Ossolińskich, 1979.

Mazzeo, Joseph Anthony. *Varieties of Interpretation*. Notre Dame: University of Notre Dame Press, 1978.

Medvedev, P. N./Bakhtin, M. M. *The Formal Method in Literary Scholarship: A Critical Introduction to Sociological Poetics*. Trans. Albert J. Wehrle. Baltimore: Johns Hopkins University Press, 1978.

Mehlman, Jeffrey. *Revolution and Repetition: Marx/Hugo/Balzac*. Berkeley: University of California Press, 1977.

Merleau-Ponty, Maurice. "The Film and the New Psychology." In his *Sense and Non-Sense*. Trans. Hubert L. and Patricia Allen Dreyfus. Evanston: Northwestern University Press, 1964, pp. 48–59.

Metz, Christian. *Film Language: A Semiotics of the Cinema* (1968). Trans. Michael Taylor. New York: Oxford University Press, 1974.

Miner, Earl. "The Objective Fallacy and the Real Existence of Literature." *PTL: A Journal for Descriptive Poetics and Theory of Literature* 1 (1976): 11–31.

Mink, Louis O. *Mind, History and Dialectic: The Philosophy of R. G. Collingwood*. Bloomington: Indiana University Press, 1969.

Momigliano, Arnaldo. *Essays in Ancient and Modern Historiography*. Oxford: Blackwell, 1975.

Monod, Jacques. *Chance and Necessity: An Essay on the Natural Philosophy of Modern Biology*. Trans. Austryn Wainhause. New York: Random-Vintage, 1971.

Morris, Charles W. "Foundation of the Theory of the Signs." In *International Encyclopedia of United Science*. Vol. 1. Chicago: University of Chicago Press, 1938.

———. "Esthetics and the Theory of Signs." *Journal of Unified Science (Erkenntnis)* 8 (1939): 131–50.

———. *Signs, Language and Behavior*. New York: George Braziller, 1946.

Morris, Wesley. *Toward a New Historicism*. Princeton: Princeton University Press, 1972.

Moulton, William G. "Types of Phonemic Change." In *To Honor Roman Jakobson: Essays on the Occasion of His Seventieth Birthday*. The Hague: Mouton, 1967, pp. 1393–1407.

Naumann, Hans, ed. *Der moderne Strukturbegriff: Materialien zu seiner Entwicklung*. Darmstadt: Wissenschaftliche Buchgesellschaft, 1973.

New Literary History. Special issues *History and Criticism* 5 (Spring 1974) and 6 (Spring 1975).

Ogden, C. K., and I. A. Richards. *The Meaning of Meaning: A Study of the Influence of Language upon Thought and of the Science of Symbolism*. New York: Harcourt, 1923.

Ortega y Gasset, José. *History as a System and Other Essays toward a Philosophy of History*. New York: Norton, 1961.

———. *The Dehumanization of Art and Other Essays on Art, Culture, and Literature*. Trans. Helene Weyl. 2nd ed. Princeton: Princeton University Press, 1968.

Patočka, Jan. "Husserlův pojem názoru a prafenomén jazyka" (Husserl's Notion of Intuitive Idea and the Primal Phenomenon of Language). *Sl. sl.* 29 (1968): 17–22.

Peirce, C. S. "Logic as Semiotic: The Theory of Signs." In *Philosophical Writings of Peirce*. Ed. Justus Buchler. New York: Dover, 1955, pp. 98–119.

Pettit, Philip. *The Concept of Structuralism: A Critical Analysis*. Berkeley: University of California Press, 1977.

Piaget, Jean. *Structuralism*. Trans. Chaninah Maschler. New York: Harper, 1970.

Picard, Raymond. *Nouvelle critique ou nouvelle imposture*. Paris: Pauvert, 1965.

Pike, Christopher, ed. *The Futurists, the Formalists, and the Marxist Critique*. Atlantic Highlands, N.J.: Humanities Press, 1979.

Pomorska, Krystyna. *Russian Formalist Theory and Its Poetic Ambiance*. The Hague: Mouton, 1968.

——. "The Legacy of the Opojaz." *Russian Literature* 14 (1983): 229–40.

Popper, Karl R. *The Poverty of Historicism*. London: Routledge, 1957.

——. *The Logic of Scientific Discovery*. Rev. ed. New York: Basic Books, 1968.

Posner, Roland. "Poetic Communication vs. Literary Language: The Linguistic Fallacy in Poetics." *PTL: A Journal for Descriptive Poetics and Theory* 1 (1976): 1–10.

Pospíšilová, Anna. "Ruský formalism." *Listy pro umění a kritiku* 1 (1933): 407–12.

Richards, I. A. *Principles of Literary Criticism*. New York: Harcourt, 1925.

——. *Poetries, Their Media, and Ends: A Collection of Essays*. Ed. Trevor Eaton. The Hague: Mouton, 1974.

Ricoeur, Paul. *Interpretation Theory: Discourse and the Surplus of Meaning*. Fort Worth: Texas Christian University Press, 1976.

——. *The Rule of Metaphor: Multi-Disciplinary Studies of the Creation of Meaning in Language*. Trans. Paul Czerny et al. Toronto: University of Toronto Press, 1977.

——. "*Anatomy of Criticism* or the Order of Paradigms." Trans. David Pellaner. In *Centre and Labyrinth: Essays in Honour of Northrop Frye*. Ed. Eleanor Cook et al. Toronto: University of Toronto Press, 1983, pp. 1–13.

Riffaterre, Michael. *Semiotics of Poetry*. Bloomington: Indiana University Press, 1979.

——. "Toward a Formal Approach to Literary History." In his *Text Production*. New York: Columbia University Press, 1983, pp. 90–110.

Robey, David, ed. *Structuralism: An Introduction*. Oxford: Clarendon Press, 1973.

Rosengrant, Sandra. "The Theoretical Criticism of Jurij Tynjanov." *Comparative Literature* 32 (1980): 355–89.

Rudnick, Hans H. "The Concretization of Meaning: Roman Ingarden." *Semiotica* 41 (1982): 247–55.

Sacks, Sheldon, ed. *On Metaphor*. Chicago: University of Chicago Press, 1979.

Said, Edward W. "*Abecedarium Culturae*: Absence, Writing, Statement, Discourse, Archeology, Structuralism." In his *Beginnings: Intention and Method*. New York: Basic Books, 1975, pp. 277–343.

Sapir, Edward. *Language: An Introduction to the Study of Speech*. New York: Harcourt, 1921.

Saussure, Ferdinand de. *Course in General Linguistics*. Trans. Wade Baskin. New York: McGraw-Hill, 1966.

Schlaffer, Hannelore, and Heinz Schlaffer. *Studien zum ästhetischen Historismus*. Frankfurt: Suhrkamp, 1975.

Schmidt, Siegfried J. "Selected Bibliography on Interpretation (1970–1982)." *Poetics* 12 (1983): 277–83.

Scholes, Robert. *Structuralism in Literature: An Introduction*. New Haven: Yale University Press, 1974.

Schon, Donald A. *Invention and the Evolution of Ideas*. London: Tavistock, 1963.

Sebeok, Thomas A. *Contributions to the Doctrine of Signs*. Atlantic Highlands: Humanities Press, n.d.

————, ed. *Style in Language*. Cambridge, Mass.: MIT Press, 1960.

Segers, Rien T. "Readers, Text and Author: Some Implications of *Rezeptionsäs-thetik*." *Yearbook of Comparative and General Literature* 24 (1975): 15–23.

Segre, Cesare. *Structures and Time: Narration, Poetry, Models*. Trans. John Med-demmen. Chicago: University of Chicago Press, 1979.

Serres, Michel. *Hermes: Literature, Science, Philosophy*. Ed. Josue V. Harari and David F. Bell. Baltimore: Johns Hopkins University Press, 1982.

Seung, T. K. *Structuralism and Hermeneutics*. New York: Columbia University Press, 1981.

————. *Semiotics and Thematics in Hermeneutics*. New York: Columbia University Press, 1982.

Simmel, Georg. *On Individuality and Social Forms: Selected Writings*. Ed. Donald N. Levine. Chicago: University of Chicago Press, 1971.

Singleton, Charles S., ed. *Interpretation: Theory and Practice*. Baltimore: Johns Hopkins University Press, 1969.

Smirnov, I. P. *Chudožestvennyj smysl i evoljucija poetičeskich sistem* (Artistic Mean-ing and the Evolution of Poetic Systems). Moskva: Nauka, 1977.

Smuts, J. C. *Holism and Evolution*. New York: Macmillan, 1926.

Sontag, Susan. *Against Interpretation and Other Essays*. New York: Dell, 1966.

Sparshott, F. E. *The Structure of Aesthetics*. Toronto: University of Toronto Press, 1963.

————. *The Theory of the Arts*. Princeton: Princeton University Press, 1982.

Spitzer, Leo. *Linguistics and Literary History: Essays in Stylistics*. Princeton: Prince-ton University Press, 1948.

Starobinski, Jean. "The Meaning of Literary History." *New Literary History* 7 (1975): 83–88.

————. "Criticism and Authority." In *Discoveries and Interpretations: Studies in Contemporary Scholarship*. Vol. 2. Special issue of *Daedalus* 106 (1977): 1–16.

Steiner, Peter. "Three Metaphors of Russian Formalism." *Poetics Today* 2 (1980–1981): 59–116.

————. *Russian Formalism: A Metapoetics*. Ithaca, N.Y.: Cornell University Press (forthcoming).

Stern, Fritz, ed. *The Varieties of History: From Voltaire to the Present*. 2nd ed. New York: Random House, 1972.

Stern, J. P. "The Weltangst of Oswald Spengler." *Times Literary Supplement*, 10 October 1980: 149–52.

Striedter, Jurij. "The Russian Formalist Theory of Prose." Trans. Michael Nichol-son. *PTL: A Journal for Descriptive Poetics and Theory of Literature* 3 (1977): 429–70.

————. "The Russian Formalist Theory of Literary Evolution." Trans. Michael Nicholson. *PTL: A Journal for Descriptive Poetics and Theory of Literature* 3 (1978): 1–24.

Sturrock, John, ed. *Structuralism and Since: From Lévi-Strauss to Derrida*. Oxford: Oxford University Press, 1979.

Suleiman, Susan R. and Inge Crosman, eds. *The Reader in the Text: Essays on Au-dience and Interpretation*. Princeton: Princeton University Press, 1980.

Svoboda, Karel. "La théorie gréco-romaine du signe linguistique." *Časopis pro moderní filologii* 26 (1939): 38–49.

Szondi, Peter. *Poetik und Geschichtsphilosophie.* Vols. 2 and 3 of his *Studienausgabe der Vorlesungen.* Frankfurt: Suhrkamp, 1974.

Thom, René. *Structural Stability and Morphogenesis: An Outline of a General Theory of Models.* Trans. D. H. Fowler. Reading, Mass.: W. A. Benjamin, 1975.

Thompson, Ewa M. *Russian Formalism and Anglo-American New Criticism: A Comparative Study.* The Hague: Mouton, 1971.

Todorov, Tzvetan. "Some Approaches to Russian Formalism." Trans. Bruce Merry. In *Russian Formalism.* Ed. Stephen Bann and John E. Bowlt. Edinburgh: Scottish Academic Press, 1973, pp. 6–19.

———. *Symbolisme et interprétation.* Paris: Seuil, 1977.

———. *Théories du symbole.* Paris: Seuil, 1977. (*Theories of Symbol.* Abridged version. Trans. Catherine Porter. Ithaca, N.Y.: Cornell University Press, 1982.)

———. *Introduction to Poetics.* Trans. Richard Howard. Minneapolis: University of Minnesota Press, 1981.

———. *Mikhaïl Bakhtine: Le principe dialogique.* Paris: Seuil, 1981.

———, ed. *French Literary Theory Today: A Reader.* Cambridge: Cambridge University Press, 1982.

Tomkins, Jane P., ed. *Reader-Response Criticism: From Formalism to Post-Structuralism.* Baltimore: Johns Hopkins University Press, 1980.

Turner, Victor. *The Ritual Process: Structure and Anti-Structure.* Ithaca, N.Y.: Cornell University Press, 1969.

Uitti, Karl D. *Linguistics and Literary Theory.* Englewood Cliffs, N.J.: Prentice-Hall, 1969.

Ullmann, Stephen, *Semantics: An Introduction to the Science of Meaning.* Oxford: Blackwell, 1962.

Utitz, Emil. *Grundlegung der allgemeinen Kunstwissenschaft.* 2 vols. Stuttgart: Enke, 1914.

Van der Eng, Jan, and Mojmír Grygar, eds. *Structure of Texts and Semiotics of Culture.* The Hague: Mouton, 1973.

Vietor, Karl. "Deutsche Literaturgeschichte als Geistesgeschichte: Ein Rückblick." *PMLA* 60 (1945): 899–916.

Vološinov, V. N. *Marxism and Philosophy of Language.* Trans. Ladislav Matejka and I. R. Titunik. New York: Seminar Press, 1973.

Wellek, René. "The Fall of Literary History." In *Geschichte—Ereignis und Erzählung.* Ed. Reinhart Kosselleck and Wolf-Dieter Stempel. München: Fink, 1973.

———. "Reflections on My *History of Modern Criticism.*" *PTL: A Journal for Descriptive Poetics and Theory of Literature* 3 (1977): 417–27.

———. *Four Critics: Croce, Valéry, Lukács, and Ingarden.* Seattle: University of Washington Press, 1981.

———. *The Attack on Literature and Other Essays.* Chapel Hill: University of North Carolina Press, 1982.

———, and Austin Warren. *Theory of Literature.* New York: Hart, 1949.

Wertheimer, Max. "Gestalt Theory." *Social Research* 11 (1944): 78–99.

White, Hayden. *Metahistory: The Historical Imagination in Nineteenth-Century Europe*. Baltimore: Johns Hopkins University Press, 1973.

———. *Topics of Discourse: Essays on Cultural Criticism*. Baltimore: Johns Hopkins University Press, 1978.

White, Morton. *Foundations of Historical Knowledge*. New York: Harper, 1965.

Whorf, Benjamin Lee. *Language, Thought and Reality: Selected Writings*. Ed. John B. Carroll. Cambridge, Mass.: MIT Press, 1956.

Wilden, Anthony. *System and Structure: Essays in Communication and Exchange*. 2nd rev. ed. London: Tavistock, 1980.

Williams, Raymond. *Problems in Materialism and Culture: Selected Essays*. London: NLB, 1980.

———. *The Sociology of Culture*. New York: Schocken, 1982.

Wimsatt, W. K., Jr. *The Verbal Icon: Studies in the Meaning of Poetry*. Lexington: University of Kentucky Press, 1954.

———. "Organic Form: Some Questions about a Metaphor." In his *Day of the Leopards: Essays in Defense of Poems*. New Haven: Yale University Press, 1976, pp. 205–23.

Winner, Irene Porter. "Cultural Semiotics and Anthropology." In *The Sign: Semiotics around the World*. Ed. R. W. Bailey et al. Ann Arbor: Michigan Slavic Publications, 1978, pp. 335–63.

Wölfflin, Heinrich. *Principles of Art History: The Problem of the Development of Style in Later Art* (1915). Trans. M. D. Hottinger. New York: Dover, 1950.

Yale French Studies nos. 36–37 (1966). Issue on structuralism.

Zabeeh, Farhang, E. D. Klemke, and Arthur Jacobson, eds. *Readings in Semantics*. Urbana: University of Illinois Press, 1974.

Žirmunskij, V. M. "O sinchronii i diachronii v jazykoznanii" (Synchrony and Diachrony in Language Studies). *Voprosy jazykoznanija* 5 (1958): 43–52.

Zolkiewski, Stefan. "Conceptions for a Theory of Literary Production." Trans. Elias J. Schwartz and Valentine Urbanek. In *Language, Literature and Meaning II: Current Trends in Literary Research*. Ed. John Odmark. Amsterdam: Benjamins, 1980, pp. 141–99.

Index

actualization (*aktualizace*), 19–22;
  Mukařovský on, 29–30, 45, 55, 203;
  Vodička on, 153, 155, 157
aesthetic experience, 73, 153–155. *See
  also* reception theory
aesthetic object, 57, 58, 69, 204; Mukařovský on, 75, 121–122, 153, 171;
  Vodička on, 153, 154, 159–161
aesthetics, 32, 59; Herbartian, 23, 43*n*;
  Hussite, 128; Mukařovský on, 57, 63,
  172, 175, 184, 188
anthropological constants, 168–174, 177,
  181
Antonioni, Michelangelo, 95; *The
  Eclipse* (*L'Eclisse*, 1962), 95
Aristotle, 76–77, 89, 91, 92, 96, 117,
  152, 161, 205; *Poetics*, 76, 117, 161
Arnheim, Rudolf, 95, 102
artist, 168–172, 180, 184–193, 204.
  See also author; individual, the;
  personality
Ascham, Roger, 47
asymmetric dualism, 87–89, 109
audience, 105, 182. *See also* reception
  theory; viewer
Auerbach, Erich, 57
Augustine, Saint, 82–83, 94; *Confessions*, 82
author, 157, 159, 179–182, 186–189. *See
  also* artist; individual, the; personality
automatization (*automatizace*), 19, 157;
  Jakobson on, 109, 114; Mukařovský
  on, 29, 45, 55, 153, 203. *See also* deautomatization

Bachtin, Michail, 82, 133*n*
Bachtin, Nicholas, 133*n*
Balázs, Béla, 136*n*
Bally, Charles, 10
Banville, Théodore de, 144–146
Baroque, 118, 128, 151, 178, 191
Barthes, Roland, 3, 77*n*, 136*n*
Baudelaire, Charles, 144–147
Bazin, André, 97
Beer, Kurt. *See* Konrad, Kurt
Bém, Alfred, 62–64, 67
Benjamin, Walter, 3
Béranger, Pierre Jean de, 144, 146–
  148
Bierce, Ambrose, 104
Bishop, Elizabeth, 205
Blake, William, 157, 202*n*; Prophetic
  Books, 157
Bogatyrev, Petr, 55, 59, 62
Boileau-Despréaux, Nicolas, 158
Bréal, Michel, 83; *Essai de sémantique*,
  83
Brentano-Gesellschaft, 175
Breton, André, 62, 123; *Les vases com-
  municants*, 123
Březina, Otokar, 144, 145
Brik, Osip, 23
Bruford, W. H., 24
Brunetière, Ferdinand, 67
Bühler, Karl, 70–72, 77, 80*n*, 82, 118,
  175; Organon-model of, 71, 73, 169;
  *Sprachtheorie: Die Darstellungsfunktion
  der Sprache*, 71
Byron, George Gordon, 24, 146, 148

canon, literary, 21, 30, 33, 45, 110, 129.
    See also norm
Čapek, Karel, 197n
Carducci, Giosuè, 145
Cassirer, Ernst, 68, 82
Cercle Linguistique, 175
Cercle Philosophique, 175
Cervantes, Miguel de, 37; Don Quixote,
    37, 51
Červenka, Miroslav, 200n
Chaplin, Charles, 27–28, 98; City Lights
    (1931), 27–28
Charles IV, 127
Charles University, 56, 199n
Chateaubriand, François René de, 163–
    164; Atala, 163
Cheke, Sir John, 47
Chicago School, 76
Chlebnikov, Velemir, 109, 110
Christiansen, Broder, 57
classicism, 110, 118, 122, 123, 127, 158,
    159, 166, 169; mimetic orientation of,
    152
Coleridge, Samuel Taylor, 30
concretizations, 73, 153–158, 160–162
contexture, 115, 116, 123, 203
Copenhagen School, 17
Counter Reformation, 151
Curtius, E. R., 57
Cyril, Saint, 126, 130, 132
Czech language, 14, 17, 40n, 47, 49,
    127–130, 132, 149, 150, 190
Czech literature: Jakobson on, 108,
    126–133, 142; Mukařovský on, 36,
    46–53, 56, 65, 149–152, 173, 190;
    Vodička on, 144, 163. See also names
    of individual authors

dadaism, 110, 113
deautomatization, 99, 103, 153. See also
    automatization
dephonologization, 88
diachrony, 6–17, 40n; Jakobson on, 129,
    202; Mukařovský on, 23, 30, 165, 172,
    184, 193; Vodička on, 153, 156, 157,
    160
Dilthey, Wilhelm, 2
dominant (dominanta), 27–32, 36, 54–
    56, 59, 60, 65, 158; defined, 29;
    Jakobson on, 108, 133; Mukařovský
    on, 33, 35, 122, 150, 153

Donne, John, 157
Dostoevskij, Fedor, 62, 117, 172; Crime
    and Punishment, 117, 172
Durkheim, Emile, 83

Eichenbaum, Boris, 99, 112, 136n
Eighth International Congress of Phi-
    losophy, 114
Einstein, Albert, 62
Eisenstein, Sergei, 95
Eliot, T. S., 6, 45, 196n
Erben, Karel Jaromír, 192
Erlich, Victor, 9, 110
Ermantiger, Emil, 3; Philosophie der Li-
    teraturgeschichte, 3
evolution, literary: 2–4, 23, 36–38, 122,
    126, 142, 166; Jakobson on, 8–10, 21,
    22; Mukařovský on, 25–27, 31, 36,
    46, 47, 53–55, 61, 63, 74–76, 123,
    124, 143, 150–151, 189–193, 202, 203,
    205; Saussure on, 11; Vodička on, 148,
    152, 153, 156, 158, 160, 163; Wellek
    on, 65, 67, 70

Fechner, Gustav Theodor, 74
film, 82, 94, 133, 182, 203; Jakobson on,
    93–97, 100, 106, 109, 110; and litera-
    ture, 99–101, 149; Mukařovský on,
    97–106; space in, 98, 99, 102; time in,
    97, 102–105, 110
First Congress of Slavicists (1929), 17, 76
First Congress of Soviet Writers (1934),
    60
First International Congress of Lin-
    guists, 10
First Phonological Congress (1930), 13
Flaubert, Gustave, 134n; Madame Bo-
    vary, 134n
form/content, 37, 130, 150
formalism, 29, 32, 38, 43n, 56, 59, 76,
    82, 83, 114, 143, 152; Bém and, 62–
    64; Jakobson and, 42n, 106, 107, 109,
    119; Mukařovský and, 24, 26, 27, 31,
    35–37, 44, 51–53, 74, 78n, 89, 93,
    97, 110, 119, 177, 180, 183, 204; on os-
    tranenie, 110; Russian, 2–4, 6, 10,
    22–23, 60, 115, 144, 202, 203 (see also
    Opojaz)
Frankfurt School, 61
Frege, Gottlob, 83; "Über Sinn und
    Bedeutung," 83

Frye, Northrop, 6, 47, 57, 64, 67, 162; *Anatomy of Criticism*, 6

function: aesthetic/poetic, 19, 23, 34, 46, 55, 56, 72, 91, 106–108, 113, 117, 119, 129, 150, 152, 168, 175, 179, 203–205; appellant/conative, 72, 118, 152; expressive, 28, 72, 118, 119, 152; informational, 119; metalinguistic, 72, 124; Mukařovský's typology of, 176–179; phatic, 72; referential/communicative, 19, 72, 107, 118, 119, 124, 152, 203; representational, 118, 119; social, 35, 55

functional dialects, 41n, 72, 115, 167

Geistesgeschichte, 2, 3, 143

Geneva School, 3, 10, 84

genre, 25, 57, 65, 75, 119, 120, 128, 150, 157, 167; defined, 26; epic, 24–26, 33, 52, 128, 131; lyric, 105, 106, 111, 119, 128, 148; Jakobson on, 111–112; Mukařovský on, 52, 53, 126, 191; "Theses" on, 21; Tomaševskij on, 22; Vodička on, 146, 147, 163

German language, 149

Gestalt, 73, 96, 150, 195n

Goethe, Johann Wolfgang von, 157

Hálek, Vítězlav, 24, 25, 146, 192; *Alfred*, 24, 25

Hartman, Geoffrey, 2

Hartmann, Nicolai, 68, 69; *Das Problem des geistigen Seins*, 68

Harvey, Gabriel, 47

Havránek, Bohuslav, 41n, 124

Hegel, G. W. F., 23, 38, 51, 52, 53; *Vorlesungen über die Philosophie der Geschichte*, 53

Herbart, Johann Friedrich, 23, 43n

Herben, Jan, 147

Herder, Johann Gottfried von, 159

Hessen, Sergius, 62

Heyduk, Adolf, 192

Hlaváček, Karel, 31, 32, 200n

Homer, 96, 158, 159, 167

homonymy, 84–87, 89

Honzl, Jindřich, 96

Horálek, Karel, 194n

Hostinský, Otakar, 43n

Hrabák, Josef, 76, 194

Hugo, Victor, 145, 147, 149

Humboldt, W. von, 68

Husserl, Edmund, 71, 82, 160, 175

Hussites, 127–133

Hýsek, Miroslav, 56

individual, the, 75–76, 85, 87, 121, 158, 171–175, 184–193, 204

Ingarden, Roman, 58, 70, 73–75, 153, 155, 160, 161, 164; *Das literarische Kunstwerk: Eine Untersuchung aus dem Grenzgebiet der Ontologie, Logik und Literaturwissenschaft*, 71

Institut für Sozialforschung, 61

intentionality, 36, 110, 113, 132, 153, 160; Ingarden on, 73–75; Mukařovský on, 116, 117, 172, 179–184, 186–189, 204

intertextuality, 8, 21, 53

Jakobson, Roman, 42n, 44n, 62, 113–115, 118, 139n, 142–144, 147, 148, 184, 203–205; on Czech verse, 127–133, 197n; on diachrony, 6–7, 129, 202; on evolution of language, 11–17, 31, 36, 63–64; on evolution of literature, 8–10, 21, 22; on film, 93–97, 100, 106, 109, 110; functional approach of, 71, 72, 177; on genre, 111–112; on phenomenology, 175; on phoneme, 40n; on phonology, 54–55, 88; on semiotics, 110, 112, 119, 124, 125, 152; "The Concept of the Sound Law and the Teleological Criterion," 9; "The Czech Share in the Church Slavonic Culture" (under the name Olaf Jansen), 142; "Linguistics and Poetics," 124; "Old Czech Verse," 36, 127; "Prinzipien der historischen Phonologie," 13; "Problems in the Study of Literature and Language," 6–9, 16, 22, 23, 31, 39n, 55, 66, 107, 141, 193; "Reflections on the Poetry of the Hussite Era," 127–133; *Remarques sur l'évolution phonologique du russe comparée à celle des autres langues slaves*, 11; *Selected Writings*, 15; "What Is Poetry?" 106–108, 110

Jakubinskij, Lev, 19, 23

Jauss, Hans Robert, 3

Joyce, James, 111

Kalandra, Záviš, 61, 62, 63
Kalatozov, Michail, 103; *The Cranes Are Flying* (*Letjat žuravli*, 1957), 103
Kallab, Jaroslav, 198n
Kant, Immanuel, 115
Kant-Gesellschaft, 175
Karcevskij, Sergei, 39n, 84–88, 109; "Du dualisme asymétrique du signe linguistique," 84–88
Keaton, Buster, 98, 103; *Sherlock, Jr.* (1924), 103
Kermode, Frank, 105
Kerouac, Jack, 157
Konrad, Kurt (pseudonym of Kurt Beer), 60, 61, 62, 63
Konstanz School, 3
Král', Janko, 111, 112
Kubrick, Stanley, 100; *2001: A Space Odyssey* (1968), 100
Kuhn, Thomas A., 67
Kultursoziologie, 58

Landgrebe, Ludwig, 199n
language: evolution of, 4, 12–17, 68, 87, 88, 110, 126, 166; poetic (*see* poetic language); social character of, 6, 14, 17–19, 21; standard (*see* standard language)
langue/parole, 6–8, 19, 30, 31, 35, 36, 63, 85, 154, 164, 184, 193; Mukařovský on, 172, 173; Saussure on, 12, 70, 88, 121, 134n, 141
Laterna Magica, 103
Latin language, 129, 130, 149
Lautréamont, Comte de (pseud. Isidore Ducasse), 120–121
Lawrence, D. H., 111
Lelouch, Claude, 98, 138n; *The Crook* (*Le voyou*, 1970), 138n; *Happy New Year* (*La bonne année*, 1972), 138n; *A Man and a Woman* (*Un homme et une femme*, 1966), 98
Lifšic, Michail, 60
Linguistic Circle of New York, 68
literariness (*literaturnost'*), 107
Louis XIV, 159
Lukács, György, 3, 60, 185; "Zur Theorie der Literaturgeschichte," 3
Lumière brothers, 98; *L'Arrivée d'un train en gare de la Ciotat* (1895), 98
Lumír, 147, 151

Lumírians, 147, 149–151, 155
Lydgate, John, 47

Mácha, Karel Hynek, 23–27, 45, 56, 61, 89–91, 93, 111–113, 140n, 146–148; *Máj*, 23–25, 27, 45, 89–91, 146, 151, 191, 192
Mailer, Norman, 113
Majakovskij, Vladimir, 112, 201n
Mallarmé, Stéphane, 32
Mannheim, Karl, 58
Marlowe, Christopher, 47, 64
Marx, Karl, 44n, 60
Marxism, 22, 56, 59–64, 70, 143, 174, 190, 200n
Mathesius, Vilém, 10, 39n, 124, 142; (ed.), *The Contribution of Czechoslovakia to Europe and to Humanity*, 142
"May" group, 146, 155, 192
Mehring, Franz, 62
Menzel, Jiří, 104; *Closely Watched Trains* (*Ostře sledované vlaky*, 1966), 104
metaphor, 91–93, 120, 130, 145; in film, 94, 95, 97, 99, 100
Methodius, Saint, 126, 130, 132
metonymy, 91–93; in film, 94, 96, 98, 104
Middle Ages, 126–132, 185
Milton, John, 123; *Lycidas*, 123
mimesis, 73, 76, 94, 101, 106, 152
modernism, 150, 166, 184, 185
montage, 94, 97, 100, 105
Morris, Charles W., 76, 77, 80n, 83, 114, 152, 202, 203
motif, 24, 91, 93, 101, 145
Mukařovský, Jan, 88, 141, 148; on artist, 184–193; on collective consciousness, 64, 69; criticism of, 56–57; on Czech verse, 36, 46–53, 65; and dialogic conception of art, 186–187; on evolution of literature, 6, 21–23, 25–27, 31, 36, 38, 46, 47, 53–55, 61, 63, 74–76, 143, 150–151, 189–193, 205; on film, 27–28, 97–106; formalism and, 78n, 180, 183, 204; Marxism and, 60, 174, 200n; on metaphor and metonymy, 92, 93; on norm, 74–75, 122, 167–170; on poetic reference, 117, 125; on psychologism, 29; reception theory and, 118, 119, 123, 168–193; on semantics, 32, 88–89, 116,

142, 203; on semiotics, 59, 110, 115, 120–122, 124, 142; 75th birthday of, 1; on sign, 72, 73; on Šklovskij, 36–37; on sociology, 34; on *structure*, 30, 35; on values, 33, 198n; Vodička and, 144, 147, 153, 159–161, 164, 165; Wellek and, 69, 70, 72; "Aesthetic Function and Norm as Social Facts," 165; "Art as Semiotic Fact," 121, 122; "L'Art comme fait sémiologique," 114; "The Artist's Personality in the Mirror of the Work," 29, 111; "An Attempt at a Scheme of the Structural History of Czech Literature," 76; "An Attempt at a Structural Analysis of Acting," 27–28; "Can There Be a Universal Value in Art?" 175; "On Current Poetics," 26; "La dénomination poétique et la fonction esthétique de la langue," 114; "The General Principles and Evolution of Modern Czech Verse," 36; "The Individual and Literary Development," 188, 191; "Intentionality and Unintentionality in Art," 179; "A Literary Work of Art as a Complex of Values," 33; *Mácha's "May": A Study in Aesthetics*, 23–25, 27, 61, 89–91, 93; "Personality in Art," 185; "The Place of the Aesthetic Function among the Other Functions," 175; "Polák's *Sublimity of Nature*," 36, 45–62, 65, 71, 72, 74, 76, 121, 126, 142, 150–152, 159, 170, 174, 189–191, 197n, 204; "On the Problems of Czech Structuralism: The Poetry of Karel Hlaváček," 31; "Standard Language and Poetic Language," 29, 30, 32, 41n; *Studies in Aesthetics*, 1, 174; "The Tradition of 'Form,'" 148–152; "Variants and Stylistics," 26; "The Work of Poetry as a Complex of Values," 108
music, 82, 94, 95, 119, 128

Nabokov, Vladimir, 138n
neoclassicism, 161, 190
neogrammarian philology, 7, 10, 109, 126
neologisms, 14, 20, 32, 40n, 45, 50, 86, 190
Neruda, Jan, 155, 158, 161–163, 192
New Criticism, 3, 32, 51, 80n

Nezval, Vítěslav, 111, 150
norm: aesthetic, 30, 33, 34, 75, 154, 156, 159, 163, 164, 166, 167, 169, 181, 204; cinematic, 97, 98, 149; dynamism of, 155; linguistic, 18, 19, 29, 30, 33, 34, 63, 86, 164, 173; literary, 8, 25–26, 35, 58, 66, 67, 70, 75, 122, 123, 134n, 157; period, 158–162, 165, 167, 168, 170; social, 34, 154; theatrical, 102
Novák, Arne, 148, 149
novel, 94, 109, 119, 120; and film, 98, 102–105
Novyj Lef, 6

Old Church Slavonic, 17, 127, 129, 130
Olivier, Laurence, 97; *Henry V* (1945), 97
Opojaz, 6, 9, 19, 41n, 51, 60, 64, 82, 106, 115. *See also* formalism

painting, 94, 109, 119, 120; and film, 98–99, 102; and photography, 133
Palacký, František, 190
Panofsky, Erwin, 95, 102, 137n
Parnassians, 147, 148, 149
Patočka, Jan, 199n
Peirce, C. S., 77, 80n, 84
periods, literary, 147, 157–162, 165–167, 174, 181, 192
Perrault, Charles, 159
personality, 180–182, 185, 188, 191, 193
phenomenology, 56, 76, 109, 154, 175, 199n; Ingarden and, 58, 71, 73–75, 153, 160; Mukařovský and, 69, 121, 122, 174–181, 185–186, 188, 204
phonemes, 14–15; defined, 40n
phonology, 10, 12–15, 17, 20, 41n, 54–55, 68, 82, 84, 86–88
photography, 133; and film, 99
Plato, 67, 71, 205
Plechanov, G. V., 62
poetic devices, 23, 26, 107, 109, 110, 112, 116; art as sum of, 22
poetic epithet, 89, 90, 91, 167
poeticity (*básnickost*), 107–110, 112, 133, 179
poetic language (*jazyk básnický*), 18–22, 29, 30, 107, 109, 115–119, 124, 127, 147, 148, 153, 161, 167, 202
poetic reference, 115–117
Polák, Milota Zdirad, 36, 45, 56, 57,

59–62, 71, 151, 171, 190, 191; *The Sublimity of Nature*, 36, 45–61, 65, 71
poststructuralism, 1, 205
pragmatics, 83, 114, 152, 202, 203, 204
Prague Linguistic Circle (PLC), 1, 19, 39n, 56, 68, 96, 106, 164, 174; Bühler and, 71, 72; formalism and, 9, 23, 64, 106, 115; founding of, 9; Kalandra and, 62; Karcevskij and, 88; Konrad and, 60, 61; on language, 7, 13, 17; on literary history, 6–10, 33, 76, 108; Marxist critique of, 59, 60, 143, 190; medieval studies by, 127; Mukařovský and, 57; Šalda and, 59; semantics of, 74, 84, 142; semiotics of, 80n, 82, 152, 193; Weingart and, 57; Wellek and, 70; "Theses," 17–22, 27, 29–31, 41n, 42n, 45, 72, 124, 169
psychologism, 60, 72, 73, 84, 111, 112, 143, 164; Mukařovský and, 29, 180, 184–186, 188, 200n; Vodička and, 144–145, 147, 148, 155, 158, 162
psychology, 107, 123; cognitive, 83; Gestalt, 76, 195n
Puchmajer, Antonín Jaroslav, 47, 49
Puchmajerians, 56, 150, 190
Puškin, Alexander, 111

Racine, Jean Baptiste, 3
reader, 63, 113, 117, 118, 121, 123, 126, 143, 180. *See also* reception theory
Readings in Russian Poetics, 8
reception theory, 3, 4, 58, 72, 112, 118, 121, 141–151, 203–205; Mukařovský on, 142, 168–193; Vodička on, 144, 146, 152–164. *See also* audience; reader; viewer
Reisz, Karel, 95; *Morgan!* (1966), 95
Resnais, Alain, 97
Rezeptionsgeschichte, 3, 153, 164. *See also* reception theory
rhetorical devices, 89, 110
Richards, I. A., 162
romanticism, 34, 91, 110, 111, 127, 128, 148, 159, 166, 169, 185; expressive orientation of, 152
"Ruch" (Rush) group, 147
Russell, Bertrand, 62
Russian language, 11, 14, 87

Šafařík, Pavel Josef, 190
Šalda, F. X., 59, 147; "An Example of Structural Literary History," 59
Saussure, Ferdinand de, 6–11, 40n, 54, 67, 70, 82, 134n; 172; Jakobson and, 12, 15, 17; on *langue*, 88, 121, 141; Mukařovský and, 164, 184, 189; semiology of, 77, 83, 84; on sign, 27, 80n; on social nature of linguistic facts, 72; Vodička and, 160, 164; *Cours de linguistique générale*, 6, 7, 11, 12, 17, 88
Sborník filologický (*Philological Miscellany*), 56
Schopenhauer, Arthur, 66
Sechehaye, Albert, 10
Second International Congress of Slavists (1934), 76
semantics, 82, 86–92, 130, 142, 154, 155, 203; defined, 83; of film, 97, 100, 101; Jakobson on, 114, 127; Karcevskij on, 85; Mukařovský on, 32, 93, 114, 116, 120, 122, 180–185
semiotics, 27, 32, 36, 59, 68, 72, 87, 115, 130; of film, 93–102, 106; Jakobson on, 108, 109, 112, 152; Mukařovský on, 114, 120–122, 152, 153, 183
Shakespeare, William, 47, 64, 92
sign, 32, 71, 77, 87, 99, 112, 116–120, 125, 130, 166; arbitrary nature of, 121, 159; auditory, 94–96, 99; in film, 94, 100; functions of, 72, 84–85; Jakobson on, 93, 109, 110, 127, 133; Karcevskij on, 88; Mukařovský on, 27, 72–73, 89, 153, 176–179, 183, 188; Schoolmen on, 86; as social fact, 28, 72, 83; visual, 94, 96, 99, 106; Vodička on, 161; work of art as, 21, 22, 27, 29, 106, 114–115, 152, 154, 159, 181, 182, 185–188, 203, 204
signans/signatum, 83, 126
sign-gestures, 28, 29
signifiant/signifié, 83, 87–88, 121, 126, 153, 159
sjužet/fabula, 104
Šklovskij, Viktor, 36–37, 51, 104–106; *Theory of Prose*, 36
Slovo a slovesnost, (*The Word and Verbal Art*), 124–125, 174
social consciousness, 59, 68–70, 122, 123, 159

Society for Cultural and Economic Relations with the USSR, 44*n*
Society for Literary History, 142
sociology and literature, 38, 63, 82, 83, 142, 144, 146, 157, 164, 204; Mukařovský and, 55, 74–76, 114, 173
Song of Songs, 155
Sophocles, 159
space: and meaning, 99, 106; in painting and film, 98, 99, 102
space-signification, 99–101
Spitzer, Leo, 57
Stalin, Joseph, 174
standard language (*jazyk spisovný*), 18–21, 29, 30, 45, 107, 109, 115, 117–119, 125, 129, 148, 153, 161, 167, 202
Stendhal (Marie Henri Beyle), 192
Stevens, Wallace, 82
Stroheim, Erich von, 103; *Greed* (1923), 103
structuralism: Anglo-American, 1–2, 164; French, 2–3, 7–8, 39*n*; German, 164
structure, defined, 30, 34, 35, 36, 44*n*
Structure and Sense of a Literary Work of Art, 1
struktura / tvar, 27, 149–150, 195*n*
subject, 72, 176, 177, 179, 180. *See also* artist, author, reception theory
surrealism, 61, 105, 110, 113, 120, 122, 155
Syberberg, Hans-Jürgen, 103; *Hitler, a Film from Germany (Hitler, ein Film aus Deutschland*, 1977), 103
symbol, 82, 130, 131, 176
symbolism, 31, 32, 148, 149, 170, 184, 185
synchrony, 6–17, 19, 24, 26, 40*n*, 103, 160; Mukařovský on, 23, 30, 165, 172, 184, 193
synecdoche, 92, 94
synonymy, 84–87, 92, 124
"system of systems," 9, 55, 60, 141

teleological explanation of language, 7, 16–17, 63, 67, 72, 115
Tennyson, Alfred, 145
tertium comparationis, 86, 87, 93, 203
text pragmatics, 73
theatre, 82, 109, 182, 187; and film, 95, 96, 98, 99, 102, 105, 133
theme, 52–55, 61, 110, 114, 119, 120; Mukařovský on, 93, 123, 187
Thomson, James, 45; *Seasons*, 45
time: in film, 97, 102–105, 110; in prose narrative, 103–105; and sign, 105–106; in theatre, 102–104
Tolstoj, Leo, 42*n*, 112
Tomaševskij, Boris, 22, 23, 91; "La nouvelle école d'histoire littéraire en Russie," 22
tradition, 126, 155, 160, 163, 170, 171
Trnka, Bohumil, 84, 124; "Semasiology and Its Significance for Linguistics," 84
Troeltsch, Ernst, 65
Trubeckoj, N. S., 10, 39*n*, 71
Tynjanov, Jurij, 6–10, 16, 24, 31, 38*n*, 51, 63, 136*n*; "The Problem of Literary Evolution," 9; "Problems in the Study of Literature and Language," 6–9, 16, 22, 23, 31, 38–39*n*, 55, 66, 107, 141, 193
type-token relation, 88

universals, 152, 170–173, 185

value judgments, 33, 46, 64–66, 69, 70, 154, 155, 165
values, 124, 126, 130, 169, 181; aesthetic, 46, 58, 64, 65, 75, 129, 153, 156, 162, 171, 174; cultural, 132; extra-aesthetic, 33–35, 37, 45, 107, 119, 144, 167, 198*n*; social, 33, 34, 114, 118, 132, 133, 155, 172
Vančura, Vladislav, 96, 197*n*
versification, 20–21, 65, 76, 108; metre, 47–51, 56, 128, 149–151, 167, 173, 181, 190; Mukařovský on, 150–152, 173, 190; Vodička on, 145, 147
Vertov, Dziga, 101; *The Man with a Movie Camera (Čelovek s kinoapparatom*, 1929), 101
Vodička, Felix, 58, 76, 142–148, 165, 183; on reception theory, 152–164, 168, 170, 173, 197*n*, 204; *The Beginnings of Modern Czech Prose Fiction*, 197*n*; "Březina and Baudelaire," 144–147; "The Echo of Béranger's Poetry in Czech Literature," 146–147; "Lit-

erary History: Its Problems and Its Tastes," 142, 163, 165; "Mácha as Playwright," 147; "Methodological Remarks on the Study of the Literary Work's Reception," 152, 163, 165; "The Period and the Work," 147; "Vrchlický and Banville," 144–147; "The Western Orientation in the New Czech Literature," 148
Vosslerian stylistics, 18
Vrchlický, Jaroslav, 24, 25, 31, 144–147; "A Ballad on Ballad," 146; *Satanela*, 24, 25

Warhol, Andy, 101
Weingart, Miloš, 56–57

Wellek, René, 57, 62, 64, 65, 76, 80*n*; on Jakobson, 110; on Mukařovský, 72–74, 153, 164, 174; on values, 66–72, 75; "The Theory of Literary History," 65, 70
Weltanschauung, 73, 74
Weyr, František, 198*n*
Wilder, Billy; 138*n*; *Sunset Boulevard* (1950), 138*n*
Wittfogel, Karl August, 61

Yeats, W. B., 141

Ždanov, A. A., 62
Zich, Otakar, 43*n*, 147
Zola, Emile, 157